Bereft of Reason

Odilon Redon
The Eye, Like a Strange Balloon Mounts towards Infinity, 1882.

Charcoal, 16 ⅝ x 13 ⅛. The Museum of Modern Art, New York. Gift of Larry Aldrich.

Bereft of Reason

*On the Decline of Social Thought
and Prospects for Its Renewal*

Eugene Halton

The University of Chicago Press
Chicago & London

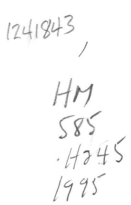

Eugene Halton teaches sociology and humanities at the University of Notre Dame. He is the author of *Meaning and Modernity* (University of Chicago Press, 1986); and coauthor of *The Meaning of Things* (1981). He has also performed blues harmonica internationally, and his blues band, The Mighty Hurricanes, is completing its first compact disc.

The University of Chicago Press, Chicago 60637
The University of Chicago Press, Ltd., London

ISBN: 0-226-31461-8 (cloth)
        0-226-31462-6 (paper)

Library of Congress Cataloging-in-Publication Data

Halton, Eugene
    Bereft of reason : on the decline of social thought and prospects
for its renewal / Eugene Halton.
        p.   cm.
    Includes bibliographical references and index.
    1. Sociology—Philosophy.   2. Social sciences—Philosophy.
    I. Title.
    HM24.H353   1995
    301'.01—dc20   94-28377
                                                                CIP

for Gemma

One must live with ideals, but never by ideals.

Men live and see according to some gradually developing and gradually withering vision. This vision exists also as a dynamic idea or metaphysic—exists first as such. Then it is unfolded into life and art. Our vision, our belief, our metaphysic is wearing woefully thin, and the art is wearing absolutely threadbare. . . . We've got to rip the old veil of a vision across, and find what the heart really believes in, after all: and what the heart really wants, for the next future. . . . Rip the veil of the old vision across, and walk through the rent.

—D. H. Lawrence

Contents

1 The Codification of Social Theory   1

2 Of Life and Social Thought   37

3 The Cultic Roots of Culture   79

4 Lewis Mumford's Organic Worldview   121

5 The Transilluminated Vision of Charles Peirce   167

6 Jürgen Habermas's Theory of Communicative
   Etherealization   191

7 The Neopragmatic Acquiescence: Between Habermas
   and Rorty   219

8 The Modern Error and the Renewal of Social
   Thought   247

   Notes   281

   Acknowledgments   295

   Index   297

I

The Codification of Social Theory

Free speech? Yeah, tell me another one.
                    —*Stanley Fish, Literary Theorist*

Let not theories and "ideas" be the rules of your being. The Führer *himself and he alone* is *German reality and its law, today and for the future.*

                    —*Martin Heidegger*

I philosophize only in terror, *but in the* confessed *terror of going mad.*

                    —*Jacques Derrida*

I admit to having a perfect horror of a dictatorship of theorists.
                    —*George Orwell*

WHY THEORY NOW?

The comedians Mike Nichols and Elaine May used to have a routine going back to their days with the Second City Comedy Club in Chicago, in which they would toss words back and forth which would qualify as "cleans" and "dirties." For example, the term "Lake Michigan" is a clean, while "Lake Titicaca"—enunciated very slowly—is a dirty. "Sword" is a clean, while "rapier" is a dirty. Are you with me, dear reader? We can apply the same method to a number of terms in intellectual life today.

In this general mindset, contingency, pluralism, and social constructionism are cleans, while essences, foundations, experience, and universals are all dirties. "Reality" is a dirty while "fiction" is a clean. The "I" is a dirty, and so is "we." An "author" is a dirty, while a "text" is a clean. "The body," formerly a dirty, can be redefined as a text and made into a clean. Local cultures are clean, while "humanity" is a dirty. "Privileging" and "valorizing" something is a dirty, while using the terms "privilege" and "valorize" as verbs is a clean. Postmodernism is a clean, while modernism is a dirty. Nonhierarchical multiculturalism is a clean, while a canon is a dirty. Both those who characterize certain people as "politically correct" and those who are so characterized agree that it is a dirty. John Dewey used to be a dirty for most post–World War II academic philosophers, but now that "the public intellectual" has become a clean, Dewey has become a clean. Even more remarkable—Dewey, the philosopher who lamented what he termed "the eclipse of community," has become a clean for many who also regard "communitarianism" as a dirty. Figure that one out!

Central to contemporary intellectual life is the assumption that "the big picture" traditionally sought by philosophy is a dirty, while "little pictures" are clean. I wish to claim that fallible big pictures are not only still possible but are requisite for comprehending the modern and postmodern world. Also central to intellectual life today, although more problematic, is the assumption that organic nature is a dirty, while culture is a clean.

When the term "nature" is used in the context of ecology it can be put safely within a political context and then regarded as a clean. But the idea that organic biology may have some direct and inward influence on persons, institutions, societies, and civilizations, that human conduct cannot be completely reduced to sociohistorical cultural constructions categorically distinct from nature—such an idea is a dirty, even if John Dewey, the newly reconstructed clean public intellectual, might have sought such a naturalistic basis for human conduct. That side of Dewey is declared a dirty and consigned to the dungheap of history.

The term "public intellectual" is clearly a clean, while for many the term "tenured radical" is a dirty. Philosophy is regarded by many today as a dirty, while social theory is a clean. There is, of course, a long tradition, going back at least to Marx's last thesis on Feuerbach, to call for the end of philosophy. But today antiphilosophical philosophers, such as Richard Rorty, to take a notorious example, gloatingly decry as obsolete the very idea of the love of wisdom—philo-sophia—and the quest toward a comprehensive understanding the term connotes.

Social theory has attained a curious currency today among intellectuals. Many literary critics and philosophers, for example, view theory as liberating, as a means of breaking down unnecessary boundaries and overturning literary and philosophical canons. High-powered social theories are often regarded, ironically enough, as a means of making literary and philosophical questions more "practical," by showing how these questions need to be viewed in their proper social or historical contexts. In this sense, social theory seems to signify a radical break with the disciplines of literary studies and philosophy and, more broadly, with disciplinary thought in general. Literary studies become "cultural studies" in this new order, with the promise of breaking out of the arid specialization that has characterized the development of the twentieth-century university.

One prominent philosopher, Rorty, prefers the term "social theory" to "philosophy," because it does not imply "the love of wisdom," or a pursuit of and devotion to something more than a "mere idiosyncratic historical product." He prefers instead the etymological visual sense of the term "theory" as looking at something or taking an overview. In Rorty's perspective of "ironist theory," which is representative of the postmodern temper, theory has the advantage of "taking a view of a large stretch of territory from a considerable distance" rather than "the belief in, and love of, an ahistorical wisdom." As he says in his book *Contingency, Irony, and Solidarity,* such a belief in and love of wisdom "is the story of successive attempts to find a final vocabulary which is not just the final vocabulary of the individual philosopher but a vocabulary final in every sense—a vocabulary which is no mere idiosyncratic historical product but the last word, the one to which inquiry and history have converged, the one which renders further inquiry and history super-fluous. The goal of ironist theory is to understand the metaphysical urge, the urge to theorize, so well that one becomes entirely free of it. Ironist theory is thus a ladder which is to be thrown away as soon as one has figured out what it was that drove one's predecessors to theorize."[1]

In Rorty's statement we see the now conventional urge to overthrow or tran-scend philosophy or metaphysics, which numerous philosophers, including Marx, Nietzsche, Dewey, Heidegger, Wittgenstein, and the logical positivists have under-taken. Rorty's ladder metaphor is taken directly from early Wittgenstein. His aim to replace philosophy with social theory inverts Marx's call to replace philosophy with a criticism capable of changing practical life. Rorty does not believe that there are connections between private and public life, or in a general historical develop-ment or in a greater human condition or community, whether in Marx's sense or any other, as shown in Chapter 7. The goal of theory, according to Rorty, is to un-derstand the metaphysical "urge to theorize" and, in so doing, to become "entirely free of it."

Thus one can see how the "urge to theorize" which has gripped contempo-rary intellectual life signals the desire for liberation from metaphysics—from the idea that literary works of art depend on aesthetic qualities of feeling communica-ted by authors to readers, and from the idea that truth, goodness, or beauty may cause wisdom in devoted pursuers. The objects of literary or philosophical criti-cism do not compel or inspire the gaze of the theorist, but seem to function as transitory or arbitrary images.

Postmodern literary theorists have come to value the social context of litera-ture as more significant for interpretation than literature itself, a tendency at least more understandable among sociologists of literature and art, if equally erro-neous. These theorists, following Jacques Derrida, would attack "logocentrism," yet they are suffering from what could only be called "sociologocentrism." The "Eureka, it is social!" insight need not override the inherent communicative quali-ties imparted by a work of art. Only a willful and uncritical self-inflation would blind critics to the art of literature or cause them to declare that the difference between criticism and art has become obsolete. In considering literature as worthwhile only when it serves some critical purpose, such as illustrating themes of class, gender, or race, thereby denying that literature is a primary activity and criticism or critique a secondary one, postmodern lit critters reflect the way that the contemporary mind has come a cropper.[2]

One gets a sense of the postliterary theorist in Stanley Fish, who went from a decidedly objectivist position in his first book on Milton, advocating a version of "reader response" in which the author sets strict limits of control on the interpretation of the work, almost as the objective stimulus to determinate responses— to a postworld in which objectivity and other "metaphysical" concepts are obsolete. Fish claimed, and apparently later repudiated that critical theory "relieves me of the obligation to be right . . . and demands only that I be interesting."[3] Though the pendulum may swing between authorial objectivity and critical subjectivism, there remains the supremely self-confident and self-possessed critic in Stanley Fish, who seems to have increasingly replaced the object of literature with the object of his own "interesting" protean persona.

Like Rorty, Fish illustrates the temper of the time toward antimetaphysical relativism. In his view knowledge consists of what a given community of interpretation happens to believe. Beliefs are not capable of being shaped by compelling facts or truths which transcend the community but only by the power and authority of persuasion. For, according to Fish, "we live in a rhetorical world" determined by persuasion in a radical sense involving "the characterization of persuasion as a matter entirely contingent, rational only in relation to reasons that have themselves become reasons through the mechanisms of persuasion . . . [and] the insight that contingency, if taken seriously, precludes the claims for theory as they are usually made. . . . It might seem that in travelling this road one is progressively emancipated from all constraints, but, as we have seen, the removal of *independent* constraints to which the self might or might not conform does not leave the self free but reveals the self to be always and already constrained by the contexts of practice (interpretive communities) that confer on it a shape and a direction."[4] No one could deny Fish's claim that we "live in a rhetorical world" in the sense that human conduct is irremovably situated within interpretation. Only Fish's view of what constitutes interpretation is utterly narcissistic, incapable of allowing that genuine spontaneity and brute otherness are also involved in interpretation and reasonableness.

As with Rorty, one is instead locked between a fixed set of arbitrary beliefs and pure contingency: both Fish and Rorty reify objectivity and truth and then declare it obsolete in the name of contingency. Does Fish really mean to characterize "persuasion as a matter entirely contingent," or is he just ritually intoning the magic postmodern word "contingency"? In his antifoundationalist enthusiasm Fish ignores the possibility of knowledge as capable of being both antifoundational and fallibly true. Though power, authority, and prestige clearly pervade social practices, rhetorical persuasion might also involve something more than converting someone from one set of beliefs to another on the basis of ultimately contingent beliefs: persuasion is more than a hinge between convention and contingency. It might sometimes require our changing our beliefs in the face of objectively better beliefs or of undeniable experiences. This is called learning and is a category Fish's philosophy seems to me to deny. Rhetorical persuasion might be better defined as the art of learning through mutual dialogue. There is, quite simply, more to being human than living in Fish's rhetorical pond, with its definition of the situated self as "a self whose every operation is a function of the conventional possibilities built into this or that context."[5] In this definition one sees the hidden connection between contemporary antifoundationalism and foundationalist positivism: both deny to the self the ability to engage in spontaneous conduct by reducing it to a "function" of its conventional or behavioral context.

It gets even curiouser when one realizes that Fish and Rorty are associated with pragmatism, which, after all, was a philosophy of purport and not a religion of contingency. The pragmatists are distinguished for the ways they included contingency and spontaneity within a philosophy of self-interpretive conduct, but the purposive side of pragmatism does not fit the postmodernist's outlook, so it is dispensed with while the shell or name of pragmatism is retained. For this reason such an outlook should not be called "neopragmatism," and should not be confused with "pragmatism," but rather I propose that it be called "fragmatism."

Nothing could be further from the philosophy of pragmatism than Fish's slippery denial of the possibility of achieving fallible truth through inquiry when he says:

> The difference then between science or law, on the one hand, and literary criticism, on the other, is not the difference between rhetoric (or style) and something else, but between the different rhetorics that are powerful in the precincts of different disciplines; and the difference between the rhetoric of science—the rhetoric of proof, deduction, and mathematical certainty—and other rhetorics in modern society is a difference between a prestige discourse, a discourse that has for historical reasons become associated with the presentation of truth, and the discourses that will for a time

measure themselves against it. I am not saying that these differences are illusory or that they don't have real consequences, only that their reality and their consequentiality are historical achievements—achievements fashioned on the anvil of argument and debate—and that as historical achievements they can be undone in much the same way as they were achieved.[6]

Fish seems to be saying that rhetorical persuasion is based purely on power and prestige, yet the "prestige discourse" of science and law is a historical achievement "fashioned on the anvil of argument and debate," which makes it seem as though it is tempered by experience. But the historical achievements "can be undone in much the same way as they were achieved," implying here, and explicitly stated throughout Fish, that persuasion is grounded neither in a fallible conception of truth nor in experience but simply in the power and prestige of cultural conventions and the persuaders who speak for them. Rhetorical persuasion is a power game, much like advertising.

Where such unbridled subjectivism can lead can be found in the marvelous parodies of Fish and the "literature racket" in David Lodge's novels *Changing Places* and *Small World*. There, Fish is portrayed as Morris Zapp, and, in a lecture comparing reading to watching striptease, Zapp/Fish expounds a basic postulate of contemporary theoretical narcissism: "The attempt to peer into the very core of a text, to possess once and for all its meaning, is vain—it is only ourselves that we find there, not the work itself." No wonder then that Fish, in a discussion with students and faculty cited in *The New Republic,* says: "I want them to do what I tell them to. . . . I want to be able to walk into any first-rate faculty anywhere and dominate it, shape it to my will. I'm fascinated by my own will."[7] So, one might add, were Hitler and Stalin and other great dictators, with whom Fish's words and ego resonate ominously.

Earlier in the twentieth century, the logical positivists sought to eradicate metaphysics through hard universal scientism. Today theorists in the humanities seek to eradicate metaphysics through soft forms of relativistic conceptualism. Both share, however, the desire to obliterate metaphysics, possibly because it involves the threat that general reason may be as much or more a producer of humans as humans are producers of it, and because reason may therefore place unavoidable limits on human conduct.[8] It is obvious to many today that the positivist attempt to deny metaphysics only resulted in the extreme metaphysics of semantic reference—an inarticulate pointing at "facts" as the foundation of knowledge. Yet contemporary antipositivists such as Rorty and Fish little suspect that their dismissal of metaphysics may also result in a revenge of the repressed: that they may be merely living an unconscious metaphysics rather than becoming, as Rorty puts it, "entirely free of it." I will claim throughout this book that both modernists and postmodernists have, in fact, been living within the metaphysics of the "ghost in the machine," a worldview combining reified materialism and spectral knowledge.

The term "ghost in the machine" was coined by Gilbert Ryle as a way of depicting the Cartesian outlook, with its dualism of incorporeal mind and mechanistic body. It resonates with the old expression "deus ex machina," the god out of the machine, which derived from the use in Greek theater of a device to transport a god to the scene of the action or to rescue someone from an otherwise unsalvageable situation. Ryle meant to counter the dualism with a physicalistic philosophy which would evict the ghost but not the machine. I believe his expression to imply a broader critique than he made of it, however, and I will be using the term to denote the split worldview which arose in modern Western civilization, usually associated with the Cartesian/Kantian outlook, which implies a dualism between the material world and a spectral mind or culture. One side of the split implies a positivist scientism, the other side implies that culture is simply conventions. Both sides of the modern split-brained worldview are inadequate to account for human social life in my view.

"THE BIG PICTURE," WHETHER OF A PLATONIC REALM OF IDEAS beyond human history, or of the idea of History itself as a progressive unfolding of some grand design, is one of the chief targets of contemporary criticism. For many thinkers today, the Big Picture view of the world represents mistaken tendencies toward foundationalism and metaphysics, which obscure socially rooted conventions. The Big Picture is seen as a particular kind of ideology, whether disguised as Philosophy, Evolution, or Religion, or as seen in recent debates over the presumed canonical texts or universality of Western Civilization. At the end of the twentieth century, we ought to be skeptical of the kinds of Big Pictures which have dominated modern life, including the modern worldview itself. Yet rejecting infallible foundationalism does not by itself assure that there might not be large historical narratives and forms of reasonableness greater than human cultures have thus far constructed, and which we can at best fallibly, or even dimly, understand. Even the rejection of big pictures can become a form of dogmatism, if not foundationalism. It strikes me as peculiar that critics of the Big Picture modes of thinking never seem to ask whether a non-foundationalist and thoroughly fallible Big Picture is not only still possible to frame, but whether the act of framing such a worldview might be an inescapable dimension of human conduct—especially that portion of human conduct which is theoretical or intellectual. This leads me to suspect that the widespread denial of the possibility of a Big Picture, or of metaphysics, may be part of an ideology unwilling to examine its own premisses. I simply do not see why a forced dichotomy between situational, relativist, or multicultural views versus large-scale universal frameworks is necessary.

The peculiar situation in contemporary intellectual life is further revealed in the ways in which literary critics attempted to transform themselves into social theorists, particularly those under the influence of French postmodernism and semiotics. By the end of the 1980s, Americans had made Jacques Derrida's theory of deconstructionism into a quasi-vernacular buzzword, an "ism" guaranteed to ward off anxieties about "the end of isms" which the downfalls of modernism and communism seemed to herald. Deconstructionist "postpeople" sang the praises of pluralism, "polyphonic textuality," and multiculturalism, while chorusing a one-dimensional theory of meaning as limited to arbitrary social and linguistic conventions, a French-inspired social theory which scarcely tolerated deviations. The 1980s were, if anything, a decade of glitter and scandals, and deconstructionists, like televangelists, politicians, and Wall Street sharps, rose to a shining prominence before the bubble burst. The immediate cause was the revelation that Paul de Man, the major promulgator of deconstructionism in America who died in 1983, had written antisemitic Nazi propaganda in Belgium during the war. De Man also conveniently forgot his wife and three children when he came to America in the late 1940s and remarried. As David Lehman says, de Man was suffering from "Waldheimer's disease," a total loss of memory regarding one's Nazi past.

With the exposure of de Man and the incontestable assembling of evidence concerning Martin Heidegger's Nazism in a controversial 1989 book, *Heidegger and Nazism,* by Victor Farias, the radical chic of the theory world were forced either to confess the fatal flaws of their masters or profess their unquestioned loyalties. Some of the rationalizing fancy footwork by loyalists was every bit as remarkable as the patriotic appeals of the Iran-Contra scandal loyalists and godly appeals of the remaining true believers in televangelists. Jacques Derrida, who coined the term "deconstruction" and who called Heidegger its progenitor, defended both Heidegger and de Man.[9]

Derrida defended de Man in the same way that the minions of Heidegger have defended his Nazism: by reading mountains into molehills, and, where molehills did not exist, by inventing them. A positive mention of Kafka by de Man could be used to refute his explicitly antisemitic articles, just as essays on Hölder-lin by Heidegger in the 1930s could be used to reveal a disguised anti-Nazi turn. In both cases the authors are seen as circumventing the pressures of Nazi censorship through indirect discourse, and the problem that they never explicitly repudiated their positions in the decades after the war is totally ignored. Derrida also published a book which claimed that Heidegger's use of the word "spirit" in pro-Nazi speeches, without quotation marks, showed that, "by celebrating the freedom of spirit, its glorification resembles other European discourses (spiritualist, religious, humanist) that people generally consider opposed to Nazism."[10] But this contemptuous rationalization of Heidegger's Nazism into its opposite should not be surprising given that Derrida once stated that deconstruction "amounts to annulling the ethical qualification and to thinking of writing beyond good and evil."[11] Perhaps the exacerbated Nietzschean lunacies of deconstruction would be better characterized as the Derridada philosophy. Though the 1980s began with the promise of a loosening up of overly disciplinary specialization—signaled, for example, by Clifford Geertz's 1980 essay "Blurred Genres: The Refiguration of Social Thought"—the end of the decade revealed a new orthodoxy of "politically correct" postmodernism busily institutionalizing itself.

While a number of sociological social theorists have been influenced by the same impulses toward genre blurring, there has also been a strong countertendency to reestablish the grand tradition of social theory "classics." Sociologists, forever theorizing about "the problem of order," also provide fascinating sociological data in the ways they invoke orthodoxy to solve "the problem of theoretical order." At the moment, the battle lines are drawn between "rational choice" orthodoxers and "classics" orthodoxers. And, oddly enough, despite an apparent blurring of boundaries and promiscuous intermingling of disciplines, many sociologists continue to view social theory as a subdiscipline within academic sociology. Admittedly, though, "theory" is an accepted subdiscipline within all of the academic disciplines. For the remainder of this chapter, I will consider the codification of "classic" social theory and its implications for contemporary thought. But the ongoing codification of contemporary social theory will remain a central concern throughout the book.

The transformation of what in earlier times was known as social philosophy into social theory is perhaps due, in part, to the professionalizing of sociology and other academic disciplines since the turn of the century. Professionalized and institutionalized sociology has resulted in a perceived tradition of "classical" social theory, and an intense socialization of students into the perceived tradition. Karl

Marx, Max Weber, and Emile Durkheim constitute a virtual triumvirate of "classical" social theory for sociologists, though some would want to include George Simmel, George Herbert Mead, Talcott Parsons, and a few others within the "classical" pantheon.

In effect, the term "classical" is an honorific term used by sociologists both in a vague sense to mean "old"—and thereby authoritative—and also to signify the creation myth of sociology in which a few select authors and their foundational texts form a pantheon of "theorists." That these authors may have viewed themselves as philosophers, historians, economists, as well as sociologists, but rarely, if ever, as "theorists" is seldom considered. The concept of "classical social theory" resembles the conditions under which the ancient Mesopotamian scribes attributed the transmission of divine knowledge to the seven mythic sages from before the Great Flood. These antediluvian sages were thenceforth regarded as the authors of the scholarly canon of texts.

The institutionalizing of sociology, philosophy, and other disciplines in universities over the past hundred years, far from signaling the progress of reason, was a process of bureaucratic codification, or even worse, of progressive petrification: Professor Pigeonhole builds a cozy nest for himself or herself out of the expected ideas of a discipline or ideology, feathers it with institutional power and reputation, and trains a brood of students to replicate the idea. The end result of this process has been the growth of nearsighted specialists without spirit and grandiose theorists utterly lacking in imaginative, humane vision.

Antidisciplinary postmodernism provides no real alternative to the petrified professor syndrome but only a variation of the theme. Take the example of Molefi Kete Asante, director of African-American studies at Temple University, author of *The Afrocentric Idea* and *Kemet, Afrocentricity, and Knowledge,* and propagator of "Afrocentrism," a racially based form of relativism. Professor Asante says, "We are producing the first African-American graduate students with no traditional discipline. Their discipline is African-American studies. We are producing the next crop of scholars who will leave here and pursue Afrocentricity, not just at Temple, but across the country."[12] Surely Professor Pigeonhole sees a like-minded colleague in Professor Asante, with his desire to clone his beliefs and thereby maximize his base of power. Asante is against the claims of "Eurocentrism" to be universal, and believes that knowledge is basically ethnocentric and therefore relativist: white Europeans, Americans, and Australians are Eurocentric, black Africans and Americans are Afrocentric, and yellow Asians and Americans are Asiocentric. Biology does not determine ethnicity but will influence a person toward an ethnic identity in keeping with one's biological inheritance, so that people of mixed races can identify with one or another of their parental lineage.

In the place of disciplines, the new academic post–world order is based on an ideology of "pluralism" in which everything counts the same. In this ideology there are no universal human qualities or essentials, no better or worse, but only conventional signifiers. There is no art or politics to live for or to die for in earnest but only fictions to be made and remade, as lightly as the water spider which dances on the surface of the pond; or there is no art but only politics (we should remember that "the personal is the political," a popular feminist motto, also happened to serve totalitarian socialist realism quite well); or no politics but only "art"—taken to mean that a public way of life rooted in some community is illusory and that all that one does is to make or live out ideas in no way inspired or bound by or contributory to a greater good. Art becomes synonomous with an effete aestheticism while politics becomes synonomous with power, and both ironically yearn to be egalitarian. Unconscious irony abounds in this world of postmodern pluralism, where opposing ideas are frequently reduced to a singular monolithic position: Western Civilization and its works are reduced to the abstract concept of a canon; critics of feminism, while being reminded that there are a plurality of feminisms, are viewed as holding a one-dimensional view of "antifeminism." Such a tendency to reify the other position in this way may be called "the pluralism versus the monolith syndrome." In the name of pluralism, the generalized "other" is reduced to the unitary or monolithic.

Only people divested of passion could actually believe that the myriad qualities which comprise a life or a culture—or an education—can be subsumed under "ideology." When one sees how the ideologues of a relativist multiculturalism, expressed, for example, in ethnocentric "Afrocentrism," assert a unidimensional "pluralist" curriculum over the entire educational system, it is clear why postmodern pluralism breeds ideological conformity and theoretical hubris. With every individual educational situation bounded by the same pluralistic quota system, there is little possibility of an educational system in America which could do the work of conveying the knowledge and history of American ethnic groups *before college,* or in specialized college courses, in order that students could be encouraged to go on in general education courses to learn a broader history of the world, one which could convey a sense of their Western and world identities.

Although it is a truism that humans live in and through institutions, the purpose of institutions is to enhance the human spirit. Individual thought, creative and critical, ought to be the result of intellectual institutions and traditions, but the opposite seems to be the case at the end of the twentieth century. When the struggle for literary interpretation is given up in favor of ideology, as is going on in literature departments throughout the United States, then there is no contradiction between students reading *Cliff's Notes* instead of actual works, and their professors' claims that there is no authorship or intrinsic merit to a work of art but only generic texts to be decoded.[13] According to Houston Baker, the 1992 president of the Modern Language Association, choosing between Pearl Buck and Virginia Woolf is "no different than choosing between a hoagy and a pizza. I am one whose career is dedicated to the day when we have a disappearance of those standards."[14] Total homogenization is the ultimate standard for the new Levelers of the theory world. The case of Baker, the pizza-hoagie theorist, is particularly dyspepsic, when one sees a person dedicated to the elimination of standards of taste and discrimination raised to the presidency of an association which is the chief representative of literature in higher education. Baker delights in describing how he combines teaching Shakespeare's *Henry V* with rap music, with which I have no great quarrel as a possible pedagogical technique. But he goes on to state that rap music is a necessary means of instruction for those between twelve and twenty-five years of age and of how proud he was to be pictured in *Jet* magazine with rappers.[15] Baker perfectly illustrates why the sordid, looney bin reputation of the Modern Language Association, with its Morris Zapps and celebrity scholarship, is well-deserved. But worse, in his inability to distinguish between the commercial values and technoid, aggressive barbarism of rap music and the sheer power of expression and human tragedy in *Henry V,* he is a good indicator of the institutional disintegration of intelligence well underway in American life and more broadly in contemporary civilization. That such a person could be elected the president of the Modern Language Association, either out of White Guilt or out of Baker's hip postmodern political currency, reveals an institution whose intellectual values are deeply corrupted.

The codified intellect has increasingly reproduced itself in its leading social theories today. Such structures as the American Sociological Association, the Modern Language Association, or the American Philosophical Association will undoubtedly continue to exert ideological power and to promote intellectual mediocrity when fueled by research moneys and university affiliations. Yet if "critical thought" is to have any significance in intellectual life beyond that of a cryptoreligious aura, there comes a time when honest questioning is required. Sometimes even the emperor realizes that the new clothes he is allegedly wearing are a naked lie (and the same is true of the empress's new clothes), when the ghost in the machine needs to be exorcised, and the machine dismantled.

As mentioned, one of the central debates in sociology over the past two decades has been concerned with the value of the so-called classics. This debate is perhaps best understood within the context of a return to the problem of meaning which exploded in the cultural and intellectual life of the 1960s.

A renewed interest in Marx, Weber, Durkheim, and others signaled not only a need to broaden the critical understanding of contemporary events but also a rejection of the establishment paradigm of structural functionalism associated with Talcott Parsons. The irony, of course, was that Parsons himself had helped to bring Weber to the attention of American sociologists, especially through his 1937 book *The Structure of Social Action.* Through this work, which claimed a "convergence" in the theories of Weber, Durkheim, and a few others, Parsons was probably the most influential person in the establishment of the sociological canon and the "pure" theorist. He exerted enormous influence over the social sciences in the 1950s and 1960s and was instrumental in establishing an ahistorical, jargon-ridden style of writing which C. Wright Mills derisively termed "grand theory."

Yet the story Parsons had fashioned out of Weber and Durkheim, a story in which the tragic implications of modern rationality and anomie had been magically transformed into the comedy of "modernization theory," no longer held together. By the 1960s a studied indifference to the social consequences of social theories and empirical social research, proclaimed as "value-free" sociology, achieved virtual hegemony in rapidly expanding sociology departments, as it already had throughout a scientific establishment only too eager to accept lucrative research grants for military projects. Yet this was also a time when the values of American domestic racial and foreign military and economic policies were being fundamentally questioned. The system of racial inequality could no longer be tolerated, and the systems theory directing the Vietnam War, embodied in the secretary of defense, Robert Strange MacNamara, produced increasing moral outrage, even as its own decisions proved increasingly disastrous. In that time when, to paraphrase Yeats, unholy anarchy was loosed upon the world, when the "rough beast" of "laughing ecstatic destruction" was everywhere visible, the brave new world of Parsons, where all things converged in evolutionary systemic progress, seemed to the unindoctrinated to be just another aspect of the military-industrial-academic complex of Americanism.

And what sociologist even today, if I may digress briefly, has taken seriously the remarkable conjunction of events which shook the world in the 1960s, when red guards in China and avant-gardes in the West ruthlessly sought to destroy the past altogether and regarded stability per se as corrupt? When students in Paris, America, and elsewhere revolted for widely different reasons? It was not a simple "world economy" that caused these events to coincide but a fever in the modern temper itself. And some twenty years later the fever again heated up, but as a revolutionary movement against reactionary communism and perhaps as part of an ongoing and problematic revolt against modernism per se, one which includes such contradictory elements as religious fundamentalism, nationalism, and environmentalism. These sorts of facts don't seem to fit neatly within the airless boxes of optimistic Parsonian modernization ideology.

With the passing of time, Parsons's "general" theory looks increasingly to be the provincial expression of the American Age of Abstraction, with its "international style," glass box corporate buildings of the 1950s and 1960s, its "organization man," its formulaic abstracted art, its Doctor Strangeloves. As Parsons's own tepid and self-enclosed responses to the enormous challenges of the times—from the 1930s onward—demonstrate, "Parsonianism" was not "value-free" sociology but rather functioned as part of the "pattern-maintenance" of the great machine of modernity, the Big System.

Parsons preached the ideology of scientism, "modernization," and a dehumanized "systems" model of American society and human development. In my opinion he was representative of the triumph of post–World War II "Americanism," with its imperial optimism and uncritical technical outlook, just as others, such as behaviorist B. F. Skinner in psychology, Charles Morris in semiotics, W. V. Quine in philosophy, also expressed a collective personality marked by unswerving devotion to technicalism. His work could not be more opposed in spirit to that of Lewis Mumford, who is roughly his contemporary. A comparison of these two prodigious writers would reveal the inner history of the twentieth-century intellect: both Parsons's *The Structure of Social Action* of 1937 and his introduction to the second printing of the book in 1949 remain utterly untouched by the catastrophic events of the decade, whereas all of Mumford's works of the period convey the gravity of those dark times. Compare Parsons's record to that of Mumford, the advocate of U.S. military intervention against Germany in the late

1930s, who became the passionate critic of American militarism in the nuclear era and the Vietnam War. Parsons, who died in 1979, still wields enormous influence over contemporary theorists despite a lapse in his hegemony. By contrast, the thought of Lewis Mumford has been in virtual eclipse in the contemporary marketplace of ideas, despite some signs of renewal, perhaps because such an unquestionably independent thinker can prove an intolerable threat to what William James so aptly termed "the Ph.D. Octopus."

Where Parsons celebrated the powers-that-be, Marx called for relentless criticism (and perhaps this contributed to Parsons's exclusion of Marx from the canon); where Parsons thought modernization and cybernetic rationalization to be the glorious wave of the future, Weber suggested darker implications; where Parsons talked about norm conformity, Durkheim had at least questioned our "age of transition" and sought the means for symbolic renewal. Durkheim and Mead seemed to reopen avenues of symbolism, along with Freud and structuralism. In short, the "classics"—which Parsons himself had helped to formularize— seemed to breathe fresh air into American social theory in the 1960s.

But history has a way of confounding things. Parsons died and was reborn in "neofunctionalism"; the "classical" road to freedom turned into a canonical orthodoxy of Marx, Weber, Durkheim, with a sprinkling of Simmel and Mead, and—thanks to the Conning of Reason—Parsons himself. As Yogi Berra once said, "It's déjà vu all over again." Nostalgia is clearly not what it used to be.

It is not as though there does not exist a wild diversity of theories and theorists today. But there is an established orthodoxy in sociology which has regained the center with a stranglehold called the "classics." The basis for this orthodoxy seems fair enough at first glance—a theorist should be familiar with the traditions of theory. But "traditions" usually amounts to familiarity with the accepted theorists and rarely implies a knowledge of the intellectual Zeitgeist of those theorists. Durkheim and Mead, for example, are often credited with ideas they drew from their respective milieus rather than originated. Similarly, one of the most irritating qualities of many postmodern theorists is a lack of awareness of the history of social thought. If we consider that the renewal of the classics began as a reaction against the theoretical amnesia prevalent in the 1950s and 1960s, when earlier theory seemed to be merely "historical" and superseded by recent developments (as Parsons liked to put it, meaning by "recent developments" his latest work), it is clear why a familiarity with the corpus of the sociological tradition might be important. But when the stronger claim is made that certain theorists, namely, Marx, Weber, and Durkheim (and the lesser saints who fall outside of the trinity), made foundational contributions on which succeeding theory must build, the facade of science gives way to the dogmatism of religion and the "classics" are revealed as the creation myth of social theorists. One would have thought that such foundationalism has been shown repeatedly to be unnecessary to science in general as well as to historically informed social inquiries.

The "social theorist," as sociologists use the term, is also part of the myth, whereby the philosophers Marx, Durkheim, Simmel or Mead, or the economic and political historians Marx or Weber, or the social psychologists Durkheim, Simmel, or Mead, or the anthropologist Durkheim, just to name the classic lights, are chopped up to fit into the generic category of "social theorist." This transformation serves to legitimize the theorist, while enabling him or her to avoid the charge of being a "philosopher" or "historian" rather than a "sociologist" (this is becoming admittedly more difficult, now that literary critics and philosophers have taken to calling themselves social theorists). Simultaneously, in many cases, the theorist avoids the immersion into the common background of philosophy and history central to the so-called classics. "But is it sociology," asks the good Professor Pigeonhole? "Yes, it is classical sociology," the sociological social theorist loyally replies.

If the renewal of interest in earlier theorists arose in rebellion against the Parsonian hegemony and was subsequently absorbed to a great extent by a new orthodoxy with strong Parsonoid overtones (specifically Jürgen Habermas, Niklas Luhman, and Jeffrey Alexander), perhaps it is time for another reconsideration of the powers that be: the "classics." Is it possible that Parsons remains as inadequate today—and for the same reasons—as when his empire went into temporary decline? Is it possible that the accepted history of American sociology is but the face of bureaucratization over a few generations? Is it possible that even the one, true reading of the canonical authors remains inadequate to the post-Hiroshima world? Is it possible that sociology really is, as Weber so classically stated it, "a swindle"?

THE PRESUMED INEVITABILITY OF THE MODERN

Modern social theory is usually regarded as founded on responses to the Enlightenment and the emerging conditions of industrial civilization. As will become evident later, the concept of life—both in Darwin's and Spencer's theories of evolution and in the positive and negative reactions they produced—also played a crucial role in the development of social theory which is too easily overlooked today. Nonetheless, thinkers such as Marx, Weber, Durkheim, and Simmel were nourished by the legacy of the Enlightenment and its ideals of freedom, scientific understanding, and social criticism. These theorists were particularly influenced by the German tradition of Kant and Hegel. But they turned their Enlightenment foundations toward the new and unsettled conditions of industrial capitalism and its effects on social relations, work, families, individuals, cities, and particularly on the meaning of modern life. Marx's phrase in *The Communist Manifesto,* "all that is solid melts into air," captures the revolutionary world that capitalism was beginning to bring about, a world in which not only workers but monarchs, too, had much to fear. And Marx's manifesto with Engels itself acted as an incendiary to the revolution of 1848 which swept across the nations of Europe like a specter, a revolution they hoped would cause the bourgeoisie to melt into air: "What the bourgeoisie, therefore, produces, above all, is its own grave diggers. Its fall and the victory of the proletariat are equally inevitable."

The revolution of 1848 failed, but Marx still held out for an inevitable fall of the bourgeoisie and victory of the proletariat. Although he developed a materialist view of history, in contrast to Hegel's philosophy that history was the progression of *Geist*—spirit or mind—Marx retained Hegel's faith in the dialectical advance of history and its culmination in a utopian end of history. As he said almost twenty years later in the 1867 preface to *Capital:* "Intrinsically, it is not a question of the higher or lower degree of development of the social antagonisms that result from the natural laws of capitalist production. It is a question of these laws themselves, of these tendencies working with iron necessity toward inevitable results."[16] Marx achieved a concrete, critical theory of human history as rooted in the social practices of production, yet he did not critically confront the Enlightenment ideal of inevitable progress.

Max Weber held a more dour view of the modern ethos, a view that linked the forms of belief and conduct produced by the Reformation with the rise and dominance of capitalism and its marked rationalism. Capitalism and its brand of "instrumental" or "formal" rationality were not historically inevitable in Weber's form of cultural relativism—other types of development were also possible. Yet once selected and embodied as the modern Western ethos, the peculiar rationalism at work in the institutions of science and technics, economy, and politics formed an "inevitable" internal logic. This system, built on the "mechanical foundations" of rational capitalism, was viewed pessimistically by Weber as producing a "steel-hard casing" of rational materialism, the "iron cage" of modernity, whose legacy would be soul-less specialists and heartless hedonists. Socialism provided no alternative in Weber's eyes but only a variation on the theme of an ever-enlarging bureaucracy.

One sees the same disturbance and foreboding in Emile Durkheim, who interpreted suicide statistics as revealing patterns of normlessness and norm-breaking individualism. In his search to find the basis of religious and social belief, Durkheim said in his concluding remarks to his *Elementary Forms of the Religious Life* in 1912 that "we are going through a stage of transition and moral mediocrity. The great things of the past which filled our fathers with enthusiasm do not excite the same ardour in us, either because they have come into common usage to such an extent that we are unconscious of them, or else because they no longer answer to our actual aspirations; but as yet there is nothing to replace them. . . . In a word, the old gods are growing old or are already dead, and others are not yet born."[17]

Written on the eve of World War I and in the midst of revolutionary modernism, Durkheim's words were indeed prescient. Yet though he questioned the "moral mediocrity" of the modern "stage of transition," he never lost his Enlightenment faith that continuing progress would eventually forge new gods of belief from modern conditions. These gods would most likely arise from science, since Durkheim believed "scientific thought is only a more perfect form of religious thought," both being systems of knowledge. Perhaps the new gods could be formed from the science of sociology, as Durkheim's predecessor Comte, who had coined the term "sociology," had hoped that religion would be refounded on a secular basis: many a "classical theorist" today believe Durkheim himself to be one of these gods, along with Marx and Weber!

One finds then, in these three admittedly exemplary thinkers, theories that attempt to come to terms with industrial conditions through scientific investigation, to criticize or interpret modern life, to reveal its intended and unintended consequences. Yet despite the range and power of their theories, none of these theorists questions the inevitability of the unfolding modern ethos itself. The same might be said for other leading philosophers and social theorists, ranging from a Herbert Spencer's endorsement of modern progress as the advance of evolution to Simmel's understanding of the problematic, yet liberating effects of modern culture on the development of forms of individuality. Yet other intimations of the destructive powers of the modern were being sensed by writers such as Herman Melville, Feodor Dostoevsky, Henry Adams, and H. G. Wells. It is, of course, one of the peculiar qualities of the modern ethos that Melville and Dostoevsky were two of the greatest expressions of modern culture as well as two of its most profound critics.

Central to the development of academic social theory since the early decades of the twentieth-century has been its progressive self-alienation from an organic conception of life. Yet, as I shall argue throughout this book, it is precisely by means of such supposedly obsolete ideas as the ascription of reasonableness to nature, of nature to culture, and of reality to mind, that a transformation to a new outlook may be effected.

On the Inadequacy of the "Classics" for Social Theory

In his masterwork *Capital,* Marx exposed in relentless detail the paradoxes of industrial capitalism, with its ideals of freedom of competition and individual liberty and its actualities of slave-like working conditions and suppression of competition and workers' rights. His compelling view of the rise of capitalism reveals the radically changed conditions of modern society: the development of mechanized manufacture; the rise of the bourgeois class which displaced traditional ties and personal worth with "the icy water of egotistical calculation"; the need of forcing people into the emergent work conditions of the factories, the diabolical contrast between an ideal of less work through machines and the harsh reality of brutal working conditions for industrialized workers and loss of work for those displaced by machines. Marx saw clearly how technical innovations in the machines of industry were inseparable from the development of capitalism itself.

Capitalism was a systematic distortion of the practice of production, one which inverted the relationship of the means of work to the ends of work. Instead of "the good life" as the object and aim of work, capitalism made the goal of work to be "the life of goods"—the products of human creation were endowed with an independent life of their own in Marx's view, just as religion projected human experience and suffering on to a make-believe world. In capitalism, as in religion, humans surrendered authority and responsibility for their productions to a human projection which was treated as an alien reality. Hence, in his discussion of the place of machines in capitalism Marx says, "In the first place, in the form of machinery, the implements of labour become automatic, things moving and working independent of the workman. They are thenceforth an industrial *perpetuum mobile,* that would go on producing forever, did it not meet with certain natural obstructions in the weak bodies and the strong wills of its human attendants. The automaton, as capital, and because it is capital is endowed, in the person of the capitalist, with intelligence and will; it is therefore animated by the longing to reduce to a minimum the resistance offered by that repellent yet elastic natural barrier, man."[18]

Marx was a true pioneer in revealing the displacement of the human being by the purely quantitative being of the machine and money—the body and soul of modernity—even if he remained insufficiently critical of the machine in its social-ized form. Still, he was a powerful critic of ethereal mind, whether in his critique of Hegel's conception of history as the progression of *Geist*—spirit, mind, or culture—or in his account of money's ascendancy in capitalism. Yet his attempt to counter etherealization through a concrete, materialist conception of history was itself a partial manifestation of the other tendency of modernity toward scientific materialism. Though Marx did not fall prey to the severe form of scientific mate-rialism found in utilitarianism, which indeed was a central object of his critique, he nevertheless was not completely free from its influences. He could thoroughly reject the legacy of Descartes's *res cogitans*—ethereal mind—but he retained prej-udices favoring *res extensa*—material embodiment per se—that left him insuffi-ciently critical of the machine and insufficiently free from the false dichotomy between thought and things. This gap in Marx's thought, greatly exaggerated and amplified in the positivist form of Marxist-Leninism that assumed control of the Soviet Union, led ironically to a nation relatively inept in the machines of life, though less so in the machines of death, and thoroughly dominated by the deadly bureaucracy of ethereal mind.

Marx's interest in man the self-producing animal leaves open the question of what counts as production and the place of production in the relative scheme of things. In articulating a consistently materialist viewpoint in the name of science, he ignored or reduced other dimensions of human existence that are either non- or extraproductive.

Self-creation remains a deeper category than self-production. Or one might say, in the language of Charles Peirce, that *abduction,* the capacity to generate novel conditions or emergent inferences, is even more fundamental to the human capacity for self-transformation than *production.* Abduction was originally intro-duced by Peirce as a form of logical inference distinct from induction and deduc-tion, thoroughly logical though not limited to conscious rationality, and rooted in the human capacity of "the well-prepared mind" to make better than chance guesses or hypotheses. Transposed to a broad context of human conduct, abduc-tion means not simply to solve problems better, or to meet current needs in an efficient and equitable way, but the ability to create wholly new premises for hu-man existence. Abduction is the bodying forth and incarnation of new ideas in fruitful modes of conduct and is viewed by Peirce as rooted in our biocosmic na-ture. Marx went further than most other social theorists toward a recognition of our purposeful nature, and in this he shares a relation to Aristotle with Peirce. But his Enlightenment humanism also prevented him from going still further, as Peirce and later Lewis Mumford did, toward a biocosmic perspective rooted in the ascription of generality and purpose to nature, and even further again to the ascription of nonpractical Imagination to nature in general and human nature in particular. We are dream creatures even more fundamentally than rational producers. As we shall see in later chapters, Mumford and Peirce, in vastly different ways, both echo William Blake's idea that the Poetic Imagination dreamed us into existence.

Such ideas would have sounded impractical to Marx, merely ideological pipe dreams, and would probably strike the contemporary reader as unrealistic or unscientific, despite the fact that abductive conjecture is at the heart of Peirce's invention of pragmatism and his contribution to the logic of science. There can be no science, in Peirce's view, without the ability to conjecture. Yet these ideas are not limited to an overly "aestheticized" conception of society but can be extended to the heart of Marx's thought as well: revolution. Revolution need not be limited to the lightning rod of human social change struck by the forces of history but can be viewed as a transhuman fact of nature. From this perspective, Marx's category of revolution forms one aspect of a much broader category of renewal or transformation: the birthing of new ways of being. In addition, other kinds of change, such as what John Dewey characterized as "reconstruction," remain possibilities too little used in Marx's outlook.

The sudden rusting away of the iron curtain of Eastern Europe in the last couple of months of 1989 is an ideal example of the way nonviolent change through peaceful negotiation and political dialogue can take place effectively. With the exceptions of Rumania and Albania, fragile democracies began to emerge to face the enormous problems of overhauling the revolting legacies of corrupt "revolutionary" communism. As time passes, the thawing out of the Cold War era will come to be viewed as part of the larger context of the exhaustion of the modernist impulse in the late twentieth century. By the end of the 1960s, architects began to move out from the thrall of the "International Style" and its panoptic glass and steel grid, and academic philosophers in America began to try to break out of the grip of analytical philosophy and its windowless architectonic. By the 1980s the Soviet power holders from the Stalinist era began to die out and be replaced with new blood, a senseless war in Afganistan sewed bitter resentments even within the system, and the abysmal economy was in a state of collapse. The Potemkin empire began to look at itself critically for the first time in its history. Though "relentless criticism of everything existing" was Marx's motto, the translator of Marx's early work was an early victim of the Stalinist purges, as Marx himself would probably have been. Criticism was one of the first casualties of Soviet modernism and may yet again be a casualty of "postcommunism": the looming specter of Dostoevsky's "Grand Inquisitor," who provides the earthly bread and releases men from the torment of freedom, has by no means disappeared from Russia, despite the marvelous success of the democratic forces against the attempted coup d'état in August 1991. And, though seldom acknowledged, the resurgence of murderous nationalism in Eastern Europe is one of the darker manifestations of postmodernity. Revolutionary modernism proclaimed the end of history in politics, philosophy, and the arts, and more recently neoconservatives took the end of communism to signal a new end of history and triumph of the West. But emergent violent nationalism is perhaps a true symbol of the end of the "end of history" myth of modernity.

Marshall Berman, in *All That Is Solid Melts into Air,* points out that Marx, although of the generation of Baudelaire, Flaubert, Wagner, Kierkegaard, and Dostoevsky, is seldom thought of as a modernist in the literary sense of modernism, as opposed to the socioeconomic sense of modernization. He suggests a reading of *The Communist Manifesto* which is quite compelling. By analogy, we can look at Communist states as some of the chief embodiments of the dark side of modernism. The sardonic ironies of Communist Russia and China ruled from the walled-off private quarters of the Czar's Kremlin and the Emperor's "Forbidden City," and the mummification of Lenin within a pyramid-like tomb in Red Square, strike one more like bizzare fantasies from the realm of Kafka than actual events in the history of "socialist realism" or modern materialism. Consider the social drama of thousands of Chinese and Russian citizens attempting to create a democratic life in the public squares of Beijing and Moscow around the beginning of the 1990s as the invisible dictators within the Forbidden City and the Kremlin sought to crush public life.

The human creature is distinguished by critical activity in Marx, and indeed "critique" is one of the chief projects of the modern era. Through critique the Enlightenment sought to bring forth a new kind of human, freed from the irrational constraints of tradition, ignorance, religion, and myth. This new human was to be a rationally autonomous being and member of a rationally and scientifically based society. Hence, Marx, the modernist, celebrated modern civilization as containing within its brutal and destructive capitalist industrialism the necessity of revolutionary critique and the eventual emergence of critical communism as realization of the Enlightenment. Yet critical activity is but a tiny portion of extracritical, extrarational activity, which includes human social capacities for imagination, dream, ritual communication, and mythmaking. Our critical capacities are much more immature than our precritical ones: we instinctively purpose myths and deviate from the mythmaking mind at our own peril. Perhaps our most extreme myth, the moving but wrongheaded spirit of modern life, is that we are rationally autonomous beings capable of creating rationally grounded, thoroughly materialistic societies.

Whether scientific materialism, utilitarian capitalist materialism and its consumerist culture, or Marx's historical materialism, the assumption that mind is limited to material causality was the faulty result of the nominalist ethos which created the modern world. This antimyth, the myth of modernity, reveals itself to be what Mumford termed the myth of the "megamachine," the tendency toward self-alienation, toward treating the powers of the human mind as either independent of or solely determined by increasingly inevitable forces of nature or history.

Neither *possibility* nor *generality* depend on the actual material state of affairs, but are independent and irreducible modes of being, if you will pardon my metaphysics. New ideas may arise, not solely as part of an "inevitable" march of history but as the emergence and shaping of a new historical departure. Similarly, there are some general truths, such as $2+2=4$, which are true regardless of what kind of society expresses them or even regardless of the actually existing physical state of affairs: to paraphrase Peirce, two plus two would equal four even if there were not four things in the universe: the reality of truth is ultimately conditional, not actual. If Marx had not been so fixated on dialectically inverting Hegel's historical idealism into historical materialism, a recognition of the idealistic nature of $2+2=4$ as a general, universal truth might have given a more complicated picture for twentieth-century Communist ideologues to ingest. It was the attempt to produce a politically correct realism which produced the $2+2=10$ unreality of modern Communist totalitarianism.

Marx's ingrained scientism helped not only to temper and concretize his Hegelianism but also caused him to succumb to the same *unvermeidlich* or inevitable view of historical progress that marked Hegel's dialectic. The laws of economic production that marked the stages of history inevitably led to the darkness of capitalism as they would lead inevitably toward goodness and light and socialized society. As Mumford put it, Marx's philosophy "rested on the conception of the continued expansion of the machine, a pushing forward of all those processes that had regimented and enslaved mankind, and yet out of this he expected not only a liberation from the existing dilemmas of society but a final cessation of the struggle. . . . Despite all Marx's rich historical knowledge, his theory ends in non-history: the proletariat, once it has thrown off its shackles, lives happily ever afterward. . . . Historic observation shows that there are many modes of change other than dialectic opposition: maturation, mimesis, mutual aid are all as effective as the struggle between opposing classes."[19] Although Marx's theory was rooted in the very ideas of praxis, process, and development, it projected a finality of communism which seemed to deny these ideas. Communist society was a sort of practical version of Hegel's Absolute and shared with it the utopian aspect of a world beyond struggle, evil, and human shortcomings. Hence Marx's reliance on the so-called inevitable links his ideal society with the very reified power complex it sought to undo. As with most attempts to fit life into an ideal scheme, the actualization of Marx's ideas in human history resulted in the diabolical opposite of what he intended: droning, brutal, Communist slave machines run by elites of ruthless power mongers and ideologues.

Yet despite the obvious failings of Marxism, Marx remains an astute social critic and historian, and many aspects of his critique of capitalism, the machine, and modern life, as well as his rooting of human life in experience or practice, when shorn from the vision of an inevitably progressing history and an all-powerful state, will remain valuable resources to social thought. Lewis Mumford's concept of the megamachine, for example, which I discuss in Chapter 4, can be seen as a more refined development of the critiques of the machine given by Marx, Samuel Butler, and others, freed from the unnecessary utilitarian restrictions of Marx's materialism.

A QUITE DIFFERENT VIEW OF THE INVERTED WORLD of capitalism is given by Max Weber, who stressed the significance of the Protestant Ethic in the development of capitalism. The honest attempt to cleanse a corrupted Christianity was marked by Luther's call to the "calling" (*Beruf*), the religious significance of one's vocation, which imbued work with a greater sense of the dignity of one's duty to God. Weber shows how Calvinism proceeded much further than Lutheranism in rationalizing work itself, of centralizing it in such a way that other dimensions of human existence, such as emotional life, artistic expression, free play, and idle curiosity were devalued and even repressed. All that could not rationally justify itself within the rationalized asceticism of this ethos became suspect or lost legitimacy. All that could rationally justify itself became paramount: unlimited acquisition, frugality, the quantification of space, time, and personal life, consequently—how should one call it—the disqualification of personal life (meaning both that the nonrational qualitative uniquenesses of the world were either quantified or rejected, and also that personal life was itself predetermined in the great clockwork of predestination).

The paradoxical consequence of this ascetic attempt to purify life was that rationality became ultimate and unlimited, in effect answerable only to itself and yet based on irrational foundations. Once established, capitalism could dispense with religious motives of spiritual frugality and become transformed into the ethos of unholy hedonism. There arose also the mistaken idea of atomic individuals for whom living relation through community was a mere human artifice and convention, divorced from the nature of things. "Isolatoism" is the word Herman Melville coined to describe this new image of man.

Weber assumed throughout his varied researches a radical and unprecedented uniqueness in modern Western civilization, seeing the "rationalization" of the West as progressive, if problematic. Although the dawning of the modern West was not a necessary historical development, the dynamics of an ethos of rationality led progressively in the direction of an ever more "instrumentally rational" civilization, one requiring a "disenchantment" of the world and bringing along with it unavoidable forms of alienation. Weber held a pessimistic outlook on the emerging rationally bureaucratic world while proposing no purposive alternative other than charismatic outbreaks, because he believed that modern rationality conformed to the nature of rationality per se. The possibility that Weber's whole schematization of rational versus nonrational types of social action, of values utterly separate from "facts," might represent a fatally flawed theory and a worldview leading ultimately to de-rationalization never occurred to him.[20]

From the modern point of view, the rise of the mechanical world picture helped free the rational mind from irrational constraints, making possible great advances in science and technics. But in examining that modern perspective critically, with the hindsight of the twentieth-century experience, the elevation of rational mind to unbounded ruling principle has led increasingly to unintentional irrational consequences which threaten the continued presence of the human personality and of the fantastic diversity of organic life itself. It falsely conceived an unbridgeable gulf between first causes and final causes, between an objective world mechanism and a subjective, spectral world of values.

Weber assumed this split of "the ghost in the machine," the inherited legacy of Descartes and Kant, as a progressive development, and it pervaded his own thinking on political life and the social sciences. The mechanical world picture may have been a historical reality, but it was by no means historically necessary for the rise of sophisticated science. In its false materializing of the object and false etherealizing of the subject, the mechanical world picture represents a progressive abdication of human autonomy to the automaton. It must ignore generative, incarnating mind in favor of either objective mechanism or subjective, incorporeal spirit. This view leads to either a positivist or a conceptualist theory of science, thereby ignoring the place of living abduction, to return to Peirce's idea.

Weber claimed that action has to do with subjectively intended meaning; yet one need not begin with isolate subjects subjectively "intending" meaning, nor is human conduct exhausted by intentions. An alternative view is to see conduct as fundamentally social and derivatively "subjectively intended." One can still champion the subjective as an ineradicable element of human conduct and institutions, but the subjective expressions and intentions of the human personality are not divorced from the social medium, as Weber thought. The passionate and "intending" self is continuous with the communicative signs of the social medium.

One of the consequences of the neo-Kantian perspective shared by Weber and Simmel, as well as many contemporary theorists, is a view of meaning as a human faculty conferred on the chaos of experience. As Weber said: " 'Culture' is a finite segment of the meaningless infinity of the world process, a segment on which *human beings* confer meaning and significance." Simmel sounds even more contemporary in his 1911 essay, "On the Conflict and Tragedy of Culture," where he says: "Ocean and flowers, alpine mountains and the stars in the sky derive what we call their value entirely from their reflections in subjective souls. As soon as we disregard the mystic and fantastic anthropomorphizing of nature, it appears as a continuous contiguous whole, whose undifferentiated character denies its individual parts any special emphasis, any existence which is objectively delimited from others. It is only human categories, that cut out individual parts, to which we ascribe meaning and value. Ironically, we then construct poetic fictions which create a natural beauty that is holy within itself. In reality, however, nature has no other holiness than the one which it evokes in us."21 Simmel's Kantianism, beautifully expressed here, assumes the modern ghost in the machine perspective in denying that nature possesses qualitative differentiation (or form, in Kant's language) independent of human categories. Clearly humans do construct "poetic fictions" of nature, given that being human means being inescapably anthropomorphic to at least some degree. But admitting this does not rule out the possibility that human life, so rooted in the fantastic symboling processes of dreaming, ritual life, and language, may not itself be a "poetic fiction" evoked by nature. Nor does it rule out the possibility that Kant's dualistic view of nature and knowledge may itself be a poetic fiction of the modern mind.

From my perspective, the Lockean/Kantian view that all natural beauty is but a "secondary quality" of subjective human perception rather than a genuine transaction between a quality of nature and a human perceiver, that faculties of knowledge spring unevolved and full-blown from human heads alone rather than as tempered achievements of creatures who evolved in transaction with the inherent forms of nature, strikes me as the modern fantastic anthropomorphizing of nature into the ghost in the machine. Though Simmel, and more particularly Weber, saw more deeply into the ever-darkening consequences of modern rationalization than many of their more optimistic contemporaries, neither saw the possibility that the very process of rationalization was itself responsible for conferring meaninglessness on the world process, thereby reducing it to a sensory manifold. That is, they could not see that the Kantian perspective might itself be a product of a faulty and by no means inevitable development of rationalization.

Simmel, standing within the Kantian orbit, noted the parallel emergence of objective nature and subjective freedom over the past few hundred years: "Thus we can observe the distinctive parallel movement during the last three hundred years, namely that on the one hand the laws of nature, the material order of things, the objective necessity of events emerge more clearly and distinctly, while on the other we see the emphasis upon the independent individuality, upon personal freedom, upon independence (*Fürsichsein*) in relation to all external and natural forces becoming more and more acute and increasingly stronger. . . . Whatever difficulties metaphysics may find in the relationship between the objective determination of things and the subjective determination of the individual, as aspects of culture their development runs parallel and the accentuation of the one seems to require the accentuation of the other in order to preserve the equipoise of inner life."[22] With characteristic perspicacity, Simmel reveals an unexpected correlation in the making of the modern world, one which released previously undisclosed human potentials.

Yet although these are distinctive achievements of the modern era—the mechanical view of nature and the release of the personality (exemplified, as Milan Kundera points out, in the emergence of the novel), they came at what we must now realize was a terrible cost. What Simmel was celebrating as a modern epiphany might also be characterized as the manifestation of the split-brain world of a mechanized nature severed from organic purpose and a spectral world of subjectivity sundered from nature. The legacy of the bifurcated worlds of Descartes and Kant culminated in extreme forms of objectivism and subjectivism in the twentieth century, with deadly consequences we can no longer ignore. The Kantian view that "facts" are objective and values are subjective, which both Simmel and Weber inherited, gave license to the diabolical release and massive expansion of powers which exceeded human purpose or limitation: let us not forget that the atomic bomb is one of the great epiphanies of the modern world, and that German *Innerlichkeit* and *Kultur* could easily turn into the god-like view that I can do whatever I feel inside, apart from otherness, a view which reached its extreme terminus in Adolph Hitler.

This dark side of the modern epiphany was expressed quite clearly by H. G. Wells in his book *The World Set Free,* which detailed a world nuclear war which involved what Wells called "atomic bombs." That book was published in 1913, before the first outbreak of world war!

Weber's Enlightenment view of the logic of modernity jettisoned those extrarational, yet reasonable, tempered sources of human intelligence, such as sentiment and imagination, from the institution of scientific understanding. Though Weber is frequently viewed as a "humanistic" sociologist because of his emphasis on an interpretative, *verstehende Soziologie,* his deeply rooted belief in the Kantian worldview that so dominated German thought caused him to accept a reified conception of objectivity and science and a relativist conception of values.

Weber's logic is framed within what I have termed "cultural nominalism."[23] It is a view that says that life's highest purpose is not reasonable. The logic of rationality is to tend increasingly toward an "instrumental rationality" in which purpose is oriented by subjective interest. In moving toward the "instrumental," rationality becomes increasingly not an instrument but a calculating machine, and one in which the user of the "instrument" becomes instrument to the machine's "purpose": single-standard homogeneous system.

Is this the purport of cultural action, biological development, cosmic evolution: to become divested of human qualities in order to assume the requirements of a machine? Or is it rather the outcome of a fundamentally distorted perspective convincingly disproven by anyone with eyes to see by the events of the twentieth century?

Twentieth-century civilization is marked, in my view, by extremism, by tendencies motivated by the very dichotomies of cultural nominalism to achieve pure finality or pure primordiality, pure rationality or pure irrationality (defined as biology, originality, novelty, or charisma), pure objectivity or pure subjectivity. Even those movements of thought that did not claim one side of the dichotomy or the other as the truth tended to define the world as if these aspects of experience were truly dichotomous; as one sees, for example, in the radical splitting of facts and values, in relativism, in Freud's psychology, or, to return to mainstream social theory, in Durkheim.

If Marx's place in the "holy trinity" of canonical social theory is that of "conflict sociologist" of social structure and class, and if Max Weber's is that of "voluntarist sociologist" of social organization and bureaucratic authority, then Emile Durkheim functions as a "macro" sociologist concerned with how symbolic structures "maintain" the patterns of society and culture, to use the terminology of Talcott Parsons. Fortunately, each of these thinkers was broader than these categories in which they have now been stereotyped by professional social scientists.

Durkheim is probably most noted for his last major book, *The Elementary Forms of the Religious Life,* which was an attempt to find the fundamental structures of society through examination of ethnographies of primitive peoples. Since Durkheim's time the word "primitive" has come to be criticized and qualified—all of the most "primitive" peoples known actually exhibit complex social organization and rich emotional and imaginative lives—but Durkheim believed that the Australian aborigines represented the world's most undeveloped people and therefore provided a glimpse at the original structures of society.

By turning to Australian aborigines, Durkheim could see social structure in its most pristine primitive state, freed from the "luxuriant growth and accretions" of more developed peoples. He argues that "collective representations," symbols such as "churinga" or symbolic rocks, pieces of wood, and other totemic and ritual objects, function to focalize the "collective conscience" of a people and thereby provide the underlying conceptual basis for religion and society. Religion and collective representations are, in effect, the mirror that society holds up to itself. Durkheim claimed that this reveals that the basic faculties of knowing are social, as against Kant's individualistic faculty theory of knowledge. He sought to socialize Kant, but he nevertheless retained underlying Kantian dichotomies, such as individual versus social or knowledge versus experience.

Between the utilitarian assumption of Spencer that social solidarity derives from individuals pursuing self-interest in exchange and the collectivist assumption of Comte that solidarity derives from a common consensus, Durkheim sought to show how social evolution naturally produces a division of labor, which nevertheless creates a new kind of solidarity rather than obliterates it. Modern life did not need to choose between a Spencerian individualism wherein morality was a by-product, or a Comtean collectivism which swallowed up the individual into a homogenous morality. Instead, morality itself, as the means of social solidarity, becomes differentiated, as social evolution pursues its inevitable course.

Durkheim's theory of collective representations, religious belief, and social structure remain, however, virtually ahistorical: the same underlying structure holds, despite a diversity of collective representations, and manifests as either the "mechanical solidarity" of traditional societies in which each member can do the same tasks as others, or in the "organic solidarity" of modern society and economy, in which individuals become progressively differentiated.

In his *Division of Labor in Society*, Durkheim used the concepts of mechanical versus organic solidarity to characterize the difference between traditional tribal societies and modern life. Although one intuitively assumes that "mechanical" would illustrate modern society, Durkheim meant by mechanical a society where one member can perform the same actions as all the other members: in short, an undifferentiated society. By "organic," Durkheim meant a society wherein members functioned as specialized organs.

The more common sense of "organic" is the contextualized relations of parts to whole, which are in many ways more characteristic of traditional peoples and polytechnic civilizations. If one takes a more critical view of the culture of modern differentiation, "mechanical" is the substitution of qualitative uniqueness and multivocal expression by centralization, homogeneity, standardization, and decontextualized differentiation. The specialized worker who turns a screw all day long is not a specialized "organ" in Durkheim's sense, since he or she has been divested of those qualities of purposive spontaneity and growth associated with organic growth. The worker instead has been rendered "mechanical"—in the everyday sense—because deprived of intrinsic connection to the organic context or purposive "whole" of the activity, not to mention the capacity to limit the action or inaugurate other actions. If one knew nothing of organic life and could observe this worker it might be difficult to know which was the screwer and which the screwed.

Durkheim assumed specialization to be a natural component of progressive evolution and though he clearly saw the dangers of normlessness and alienation which the breakdown of common belief by modern diversification could entail, he never critically questioned the "differential calculus" of modern life per se. He would grow increasingly wary about the effects of modernization, but he always retained his Enlightenment faith that a social science could be created which would rationally reform society in the service of social evolution and progress. Perhaps this Enlightenment vision was personally shattered when his son and a number of his followers were killed in the first World War, followed shortly after by his own physical breakdown and death. Yet Durkheim's writings remain imbued with the faith that rational reform can remake society.

One sees a variation on the theme of the ghost in the machine metaphor in Durkheim's conception of human nature as fundamentally dualistic: "It is not without reason, therefore, that man feels himself to be double: he actually is double. There are in him two classes of states of consciousness that differ from each other in origin and nature, and in the ends toward which they aim. One class merely expresses our organisms and the objects to which they are most directly related [and are] strictly individual. . . . The states of consciousness of the other class, on the contrary, come to us from society; they transfer society into us and connect us with something that surpasses us. . . . It is evident that passions and egoistic tendencies derive from our individual constitutions, while our rational activity—whether theoretical or practical—is dependent on social causes"[24] Durkheim mistakenly assumes that the passions, the fruit of that long process of social evolution which created humans, are not social. He materializes both passion and "egoism" by ignoring how both are the *products* of evolutionary social practices and simultaneously etherealizes the social as limited to the realm of ideals or collective representations.

Durkheim was broader than more recent French structuralists and poststructuralists in including emotions within collective representations, yet his theory still remains conceptualistic and rationalistic in holding emotions as carriers of social conceptions instead of viewing social conceptions as the surface film of deeper societal, extrarational emotions. In Durkheim's conceptualist theory, collective representations, religious beliefs, science, and society form a system of knowledge rather than ways of living, just as rituals are but variable and secondary content to an underlying logic rather than enactments of life. Claude Lévi-Strauss was later to codify these ideas by combining Durkheim with Ferdinand de Saussure's theory of language, creating a structuralist social theory which captured the intellectual scene much the same way that its predecessor and opposite, existentialism, had done in the 1950s. By the end of the 1970s, however, structuralism was "out" and poststructuralism was "in." Though many hailed these movements as progress, it is my opinion that they are but another chapter in the depersonalization of the twentieth-century intellect: by contrast, one feels more of the human presence in Durkheim, even if his doctrine of collective representations remains ultimately conceptualistic.

In viewing the passions as not intrinsically social, and the individual as needing to be attuned to an outer social milieu not in any way original to the individual, Durkheim unnecessarily limited the concept of the social and what is involved in the process of socialization. Consider, for example, the passionate human activity of dreaming. All the world dreams every night, and therefore dreaming, though a private activity, is clearly one of the most social activities which characterize the human individual. The passion to dream transcends socialization from the outer environment, even if much of the imagery of dreams is culturally learned.[25] We can't help but to dream, to engage in nightly excursions of passion, often of a most fantastic nature. Yet because of its "inner" and intangible nature, dreaming is apparently not counted as significant behavior by evolutionary and social scientists.

In other words, although it is legitimate to discuss worldviews of the most fantastic natures, the imaging process itself, or what might be termed the autonomic "recombinant mimetics" of the human psyche, is overlooked as a formative influence on human development. Durkheim himself raises interesting questions about dreams in his *Elementary Forms,* but because he was committed to a conceptualist theory of representation he could not allow that dreams might form an intrinsic language of images: that dreams might "stand for" themselves, as sign presentations or icons, as well as "standing for" personal or collective experiences as representations or symbols.

Dreams not only passively symbolize experience but actively create inner experience. Jung, more than Freud, recognized this creative aspect of dreams, but like Freud he succumbed to the one-sided "inwardness" tendency of German thought, and undervalued the "outwardness" and "otherness" that are also irreducible aspects of human experience and human dreaming.

If we consider dreams as "recombinant mimetics," in which time, space, emotions, personalities, familiarities and the exotic, desires and anxieties assume fantastic juxtapositions through the language of images, it becomes possible to see how dreaming may be as or more potent—and dangerous—than recombinant genetics. If dreaming made possible for prespeaking protohumans an expanded sense of time and social relations not limited to immediate experience, it may have laid the groundwork for symbolic consciousness: dreaming, in all its fantastic diversity, is perhaps the original "collective representation" of the emergent inner life of humankind. The anxieties produced by dreams and their fantastic and sublime logic could have impelled and even compelled emergent humanity toward interpretation, the simultaneous freedom from instinctive and habituated experience and violent tearing away from the profound envelope of mature truth that instinct, in its proper environment, provides.

Although humanity has become increasingly conscious of itself, it has never stopped dreaming. Nor have its dreams become any less wondrous and terrifying. Despite the claims of modern, supposedly rational, culture, the powers which move history and human development decidedly involve more than "rationality" and may remain more dream-like than we proud moderns would wish. In my perspective there are waking dreams or myths which guide whole epochs, much as our rituals of conscious rationality would deny them. Could it be that the Enlightenment, in seeking to subdue and transcend the passions and irrational capacities of the live human creature, was simply afraid of the dark?

Exploding the Canon

The canonical social theorists may have differed in their interpretations of modernity, but they did not question the inevitability of its development. These theorists and their adherents still dominate contemporary discourse in the social sciences, despite the fact that our post-Hiroshima world and its fetishism of nuclear commodities rendered obsolete the very concept of inevitability. The dominant voices in contemporary social theory have returned to the problem of meaning that so animated the earlier theorists, but in ways that betray domination by the very theoretical techniques that they attribute to society. If the older and now canonical social theory was insufficiently differentiated from the megamachine of modernity it sought to criticize, the newer "grand theory" has become the megamachine itself: contemptuous of organic nature because of overweening pride in a rationalistic conception of culture, ignorant of or indifferent to those qualities and capacities of the human creature and human communities which cannot be fitted into the rational system, and never seriously questioning the whole premises on which modern civilization and modern social theory are built.

Human communities and civilizations are not simply talk worlds, as they are for both Karl Popper and Jürgen Habermas, who have developed theories rooted in rational discourse; nor are they bookish text worlds, as Paul Ricouer, Jacques Derrida, and poststructuralists would have us believe; nor simply a "structurating" coordination of ethereal structures and Isolato "agencies," as they are for Umberto Eco, Pierre Bourdieu, and Anthony Giddens; nor again "subsystem integrations" within the BIG SYSTEM as they were for Parsons and perhaps are again for Niklas Luhmann, Jeffrey Alexander, Richard Münch, and other neo-Parsonians. Both a local community or culture and broader civilizations are living social relations incarnate and, as such, involve orders of intelligence and organs of meaning much deeper than all of these varieties of rationalism could allow. And it is precisely in those areas repressed or excluded from meaning by rationalism—in the living, organic, biocosmic tissue of semeiosis—that both the organization of communities and members as well as human transformative possibilities are to be found. The leading theories of our time remained shackled to the modern myth of "the ghost in the machine," to eighteenth- and nineteenth-century modes of thinking clothed in late twentieth-century fashions. Far from being able to confront the self-destroying calamities of our time, they form an intellectual opiate: social theory.

In the late twentieth century, the modern myth of the ghost in the machine has approached its perfection: the transformation of organic nature into the world machine and of humane reason into the inhuman specter of rationality. Most contemporary attempts to provide better theories of rationality or alternative theories of antirationality are but variations on the ghost in the machine theme. A more fundamental questioning of the entrenched premisses of the modern era itself is urgently required. Such a questioning of the foundations of belief has been a central component in modern thought since Descartes, yet some allegedly "critical" theorists today shy away from the critical confrontation with the foundations of modern belief and its root metaphors either out of an entranced habituation to those patterns of thought or out of fear that the rejection of the premisses of modernity entails the rejection of its many positive achievements, or, even worse, that it leads to reactionary antimodernism. Such a questioning, as I hope to show, requires critically delving into the deeper sources of reason, which modern thought has tended to deny or degrade. The "disenchanted" world brought about by the mechanistic world picture of modern science and by rationalized culture then reveals itself to be a product of the cryptoreligion of modern materialism rather than the necessary ground of scientific truth. Modern culture reified physicality while etherealizing the perfusion of signs in which we humans live and by which we evolved into humankind: signs which bodied us forth from an organic nature far more mysterious than a mere machine, no matter how complex a machine nature is conceived to be.

We can no longer consign patterns of feeling, acting, and thinking which do not fit modern rationality to the self-serving category of "pre-enlightenment" thought—meaning obsolete—as many contemporary thinkers wish. Nor can we ignore or denigrate the Western legacy of self-critical reason and universal human rights, so central to the political, cultural, and intellectual institutions of contemporary world civilization—even if frequently violated—as many current antirationalists and relativists would like to do. Something more is required: a marriage of these assumed opposites.

Hence the chief question confronting contemporary social thought is not simply how to reconstruct "grandiose theory," as a number of its practitioners seem to think, or to "deconstruct" the contemporary world through a "post-theory" which would ignore the big questions by declaring them nonexistent, but rather: Can "enchantment"—the spontaneous, passionate, and mythic modes of relation to the wider world—and critical reason meet in a more fruitful relationship to provide a fuller understanding of reasonableness? By exploring neglected paths in twentieth-century social thought and philosophy of the past century, I hope to suggest some beginnings for a new and nonmodern basis for contemporary thought. My working hypothesis is that there is a broader outlook which undercuts the ghost in the machine mentality of the modern era, that a small community of thinkers have already articulated such a worldview, that overturning the ghost in the machine means rejecting many widely shared beliefs, such as scientific materialism, pure Darwinism, the nature-culture "dichotomy," and anti-naturalistic accounts of human meaning, and therefore that this perspective may appear strange and perhaps even retrograde to the sophisticated contemporary reader. I can only attempt to present my claims and arguments as clearly as I can and hope that the patient reader may find at least some of them compelling.

2

Of Life and Social Thought

The old idea of the vitality of the universe was evolved long before history begins, and elaborated into a vast religion before we get a glimpse of it. When history does begin, in China or India, Egypt, Babylonia, even in the Pacific and in aboriginal America, we see evidence of one underlying religious idea: the conception of the vitality of the cosmos, the myriad vitalities in wild confusion, which still is held in some sort of array: and man, amid all the glowing welter, adventuring, struggling, striving for one thing, life, vitality, more vitality: to get into himself more and more of the gleaming vitality of the cosmos. That is the treasure.

—D. H. Lawrence

Do not be afraid of life!

—Alyosha, in The Brothers Karamazov

On the Problem of Going beyond Life

Among the curious facts of intellectual life today is how peripheral the concept of life has become to most social theorists and philosophers. Despite a revival of Nietzsche, philosophical pragmatism, and the sociological "classics," contemporary social thought has tended to ignore the significance which the concept of life held for the late nineteenth and early twentieth centuries, producing a major blind spot in our understanding of the spirit of that age and of its import for ours. Considering how generalized the project of a philosophy of life had become at the turn of the century, inextricably connected to the parallel project for a philosophy of meaning, the history of twentieth-century thought is notable for the ways it veered away from life in the name of meaning. One might argue that the term "life" is one of those intrinsically ungraspable phantoms, capable of meaning just about anything its beholder wishes it to mean. But so too are the concepts of "meaning" and "culture" which continue to be central concerns of social thinkers, and so something more than the imprecision of the term "life" is required to explain why conceiving life as a central feature of social theory no longer animates contemporary thought.

The attempts to formulate a conception of life were key symbols of the emerging twentieth-century mind, and provide a standard by which to evaluate contemporary thought. In its tendency to deny the relevance of organic life for questions of meaning, much of contemporary intellectual life may be viewed as part of a larger metaphysic which involves the escape from organic life through rationalization. Conversely, the tendency to deny the irreducible significance of mind and its capacities to generalize and actualize reason, a denial manifest in various forms of biological reductionism, bespeaks a larger metaphysic of automatism. Together these two outlooks—roughly rationalism or idealism on the one hand and automatism or materialism on the other—express the modern ideology of the ghost in the machine.

Despite widely varying meanings of the term "life," the concept of life emerged as a central topic for the leading thinkers of the late nineteenth and early twentieth centuries although that fact also has been ignored and virtually consigned to oblivion. A possible exception to this forgetting might be the traditions of *Lebensphilosophie* and Philosophical Anthropology, terms which are today usually associated with the German thought. The terms may be German, but it is important to remember that the ideas comprising these schools of thought were pervasive throughout Europe and America in the early part of the century. The publication of Darwin's *The Origin of Species* had an immediate impact on social theorists, as one sees in Marx's admiration for Darwin's observations, despite his critique that Darwin projected the ideology of his English class-structured society onto nature.

Even before Darwin published his great book in 1859, Herbert Spencer was developing an evolutionary social theory, which idealized industrial European civilization as the pinnacle of organic life. Although he did not invent the term "evolution," Spencer, rather than Darwin, is the person responsible for its widespread use. Beginning in his 1857 article, "The Ultimate Laws of Physiology," Spencer adopted the term "evolution" as a preferable replacement for "progress," which he thought to be too anthropocentric, and it included both organic and inorganic processes. Spencer also suggested the phrase "survival of the fittest" to Darwin, and its adoption was supported by Alfred Russel Wallace, the codiscoverer of natural selection. Darwin's ideas were a significant influence on Nietzsche's conception of a "will to power" underlying the hypocritical artifices of civilization. Pragmatism, which originated in America but had profound influence throughout Europe, can be viewed in this context as a philosophy of life which undertook a critical reconstruction of Darwin.

Today, when Darwin's principle of natural selection acts as a cornerstone to evolutionary theory, the fact that there were decades of serious debate within evolutionary and social theory is not always remembered. Peter Kropotkin, to take one example, is usually remembered as a political anarchist but not as a geographer who spent years in Siberia leading geographical field explorations. Kropotkin did not deny that natural selection based on competitive fitness was a powerful factor in evolution, but he claimed that it was not the whole picture. In his observations of nature, the "mutual aid" which organisms provide to one another was a factor of evolution not reducible to competitiveness alone: "As soon as we study animals—not in laboratories and museums only, but in the forest and the prairie, in the steppe and the mountains—we at once perceive that though there is an immense amount of warfare and extermination going on amidst various species, and especially amidst various classes of animals, there is, at the same time, as much, or perhaps even more, of mutual support, mutual aid, and mutual defence amidst animals belonging to the same species or, at least, to the same society. Sociability is as much a law of nature as mutual struggle."[1]

Mutual aid or ecological symbiosis can be seen as a critique that Darwin's competitive model reduced certain social relations to by-products of self-maximizing activity. This problem of genuinely noncompetitive social behavior, such as altruism, was to plague evolutionary theory until the 1960s, when certain mechanisms, such as so-called reciprocal altruism, were invented to reappropriate the social to the great competitive machine of natural selection. "Reciprocal altruism" was a term coined by R. L. Trivers to signify "I'll scratch your back if you scratch mine." In other words, it was a theory which enabled evolutionary thought to deny that altruism—or genuinely social behavior not based on self-interest—is real. Reciprocal altruism and the emerging field of sociobiology preserved the "free market" political economy on which Darwin's model of natural selection was based, while radically individualizing the concept of fitness. But Kropotkin's objection still holds: "Sociability is as much a law of nature as mutual struggle."

When we remember thinkers as diverse as Kropotkin of Russia, Bergson of France, Spencer and the Darwinians of Britain, and Samuel Butler and later Patrick Geddes, Samuel Alexander, C. Lloyd Morgan, L. T. Hobhouse, and others, the American pragmatists Peirce, James, Dewey, and Mead, as well as Charles Horton Cooley, Alfred North Whitehead, Nietzsche, Dilthey, Rudolph Eucken, and Sigmund Freud, we are reminded of how pervasive the questions of life, nature, and evolution were. These thinkers and others all considered it important to include a conception of life in their general philosophy or framework. When we broaden further to remember writers such as William Morris and George Bernard Shaw, Strindberg, Butler's fictional works, the whole art nouveau movement, architects such as Louis Sullivan, Frank Lloyd Wright, and Antonio Gaudi, we are reminded that "life," whatever it meant, was the virtual pivot of the age. The turn to the concept of life by intellectuals was parallel to the artistic movement variously called art nouveau, *Jugendstil,* or arts and crafts, which sprang forth near the end of the nineteenth century with a program that placed the representation of life and organic form at its center.

A number of philosophers and social theorists sought to incorporate the implications of Darwin and Spencer into social theory, as was clearly the case in those connected with the "social Darwinist" movement, and Spencer was immensely influential in the founding of American sociology. Yet the word "life" also holds a nonbiological meaning, as when we speak of "social life" or "the life of the mind," and a number of thinkers developed conceptions of life in this direction. The term *Lebensphilosophie,* or "philosophy of life," for example, is perhaps most closely associated with Wilhelm Dilthey, for whom terms such as *Leben* (life) or *Erlebnis* (experience) meant primarily cultural constructs of experience, concepts signifying a specifically human nature fundamentally different from unreflective biological nature. As Dilthey put it:

> In the human studies I shall confine the term "life" to the human world; its meaning is thus determined by the sphere in which it is used and thus not open to misunderstanding. Life consists of interactions between people; the finite course of a particular life is regarded by a spectator as belonging to one person because the body in which it occurs seems to remain the same; yet, this lifetime has the strange characteristic that every part of it is consciously linked to the others by some kind of experience of continuity, coherence and identity. . . . Life is the context in which these interactions, conditioned by the causal order of physical objects including the psychological events in bodies, take place. This life is always and everywhere spatially and temporally determined—localized, as it were, in the spatio-temporal order of people's lives. . . . Then, and only then, do we discover a general property of life, not experienced in nature or even the natural objects which we call living organisms.[2]

It was Dilthey, the antinaturalistic *Lebensphilosoph,* who was a key participant in the German methodological dispute, advocating the distinction between the *Geisteswissenschaften* versus the *Naturwissenschaften* (or human sciences versus natural sciences), claiming that the cultural and social sciences were hermeneutically rooted in interpretive methods rather than naturalistic laws and methods. Dilthey's antagonists were positivists who sought to reduce the problem of meaning to one of mechanical or systemic explanation, thereby producing a general science which ignored the crucial contexts of meaning one finds in human lives. *Lebensphilosophie,* for Dilthey and many others, was clearly antinaturalistic in claiming that causal laws of nature do not provide a sufficient basis for understanding human action and that therefore a specific human science is required. As he put it in 1894, "Die Natur erklären wir, das Seelenleben verstehen wir" ("We explain nature, we interpret human life"). He developed a powerful critique against physicalistic reductionism, but remained uncritical of the idea that natural science must be physicalistic and untouched by meaning, an assumption that continues today in such apparent opposites as Hans-Georg Gadamer and Jürgen Habermas, who both regard natural science as an inherently technical activity needing to be supplemented from the "outside" by hermeneutics or "communicative rationality."

Within Germany the idea of a *Lebensphilosophie* animated the work of Dilthey, Max Scheler, and others, and Georg Simmel saw the centrality of the life-concept in philosophy and the arts as itself indicative of the character of the twentieth century. But with the nazification of *Lebensphilosophie* in the 1930s, the concept of life was perverted to racist ideology and even today retains these negative overtones for many contemporary theorists. The significance of life, the "organic," and biology was also central to the development of pragmatism and sociology in America.[3] Yet between a combination of critiques of the eugenics movement as ignoring "nurture," and the rise of behaviorism, scientistic sociology and positivism—which eschewed the kind of broad philosophy of conduct which marked pragmatism and thinkers such as Cooley—the concept of life also tended to become discredited and to drop out of sociological concern.

One does see discussions today of the "life-world" or of "forms of life," deriving from Husserl's *Lebenswelt* concept or Wittgenstein's *Lebensformen,* both signifying social constructs of experience rather than something natural. But organic life itself—biological life or nature—has been largely discredited or, rather, has come to be seen as irrelevant to questions of meaning and culture.

In his 1918 essay, "The Conflict in Modern Culture," Georg Simmel pointed out the significance of the concept of life for twentieth-century culture. He saw in the rise of artistic expressionism and in the prevalence of *Lebensphilosophie* itself, especially philosophical pragmatism, a new cultural paradox. In Simmel's view, as we will see, human cultures are marked by an ever-present dialectical tension between form and life. Yet this dialectic between form and fluid vitality had reached a peculiar turning point by the turn of the century: the form of the twentieth century was revealing itself as life itself. Simmel drew attention to the paradox that life, inherently formless, was becoming the form of the age—a formless form. His examples included expressionism in art and pragmatism in philosophy. In Kandinsky's works of the period in which Simmel was writing, color is liberated from form to become expressive in its own right. Jamesian pragmatism, with its elevation of vital existence over immovable truth, struck Simmel as a key indicator of the paradoxical transposition of life to form. One might add that Simmel himself, though still a formalist, drew from the same spirit of the time in turning to *Lebensphilosophie*. Unfortunately, he did not see the other half of the paradox, the formalization of life itself, resulting in lifeless life. Instead of a dialectical tension between life and form, a strange inversion was occurring, producing lifeless life and formless form, each, in effect, canceling the other out instead of transforming it.

The physicists say that should a piece of matter encounter a piece of antimatter, a tremendous explosion would result. With hindsight we can see the cultural equivalent in the explosive artistic, intellectual, social, and political forces released in the twentieth century, illustrating the problematic relationship which life and form had assumed. Life was central to the emerging social theories and philosophies of the early twentieth century, yet one can scarcely appreciate its importance in contemporary sanitized reconstructions of the thought of that time. The other, missing half of Simmel's equation, formalization, has frozen the life out of the current canon of social theorists and philosophers. Yet the concept of life, so indeterminate in its variegated meanings, nevertheless provides the hidden key to the critical understanding of our age, and perhaps the means to open the door to the next one.

BIOLOGICAL AND CULTURAL REDUCTIONISM

Most social theorists today would prefer to address questions of what is considered "significance," and the concept of life is generally regarded as either insignificant for the question of meaning or as a form of reductionism, except perhaps by sociobiologists and noncanonical social theorists. Sociobiologists reverse the equation and regard the question of meaning as insignificant, except as it addresses the rational calculus of individual genetic survival, or what might, in theological terms, be described as the afterlife of the sperm and egg. The social person and public life seem to be largely illusory to sociobiologists, and even life itself is directed solely toward the transmission and maximization of genetic capital.

ALL HUMAN FACTS, RELATIONS, AND CULTURAL CONVENTIONS are easily filtered through the sociobiological matrix as rational choices for individual genetic gain, echoing similar tendencies in so-called rational choice theory to view strategic individual gain as the sole basis underlying human conduct and decision, in Freudian theory for sexuality to motivate all private and social life, and in capitalism for maximal competitive profitmaking to be regarded as a law of nature. Indeed, sociobiology is itself a philosophy of greed, in which all human meaning is but an epiphenomenal instrument for genetic capitalism. Or put conversely, all evolution of life on the earth seems to have been evolving toward modern capitalism and its radical individualism, boundless maximization and struggle, and inevitable progress. It is not surprising that most social theorists reject this form of biological reductionism and naive ideology as a valid social theory. What is truly a wonder, however, is how frequently this view of biology is accepted by supposedly "critical" social theorists as an adequate understanding of biology.

Most critical theorists assume that biology must translate into some form of reductionism, such as human ethology or sociobiology, though they often neglect to see how sociobiology—even when limited to nonhuman life—is an antiorganic form of rationalism, neither social nor biological. In Germany, judging, for example, from Jürgen Habermas's attitude, biological approaches to human conduct are almost automatically suspect because of the perversities of the Nazi era. Clearly there are good grounds for this prejudice, since the authoritarian ideology in some theories of *Lebensphilosophie,* philosophical anthropology, and ethology fit in quite well with Nazi ideology and were, in fact, appropriated by the Nazis.[4] Those Nazis who sought to develop biologically oriented approaches to human conduct, such as Konrad Lorenz or Arnold Gehlen, were well rewarded in the nazification of German universities. Rudolf Hess told the assembled masses as early as 1934: "National Socialism is nothing but applied biology," and the mass medical murders of the late thirties which preceded the Holocaust were based on the concept of *lebensunwertes Leben* ("life unworthy of life"), a horrific application of "the survival of the fittest."[5] But since the Nazis were clearly false and perverse in their politics and worldview, why should one assume that their definition of biology—a big machine playing "follow the leader" (Führer = leader)—was any less false than their similar view of society? The nazification of the concept of life by the Third Reich does not invalidate the concept of life in general, just as the nazification of politics does not invalidate the concept of politics in general. By the same token, why should reasonable people today swallow whole cloth the only slightly revised biology of human ethologists, such as former Nazi advocate Konrad Lorenz (whose most famous innovation was to convince goslings to goosestep and play "follow the leader")? Why should one, in other words, not adopt the same critical attitude toward the concept of biology itself, instead of merely uncritically accepting the received mechanical perspective?

Consider the following words of a human ethologist, originally given as a lecture in June 1986 in Bonn, with the nuclear fallout from Chernobyl still fresh on the ground just outside the lecture hall: "Science and technology are a product of nature; they are the logical goal of an evolutionary process that has always rewarded a better understanding of the world with reproductive success. . . . Modern technology is a product of nature. Thus, it would be as useless to forbid its continuing use by man as it would be to forbid a bird to fly. However, indiscriminate use of technology is another matter. The conquest and transformation of the earth by a single, knowledgeable species, namely man, is an inevitable consequence of evolution. Man in the 20th century has brought nature completely under his control and can direct the evolutionary process to achieve his *own* ends. He is truly the crowning achievement of creation, its subject and object, the very *incarnation* of evolution."[6]

"Man in the 20th century . . . the very *incarnation* of evolution": only a sleepwalker could believe such bio-Hegelian claptrap in the time of Chernobyl and Bhopal, in the age of Auschwitz and Hiroshima. "Man in the 20th century" has not brought "nature completely under his control," but the machine in the twentieth century has nearly brought man completely under its control. The "laws" of nature and human destiny believed in by Neuweiler and other ethologists and sociobiologists—including continual struggle, maximization, and inevitable progress—are not the laws of organic life to anyone who observes life in its fullness but rather those of the inorganic machine.

The ethologists and sociobiologists simply ignore those fundamental facts of social communication and ecological symbiosis in nature—Kropotkin's "Mutual Aid"—or reduce them to by-products of individualism, including "social" Darwinism. And in viewing the "conquest and transformation of the earth" by humans as an "inevitable consequence of evolution" they must also ignore the possibility that many of their examples of human "progress," such as industrialization and advanced technology, may in the end prove catastrophically destructive to all life and evolution. When Neuweiler equates science and technology with reproductive success he apparently forgets about the very low rates of reproduction in Germany—in effect he is dooming his own theory as not "advanced." The very facts that the countries with the greatest "reproductive success" today are not the scientifically and technologically advanced ones, which, by contrast, have the lowest rates of reproduction, and that so-called reproductive success so frequently translates into socioeconomic chaos at least should have tempered his views of what constitutes human evolutionary success. It is apparent that ethologists and sociobiologists fundamentally ignore the possibility that the mechanical *Weltbild* may be simply an ideological by-product of certain distortions in modernity rather than the unimpeachable foundation of a scientific biology.

Compare Neuweiler's 1986 description of twentieth-century man as the "crowning achievement of evolution" with Lorenz's 1940 wartime call for Nazi evolution: "Whether we share the fate of the dinosaurs or whether we raise ourselves to a higher level of development, scarcely imaginable by the current organization of our brains, is exclusively a question of biological survival power and life-will of our people. Today especially the great difference depends very much on the question whether or not we can learn to combat the decay phenomena in our people and in humanity which arise from the lack of natural selection. In this contest for survival or extinction, we Germans are far ahead of all other cultural peoples." Was Lorenz being original here, or was he himself only playing "follow the leader," as his goslings did when they followed him? Consider what Lorenz's Führer, Adolph Hitler, had to say in *Mein Kampf*: "At this point, someone or other may laugh, but this planet once moved through the ether for millions of years without human beings and it can do so again some day if men forget they owe their higher existence, not to the ideas of a few crazy ideologists, but to the knowledge and ruthless application of Nature's stern and rigid laws."

Elsewhere in 1940, Lorenz stated as clearly as possible how the knowledge of nature's stern and rigid laws should be ruthlessly applied: "If it should turn out . . . the mere removal of natural selection causes the imbalance of the race, then race-care must consider an even more stringent elimination of the ethically less valuable than is done today, because it would, in this case, literally have to replace all selection factors that operate in the natural environment."[7] When the Nazi Lorenz called for "an even more stringent elimination of the ethically less valuable than is done today," the Nazi "applied biology" program had already murdered a couple of hundred thousand men, women, and children in the name of medicine, setting the stage for the Holocaust. And in the Holocaust, German "race-care," or, as it is usually called, Nazi genocide, effectively carried out Lorenz's call for blood in its wholesale rationalized slaughter of those millions of men, women, and children who did not fit the demented Nazi dream.

The theoretical foundations of the human ethology viewpoint come perilously close to the biology of fascism. Although contemporary ethologists clothe the human level with more liberal implications, saying that we can repress our "natural" instincts for domination and war-making aggression by limiting natural selection, they assume very much the same underlying biology of power. Perhaps one might even say that from this viewpoint the Nazis were more consistent, and would be the pinnacle of "natural man" instead of the deadly and diabolical perversion of all things natural and cultural they actually were.

A fundamental reconception not only of ethology and sociobiology but of the unquestioned assumption of modern biology and evolutionary theory in general is now required. Mere revision, such as one sees in a recent book by Robert Richards, *Darwin and the Emergence of Evolutionary Theories of Mind and Behavior*, will not do. Richards attempts to counter views of Darwinism as mechanistic materialism, individualistic, and demoralizing, through a close reading of Darwin, Herbert Spencer, George Romanes, William James, James Mark Baldwin, and others. In the end, Richards mounts an academic defense of Darwin rather than a fundamental questioning of evolutionary theory. He ignores the American thinker Charles Peirce, who had a profound influence on James and a significant one on Baldwin, and whose thoughts on evolution ultimately run deeper, I claim, than either James, Baldwin, or any of the other evolutionary theorists discussed, including Darwin.

Because of his uncritical commitment to Darwinism, Richards glosses over Konrad Lorenz's Nazi connections: "The vast bulk of Lorenz's work on instinct rests squarely in the Darwinian evolutionary tradition. Even his concern about behavioral and mental degeneration has deep roots in that tradition . . . again, recall that Darwin too warned of the dangers to human progress consequent on the disengagement of natural selection in civilized societies. . . . Certainly [Lorenz] fostered the union of biology and propaganda, but I doubt that his main concerns would have been markedly different had the Weimer Republic survived."[8] Unfortunately the Weimer Republic had not survived, and hundreds of thousands of Europeans had already not survived the Nazis and their "medical" murders when Lorenz began writing his Nazi biological propaganda in 1940. Millions of Jews, Gypsies, and others were later murdered by precisely the kind of program Lorenz called for. It was during the same period of 1939-40 that the strategies of the Holocaust were being carefully outlined. Richards tries to whitewash Lorenz's "brown stain" by showing that his "main concerns" were consistent with Darwinism, but the red blood spilled by biological Nazism cannot be covered over and reveals the vapidity and cold-bloodedness of the attempt to do so. How is it that intellectuals such as Richards can be so cut off from real history and their own feelings about such a history that they can manufacture rationalizations to explain away ethically and scientifically corrupt ideas?

Without a frank examination of the outmoded dogmas of evolutionary theory, and of the unscientific reliance on unproved but assumed foundational principles, principles that attempt to explain growth but in no way include growth itself as intrinsic to the laws of evolution, no real advances from evolutionary theories should be expected but only variations on the same tired theme. By the same token, those biophobic theories of culture that accept biological mechanism but claim it has nothing to do with cultural meaning uncritically assume principles of evolution that are in fact the by-product of modernity. The dichotomy of nature and culture must be recognized as the false and modern abstraction it is, as I hope will become clearer as we explore some philosophies of life.

To get a better sense of the ways the concept of life entered into social theory, let us turn now to some exemplary representatives who also provide thoughts for contemporary reflection. The tension between matter and mind, which marks so much of modern thought, is particularly evident in Simmel and Scheler. Similarly, philosophical pragmatism, which has become a renewed center of interest for antinaturalist "neopragmatists," takes on a different aspect when viewed as an American philosophy of organic life.

BETWEEN LIFE AND FORM: SIMMEL

Georg Simmel was a remarkably broad thinker whose writings ranged from the massive philosophical treatise, *The Philosophy of Money,* to a book on Rembrandt, to his attempts to lay a groundwork for sociology. Although he dealt with evolutionary questions in an early essay of 1895, the concept of life grew increasingly important in his later work, beginning with *Schopenhauer und Nietzsche* (1907), and culminating in his last major book, *Lebensanschauung: Vier Metaphysische Kapitel* (Life-view: Four metaphysical chapters). In this final book, and in his essay also published in 1918, "The Conflict in Modern Culture," Simmel expresses his mature philosophy of life.[9] In his outlook, human existence is characterized by a dialectical tension between life and form.

"Form" and "life" are terms which embody the fundamental dichotomy between structure and process, between the individual and the continuous. As mentioned in the last chapter, Simmel was heavily influenced by Kant and, indeed, had written his dissertation on Kant's physical monadology. Much of his sociology is rooted in Kant's bifurcated world, with its dichotomies of form and content, subject and object, and these same premisses guide his discussions of form and life. Despite what I see as fatal mistakes built into the Kantian outlook, Simmel remains a fascinating thinker whose observations are ever more perceptive than the framework he imposed on them.

The task Simmel faced was that of any neo-Kantian formalist or of any structuralist: how to relate the two sides of the dichotomy. That the two are logically distinct is clear in many remarks Simmel made:

A deep contradiction exists between continuity and form as ultimate world shaping principles. Form means limits, contrast against what is neighboring, cohesion of a boundary by way of a real or ideal center to which, as it were, the ever flowing sequences of contents or processes bend back, and which provides every circumference with a source of resistance against dissolution in the flux. . . . Form . . . cannot be altered. It is eternally invariable. . . . Form . . . is individuality. If now life—as a cosmic, generic, singular phenomenon—is such a continuous stream, there is good reason for its profound opposition against form. This opposition appears as the unceasing, usually unnoticed (but also often revolutionary) battle of ongoing life against the historical pattern and formal unflexibility of any given cultural content, thereby becoming the innermost impulse toward cultural change. Left to itself . . . life streams on without interruption; its restless rhythm opposes the fixed duration of any particular form. Each cultural form, once it is created, is gnawed at varying rates by the forces of life. . . . Life, in its flow, is not determined by a goal but driven by a force.[10]

One sees in these remarks that Simmel, as a neo-Kantian formalist, saw life as a sensory manifold, needing to be organized by something outside of itself. Or as he put it elsewhere, "Life as such is formless, yet incessantly generates form for itself." The Kantian influence on Simmel led him to define the object of sociology as *forms* of interaction, even as it prevented him from seeing that there might be form in experience and life itself: it prevented him from seeing the possibility of *living form,* continuous and yet qualitatively unique.

Yet one senses that Simmel's attempt to develop a *Lebensanschauung* was also an attempt to break out of the Kantian dualism, especially in his discussion of the "transcendent character of life." After noting the "unreconcilable opposition between life and form," Simmel goes on to say, "Nevertheless, individuality is everywhere something alive, and life is everywhere individual." He speaks of a third principle, beyond dualism and unity, which is the essence of life as self-transcendence: "In *one* act, it creates something more than the vital stream itself— individual structure—and then breaks through this product of a blockage in that stream, lets the stream surge out over the bounds and submerge itself again in the ongoing flux . . . the fundamental character of life resides precisely in that unified function which I, albeit symbolically and inadequately, have termed the transcendence of itself. This function actualizes as *one* life what is then split through feelings, destinies, and conceptualization into the dualism of continuous life flux and individual closed form."[11]

In these passages and similar ones in his *Lebensanschauung,* Simmel is struggling to account for the creative intelligence of life itself, for the generativity or natality inherent in life. Although he recognizes that his idea of self-transcendent life may not be consistent with the life versus form distinction, he never seriously questions whether the rigid separation of form and life is itself a false abstraction. Instead, he stretches the distinction to its limit, perhaps as Gustav Mahler had stretched the symphonic form to its seeming limit a few years earlier. The year 1918 was, after all, a time when all political, cultural, ethical, and intellectual boundaries seemed to be at or beyond the breaking point. In this sense, perhaps Simmel's *Lebensanschauung* is, in its very substance, its own best example of self-transcendence. One must remember, however, that it was Kant who coined the term "transcendent" to signify that realm of the noumenal beyond the forms or faculties of knowledge. And one might say that Simmel's view of the transcendent character of life biologizes Kant's transcendental ego rather than transcends Kant's framework.

Simmel applied his form versus life distinction for a fascinating interpretation of "The Conflict in Modern Culture." As mentioned earlier, he sensed very clearly that the antithesis of life and form, which he believed is the source of cultural life, had reached the peculiar position in the early twentieth century of life itself, which is inherently formless, becoming the form, so that the dominant form of our time is paradoxically formless life. He sums up the gulf between present and past at the end of World War 1 when he says, "The bridge between the past and the future of cultural forms seems to be demolished; we gaze into an abyss of cultural forms beneath our feet. But perhaps this formlessness is itself the appropriate form for contemporary life. Thus the blueprint of life is obliquely fulfilled. Life is a struggle in the absolute sense of the term which encompasses the relative contrast between war and peace: that absolute peace which might encompass this contrast remains an eternal [*göttlich*] secret to us."[12]

Yet one might say that Simmel himself, perhaps precisely because of his formalism, ignored the other half of twentieth-century culture: the sterilization of life and form, resulting in lifeless form. It remains remarkable that Simmel, a profound puzzler of modernity, could not see the other half of modern life of which he, the form giver, was a part: the relentless construction of logical forms on the contents of life. Modernity is not simply the transitory and evanescent, it is also the formalization of existence. Modern life is not simply what Baudelaire referred to as *"le transitoire, le fugitif, le contingent,"* which one interpreter of Simmel, David Frisby, thinks captures Simmel's outlook (Baudelaire himself used these terms to describe half of what art is, the other half being "the eternal"). It is also the powerful and opposite impulse to annihilate the transitory, the fugitive, and the contingent in the name of the deified machine, the almighty grid. This other side of modernity is the quest for primordial totality and finality, expressed in twentieth-century foundationalism, bureaucracy, and totalitarianism; in those systems designed as final solutions, whether in Wittgenstein's announcement in the preface to the *Tractatus Logico-Philosophicus,* written in 1918, that "I therefore believe myself to have found, on all essential points, the final solution of the problems" or in Hitler's diabolical program of genocide, whether in the "International Style" of modern architecture or in dogmatic assertions by the Stalinist Soviet Union that Marxist-Leninism constituted the only valid foundation for science and society.

The same cultural nominalism that formed Simmel's dichotomies operated to produce an either/or binary mentality in modernism. Simmel perceptively saw the dominance of life in the twentieth century but missed the other half of the split-brain of modernity: lifeless formalism, which in its virulent development in the course of the twentieth century manifested as the "cult of anti-life." The problem was not simply the overpowering of form by life, as Simmel seemed to think, but rather the severing of the cultural corpus callosum between life and form: cultural lobotomy. Simmel, who wrote his *Lebensanschauung* while suffering from terminal cancer of the liver, sought to embrace life, but his ingrained formalism prevented him from finally breaking out of Kantian nominalism to a view of life as *living form,* capable of being both spontaneous and reasonable.

Although trying to develop a *Lebensanschauung,* life seems to remain a preformed concept in Simmel's discussions, never a palpitating presence. Life occupies one side of a neat dichotomy, and even if its essence is to transcend the boundary it possesses no capacities for limiting, selecting, and arresting of its own. It is a general concept which Simmel rarely takes into specifics, and even his specific examples are those of a cosmopolitan city dweller, not an anthropologist of life.

SCHELER'S PHILOSOPHICAL ANTHROPOLOGY

A quite different approach to the life concept emerged in the work of Max Scheler. Scheler's work reveals the influence of Simmel, Dilthey, Nietzsche, Bergson, and others on his philosophy of life. Like Simmel, Scheler was concerned explicitly with Kant in his early work, but turned increasingly toward the analysis of cognition in its social and cultural contexts, as his *Habilitationschrift,* written under Max Weber's influence, indicates. He later rejected his earlier Kantian efforts but retained a growing interest in the concept of life, which culminated in his philosophical anthropology of his last years, particularly his *Die Stellung des Menschen im Cosmos (Man's Place in Nature).* This work is frequently cited as foundational to the development of German philosophical anthropology, a tradition which, as one recent work put it, "has its origin in one of the philosophical and scientific currents that were characteristic of the Weimar Republic."[13] While not denying the distinctive tendencies of the German tradition, of which Anglo-American social theorists remain too little informed, the idea that philosophical anthropology was a specifically German concern rather than a specifically German term is quite simply provincial, and reveals the extent to which the generalized concerns of social philosophy in the late nineteenth and early twentieth centuries have been obscured in the codification of social theory. The very title of Scheler's book is part of a tradition of similar titles in evolutionary theory dating back to T. H. Huxley's *Evidence as to Man's Place in Nature,* published in 1863, a fact which illustrates a common concern throughout modern civilization with "man's place in nature" far broader than German thought in the Weimar Republic. Evolutionary theory itself marks a transformation of the earlier tradition of *Naturphilosophie,* which animated Goethe, Schelling, and Coleridge, among others in Germany and England.

Unlike Simmel's undifferentiated discussion of life, Scheler brings in a variety of examples from the biological sciences and his own observations that attest to a much more comprehensive appreciation for nature than one finds in Simmel. Scheler assigned "the greatest urgency" to the development of a philosophical anthropology, by which he meant the broad study of humankind in relation to "biological, psychological, ideological, and social developments."[14]

Scheler articulates a developmental sequence of four essential stages in which all of existence manifests itself with regard to inner being. These are evolutionary stages which move from noncentered or "ecstatic," *Gefuhlsdrang,* a term revealing the influence, perhaps, of Henri Bergson's *élan vital,* through increasingly centered and reflective stages. The first stage is characterized in particular by plant life, but more generally is the undifferentiated energy force pervading all higher forms as well. Although unconscious and devoid of sensation and representation, this level of blind driving life-force includes form and even aesthetic order, contrary to Simmel's splitting of life and form: "The rich variety of forms in the leafy parts of plants suggests, even more impressively than the forms and colors in animals, that the principle at the unknown roots of life may act in accordance with fanciful play regulated by an aesthetic order."

Scheler's next stage is instinctual behavior, which in his view must include five characteristics: it must be purposive (teleoclitic) for one or more organisms; have a "definite unchanging rhythm"; respond only to typically recurring situations; be innate; and be inheritable, in the sense of transcending particular situations, because it is already "complete" as a *Gestalt* from the outset.

The further differentiation of instinctual behavior leads to Scheler's third and fourth forms of psychic life, respectively, habitual behavior and practical intelligence. These represent the further centering and bending back of psychic life upon itself as well as the progressive "dissociation" of instinct. Habitual behavior has to do with associative memory and is attributed by Scheler "to all living organisms whose behavior is modified slowly and continually on the basis of earlier behavior with respect to a purposive and useful end."

Perhaps the most interesting human manifestation of habitual behavior is tradition. Scheler's conception of tradition is biosocial, extending beyond conscious memory and "all cultural inheritance by means of symbols, sources and documents, that is, from all historical knowledge." Tradition extends even beyond humans to other social forms of animal life, such as herds and packs. Scheler poses the paradox that tradition is both "a powerful instrument of liberation in relation to instinctive behavior" and a constricting bond that is progressively decomposed in the course of evolution. Scheler's assumption of the continuous evolutionary reduction of the power of tradition seems to me open to question. He, like Weber and others, may have simply confounded the modern experience with the universal. The typical fault of the Kantian-based founders of modern social theory such as Scheler, Simmel, Weber, and Durkheim, was to assume the peculiar cultural nominalism of modernity as a valid universal principle. Yet the conception of noninstinctive social forms of learning through a deep-seated conception of tradition remains intriguing.

Having "decomposed" tradition to such an extent that even the "decomposing tradition" of modernity itself now appears exhausted, we have begun to reengage tradition as a potentially vital source for contemporary life, ranging from the widespread revival of religious life, to the reengagement of the arts with the past, to the scientific interest in traditional agriculture, diet, and knowledge of plants. Scheler and other dualists would question whether a reconstructed tradition qualifies as tradition in the prereflective sense, or whether it is simply a new form of "knowledge." But if tradition is not so much erased by the reflective consciousness of modernity as it is sublimated, or even repressed, then tradition may remain as a potential reservoir of cultural energies, for good or bad. The question then becomes, How can a culture or civilization tap deep-rooted resources of collective and habitualized memory in purposeful and not destructive ways? The answer that suggests itself is that whatever resources of the human body there may be are always engaged in a dialogue with present conditions. The organic past of the body and the cultural past of institutions are archives for possible conduct. This is not to say that collective memory or tradition is to be "utilized" to fit present conditions, such as occurs in nostalgia or political propaganda. On the contrary, there may be the potential in dormant habitualized memories to transform present conditions to new purposes. But to do so involves a dialogue between a potentially greater animating form and an ongoing and irreducible situation. My conception of what Scheler calls tradition, or what the eighteenth-century Scottish thinkers called "common sense," includes a degree of generality or *Geist* that Scheler would not allow and a degree of fallibility excluded from the Scottish conception of common sense. And my critique of Scheler's view of the inevitable decomposition of tradition is that he mistakes an artefact of modernity for a fact of evolution. Who knows but that tradition may prove in the end more enduring than modernity?

Scheler's next stage is that of practical intelligence, which involves the ability to respond to a new situation. Practical intelligence is rooted in the organism's needs and drives but transcends prior conditioning. As Scheler discusses it, it is a form of instrumental or technical behavior. Again, Scheler shows a broadened conception of the ingredients of human action, since practical intelligence is not only limited to humans but extends to other higher animals. Yet if he were to allow the active juices of life to commingle with the contemplative egg of spirit, his conception might have been more fruitful, since he would have been able to include impractical behavior, such as imagining and creative play, as aspects of practical intelligence.

After practical intelligence in Scheler's hierarchy comes *Geist* or spirit, which includes not only theoretical intelligence but also "the intuition of essences and a class of voluntary and emotional acts such as kindness, love, remorse, reverence, wonder, bliss, despair, and free decision." Spirit manifests itself within what Scheler distinguishes as the *person*—a central theme in Scheler's perspective and which is in sharp contrast to the "psychic centers" or stages of life previously developed in his anthropology. With spirit comes a radical break with and antithesis to life. For spirit completely transcends life and, indeed, is "a principle opposed to life as such, even life in man."

With the introduction of spirit, Scheler's argument becomes much more phenomenologically based. The action of spirit is similar to the phenomenological reduction of Edmund Husserl. Spirit is "originally devoid of power and efficacy, and the more this is so, the purer it is . . . inherently, the spirit has no energy of its own." Life, by contrast, is in its pure state energy devoid of mind, blind energy. The task of spirit is to "lure" this energy from life, in a kind of sublimation. This process may seem similar to Freud's understanding of the psyche, but Scheler rejects what he sees as Freud's one-sided denial of the autonomy of spirit, or biological materialism. Spirit operates phenomenologically or ascetically in blocking or canceling the resistance of the world that constitutes reality, the experience of resistance which is inherent to the vital drive. This capacity "to isolate essence from existence is a basic characteristic of the human spirit" in Scheler's view and is made possible by the "world-openness" (*Weltoffenheit*) of the human spirit. Man, as a spiritual being, is existentially liberated from the organic world, "no longer subject to its drives and its environment." Man is the being who opposes the resistance of reality with an emphatic "No!" and thereby both cancels its demands and limitations, while yet tapping its energy: "man is the being who can say 'No,' the 'ascetic of life,' the protestant par excellence, against mere reality."

Scheler was not content with a simple dualism but saw history as a dialectic between spirit and life, which he hoped would culminate in a new era of a "World-Age of Adjustment," in which an inner integration of the two principles could make possible a new kind of person, harmoniously balanced. As Scheler said: "Spirit, originally impotent, and the demonic drive originally blind to all spiritual ideas and values, may fuse in the growing process of ideation, or spiritualization, in the sublimation of the drives and in the simultaneous actualization, or vitalization, of the spirit. This interaction and exchange represent the goal of finite being and becoming. Theism erroneously puts this goal at the beginning."

Scheler was a great synthesizer, and in his ideal of a fusion of spirit and life in a new "World-Age of Adjustment" one sees why he felt the development of a philosophical anthropology held such urgency. Yet we see again in his thought the haunting traces of Kant, and of the old Kantian/Cartesian problem of an abstracted dichotomy, falsely held to be original, and needing a synthesis. In his conception of impotent spirit and blind life Scheler should have heeded Kant's statement to the effect that form without content is empty and content without form is blind. Scheler's "person" is only made possible by thwarting life and reality. There is a "synthesis" of life and spirit, in the sense that spirit draws its energies from life, but there is no inner life of the spirit. Scheler may have sought to transcend earlier dichotomies, but he too fell victim to the bifurcated world of the Kantian tradition, with its denial of the inner continuum of life and spirit.

Or perhaps we should place Scheler's ascetic view of spirit in a broader context, not simply that of Kant but of Buddha and Jesus, who inform Scheler's discussions of the "World-Age of Adjustment." But then we might say that Scheler, despite his desire to find a way to a greater synthesis of worldviews, still remains within the ascetic ethos of what Karl Jaspers and Lewis Mumford have independently described as the "axial age." By the concept of "axial," both Jaspers and Mumford sought to capture the pivotal shift of values which marked a heightened spiritualization of humanity through those personalities who sprang forth within a few hundred years of each other—Zoroaster, Plato, Buddha, Jesus and others—which marked an unprecedented transformation of humankind. The axial age, a time period beginning roughly around 600 B.C., marked the emergence of the universal religions, such as Zoroastrianism and Buddhism, and later others such as Christianity, Mithraism, Manichaeism, and Islam, and also the development of a new kind of person and a new kind of community. The term "axial age" is associated with Karl Jaspers, but Lewis Mumford also formulated the concept independently at about the same time, in the late 1940s, and claims that both were preceded by J. Stuart Glennie about fifty years earlier.[15] In Mumford's view the rise of the axial personality marked an opposition to and compensation for the bureaucratic civilizational structures.

A new kind of human and civilizational structure emerged from this period, in which the personality could be enhanced through ascetic discipline. Yet it might be said that the cost of this transformation was a devaluing of the life-process itself. The ascetic attitude harnessed life-energies and put them to its services, but this harnessing or repressing effort, the raising of spirit over flesh, unnecessarily polarized life and spirit. Should we be entering a "World-Age of Adjustment," as Scheler envisioned, it would be an age that could draw from the invaluable positive legacy of the axial age, while internally reuniting life and spirit as living spirit, and that would externally manifest as a civilization centered in organic potential, limitation, and purpose. Such an age would be opposed to Scheler's original dualism of life and spirit. Incarnate mind, not ethereal spirit, would be its source and goal.

Scheler's view leads to an inevitable etherealization of the human creature. When he says elsewhere, "The 'purer' mind is, the less potent it is in its dynamic effect upon society and history," he simply shows the impotence of beginning with a conception of spirit that is utterly divorced from life. What if "pure" mind were mind made harmonious with reality, realized in incarnate life? Pure mind in this case might be a form of instinct, and impure mind, or immature mind, precisely the canceling of reality that Scheler attributes to spirit.

PRAGMATISM AND LIFE

Turning to the American context, we note similar tendencies at the turn of the century for the life-concept to rise in importance. Herbert Spencer was widely influential in social theory, but with the advent of the twentieth century it was pragmatism that came to animate American intellectual life. Both Simmel and Scheler identified pragmatism as central to the general rise of life philosophies, and both disparaged it because it collapsed the categories of form and spirit to that of life. Simmel seemed to have William James in mind when he said, "Pragmatism . . . deprives truth [Erkennen] of its old claim to be a free-floating domain ruled by independent and ideal laws."[16] James, a friend of Henri Bergson, indeed celebrated vital philosophy, often at the expense of formal principles and rigorous philosophical clarity. And it was James who became the chief representative of pragmatism, later to be succeeded by Dewey, who in turn was succeeded by George Herbert Mead.

If Simmel had read the founder of pragmatism, Charles Peirce, who was a practicing mathematician, physicist, astronomer, geodicist, and logician, the founder of modern semeiotic, and who claimed to have almost memorized Kant's *Critic of the Pure Reason* (as he preferred to translate it) after three years of daily study, he would have had to have modified his view. Peirce clearly distinguished between "vitally important topics" and theoretical science, and claimed that truth, as the goal of theoretical science, could not be reduced to the practical affairs of life: the essence of science for the founder of pragmatism is that it is useless. How would Simmel have responded to Peirce's defense of the power of truth in his letter to William James of 1902? Addressing an imaginary interlocutor, Peirce says: "You think that the proposition that truth and justice are the greatest powers in this world is metaphorical. Well I, for my part, hold it to be *true*. No doubt truth has to have defenders to uphold it. But truth creates its defenders and gives them strength. The mode in which the idea of truth influences the world is essentially the same as that in which my desire to have the fire poked causes me to get up and poke it. There is efficient causation, and there is final, or ideal, causation. If either of them is to be set down as a metaphor, it is rather the former. Pragmatism is correct doctrine only in so far as it is recognized that material action is the mere husk of ideas. The brute element exists, and must not be explained away. . . . But the end of thought is action only in so far as the end of action is another thought."[17] These are not the kind of ideas conducive to a Bergsonian view of *homo faber* or of truth as mere practical expedience.

Simmel might have been rudely shocked to read the founder of pragmatism writing to James in 1894, concerning his ideas that "matter is effete mind, inveterate habits becoming physical laws": "[M]y views were probably influenced by Schelling,—by all stages of Schelling, but especially by the *Philosophie der Natur*. I consider Schelling as enormous; and one thing I admire about him is his freedom from the trammels of system. . . . If you were to call my philosophy Schellingism transformed in the light of modern physics, I should not take it hard."[18] Peirce not only rejected the view of science as a practical or technical endeavor but also the conception of science as systematized knowledge, in favor of science as living inquiry, as the "desire to find things out." In Peirce's theory of "abduction," instinctive proclivities act as true but vague ideas, essential to the highest flights of hypothesis, and cause the creation of hypotheses, or informed guessing, to be a logical, though not rational, process.

Pragmatism in general sought a socialized conception of nature, ranging from Peirce's doctrine of "evolutionary love," to John Dewey's critique of the reflex-arc concept in psychology as inadequately characterizing a stimulus as an unconditioned starting point rather than the social result of prior responses, and to G. H. Mead's naturalistic philosophy of the act.[19] It is this thoroughly socialized conception of nature that sets pragmatism apart not only from much in German thought, with its overly subjective view of self, but also from Darwinism.

The pragmatists carved out in scientific contexts what the literary transcendentalists, such as Emerson, Thoreau, Melville, and Whitman, had explored earlier in the flowering of the American mind in the 1850s. The significance of organic life and nature received profound expression in the nature philosophies of the transcendentalists, expressed, for example, in the observations of nature in Thoreau's *Walden,* or the titanic struggles of humans lodged between nature and modernity in Melville's *Moby Dick.* Ralph Waldo Emerson's transcendentalism, influenced by Coleridge's "misunderstandings" of Kant and Schelling's conceptions of the transcendental, and by Schelling himself, expressed itself in his conception of the "oversoul" as breaking beyond rather than being behind the faculties of cognition. The somewhat transformed transcendental "ping pong ball" then later bounced back to Germany through Emerson's influence on Nietszche's conceptions of life and the *Übermensch*.

If one were to trace the course of the life-concept in the American mind, one sees a transformation from the transcendentalists, to the scientific concerns of Peirce the logician and James the psychologist, and, in the next generation, to Dewey and Mead the social philosophers. In this transformation, the broadened metaphysical concerns of the literary transcendentalists are ignored because of the "scientific" impulse at work in James, Dewey, and Mead. Strangely enough though, Peirce, the practicing scientist and exact logician, is the one pragmatist who preserves the metaphysical concerns of the transcendentalists, though meta-morphosed, perhaps, in his scientific philosophy.

But though the scientific impulse at work in James, Dewey, and Mead stimu-lated them to broaden their philosophies, it nevertheless took on a life of its own in American thought and culture. In the establishment of scientific sociology at the University of Chicago, for example, we see the ideology of science influencing a Hobbesian conception of nature, devoid of purpose and needing to be tamed through social conventions, at work in the social ecology of Park, Burgess, and others. Here the life-concept assumed the very properties of the virulent capital-ism at work in Chicago: competition and rational maximization.[20] This trend for the assimilation of the life-concept by an ideological conception of science only continued in the rise of the structural-functionalist paradigm and its treatment of the life-concept within the frame of the great mechanical system. In other words, I am suggesting that one may find in the development of the life-concept in Ameri-can thought, the devolution of American thought and, more generally, the pro-gressive self-alienation of social theory from life.

But to return to the pragmatists, one could characterize *living habit* as the central concept animating their work. Through this concept, Dewey and Mead developed an integrated theory of the development of self and socialization, and of large-scale social structure. Habit was not seen by them in the same sense as behav-iorism developed it but, instead, included an open-endedness that could encom-pass novelty, spontaneity, the natality and growth of meaning. Dewey and Mead were animated by the ideal of a living and critical intelligence as an inherent capac-ity of the human creature. In Dewey's theory of inquiry and Mead's philosophy of the act, the human body, with its perceptive and memory capacities, and its ability to "feel" and not simply know problems, is thrust squarely into the foreground.

Scientific inquiry is thus existentially and not simply epistemologically grounded. The close attention to the context of situation, or situational determination of meaning, and the idea of emergent meaning drawing from the "emergent evolution" ideas of Alexander and Morgan are the unique contributions of Dewey and Mead to the life-concept and social theory.

But Dewey and Mead's contribution came at a cost, because they greatly underestimated or avoided the influence of trans-situational norms and forms, which led them in turn to gloss over some of the difficulties of social reconstruction. Despite their strong opposition to the violent upheavals and instabilities brought about by industrial capitalism in Chicago, and their theoretical emphasis on habit, Dewey and Mead shied away from conceptions of long term stability, expressing a kind of fear of extrasituational permanence in the name of creative transience. Their optimistic reconstructive attitude undercut the European tendency to dichotomy in general, but undervalued the significance of long-term "slower moving" structures not so transparently subject to reconstruction. They were quick to criticize Platonic realism in favor of "live" situational truth, but opaque to the idea that the most vital existence is precisely that in harmony with enduring truth *and* creative transformation. Life, from this semiotic realist perspective, is the reciprocal transformation of the eternal into the circadian, and generation or birth of existence for the potential: general truth and possible existence meet in life. In their enthusiasm for and achievement of a humane theory of scientific inquiry, Dewey and Mead also gave too little attention to the formative influence of other kinds of human expression and intelligence, such as those dealt with by the literary transcendentalists, or, perhaps, by Simmel.

Life and the Cult of Antilife

Although the concept of a *Lebensphilosophie* is a specifically modern and largely twentieth-century development, one can say that this same time period gave rise to what Lewis Mumford has termed "the cult of anti-life." In other words, the development of modernity in many ways both reified and repressed the concept of life.

Hannah Arendt, for one, calls attention to the ways the life-concept, expressed especially in the concepts of labor, necessity, and the social realm, came to dominate Western Civilization after the Middle Ages. Whereas the concept of life had traditionally been delimited to the realm of the household, life conceived as the social realm destroyed, in Arendt's view, the traditional distinction between private and public, between household as the realm of necessity and polis as the realm of freedom: "The social realm, where the life process has established its own public domain, has let loose an unnatural growth, so to speak, of the natural; and it is against this growth, not merely against society but against a constantly growing social realm, that the private and intimate, on the one hand, and the political (in the narrower sense of the word), on the other, have proved incapable of defending themselves."[21] The unbinding or false ascription of the qualities of biological life from the private to the public realm has resulted in the cancerous nature of modernity in Arendt's view, an inverted worldview dominated by a reified conception of life.

Arendt provides fascinating insights into the hidden premises of modernity, yet these insights themselves derive from the side of modernity that has served to repress life, denying intelligence to it, making it to be without intrinsic quality, without organic spontaneity, without growing purpose, or capacities for self-limitation. Her critique of the rise and domination of the life-concept accurately draws attention to the reification of the life-concept historically, but she cannot see that even her definition of the life-concept is already reified, because she is hopelessly trapped within the same neo-Kantian German nominalism. Like Simmel, she must begin her conceptualization with a divided world.

The same tendencies are to be found today in the work of Habermas, as we shall see in more detail in Chapter 6, who thinks "system" is something completely different from "life-world," and life-world something completely different from organic life itself. The "life-world," as he develops it, has nothing to do with biological life itself but rather with traditional and conventionalized forms of social knowledge, and in this regard he is in the tradition of Dilthey's antinaturalistic conception of life. Unlike Dilthey, however, Habermas wants to retain an element of the natural—or "objective world"—in his social theory, even if it has nothing to do with the life-world. In order to include the natural or objective world, Habermas surrenders to positivism the idea that the "objectivating attitude," which, in the rise of science and technics over the past few centuries has sought to disqualify the subjective element, is internally correct. But he argues that it only needs to be brought into balance with the social world (which is about "norm conformity") and the subjective world (which is supposed to be about "expressiveness," but which is really about German "innerness," though in disguised form). The resulting balance Habermas calls "communicative rationality," a "talking cure" or theory of linguistic intersubjectivity.

Like Dilthey, Arendt, Simmel, and others in the Kantian tradition, Habermas uncritically accepts the received Cartesian/Kantian abstraction of a fundamental dichotomy between nature and culture or meaning as given: it becomes more complicated in Habermas's distinction of objective, social, and subjective worlds, but preserves the gap between the world "as it is" and the world "as it is known." Cultural nominalism, the system of the machine and power complex and the "ghost" of ethereal consciousness, is the underlying source of Habermas's ideas rather than the concept of "communicative action" he believes himself to be guided by. As we shall see in more depth in later chapters, "communicative action" reveals itself to be antithetical to life, proud of its separation from organic nature.

On the other side of the picture one could cite Arnold Gehlen, who adapted Scheler's view of *Weltoffenheit,* or world openness, to his own theory of *deinstitutionalization.* Briefly stated, Gehlen argues for an evolutionary anthropology in which institutions have taken the place of instinct as guides for human behavior. Humans are "deficient beings" in that, unlike other creatures, we are biologically unspecialized and unadapted to the natural environment. We therefore require institutions. But critical consciousness and ideals of freedom, individualism, and cosmopolitanism, which are so characteristic of modern life, uproot the stability of traditional institutions, resulting in normlessness and alienation. Therefore disciplined institutions are required which can mimic the guidance formerly provided by instincts.

Gehlen also drew on the attempts of the pragmatists to reconstruct a socialized biology, but he reached quite different conclusions regarding the openness of human communities and communication. Perhaps this was due to his inability to free himself from the German tendency to dichotomy: against the *Weltoffenheit* of human institutions stands an ideal of what might be termed *Instinktgeschloßenheit,* the closedness or rigidity of nature and instinct. Gehlen may have been influenced by his teacher Driesch, who defined instinctive behavior as "a complicated reaction that is perfect the very first time." Driesch's definition ignored how instinctive behavior, though innate, may develop through learning and may, in many cases, even require experience for its expression. Gehlen's view of instinct is that of the "harmonious ant-hill where there are no dissenting voices," as Dostoevsky's Grand Inquisitor expressed it. Like the Grand Inquisitor, he would free us from the torment of freedom with an image of society resembling that achieved by ants sixty million years ago. Yet instinct is not the all-or-nothing view Gehlen held, even perhaps for insects. Consider naturalist J. Arthur Thomson's remarks: "But the rigidity of instinctive routine must not be exaggerated. . . . On the whole it works like clockwork, but there may be variations and mistakes at every step! Moreover, in the wasp's routine there is probably help from intelligence—in choosing a good site, in adapting the shape of burrow to the soil, in remembering the locality, in biting at the prey to suit the size of the hole, and so on."[22]

Gehlen's discussions provide a critique of the instabilities and pronounced emphasis on subjectivity in modern civilization. Yet a disturbing implication of his thought is that he held an ideal of rigid and authoritarian institutions, modeled after the rigidity of instinct. Consider, for example, Gehlen's remarks in 1969 on national self-preservation as requiring an immunization against self-criticism: "It is the most significant achievement of a nation simply to maintain itself as a duly constituted unity, and such a fortune has not fallen to the Germans. Self-preservation includes the spiritual affirmation and profession of a nation to itself before the whole world as much as security in terms of international politics, and this consists of the power of a people to make moral and physical attacks upon itself impossible."[23] Gehlen laments the partition of Germany here, blind to the fact that it was precisely "the affirmation and profession of a nation to itself before the whole world," namely, Nazi Germany, and its use of power "to make moral and physical attacks upon itself impossible" that brought about its self-destruction and dismemberment. Arnold Gehlen was himself an ardent Nazi and prominent intellectual who played an active role in that destructive process, and therefore bore moral responsibility for it, and for the ruination and suffering it produced. Was it Nazi "self-preservation" that immunized the opportunistic Gehlen from ethical self-criticism when he replaced the exiled Paul Tillich or his own teacher Hans Driesch, whom the Nazis forced into early retirement because of his "pacificism." In his 1934 inaugural lecture on taking over Driesch's post, one can imagine Gehlen's right arm going erect as he spoke about a new "reinstitutionalization" for the German people: "[T]he National Socialist movement [has given] a new drive for life and new structures for existence."[24]

Would a victorious Third Reich or any bloody tyranny of power constitute a successful "self-preservation" harmonious with nature? Gehlen, in his apparent support of the Leninist/Stalinist Soviet invasion of Czechoslovakia in 1968 as a renunciation of an overly rational intelligentia by a unified institution of power, seems to say so.[25] His ideal seems to be a political order immunized from politics, a dream that harmonizes with that of Reagan's America in the 1980s. In this dream a "star wars" automatic defense mechanism in the heavens was to immunize the United States from physical attack, deus ex machina, while the secret police, authorized and unauthorized, sought to immunize the administration's policies from constitutional law and moral attack. When discovered, presidential aides realized that they too required an immunity system to avoid prosecution.

Whether presidential aides or biological AIDS, the 1980s introduced the "Age of Immunity," contained in the threat and terror of the loss of the biological immune system, in the political dreams of total immunity from political life, and in the decay of standards of judgment by the spirit of postmodernism to the cultural "immune system" which wards off kitsch. In this regard Gehlen's very German idea of self-immunization against self-critique (or, point the finger at the other, not at oneself), and the very American Reagan "star wars" or "strategic defense initiative" idea of technical immunization against political negotiation, both reveal the irony of the Latin negative adjective, *immunis,* which meant to be free from public obligation or service, to be immune to the municipal. Just as *immunis* had political connotations, two related words were essential to the ancient ideals of public and republic: community and communication. And immunity through power and secrecy provides protection from the open community and its media of communication.

Gehlen's ideal society would ignore experiential uncertainty and the emergence or generation of new habits of conduct. He would immunize us from self-criticism, whereas Habermas would immunize critical communication from organic life.

Yet in viewing humans as "instinctually deprived" against an ideal of rigid instinct, Gehlen ignored the possibility that human instinct is not so much absent as it is *intrinsically vague.* About two hundred years ago even Johann Gottfried Herder, who believed that reason is not innate in man but acquired, could see that instinct can be more than a question of all or nothing: "Men repeat, after one another, that man is devoid of instinct and that this is the distinguishing character of the species; but he has every instinct that any of the animals around him possess; only, in conformity to his organization, he has them softened down to a more delicate proportion. . . . Man therefore is not properly deprived of instincts; but they are *repressed* in him, and made *subordinate* to the dominion of the nerves and finer senses. Without them the creature, who is in great measure an animal, could not live."[26] Though human instincts could be "softened down," they remain as vital though vague sources of conduct.

Consider sexuality, for example, as the chief expression of a generalized instinct for reproduction, and one immediately sees the variety of behavior and institutions—ranging, for example, from family organization to religious celibacy —in which such an expression can take place. Human desire may determine a broad range of conduct, and even set built-in limits to conduct, but does not necessarily determine that such limits must be heeded. Similarly, humans are not only not born knowing how to mate but require extensive socialization into what biologists call "courtship behavior" or what could more broadly be called the conduct of erotic love. Whether one purchases flowers or condoms—or both—can, in some situations, make or break erotic consummation of new love in a way that birds and bees never have to consider. Despite the presence of "love tokens" in other species, such as the ritualistic shelter of twigs which the Australian Bower bird builds, and the widespread use of dowries in traditional wedding exchanges among humans, the achievement of romantic love is based on the qualities of the specific other rather than familial, social exchange rules. Yet even romantic love draws from a process of infatuation which has a general physiological profile, and from traditional forms of love conduct.

Human instincts continue to operate in the view I am proposing, but merely suggestively, feeding the imagination, will, and thought, and requiring, precisely because of their vagueness, viable, believable, and self-critical institutions that can be guided by the undercurrents of instinct while channeling them. Critical human communication, in the sense of a frank acknowledgement of a problematic situation, is not something that a people should be immunized against, but may itself be one of the most essential expressions of human social instinct, "grown into" the human body and its vocal cords and hands.

The concept of life in German *Lebensphilosophie* and philosophical anthropology can be seen as a continuation of the older *Naturphilosophie,* and I want to touch on this theme briefly to highlight the place of the life-concept in contemporary social theory. German *Naturphilosophie* was a reaction against the sensationalistic and rationalistic materialism of English and French science. This tradition, whose greatest representatives include Jakob Boehme, Goethe, Leibniz, and Schelling, rejected the Newtonian-Cartesian transformation of all physical existence into mathematical points and extension.

Commenting on Holbach's treatise of 1770 on mechanical materialism, *System of Nature,* Goethe expressed the opposing inward German vision: "But how hollow and empty did we feel in this melancholy, atheistical half-night, in which the earth vanished with all its images, the heaven with all its stars. There was to be matter in motion from all eternity, and by this motion, right, left, and in every direction, without anything further, it was to produce the infinite phenomena of existence. . . . We indeed confessed that we could not withdraw ourselves from the necessities of day and night, the seasons, the influence of climate, physical and animal condition: we nevertheless felt within us something that appeared like perfect freedom of will, and again something which endeavored to counterbalance this freedom."[27]

The *Naturphilosophie* tradition provided a bulwark against Western materialism, especially in preserving the inner world as an essential ingredient of human reality and the world spirit. It continued the great German humanist tradition of Luther and, even earlier, of Meister Eckhardt, which spoke powerfully for the inner human voice, the autonomy of the subjective spirit and will. But it also continued and transmitted the chief vice of this tradition: that the inner subjective realm is untempered by the external world and, indeed, that what is inner somehow has a higher claim to truth than either external world or transpersonal community. This vice is probably one reason why *Naturphilosophie* after Kepler seemed to lose out to modern science, and is also one reason why turn-of-the-century *Lebensphilosophie* is insufficient for the needs of contemporary thought. This overextended autonomy given to inner feeling and to will also gave voice to the sense of inner superiority of German *Kultur* and the German state that one reads in a variety of writers—including Simmel and Scheler in their propagandistic writings during World War I and Weber in his political tracts—and which, in its logical irrational endpoint contributed to the successful rise, domination, and self-destruction of German Fascism. What began as a healthy skepticism toward materialism culminated in the degenerate cult of "Aryan physics."

This *Weltanschauung*, with its indifference or scorn for *Otherness*, would be an adequate view if we were gods, as Charles Peirce once said. But since we are not, since Otherness is an irremovable and irresistible facet of human existence, it leads eventually to precisely those problems of a world of god-men leading a world of beast-men: two incommensurate and inhuman worlds, devoid of that living cultural corpus callosum which mediates human life with those transilluminative forms of meaning projected out of nature.

If the innerness of German humanism or romanticism deprives itself of Otherness, it is equally true that English empiricism and French rationalist materialism and much in pragmatism deprive themselves of the full reality of innerness, and of the significance of inward or extramaterialist forms in human affairs and the evolution of nature.

What we see in these traditions, perhaps, is the rending of Medieval Civilization into an external/material versus internal/idealist split, in which the English, French and German traditions each contributed genuinely new perspectives on individualism. Each tradition enlarged the arena of human understanding, but this enlargement came about at the cost of a greater whole, which was split into false dichotomies. Modern philosophy and social theory can be characterized as the attempt to achieve a synthesis of the false dichotomy, an attempt rooted in nominalism and fated to failure, because of its acceptance of the dichotomy as given. In my view the emergence and evolution of these divergent traditions represent an epoch of cultural nominalism, characterized by an artificial splitting of evolutionary reasonableness into spiritual and material, of thought and thing, subject and object, culture and nature.

By cultural nominalism I mean that modernity can be characterized as a culture rooted in the dichotomous principles of philosophical nominalism, whereby all signs, including language, knowledge and beliefs, are general names standing for individual particulars. I do not mean that modernity was caused by nominalism, but that the philosophy which rose in opposition to scholastic realism was itself a symptom of the shift of epochs, one which put into philosophical form underlying antipathies of the emergent ethos. That ethos saw the expansion of forms of conduct and thought in which rational, quantifying mind came to an ever-increasing predominance in economic and scientific life. Yet it should also not be forgotten that philosophy and theology had significant influences on the development of Western Civilization in the middle ages. Luther and Calvin, and later Hobbes, all studied philosophy and theology under nominalist influences.

Max Weber's idea that modern capitalism should be viewed as a sixteenth-century product of the Protestant ethos undervalues the clear emergence of capitalism out of Medieval Catholic culture and the rising nominalism which gave birth to Protestant theology. Early nominalists, following the *via moderna* of William of Ockham, rejected the idea of scholastic realism (out of which the Medieval Latin term *realis* was coined) that some general signs are real. Nominalists claimed that reality could be found only in particulars, that general laws or knowledge are fictions or conventions, and that conventions are simply names for particulars, hence nominal. To express it as simply as I can, nominalism holds that things are real, thoughts are not. Things are objective or natural, thoughts are subjective or artificial. The law of gravity is a general sign, a human fiction, standing for the reality of actually interacting physical particles and forces. Nominalism, in effect, created two worlds by driving a wedge between thought and things, and then faced the problem of how to put them together, the problem of modern philosophy.

What the scholastics might have accepted on a foundation of faith or revelation becomes increasingly inexplicable in the nominalist ethos. Descartes, for example, assumed a dichotomy between thinking substance and extended substance, the "ghost in the machine," and faced the problem of how we can have valid knowledge of objects if the only basis for knowledge is a foundation of intuitive individual self-consciousness. The whole ideal of systematic, rational science modeled on the mechanical conception of the universe that one sees in Descartes and Hobbes, who both believed that life, as Hobbes put it, "is but a motion of Limbs," grows directly out of the spirit of nominalism. We have inherited this spirit and its machine in the assumed dichotomy of nature and culture, and in the assumed alienation of the human self from organic life. It was an ethos which produced great and powerful ideas, many of which will endure. But the ethos as a whole produced a world, to paraphrase Henry Adams, in which law disappeared as theory or a priori principle and gave place to force, in which morality became police, in which explosives reached cosmic violence and threatened total obliteration, in which the disintegration of the moral and ecological fabric overcame integration: in short, in which a massive rational and mechanical expansion has taken place at the cost of an equally massive organic regression. By organic regression I mean both the living biosphere without and the inner world of imaginative reasonableness, whose chief locus seems to be the human self and human culture.

LIFE AND THE INCARNATE COSMOS

In recalling to mind the many-sided conceptions of life which flourished in the decades surrounding the turn of the last century, we gain another perspective in which to view the roots of twentieth-century thought and the possibilities for social thought in the coming turn of the century. It is clear that a simple return to *Lebensphilosophie* is not adequate to face the challenges of the contemporary world, but by the same token there remain valuable insights to be gained by conceiving human meaning against conceptions of life. The Darwinian tradition, though still providing a powerful critique of *homo sapiens* as the loving and rational captain of his fate, remains as inadequate today as it always has in coming to terms with human reason in all its elevated and suicidal varieties. Similarly, *Lebensphilosophie* and philosophical anthropology do not successfully free themselves from the false dichotomies of cultural nominalism, and neither do the situational pragmatisms of Dewey and Mead.

The concept of life and, more generally, of naturalism, were in part discredited because of the wrong-headedness of eugenics and the perversities of the Nazis. Yet one can also see a repression of the concept of organic life through the rise and institutionalization of antinaturalistic rationalism in the course of twentieth-century thought. The attempts, for example, by Dewey and Mead to develop social theories rooted in socialized reconstructions of organic life were obliterated by the rise of antinaturalistic "symbolic interactionism" in sociology, which was supposedly influenced by Mead, and by the "neopragmatism" of Rorty, supposedly influenced by John Dewey. European *Lebensphilosophie,* where it has continued to be influential, has tended to preserve antinaturalistic conceptions of life, such as found in Dilthey or in the use of the concept of "life-world," or has fallen into the old problems of biological reductionism, as in human ethology, or in Gehlen's views of human "instinctual deprivation." By and large, with key exceptions, contemporary social theory has removed itself from concerns of reconstructing a critical and organic conception of life—thereby surrendering life to the biological reductionists—because it falsely assumes life to be irrelevant to meaning. Only a larger perspective, capable of undercutting cultural nominalism and encompassing its lost, abstracted halves can fashion a conception of life capable of animating social theory and ending its current lifelessness and, more significantly, of beginning to answer the needs of this age, which has so insulted life.

Modernity is in one sense, to use a term expressed to me by painter Ernst Fuchs, a vast "invisible dictator" dedicated to repressing or extinguishing those deeper, biocosmic powers of transformative nature. Modern power conceived as force must extinguish the older sense of power as potentiality, must materialize and etherealize it to gain control over it. Those living potentials of our inner being, those instincts or beings of our inner nature which imperceptibly shape our existence have suffered greatly from the modern experience. Yet from the moment of conception and the mingling of the genetic codes to the great procession in which the neurons of the brain are laid out in precise sequence and fixed for lifetime, to the abductive inferences which come to us in the practice of life, we are creatures not entirely of our own making. Consider the fact that retroviruses have inscribed themselves into the DNA of human and other species, and thereby have become part of the genetic code itself: even the human genetic code is not entirely human and contains retroviruses embedded from before the human species differentiated itself from other hominids! That slim sliver of verbal consciousness which floats on a vast brain sea of nonverbal consciousness within us deludes us into thinking that being most fully human is being rational, is being modern, is being creatures of our own invention.

One must hope that our insults to nature have not been too severe and that the repressed powers of inner being can displace the gods of blind particulars and disembodied generalities without large-scale destruction: our dubious uniqueness may be to place the great catastrophe squarely within the emerging human consciousness of world culture as the ancient tragedies did for local cultures.

The iron cage of rationalization flourishes today in those systems of social theory—whether critical, interpretative, deconstructive, or rational choice, or even sociobiological—which all remain unwilling to consider the possibility of organic, purposeful life as animating human meaning. Weber himself saw that modern life had taken on the qualities of a "steel casing" or iron cage, rooted in the mechanical principles of capitalism, but he was blind to the possibility that his own Kantian rationalism, which decreed a gulf between meaning and nature, was itself part of the iron cage.

Those earlier attempts to incorporate the concept of life into social theory were largely cast aside or perverted in the "dead zone" that rose to full dominance in mid-century and continues now: the dead zone of the invisible dictator of modernity, the ghost in the machine. Modernization, in all of its megatechnic glory and medical progress, remains yet an escape from life. The question now is: Can social theory be brought back to life?

Let me suggest an unlikely direction, switching metaphors from Weber's "iron cage" to D. H. Lawrence's commentary on the apocalyptic meaning of the *Book of Revelation* for the twentieth-century:

> The Apocalypse shows us what we are resisting, unnaturally. We are unnaturally resisting our connection with the cosmos, with the world, with mankind, with the nation, with the family. All these connections are, in the Apocalypse, anathema, and they are anathema to us. We *cannot bear connection*. That is our malady. We *must* break away, and be isolate. We call that being free, being individual. Beyond a certain point, which we have reached, it is suicide. Perhaps we have chosen suicide. Well and good. The Apocalypse too chose suicide, with subsequent self-glorification.
>
> But the Apocalypse shows, by its very resistance, the things that the human heart secretly yearns after. By the very frenzy with which the Apocalypse destroys the sun and the stars, the world, and all kings and all rulers, all scarlet and purple and cinnamon, all harlots, finally all men altogether who are not "sealed," we can see how deeply the apocalyptists are yearning for the sun and the stars and the earth and the waters of the earth, for nobility and lordship and might, and scarlet and gold, splendour, for passionate love, and a proper unison with men, apart from this sealing business. What man most passionately wants is his living wholeness and his living unison, not his own isolate salvation of his "soul." Man wants his physical fulfillment first and foremost, since now, once and once only, he is in the flesh and potent. For man, the vast marvel is to be alive.

For man, as for flower and beast and bird, the supreme triumph is to be most vividly, most perfectly alive. Whatever the unborn and the dead may know, they cannot know beauty, the marvel of being alive in the flesh. The dead may look after the afterwards. But the magnificent here and now of life in the flesh is ours, and ours alone, and ours only for a time. We ought to dance with rapture that we should be alive and in the flesh, and part of the living, incarnate cosmos."[28]

In his extended commentary on the *Book of Revelation,* Lawrence resonates with both Dostoevsky and Nietzsche's critiques of Christianity as a civilization marked by the repressed hatred of the greater man by the common man, a theme also taken up by Scheler in his work *Ressentiment.* Yet Lawrence reaches quite different conclusions from Nietzsche or Scheler, though perhaps closer to those of Dostoevsky. In Lawrence's view the admirable ideal of Christian love, so crucial in the development of Western Civilization, carries with it the danger of causing its adherents to live too much by ideals, by an idealized conception of love and life which, because isolated from or repressive of the nonidealist conditions of life, could, in its imbalance, call forth opposite impulses. The hatred-motivated quest toward Apocalypse is then a compensation for the one-sided Christian ideal of the inwardly powerful man (meaning the perceptive, the morally sensitive and self-disciplined, the imaginative) giving himself to the inwardly weak. "Inwardly weak" might be defined as "normalized man," socialized into habits of conduct which are closed to the spontaneity and organic social autonomy of the person. The "inwardly weak" person is one of the usually unacknowledged developmental goals of civilization—or what Melville derisively termed "snivelization"—and culminates in organization man and, ultimately, in mass man, whose moral and aesthetic life has been deadened to outer conventions. Consider the fable of The Grand Inquisitor, from Dostoevsky's *The Brothers Karamazov,* where the Grand Inquisitor of the Spanish Inquisition in Seville tells Jesus:

> "You thirsted for love that is free, and not for the servile raptures of a slave before a power that has left him permanently terrified. But here, too, you overestimated mankind, for, of course, they are slaves, though they were created rebels. Behold and judge, now that fifteen centuries have passed, take a look at them: whom have you raised up to yourself? I swear, man is created weaker and baser than you thought him! How, how can he ever accomplish the same things as you? Respecting him so much, you behaved as if you had ceased to be compassionate, because you demanded too much of him—and who did this? He who loved him more

than himself! Respecting him less, you would have demanded less of him, and that would be closer to love, for his burden would be lighter. He is weak and mean. What matter that he now rebels everywhere against our power, and takes pride in this rebellion? The pride of a child and a schoolboy! They are little children, who rebel in class and drive out the teacher. But there will also come an end to the children's delight, and it will cost them dearly. They will tear down the temples and drench the earth with blood. But finally the foolish children will understand that although they are rebels, they are feeble rebels, who cannot endure their own rebellion. . . . Is it the fault of the rest of feeble mankind that they could not endure what the mighty endured?"

The deeply troubling message of the Grand Inquisitor is that humans are created as rebels desiring freedom and as slaves unable to endure it. Jesus promised the way of freedom, a "love that is free," but thereby held up an ideal destined ultimately to frustrate a humanity moved and obsessed by other desires, needs, and torments. One might say that the rebel/slave dialectic is too specifically Russian and that the ideal of freedom has proven more durable in the politics of the West. But the beauty of the fable of the Grand Inquisitor is that it questions the whole basis on which modern culture grew out of the West and exists today. The Grand Inquisitor, correcting Jesus's mistaken calling for a love that is free by basing it on "miracle, mystery, and authority," is a prophecy of the twentieth-century great dictators, of "Uncle Joe" Stalin, Hitler, Mussolini, and the others. But he remains a troubling cipher for the postmodern world, where democratic life is viewed as a mere figment and "mode of authority," and where power is the only reality. The whole idea of freedom, originating in such axial-age prophets as Socrates and Jesus, formed a guiding ideal in the development of the West and specifically modern Enlightenment culture. The ideals of freedom, enlightenment, and progress emphatically declared that humans could become completely self-conscious and critical masters of their fate, transcending the limits of organic being. This was a bold worldview, whose power seemed unquestionable until the twentieth century exhibited its shortcomings.

In not acknowledging the countertendency of the inwardly weak desiring to destroy the inwardly strong, of the long-term consequences of frustrated promptings of the nonideal in human affairs, the Western ethos set itself up to turn into its opposite, symbolized by the Apocalypse, the dream of final vengeance, of final isolate salvation at the cost of all earthly and cosmic relations. Such an inversion begins to be visible, perhaps, in Hobbes's characterization of the state of nature as a "warre of every one against every one": a complete inversion of Aristotle's view that Humankind is by nature determined to live in community and of Jesus's message that love or relation is the basic human condition. In Lawrence's opinion, the symbolism of the Apocalypse is deeply connected with the story of modern materialism and the twentieth-century: the legacy of modern life is not simply an iron cage of rationality that we unknowingly constructed for ourselves in the name of freedom, which is true enough, but it is further a tragic project of collective suicide.

It is precisely those continua between self, social relations, and nature that Lawrence claims underlie the isolating ideology of the religious Apocalypse of John of Patmos and of the Apocalypse of modernity, and that motivate the deepest wellsprings of human life: the incarnate cosmos in which we bodily participate. The concept of a "living, incarnate cosmos" falls outside of the narrow boundaries of biological mechanists and sociocultural rationalists, for it grants both emergent reasonableness to nature and organic life to culture. Yet it is just such a critical reconstruction of the concept of nature and an organically rooted renewal of the concept of culture that social theory, biology, and contemporary life desperately need.

Lawrence's critique of the Apocalypse of John of Patmos as the dark side of Christian/Western Civilization, realized in the twentieth century, seems to me entirely on the mark: the inwardly weak, desiring to destroy the inwardly strong. This is the destructive ethos of the Grand Acquisitors of capitalistism and Fascists and Stalinist/Maoists, who have acted in varying ways to smash the free, imaginative, whole person.[29] It is technical civilization, ever more externalized, desiring to eradicate "man's glassy essence": our inborn needs to dream and to dramatize our way in the world. It is the "peoples' republics" and the American distraction industries, which all have gone by the name of "democracy," while creating antidemocratic mass civilization. The peoples republics sought to undo the human person by punishment and terror, while the Western consumer societies have pursued a more successful route of undoing the person by reward, by bread and circuses, hamburgers and television, by creating conditions which relieve the whole person from the spontaneous engagement with life.

Lawrence is for the potential wholeness of the human being, and feels that the West has come to raise ideas up above their proper context within a triune whole including tradition and spontaneous impulse: "There is a continual conflict between the soul, which is forever sending forth incalculable impulses, and the psyche, which is conservative, and wishes to persist in its old motions, and the mind, which wishes to have 'freedom,' that is spasmodic, idea-driven control. Mind, and conservative psyche, and the incalculable soul, these three, are a trinity of powers in every human being. But there is something even beyond these. It is the individual in his pure singleness, in his totality of consciousness, in his oneness of being. . . . Every man must live as far as he can by his own soul's conscience. But not according to any ideal."

These words form a powerful critique not only of rationalism but also of religion, nihilism, conservatism, progressivism, and even hedonism—and especially ismism! They reveal a depth of insight far more penetrating than Gehlen, who merely supports the view that specifically human meaning exists in alienation from nature, and at best can try to mimic nature through external institutions. There is here an anthropology in which the thoroughly social and unique individual is a composite of opposing tendencies, which need to live in balance for the human person and human cultures to thrive. The implication is that on the cultural side we are not deprived of biology but have a specifically meaning-seeking biology, while on the biological side, organic nature includes far more of the stuff of reason than most biologists have wanted to admit. The roots of narrative go deep into our biological constitution, emanating from soul, or from what we nowadays call the unconscious, which sends forth impulses beyond what our rational minds can comprehend at a given point. The reasonable is far more than the rational and runs deeper than cultural and biological reductionists can admit. It includes empathic intelligence, which can feel what rational mind cannot know, as well as projective intelligence, which can body forth ideas, images, feelings, and forms utterly irrationally, though reasonably.

I am not claiming that we should become noble savages, ignoble savages though we may be: but simply that modern civilization has become dominated by rational madness, that rationality per se—of whatever description—is insufficient as a foundation for a culture or civilization, or even for the practice of science, and that rationality needs to be reconnected to deeper human imaginative and emotional capacities. Some say that it is possible to be a modernist without being a total rationalist, and I agree. Only it is no longer valid to remain a modernist, in my opinion. The time has come to salvage the valuable parts of the legacy, and to move on to project a new mind, freed from the compulsions and excesses of modern civilization, because mindful of the terrible consequences they brought about.

Such a perspective has already been developed, in scattered places, but has not yet been allowed to enter the scholarly canon of social theory. When one reads master ethnographer and cultural theorist Victor Turner's late work on how

deeply embedded brain patterns and functions may be related to human ritualization, for example, one sees how a turn toward organic life can deepen our understanding of human signification. It goes without saying, however, that most of
Turner's closest colleagues automatically assumed that he had gone astray. In their
eyes he had committed "the naturalistic fallacy" in claiming that the depths of human cultural meaning might be organically motivated. Similarly, as we shall see
later, the surprisingly little-known philosophical and anthropological aspects of
Lewis Mumford's work suggest the outlines of a reconception of human nature
and meaning, one which pervades all of his varied researches on technics, cities,
and the modern power complex. Such pleas for an organic conception of homo
symbolicus, which treat the dramas and purposes of life as real, remain marginal to
the major currents of contemporary social thought.

The dogmas of Darwin have coalesced with the ideology of "post" culture at
the end of the twentieth century to negate evolutionary reasonableness in favor of
blind, purposeless chance or contingency as the sole agent of change. It may seem
at first glance that biological reductionists and cultural reductionists make strange
bedfellows, given that they seem to deny what the other holds as determinative of
human conduct. Yet whether one reads Stephen Jay Gould's defenses of Darwinism, Richard Rorty or Stanley Fish's happy-go-lucky attacks on truth, beauty, and
natural meaning, or even art historian and director of the Museum of Modern Art
Kirk Varnedoe's history of modern art, we are by these accounts simply the nominal product of particular contingencies bound together by mere social fictions.

In this mindset, the admittedly real element of chance is raised to the sole
legitimate principle, while the equally real element of evolutionary reasonableness
—the marked increase in sentience and foresight one sees in the course of biological evolution—is denied autonomy. To allow reasonableness as a real and irreducible element in the evolution of organic life would be to allow teleology into
science and that has been forbidden since the seventeenth century. As Stephen Jay
Gould said recently in describing human evolution, "We are an improbable and
fragile entity . . . an item of history, not an embodiment of general principles."[30]
Though Gould remains true to Darwin, his words could be those of Rorty describing human community or of Fish describing the literary canon. What then would
be an "embodiment of general principles" in organic nature? Gould begins with
the premiss of Darwinian chance and works it to its ultimate conclusion: everything is a result of chance. In order to do this, he must at the least deny to human
evolution the rapid accumulation of ritualizing, habitual mind in the face of
chance, the development of practices which sought to control chance and

contingency—or at least limit its effects—through ritual repetition, collective memory, or divinitory foresight.

Consider, by contrast, the following from Lewis Mumford, whose life's work was rooted in a concept of organic life that does full justice to the concerns of Simmel and Scheler, Dewey and Mead, Kropotkin and Gehlen, while, in my view, compensating for many of their lacks and excesses. Mumford reverses the happenstance view of the universe:

> Sentient creatures of any order, even the lowly amoeba, seem to be extremely rare and precious culminations of the whole cosmic process. . . . When we view organic change, not as mere motion, but as the increase of sentience and self-directed activity, as the lengthening of memory, the expansion of consciousness, and the exploration of organic potentialities in patterns of increasing significance, man's relation to the cosmos is reversed.
>
> In the light of human consciousness, it is not man, but the whole universe of still "lifeless" matter that turns out to be impotent and insignificant. That physical universe is unable to behold itself except through human intelligence: unable in fact to realize the potentialities of its own earlier development until man, or sentient creatures with similar mental capabilities, finally emerged from the utter darkness and dumbness of pre-organic existence."[31]

We shall turn to Mumford's organic vision and its implications in more depth in Chapter 4.

In exploring the organic potentialities of human memory, feeling, and transhuman needs for social relation and biosocial transformation, in critically examining and revising the received view of nature, in taking seriously the implication that *evolution itself grows* (which contemporary evolutionary theories seem not to do), that is, the very laws of evolution themselves were products of evolution and continue to evolve, potentially growing into a reasonableness by no means necessary, predetermined, or inevitable, we pose the very questions that could bring about the transformation of social theory from the outworn and now deadly premises of cultural nominalism. In order to overcome the arrogant claims of ethereal rational intellect to dominance in the conduct of life, and the alienation of social theory from life, a renewal of social thought is required, one that involves acknowledging that we, as living forms of intelligence and emergent products of the cosmos, are also coparticipants in a living, incarnate cosmos still very much in the process of creation.

If we entered the twentieth century led by economics, we leave it with the hope of a revolutionary biology in the making, one that may finally come to grips with the living spontaneity of life, the great organic continuum of the living earth. Given the controversial revival of old ideas about the earth as a living organism in the "Gaia hypothesis," the increased attention being paid to social cooperation by ecologists, and other questionings of the Darwinian worldview, there may be good reason to hope that the machine of modernity may give way to a more life-sustaining epoch. But given the seemingly inexorable march of megatechnic modernity toward ecological disaster, hope may be all that is left. The machine has never been more powerful, yet its very successes—and not only its failures—have created grave threats to life and are forcing reconsiderations of what life science and social theory must include and, more generally, what a world civilization can be—and must not be—if we hope to remain on a living earth.

3

The Cultic Roots of Culture

> . . . *man, proud man,*
> *Drest in a little brief authority,*
> *Most ignorant of what he's most assur'd,*
> *His glassy essence, like an angry ape,*
> *Plays such fantastic tricks before high heaven*
> *As makes the angels weep.*
>
> *—Shakespeare*[1]

> *"Sleep-pictures"—New word coined in sign language by an ape to describe what it did at night.*

> *It seems to me that man has what we call a human heart, but that he also has something of the baboon within him. The modern age treats the heart as a pump and denies the presence of the baboon within us. And so again and again, this officially non-existent baboon, unobserved, goes on the rampage, either as the personal bodyguard of a politician, or wearing the uniform of the most scientific police force in the world.*
>
> *—Vàclav Havel*

INTRODUCTION: A REPORT TO THE ACADEMY

In Franz Kafka's "A Report to an Academy," an ape gives a lecture on his acquisition of symbolic consciousness. He describes his long months in a tiny iron cage on board the ship that brought him to occidental civilization, and the unbearable loneliness that tortured him into a state of cultivation. Becoming communicative, as he put it, was his "only way out." He learned to become rational, to communicate, to drink schnapps and wine. He became socialized into a "cultural system," and, in ways quite consistent with what most contemporary theorists of culture believe, he became utterly estranged from his animal nature. Thus, when presented with a female ape mate, he could only see "the insane look of the bewildered half-broken animal in her eye," a dim-witted unconscious creature of nature, uncivilized, incapable of drinking schnapps or wine.

I would like to propose Kafka's ape, this hairy biped virtually reduced to a talking head, as the ideal type of creature proposed by most contemporary theories of culture. This creature, regardless of whether one reads of him in structuralist, structural-functionalist, poststructuralist, or critical accounts (or whether one reads of her in much of radical feminism), is a product of unfeeling systems; his or her actions thoroughly stamped with the impress of an inorganic, rational system. While granting that there are exceptions to these tendencies—some feminists, such as Nancy Chodorow, Carol Gilligan, or Edith Turner want to heighten the emotional character of the person and acknowledge the possibly biological sources of some gender differences and incorporate them into overly rationalized social theory—nevertheless, the dominant approaches presume a nature-culture dichotomy and an utterly ungrounded and unbounded conception of culture.[2]

Like the concept of life, the "culture concept" remains a profound indicator of contemporary intellectual culture. "Cultural studies" has become a focal point for multidisciplinary studies throughout the humanities and social sciences, often with a decidedly postmodern "theoretical" emphasis. Academic sociology has seemed to rediscover the importance of culture, as seen in the recent creation of cultural sociology sections of the American and German sociological associations in the past few years, and a similar return of interest has been underway in psychology.

Indeed, the sociology of the recent culture section in the American Sociological Association suggests that the objectivist and positivist prejudices of mainstream American sociology are appropriating the "soft" concept of culture by making it "hard," and thereby safe for "science" and career advancement. A peculiar irony of this development is that the objectivists share a tendency with relativists to view culture in purely conventionalist terms. Hence the inner social aspects of culture—subjective meanings, aesthetic qualities of works of art or common experience, the "spontaneous combustion" of new ways of feeling, doing, and conceiving—are either proclaimed not to be sociological, reduced to external considerations, or are virtually ignored. The outer aspects, the externals of culture—such as reputations, "tool kit"–like strategies of action, social networks, and production standards, although admittedly social and legitimate topics of study, are overenlarged to cover the whole meaning of culture.[3] Such approaches, by no means limited to sociology, amount to a *doughnut* theory of culture, after the American pastry which is hollow at the center. In seeking to examine "context," they in effect reduce the object of investigation and its significance to the context in which it is embedded: foreground is reduced to background. They are, in my opinion, reflections of general societal tendencies toward technical externalism, toward culture as a "package." The result is that culture legitimates new topics of study while simultaneously being tamed to meet the expectations of actually existing sociology.

Just what then is "culture," a term so indeterminate that it can easily be filled in with whatever preconceptions a theorist brings to it? The usual way of answering this question is to trace the modern history of the "culture concept" from E. B. Tylor to the present. Such a history can be quite revealing, because the culture concept itself is a cultural indicator of the major intellectual tendencies and battles over the past century. The joint statement in 1958 by A. L. Kroeber and Talcott Parsons on culture, for example, formalized a kind of a truce between structural functionalism and cultural anthropology, ratified by the two leading proponents of each camp (some may have regarded it as what in business is called a "hostile take-over attempt" of the culture concept by Parsons, although "corporate merger" might be a more apt expression).

By beginning with a brief tour of the contemporary landscape of culture theory, I hope to show how current conceptions of meaning and culture tend toward extreme forms of disembodied abstraction, indicating an alienation from the original, earthy meaning of the word *culture*. I will then turn to the earlier meanings of the word and why the "cultic," the living impulse to meaning, was and remains essential to a conception of culture as semeiosis or sign-action. Culture and biology are often treated by social scientists as though they were oil and water, not to be mixed. I am fully aware of the assumed nature-culture dichotomy, but I reject it, not because I am a sociobiologist, quite the contrary, but rather because I am a semiotician, and my studies of signs have led me toward a critical reconstruction of the concepts of nature and culture. In my perspective, culture is a living, social metaboly of signs, not limited to a convention but in transaction with the inmost recesses of the person and with the qualitative, physical, and significant environment. The question is not whether culture is a "system" or not but whether we shall continue to conceive of culture as an inert, mechanical system or code, incapable of self-critical cultivation, or as a "living system"—a way of living—fully open to contingency, spontaneity, purposive growth and decay.

Putting the "cult" back into culture requires a reconception of the relations between human biology and meaning, and between nondiscursive, nonrational reason and modern rationality. Such a reconception involves considering how the technics of the biosocial human body itself form the primary source of culture. In contemporary modern culture in general, and intellectual culture in particular, we have unnecessarily narrowed our conceptions of meaning and culture. By outlining a broad historical reconstruction of human consciousness and communication —that is, by reopening the questions of evolution and philosophical anthropology, which have been pushed to the periphery of social theory—we can see why culture seeps into our very biological constitution: *cultus,* the impulse to meaning.

To the extent that we deny our organic apehood, we remain ignorant of what we are most assured—our deeply embedded signifying nature—and become not much more than Kafka's thoroughly civilized, yet utterly devitalized, ape.

Culture Is More Than Convention

In the "culture is convention" view, it is usually assumed that meaning is a systemic property, that signification forms a logical or ideological system, and that culture is a code for order. Such a view, when found in extreme, for example, in French structuralism, amounts to little more than intellectual totalitarianism in which there are no meaningful deviations from the "code." Yet even the antirationalist opposites proposed by the "post" theorists, such as Jean Baudrillard, Jean-François Lyotard, and Jacques Derrida, remain tethered to the structuralist ideology they flamboyantly act out against, and infected with the old Cartesian "ghost in the machine" dichotomy: the ethereal ape of deep structural code and post-structural fission, a mere "simulacrum" without presence—his or her body reduced to a text. Take the example of Lyotard, who in his book, *The Postmodern Condition,* proclaims a pseudorevolutionary postmodernism:

> The postmodern would be that which, in the modern, puts forward the unpresentable in presentation itself; that which denies itself the solace of good forms, the consensus of a taste which would make it possible to share collectively the nostalgia for the unattainable; that which searches for new presentations, not in order to enjoy them but in order to impart a stronger sense of the unpresentable. A postmodern artist or writer is in the position of a philosopher: the text he writes, the work he produces are not in principle governed by preestablished rules, and they cannot be judged according to a determining judgment, by applying familiar categories to the text or to the work. Those rules and categories are what the work of art is itself looking for. The artist and the writer, then, are working without rules in order to formulate the rules of *what will have been done.* . . . It must be clear that it is our business not to supply reality but to invent allusions to the conceivable which cannot be presented. Let us wage a war on totality; let us be witnesses to the unpresentable; let us activate the differences and save the honor of the name.

We see here yet another avatar of *the invisible dictator,* a servant of the ghost in the machine mentality of modernity who happens to reside on the spectral side of the dichotomy. He would do away with "totality" by replacing it with the artist as philosopher-king. The brave new postmodern artist is not possessed of a need to body forth feelingful forms but works "to formulate the rules," while denying himself or herself "the solace of good forms." Far from presenting us with the unpresentable, Lyotard is simply mouthing the old avant-garde delusion of art as pure novelty. Surely we can see at the end of the twentieth century that the Cartesian quest to doubt away all beliefs to a pure starting point, echoed in the avant-garde all-out assault on tradition, resulted not in originality but in the evaporation of the human subject. Both structuralism and poststructuralism were conscious agents of antisubjectivism, as seen, for example, in the ideal of the decentered self, but in attacking Cartesian individualism they unwittingly embodied intellectual versions of the more general process of depersonalization at work in the twentieth century.

One does not overcome conventional signification through idiosyncrasy or through an ideology of the "unpresentable" or "absent" but through constantly cultivating one's honesty and perceptiveness in the practice of living. If modernity be characterized as cultural nominalism—a dichotomous worldview that falsely divides thoughts from things, producing a conventional conception of mind and a materialized conception of nature—then we can well understand why Lyotard suddenly waxes nostalgic to "save the honor," not of a flesh and blood creature but of "the name" itself in its abstract generality.

The same etherealizing and mechanizing tendencies reside on the other half of the great divide of cultural nominalism, for humanity incarnate is also the unacknowledged enemy of many current biologically based theories of culture, such as those of human ethology or sociobiology. As I claimed in the previous chapter, the seeming antithesis to the ethereal ape of structuralism and poststructuralism, the so-called natural man of ethology and sociobiology, likewise shares a domination by the calculating character of modern rationality. Like Caliban in *The Tempest,* that nasty and brutish subhuman, the creature of ethology and sociobiology is all appetite and impulsive greed. Yet these Hobbesian "state of nature" emotions are themselves facades for a cunning, underlying, rational genetic choice theory. Indeed structuralism, poststructuralism, rational-choice theory, and the rational calculation imputed to the genes by sociobiology are only apparently opposed; inwardly they speak the same disembodied language. The incarnate human body, with its stored capacities of memory and tempered abilities to suffer experience and engender meaning, is epiphenomenal in the sociobiologists' accounts; all that truly matters is the ethereal rational self-interest and its total willy-nilly maximalization.

We see variations of the same mindset in those theories that view culture as "a system of symbols and meanings," as though system were the be-all and end-all of culture and human action. Such theories, from that of Talcott Parsons to those of more up-to-date postmodernists, claim to do justice to the systematic nature of human signification, but in reality they grossly exaggerate those aspects of signification concerning conceptual systems—as though culture were only a domain of knowledge instead of being a way of living—while ignoring or distorting those aspects of signification that reside outside the boundaries of rationality and systems. These latter forms of signification include dreaming, imaginative projection, lived and suffered experience and its contingencies—what Charles Peirce termed *iconic* (or *qualitative*) *signs* and *indexical signs* (signs of physicality or existence)—as well as *symbolic signs* that are conceived within a living context and larger purport beyond the narrow confines of system and rationality.

In founding modern semeiotic toward the end of the nineteenth century, Peirce proposed that signification occurs through three modalities of being. He demonstrated logically not only why signs can represent their objects qualitatively, existentially, and conventionally but also why all three modalities are inherently social.[4] His existential signs, or indexical signs, are therefore fundamentally unlike the positivist notion of semantic reference with which they are sometimes confused. Similarly, iconic signs, in being wholly within semiosis, or sign-action, convey *essences* or the qualities of their objects, within the social process of interpretation. Iconic signs may exist within social conventions, yet are not reducible to conventional signification. Advocates of *essentialism* tend to view essences as outside of the realm of signs, while critics believe that what are called essences can be subsumed under social conventions or "constructions," and in fact are merely products, as all facets of culture are, of ideological systems. Yet Peirce's concept of iconic signs undercuts both positions, revealing how essences or qualities are indeed both social and significatory, while simultaneously not reducible to conventions, constructions, or ideological systems. One can admit that anything can be used for ideological purposes—such as nature or art or *Kultur*—without denying the possibility that there may be laws of nature, or qualities of feeling or craftsmanship, which are not reducible to the ideology appropriating them, or to human construction, as in the example of biologically caused schizophrenia, or even, in the case of art, to the conventions out of which they grew. Even Peirce's concept of symbolic signs is not limited to conventions. As he put it, a symbol "depends either upon a convention, a habit, or a natural disposition of its interpretant or of the field of its interpretant."[5] Even a conventionalist must account for the evolution of the first symbol and the first convention as coming into being without being dependent upon prior convention or essences. Such nonconventional modalities of signification as found in Peirce's iconic and indexical signs are fundamental to a vital culture and civilization, I claim, though they may fall outside the pale of conventionalist theories, such as those of Pierre Bourdieu, Jürgen Habermas, or James Clifford.

Being human is being a living sign-complex, immersed within innumerable layers of signs which represent and interpret—and misinterpret—our personal, familial, ancestral, cultural, and evolutionary pasts, and out of which we project our selves. To say that we are the stuff of which signs are made is not to reduce us to language, text, or convention but to acknowledge that organic significance is the fruit of nature and the wellspring of culture. In the denatured language of contemporary theory, however, the "natural" human of sociobiology and the "cultural" one of individualistic or systematic conceptualism are equally divested of organic nature and personhood. Even Kafka's ape could see that these creatures are simply lackeys of rationalism, ignorant of their biosemiotic "glassy essence."

CORPUS AND CULTUS

> *Thought must live with and be inspired with the life of the body.*
>
> —*Henry David Thoreau*

Culture theory is facing the problem portrayed in the 1950s American science fiction movie, *The Invasion of the Body Snatchers*. In this movie the citizens of a small American city are secretly replaced gradually by alien replicas grown from pods that have fallen from outer space. When placed near a sleeping human body, the pods assume control by appropriating memory, personality characteristics, and a perfect physical resemblance; all they lack is human emotions. As the pod creature blooms in the night, the human creature withers, so that the next morning—presto!—a real vegetable substitute walks and talks in embodied form, and the "system of symbols and meanings" is virtually unchanged: people still drink coffee and read the newspapers in the manner criticized by Camus, though fornication has become obsolete. But of course there is one major change in the culture of this town, for the system of symbols and meanings has taken on a distinctly alien life of its own, and the one passion left to the quasi-carnivorous vegetarians—if I may describe creatures who absorb human flesh while remaining vegetables—is to transform all human life to their system of perfect dispassionate being, to their rational system of symbols and meanings.

Many valid interpretations of *The Invasion of the Body Snatchers* can be given. It could signify the paranoia of the McCarthy era in the 1950s. In that scenario, red-blooded Americans feared the takeover by the "red menace" of communism, whose bloodless agents could be your own neighbors, and projected these fears into pop-mythic aliens. Or, in its remade version from the 1980s, it might signify the neo-1950s paranoia of the neo-McCarthyite neoconservatives. It could also be taken to signify the deadliness of "organization man," as a sort of collective synonym for Willy Loman of Arthur Miller's *Death of a Salesman,* or the role played by Gregory Peck in the movie *The Man in the Grey Flannel Suit.* We could also interpret this movie as a prophecy of the evisceration of the American city by the "alien" automobile and shopping mall, a process that began in earnest in the 1950s and continues unabated today, leaving in its wake "urbanoid tissue." For my purposes the movie is a popular narrative of mythic rationality: the progressive loss of natural human capacities resulting from the dictatorship of the machine of modernity: we moderns, we half-barbarians, we total vegetables brainwashed in the service of expanding a great unfeeling system. The cultural processes which emanated from that movie in phobic form are being expressed in recent culture theories in intellectual form.

Culture theory, in its dominant contemporary manifestations, is an old science fiction movie, practiced by would-be body snatchers: some claim to transform the body into a text or into communicative "talking heads"; still others seek to appropriate the human capacity to body forth meaning to the depersonalized system, for example, Niklas Luhmann's concept of *autopoeisis.* A considerable number of so-called feminists have as their goal not the reform of gender relations but the eradication of gender, taking a neutered androgeny as an ideal instead of as a form of deprivation. Camus regretted modern man, reduced to a life of coffee drinking, newspaper reading, and fornicating. What would he say of our genderless, eviscerated, postmodern person, reduced to the status of a text? At least Camus' modern man could have a little coffee and sex along with his text. The point is that whether one regards gender as limited to conventional social roles or, as I believe, an aspect of one's identity with deep biosemiotic roots in the human body, femininity and masculinity ought to be celebrated as part of what it means to be human. The attempt to eradicate gender differences is based on the mistaken assumption that genderlessness is requisite for social equality. Those who would devalue gender are unwitting accomplices of the invisible dictator of modernity, the neutered ghost in the machine.

The body has recently emerged as a major theme in intellectual life, but it is for the most part a conceptualized and etherealized body modeled on the text: the anticorporeal gospel of postmodernism seems to proclaim that "the flesh was made word and dwells among us!" In other words, it is not so much "body language" that is now fashionable as the body as language. The rhetoric of the body, the conventionalization of the body, and the symbolism of gender differences can all be significant topics. But when we note how little is said about the organic, biological body in these discussions, we begin to suspect that the academic mega-machine is continuing its work of rational reduction. Such is perhaps more clearly the case in Paul Ricouer's and Derrida's calls to view human action and social life as texts, or in Habermas's theory of communicative action, which says much about rational talkers talking but very little about actors acting: felt, perceptive, imaginative, bodily experience does not fit these theories.

Or consider the systems theorist Niklas Luhmann, who introduced the idea of *autopoeisis* to account for self-generating systems. Here we see another contemporary avatar of the megamachine. The abstract, lifeless "systems" theory, because it excludes the living humans who comprise the social "system" as significant, ignores those natural capacities of life for self-making and self-generation. *Autopoeisis* must ignore *poeisis,* the human ability to create meaning in uniquely realized acts and works that transcend mere system per se. Therefore Luhmann's theory can be seen as part of the age-old dream to give life to the machine, in this case the machine-like system. His concept of *autopoeisis* is like the robot, android, or other automaton fetishes of contemporary popular culture and movies, many of which involve (and even celebrate) a transformation of humans into automatons.

Such sociological theories are not too distant from materialist artificial intelligence and "neural network" theories, which view human beings, to quote computer scientist Marvin Minsky, as highly systematic "meat machines." One wonders whether the robots have snatched Minsky's mind, not to mention his body and soul when, in extolling the "intelligence" of the next generation of computers, he says that we mortal meat machines will "be lucky if they are willing to keep us around the house as household pets."[6] This delusional phobic fantasy is of a piece with the *Terminator* movies, where the next generations of computers are not willing to keep us around and create look-alike humanoid robots to exterminate the human race. I take these intellectual and cultural phenomena as further signs of the capitulation of autonomous life to the automaton in the late twentieth century. They remind one of the delusional fantasies of the Italian Futurists, who longed to replace humanity with an eternal avant-garde of sleek power drones. A robot-worshipping Minsky and an antihumanist, chaos-loving Derrida both coalesce in the Futurist Marinetti's remarks during World War I in an essay titled, "Multiplied Man and the Reign of the Machine": "We look for the creation of a nonhuman type in whom moral suffering, goodness of heart, affection, and love, those corrosive poisons of vital energy, interrupters of our powerful bodily electricity, will be abolished." No wonder that Marinetti later embraced Mussolini's Fascism, a point we should keep in mind today. The widespread fascination with the electronics revolution of the 1980s, visible in the transformer robot toys of young children, in the video games of older children, in the word processor computers increasingly a part of the work environment and the exercise machines, and portable "walkman" cassette machines and "internet" communications systems increasingly a part of the adult play environment, may symbolize the emergence of a new creature who prefers "virtual reality" to the real thing: perhaps the electronic version of the mechanized "nonhuman type" for whom Marinetti longed, dehabitualized to the human affections, "those corrosive poisons of vital energy."

Charles Horton Cooley described primary groups as constituted by "face-to-face" relations, as distinguished from relations determined by broader, more impersonal social roles and structural positions, which could be called secondary relations. Following this distinction I will suggest that we are seeing the ascendency since the 1980s of what I will term "tertiary groups," in which the machine has become the crucial intermediary, such that communication is predicated on indirect "face-to-machine" relations.

Hence the current interest in the body as a theme may have the further undoing of the body as its unacknowledged goal. Whether disembodied as conceptualism or reified as mechanistic system or artificial intelligence, we are still left with the ghost in the machine.

From the perspective of the organic body, however, contemporary culture theory is for the most part a form of sensory deprivation. Those who proclaim culture to be solely a "social construction" make an uncritical assumption that social life, culture, symbols, and meanings neither touch nor are touched by organic life in any deep way. Indeed the leading ideologues of culture theory—whether poststructuralists, critical theorists, or social constructionists, tend to regard any concern with the relations between culture and organic nature or evolution as a threat to the hegemony of the cultural system over meaning.

There are significant exceptions to this outlook, notably in the work of Clifford Geertz, Victor Turner, and Lewis Mumford. Geertz has written on the interaction of culture and biology in the emergence of human culture. As he says in his essay "The Growth of Culture and the Evolution of Mind": "Man's nervous system does not merely enable him to acquire culture, it positively demands that he do so if it is going to function at all. Rather than culture acting only to supplement, develop, and extend organically based capacities logically and genetically prior to it, it would seem to be ingredient to those capacities themselves. A cultureless human being would probably turn out to be not an intrinsically talented though unfulfilled ape, but a wholly mindless and consequently unworkable monstrosity."[7] By implication one can also say that a natureless human being could not be considered "civilized" but a similarly unworkable monstrosity.

As the neurological disorder of autism reveals, it is possible to perform and remember complicated human tasks and yet to live devoid of meanings. As cases of individuals who have suffered damage to the hippocampus and related areas of the brain reveal, it is possible to retain the heights of human consciousness, speech, and passion while trapped in a continual present, utterly devoid of the ability to remember anything since the time of the damage, to learn new information, or to project a course of action beyond the immediate situation. All that is solid to the experiencing self, so solid that we simply take it for granted—the encoding of experience as memory, melts away, leaving a person both passionately engaged in the present and yet truly unable to embrace it and learn from it. This misfortune tragically gives the lie to the avant-garde dream of erasing the past to achieve a "live" present: such a culture would truly be posthuman in the sense of being deprived of the means of human experience. Clearly human biology, as seen in the human brain and its meaning and memory capacities or in the vocal organs, is involved in a reciprocal relationship with culture.

Culture may be an objectified organ of meaning, but it remains connected to the organic proclivities and limitations of human bodies through the tempering effects of experience. The plasticity of culture does not signify the want of underlying instinctive motivation, as Gehlen thought, but the positive vagueness or indeterminate suggestive nature of human instinctual promptings: culture does not free us (or deprive us) of biology but has co-evolved as an intrinsic aspect of human biology.

To anyone who seriously considers how human culture came to be, Geertz's statement that culture is ingredient to organically based capacities challenges the so-called nature-culture dichotomy. Ironically though, Geertz's ideas on the interaction of culture and biology are rarely cited, whereas his more conceptualistic "cultural system" works are cited. Though Geertz is generally appreciative of the significance of organic human nature for culture, even he retains the reductionistic tendencies of the "cultural systematizers" to view meaning as limited to the mode of conventional signification.

The cultic is the springing forth of the impulse to meaning, which culminates in belief. As such the cultic is no throwback to "vitalism" but involves the deepest emotional, preconscious, and even instinctive capacities of the human body for semiosis. Although most theories of culture continue to view meaning as conventional knowledge or system, I am proposing that the essence of meaning resides in bodied sign-practices that circumscribe mere knowledge. Conventions of language, gesture, image, and artifact should be viewed as the means toward incarnate sign-practices, not as the structural or systemic foundations or ends of meaning. The very attempts to ground meaning in a theory of pure conventionalism are signs of the evisceration of meaning, the hollowing out of living human experience to the external technique or the idolatry of the "code": the doughnut theory of culture.

By "incarnate sign-practices" I mean that culture is a process of semiosis, or sign-action, intrinsically involving the capacities of the human body for memory, communication, and imaginative projection and is not completely separable from those capacities. Social structure, in this perspective, cannot be severed from the living inferential metaboly of human experience through systematic or structuralist abstraction, but it needs to be conceived in some relation to lived human experience and its requirements, limitations, and possibilities. Human life, in its organic fullness, remains the yardstick for social theory and cultural meaning, and neither the abstractionist distortions and perversions of the life-concept through biological reductionism nor the equally abstractionist repression of the life-concept through cultural reductionism will suffice any longer.

We are left, it seems to me, with centering our investigation of the roots of culture in the most sophisticated technics the world has yet known: those of the organic human body. Through human memory we have a profound connection to the past: to historic, prehistoric, and even transhuman memory as the incorporation of organic experience. Living human memory, which is something quite different from mere nostalgia, makes it possible for collective and personal past experience to infuse its wisdom into the present and so generate new prospects for future conduct. No computer memory chip can help a computer to *feel* a novel situation, as human memory can, or to generate a truly novel interpretation. The generalization of human memory in myths, rituals, traditions, and writing vastly broadened the spatiotemporal environment and human power. But power is double-edged, and as Milan Kundera has said, "The struggle of man against power is the struggle of memory against forgetting." And, I would add, it is the exercise of imagination against convention and the overvalued power of the rational intellect.

THE NOMINALISTS' CONVENTION

Conventionalism, the view that all human meaning is based upon nonnatural social conventions, holds a pervasive sway over contemporary intellectual life. The leading French schools of thought associated with structuralism and poststructuralism retain strong influences of Ferdinand de Saussure's conventionalist semiology, and even Pierre Bourdieu's attempt to develop a more experiential category of the *habitus* remains thoroughly conventionalist, viewing the habitus as a "system of dispositions."

This view is particularly clear in Bourdieu's discussions of aesthetic judgment in his book *Distinction,* in which he assumes the standard dichotomy between "essentialist" and conventionalist analysis and claims that essentialist analysis "must fail" because it ignores the fact that all intentions and judgments are products of social conventions. The term *essentialism* carries with it highly negative meanings in cultural studies today, and Bourdieu's criticism of essentialism represents the tendency to regard aesthetic qualities—the essential—as nonsocial. The producer's intention

> is itself the product of the social norms and conventions which combine to define the always uncertain and historically changing frontier between simple technical objects and objets d'art. . . . But the apprehension and appreciation of the work also depend on the beholder's intention, which is itself a function of the conventional norms governing the relation to the work of art in a certain historical and social situation and also of the beholder's capacity to conform to those norms, i.e., his artistic training. To break out of this circle one only has to observe that the ideal of "pure" perception of a work of art qua work of art is the product of the enunciation and systematization of the principles of specifically aesthetic legitimacy which accompany the constituting of a relatively autonomous artistic field. The aesthetic mode of perception in the "pure" form which it has now assumed corresponds to a particular state of the mode of artistic production.[8]

By claiming that all aesthetic experience is purely conventional and therefore social, Bourdieu is attacking the view that aesthetic judgment consists in an unmediated act of perception and that the work of art possesses inherent qualities unmediated by social signification. In the conventional view that Bourdieu takes, to be human is to be the enclosed product of those specific social norms in which one finds oneself. It is the same old world in which the social is limited to the conventional and modalities of nonconventional signification, such as Peirce's iconic and indexical signs, are thereby either ignored or falsely assumed to be nonsocial. It is a world in which the human creature, who, above all others *both is open to and needs meaning,* is denied the social capacity to germinate and body forth genuinely new feelings, perceptions, and ideas not reducible to, though growing out of, prior social norms. How little feeling must Pierre Bourdieu and other like-minded cultural theorists have, to reduce the encounter with a master work of art to an intellectualistic system! Unfortunately, Bourdieu's shrewd and anesthetic understanding of the aesthetic is compounded by a crude and uncritical theory of meaning as solely conventional.

Another route, which Bourdieu's conventionalism forbids him to take, is to view aesthetic experience as fully social, yet not necessarily conventional, so that conventions themselves are live processes of sign interpretation open to experience, growth, and cultivation or "minding." In such a view every sign can possess its own qualitative significance or essence qua socially communicative sign as well as reflect social structures. Hence, from my perspective, aesthetic experience may be truly *formative* in giving birth to new "social norms." The ability to body forth new meaning, not reducible to prior conventions, has the added advantage of being able to explain how conventions developed in the first place, a question that conventionalism usually avoids.

James Clifford is one cultural theorist and historian of ethnography who has sought to defend the emergence of new conventions in cultures which have encountered modern civilization, cultures which are too often, in Clifford's view, frozen by the West into an image of a pure, precontact past. His book, *The Predicament of Culture,* is a broad-ranging tour of ethnography, literature, and art, and a good example of the contemporary cultural predicament: Can the modern one-size-fits-all world be successfully challenged and transformed by the postmodern "one thing is as good as any other thing" world of ever-emergent pluralism? He seeks a pluralistic ethnography not distinct from literature, and thereby links up with poststructuralist, "post-literary" critics who see no difference between writers and critics, and with the postmodern horde who claim to have killed the monological author.

In Clifford one sees the standard conventions of the contemporary multi-culturalist:

> The denial of the Big Picture (to quote Clifford, "There is no master narrative which can reconcile the tragic and comic plots of global cultural history," as he puts it, no "privileged Hegelian vision").
> The denial of the author ("Recent literary theory suggests that the ability of a text to make sense in a coherent way depends less on the willed intentions of an originating author than the creative activity of a reader").
> The denial of truth or experience as something other than "modes of authority" or fictions, the selection of which by the "author" of an ethnography being merely "a matter of strategic choice."
> The denial of a human essence (to speak of "man" and "human" is to run the risk of reducing contingent differences to a system of universal essences. . . . To stress . . . the paradoxical nature of ethnographic knowl-

edge . . . does mean questioning any stable or essential grounds of human stability").

And finally the denial of the human ability to create and communicate felt forms possessed of aesthetic quality or, more simply, *beauty,* and along with it the denial of standards of discrimination and judgment—of better or worse—which transcend conventions.

Consider Clifford's use of "the doughnut theory of culture," of trendy externalism, in his critique of "the modern art-culture system." Commenting on the apparently indistinguishable system of value underlying archaeologists recovering bronze age pots and thieves looting and selling Native American Anasazi pottery from archaeological sites in the American Southwest, he says, "This system finds intrinsic interest and beauty in objects from a past time, and it assumes that collecting everyday objects from ancient (preferably vanished) civilizations will be more *rewarding* than collecting, for example, decorated thermoses from modern china or customized t-shirts from Oceania. Old objects are endowed with a sense of "depth" by their historically minded collectors. Temporality is reified and salvaged as origin, beauty, and knowledge." Because of his conventionalist presuppositions, Clifford conflates his valid criticism of the predatory consumption of the past by robbers, robber barons, and grave robbers—and by modern materialism in general—with the idea that the artifacts cannot be possessed of beauty or that the pursuit of a past culture for scientific discovery may not have intrinsic interest. In the name of pluralism, he advances a theory of meaning which reduces and homogenizes the unique characters of persons and things to belief conventions and contingent differences. Art is but a part of an ideologically bounded "art-culture system" rather than a social precipitate of human experience and the communication of feelings and beliefs in felt and unified form. He does suggest one possible alternative to the modern art-culture system in viewing objects as *"our own* fetishes," but even here we seem to be left with the dichotomy of culture as a rigid, codified system versus privatized fixation, again, the typical result of conventionalism.[9]

Clifford is against the Big System in general and in favor of the little systems, much as a poststructuralist would be against the single, Great Code of structuralism in favor of the "fissioning" of signs or creative cultural fragmentation: the pendulum may swing the other way, but somehow it is still the same Saussurean pendulum swinging. Perhaps this is why Clifford sees the connections between surrealism and ethnography in the 1920s as a possible revitalizing source for cultural pluralism today. Given the sterility of academic specialization, perhaps he may have a point, but because he avoids looking at art as the transformation of inner feeling to outer form in favor of art as both belief system and provocative critique of belief systems, one will not find a discussion of surrealism as a perception of the great disturbance underway in Western Civilization, one which would overcome Europe in the 1930s and 1940s.

In a self-critical comment, Clifford questions whether his book "goes too far in its concern for ethnographic presents- becoming-futures. Its utopian, persistent hope for the reinvention of difference risks downplaying the destructive, homogenizing effects of global economic and cultural centralization." I would agree that he downplays the effects of a global centralization in which the center cannot hold and overplays the semiological concept of "difference" as the key to cultural vitality. In the midst of a destructive global commodification of cultures and organic life, Amazonian Yąnomamö Indians can "reinvent difference" by video recording their forest being cut away around them and their family members dying of flu viruses for which they have no immunities: new cultural forms and syncretisms undoubtedly emerge, but Clifford's postmodern conventionalism, with its Panglossian "best of all possible worlds" approach is, to my way of thinking, only a continuation of the unconscious projection of Western ideology on to the diversity of cultures. Yet, apart from his utopian ideology, there is perhaps a necessary tension at work between ethnography and theory, the former tending to suffer from nearsightedness, the latter from farsightedness. In my experience ethnographers, like historians, prefer concrete particulars to generalization, just as theorists and philosophers prefer to see what the particulars add up to: rare is the temperament which can do justice to both. Clifford's own concerns for ethnographic detail and the best case for his ideas are apparent in his ethnographic chapter, "Identity in Mashpee," where he presents an account of the suit filed by the Mashpee Wampanoag Tribal Council for possession of the Cape Cod town of Mashpee. The trial focused not around the land dispute but on whether the Mashpee Tribe was, in fact, an Indian tribe, and there the strengths of including multiple perspectives in one ethnographic account become apparent. One also sees the predicament of culture for people who could not have survived if they had not assimilated, and yet who are denied their identities because they are not "pure" aliens.

Clifford traces a variety of methodological approaches in his opening chapter, "On Ethnographic Authority," including experiential, textual or interpretative, dialogical, and polyphonic—or many-voiced—"modes of authority." The experiential "mode of authority," for example, is viewed by Clifford as subjective rather than intersubjective and naive in comparison with the "sophisticated alternative" of textual interpretation. Although he cites Dilthey as a source for both modes, Clifford neglects to ask how Dilthey could have viewed the two—*Erlebnis* or experience and *Verstehen,* understanding or interpretation—as interconnecting. Experience ought to be the meeting of the ethnographer with the people studied, in which the ethnographer genuinely learns from the culture, despite what his or her subjective beliefs and cultural presuppositions happen to be. In other words, experience is an intersubjective mode of conduct, not simply a convention of subjective authority. Honest interpretative or hermeneutic ethnography, unless one is a preformed ideologue merely projecting one's theory onto a people, is likewise an intersubjective meeting of interpreter and interpreted, regardless of what Dilthey, Weber, Gadamer, or Geertz might have said. Margaret Mead or Malinowski may (or may not) have used these methods in ways to produce the "I was there" limitations Clifford described, but one need not take the concept of experience to be exhausted by these efforts and requiring more sophisticated "dialogical" and "polyphonic" approaches. Nor does one need to take the conventional postmodern interpretation of Bakhtin's concept of polyphony as antiauthorial relativism. I might add parenthetically that Clifford's methods seem to form a hierarchical organization of "sophistication," but since hierarchies are verboten by postmodern convention he does not and cannot acknowledge a hierarchical order, except by implication. Victor Turner, whom Clifford praises for allowing the voices of his Ndembu informants to enter in significant ways into the ethnography, believed that experience itself is "polyphonic," or, to use his term instead of Bakhtin's, "multivocal."

Turner and his wife Edith revealed themselves to be initiates, not only to the rites revealed to them by the Ndembu but to the centrality of ritual experience itself in tribal society and human affairs. Trained in the British structural-functionalist approach to social anthropology, Victor Turner noted how the incessant call of the drums made him feel that he "was always on the outside looking in." Soon, however, Turner and his wife and collaborator Edith discarded their theoretical earplugs and answered the invitation of the drums. As observers and co-participants in Ndembu ritual the Turners began to blaze a trail toward a new anthropology far deeper than any "mode of authority." As Edith Turner noted in her introduction to a collection of Victor's essays:

> Fieldwork became our delight. Arriving at a distant village we would be greeted by the whole population, shaking hands and thumbs with us and clapping. I would find the women's kitchens, while Vic sat in the meeting hut with the men. If you listened you could hear the warm deep buzz of voices over the beer calabashes. They liked Vic. The women took me to

visit their girl initiate in her seclusion hut, while our own three children played around the cooking fires. On the way home Vic and I discussed the going-into-seclusion ceremony of the previous week. "What's interesting," said Vic, "is the name of the spot where she was laid down under the milk tree. 'The Place of Death.' Then she becomes a 'baby,' and is carried backwards into her seclusion hut. She's sacred, and mustn't touch the earth." "The hut's sacred too. Her white beads—her 'children'—are in the roof. She mustn't look up." And so we would go on, testing out ideas and listening for clues to help interpretation.[10]

"Listening for clues to help interpretation": therein lies one of the clues to Victor and Edith Turner, anthropologists of experience, interpretation, and the multivocal human spirit. Amidst the mighty theoretical armatures in which the social sciences have been clothing themselves throughout this century, Victor and Edith Turner stand out as ethnographers who *listened,* who felt the rhythmic pulse of cultures rather than abstractly dictating their underlying grand scheme or stating hollowly, "I was there." As Victor Turner pointed out, the etymological root of "experience," *per* or *par,* means "to attempt, venture, risk," and is "from its inception ambiguous" regarding one's *participation with* and *observation of* those studied. Experience produces double loyalties, both to the undeniable uniqueness of those with whom one has lived, and to the model of objective comparison derived from modern social science. It is, in Turner's eyes, a prod toward richer interpretation rather than a mere "mode of authority."

In considering the body of Victor Turner's work and his feel for experience and the craftsmanship of ethnography, the callowness of Clifford's departmentalization of "subjective" experience from "intersubjective" polyphony is exposed. So too is what William James once called the "vicious intellectualism" infesting social thought today, which would make ideological power the be-all and end-all of life. To cite one politically correct feminist ideologue, "The appeal to experience, as the ultimate test of all knowledge, merely subtends the subject in its fantasy of autonomy and control. Belief in the truth of Experience is as much an ideological production as belief in the experience of Truth."[11] Such a view, that there is nothing outside the bubble of ideology, no obdurate facts we may bump up against regardless of our ideology, no tempering of emotions and ideas through continued encounters, no emotions—no suffering, joy, or sorrow—which are not ideological, no maturation of persons by contingencies of life which press on us despite our beliefs and intentions, no valid conclusions to be drawn on the basis of warranted assertions, that is, fallible truth rather than arbitrary ideology, such a view amounts to a mere childish delusion of autonomy and control emanating from a fevered intellectualism. "Ideological production" is a neat and closed immune system guaranteed to save ideologues from exposure to the perilousness of experience.

Clifford assumes that validity claims are based on modes of authority rather than the fullness of truth or insight gained and conveyed. In concluding that it is a matter of strategic choice which technique or techniques the ethnographer relies upon, his main concern is to preserve the openness of source material as much as possible and thereby to avoid foreclosing on alternative interpretations which might be suppressed by an author's own limitations. But are "authority" and its opposite, nondiscriminative pluralism, the only alternatives for the contemporary ethnographer and for cultural studies?

Ethnography, like politics or cultural beliefs in general, is supposedly based upon one or more "modes of authority." In this postmodern world where authors are dead fictions and authority is all that remains, truth is obviously obsolete, merely one more fiction claiming authority. Yet, in acknowledging a multiplicity of "modes of authority," is not Clifford really implying that some ethnographic fictions are better than others? Why then is ethnographic pluralism preferable, if not that it provides the best shot at truth, at the fullest presentation of evidence? Or are we simply seeing a critique of what used to be called *ethnocentrism* in new, high-tech postmodernist clothing? It is not clear to me why, in such a world, fairness to multiple voices is preferable to the ethnographer's monologue. If ethnography is simply a question of authority then why not make up any falsehood one wants, burn any dissenters, rewrite any contradictory facts, in order to achieve the maximum "authority"? "Modes of authority" is the term of an authoritarian, and though Clifford and other "postpeople" claim to be antiauthoritarian pluralists, the conventional theory of meaning, largely inherited from Saussure's total code model, betrays a reductionism which results in intellectual authoritarianism. When extended to relativist multicultural politics, such valuing of "modes of authority" over the possibility of a fallible apprehension of truths can spread out from the university and lay the societal basis for authoritarianism, and this is why such views can bespeak what could be called a "fascism of the soul." Real pluralism must rest in informed public opinion, not authority, and informed public opinion must be that which is open to the recalcitrant facts of experience as well as the emotional promptings of the heart, both of which are extraconventional sources of reason.

Both Anthony Giddens and Habermas have sought to reconstruct the basis of social theory, but both remain stalwarts of unreconstructed conventionalism at the heart of their theories of meaning. Giddens, for example, has sought to broaden the base of contemporary theory by using a French structuralist conception of structure and linking it with a theory of "agency" influenced by language analysis, ethnomethodology, and symbolic interactionism. His "structuration theory" can be seen as an attempt to deal with the old sociological problem (itself part of the older nominalist problem) of the relation of the individual with society, or "action" with "order," or subject with object. Yet even a reconstructed structuralism remains too narrow to encompass structure; while agency, even in a broad sense, remains too narrow to encompass subjectivity, and both are inadequate for the creation of a broader theory of meaning. French structuralism reifies structure, treating it as a deep code of "logical" differences divorced from human practices, habits, and memory. Structuralism provided a theory of meaning that enabled one to view the hidden sources or codes which structure meaning in everyday life, claiming that myths, language, and cultural practices are the mere surface manifestations of "deep structures," codes or conventions. In structuralism individual manifestations of speech or conduct are trivial; only the underlying code, rooted in Saussure's conception of the arbitrary and differential nature of the sign, is significant. Although structuralism struck the intellectual community as liberating, one can see how structuralism was actually a form of intellectual totalitarianism—a "one size fits all" approach to meaning which allowed no deviation from the binary logic of the deep structure. It was too inflexible to do justice to time and place in human affairs, to lived, extralogical experience, to the qualitatively unique, in short, to those features of human experience which are not reducible to the grid of cultural nominalism in its manifestation as French rationalism.

The "logic" of structuralism is that of a binary computer; it cannot encompass the living, inferential metaboly of human thought. For this reason structuralism can be viewed as one of the key manifestations of the ghost in the machine in the twentieth century, enacting its assigned role to devalue lived, human experience by etherealizing reason as immaterial structure.

Giddens's attempt to complement a structuralist approach with a concept of agency fails, in my opinion, on both sides of the attempted synthesis. Structuralism was a fundamentally flawed theory of the structures of human institutions, societies, and conduct. "Agency," as Giddens uses it, simply does not go deeply enough into the personal or individual side of meaning, which includes the being acted upon or suffering of experience—the "patient" side of the agent-patient dialectic—let alone the inner dimensions of experience that do not fall under the rubric of agency.

Richard Rorty seems to take a very different perspective, which has been called *neopragmatism,* mistakenly, in my opinion. He remains within the conventionalist fold he seems to reject, viewing meaning as limited to arbitrary language games. Unlike the pragmatists, he denies that there are qualitative and existential modalities of signification not reducible to conventional signs alone. Surely human languages involve conventions, but the full range of meaning or human communication—not to mention human social life—is simply not exhausted by conventional signification. As the neurologist Oliver Sacks expressed it, "Speech—natural speech—does *not* consist of words alone, nor . . . 'propositions' alone. It consists of *utterance*—an uttering-forth of one's whole meaning with one's whole being—the understanding of which involves infinitely more than mere word-recognition. . . . For though the words, the verbal constructions *per se,* might convey nothing [to aphasics], spoken language is normally suffused with 'tone,' embedded in an expressiveness which transcends the verbal—and it is precisely this expressiveness, so deep, so various, so complex, so subtle, which is perfectly preserved in aphasia, though understanding is destroyed. Preserved—and often more: preternaturally enhanced."[12] Given the undeniable facts of communication practices in humans and other species in which signification occurs through nonconventional modalities, why then does conventionalism hold such a power over the contemporary mind?

One way to answer this question is to view these theories as emanating from *cultural nominalism,* the term I use to characterize the modern epoch. What is interesting about the nominalistic ethos is how it systematically undercuts *cultus*—the spontaneous impulse to meaning. In the seventeenth century of Calvin, who was educated in nominalist theology, "the impulse to meaning" becomes an intolerable threat to the great clockwork system of predestination and rational self-control. Hobbes, who also was taught nominalist theology, transformed the impulse to meaning into a mythic projection of individual competitive lust and aggression in the state of nature, which had to be repressed by a social contract—a nonnatural artifice or convention. In the place of the live signifying creature of fantastic passions, delusions, and organic possibilities which no robot could ever hope to achieve, Hobbes saw only the machine: "For seeing that life is but a motion of Limbs, the beginning whereof is in some principal part within; why may we not say, that all *Automata* (Engines that move themselves by springs and wheeles as doth a watch) have an artificiall life? For what is the *heart*, but a *Spring;* and the *Nerves*, but so many *Strings;* and the *Joynts*, but so many *Wheeles*, giving motion to the whole Body, such as was intended by the Artificer?" Bentham psychologized and nominalized organic cultus yet further into individual sensations of pleasure and pain. Even Freud, who is instrumental in the return of the cultic in twentieth-century culture, based his metapsychology in a Bentham-like underlying "pleasure principle" of the reflex-arc concept. While admitting that a pure rational existence is a denial of life and life's energies—similar to Scheler's later discussion of the life versus spirit antithesis—he viewed the cultic, in its pure source, the "id," as chaotic destructive energy needing to be tricked or sublimated into a benign form. Freud's id, like Hobbes's state of nature, is a realm in which individual intentions for maximizing pleasure are carried out, despite the lack of a communicative medium in which such intentions and individuals could be formed.

One cannot deny that much of meaning is conventional, yet even conventions themselves are inherently purposive habits of life which need to be practiced and which can grow or wither in the course of experience. Granted, whether one cracks one's egg in the middle or at the end in order to eat it may make no significant difference in the practice of life, but these conventions contribute to a larger way of life or culture which has an inherent quality and which ought to sustain the vital participation of its members. When high cholesterol from a diet containing too many eggs is shown to contribute to bad health, both types of egg crackers need to reconsider their habits of life.

Conventionalism is proposed as an antidote to reductionism, yet it radically reduces the realm of significance, meaning, and the social. That which is outside the system is regarded as meaningless until it is "systematized." The conventionalist simply assumes that conventions or codes encompass culture. Hence a number of recent sociological and art historical studies take the position that art can be understood solely as social conventions, thereby denying aesthetic quality to works of art and aesthetic experience as an element of human conduct.[13] Similarly, attempts to discuss either the brute factuality or the esthetic or inherent meanings involved in human experience are frequently dismissed by cultural theorists as reductionistic or obsolete because these approaches fail to see that all meaning is conventional, that is, dependent on cultural belief systems. Hence the expressive outpouring of an artist is meaningful only insofar as it can be related to existing cultural values, beliefs, and constructions, or, in the views of some postmods, only insofar as it can idiosyncratically differentiate itself from current conventions. The inner compelling expressiveness of a work of art is reduced to outer considerations and the possibility that art may actually *create* perceptions and beliefs is sidestepped, as is the possibility that culture may involve other modalities of signification.

One can view a late work by the sculptor Ivan Meštrović, *An Old Father in Despair at the Death of His Son,* and, knowing that Meštrović's own son committed suicide, see the autobiographical source for the agonized figure. Clearly representational conventions are involved in the form of this sculpture. But ultimately one is left with the sculpture itself, the father's powerful hands covering most of the face in grief. To say that the sculpture communicates the system of artistic representation or that it is an "aesthetic-practical" form of communication (Habermas) is to miss the point that this physical thing is a bodying forth of human emotion through the hands that shaped it, directly conveying the feeling of human grief through the hands covering the agonized face. It is not a "symbol" standing for something else; it is a living icon and secretion of human experience. It may involve conventions, but these conventions form the vessel, the husk, that contains the actualized experience.

Most sociologists of art and culture do not consider that a work of art might be a spontaneous, meaning-generating gesture or sign not reducible to the conventions from which it grew. The organic, the inherent qualitative possibilities, the imaginative, the spontaneous, the contingent, the serendipitous—in short, the extrarational and nonsystematic—must be devalued or disregarded by the practitioners of conceptual SYSTEM. The result is a systematic ethereal grid that treats only the externals of culture while denying its vital, extrarational, incarnate sources. How is it that literary and cultural theorists and sociologists of literature and culture can remain immune to the power of literature and art, to masterworks which capture and convey the soul of life? How is it that theorists promote intellectual agendas in the name of humanities education which only serve the enlargement of the rational and postrational intellect at the expense of all of those qualities which are not properly "theoretical"?

It is for the same reason that postmodern nondiscursive image culture is ultimately anti-image. In the commercial images which overrun everyday life, we see rational calculations producing image-conventions, whether in rock videos, the American presidential election, or Baudrillard's apology for "hyperreality," for the postmodern world of "simulacra" as one we should celebrate. This is truly the arrival of the posthuman: deprived not only of discursive and rational communication but also of the spontaneous, integral, imaging process. These calculating im-

Figure 1. Ivan Meštrović, An Old Father in Despair at the Death of His Son, *1961. The Snite Museum of Art, University of Notre Dame. Reproduced with permission.*

ages seem to shout, "Don't think! It's all a conventional fiction," and "Don't imagine, let us do it for you."

Culture as abstract, depersonalized system denies the living source of culture as *cultus*. In its reliance on culture as system, it raises system from a means of interpretation to a virtual end of cultural life. Hence culture theory is itself by and large part of a progressive externalization of meaning in cultural life generally: meaning as technique, meaning as prepackaged script, meaning as "the honor of the name."

THE CULTURE AND MANURANCE OF MINDS

When Francis Bacon in 1605 wrote of "the culture and manurance of minds," the literal sense of culture as tending and cultivating nature was still very much in the foreground, although the metaphoric extension of the term to mind was intended. The term *culture* traces back to the Latin *colere,* which meant variously to till, cultivate, dwell or inhabit, and which in turn traces back to the Indo-European root, **Kwel-,* which meant to turn round a place, to wheel, to furrow. As Raymond Williams noted, "Some of these meanings eventually separated, though still with occasional overlapping, in the derived nouns. Thus 'inhabit' developed through *colonus,* Latin to *colony.* 'Honour with worship' developed through *cultus,* Latin to *cult. Cultura* took on the main meaning of cultivation or tending, though with subsidiary medieval meanings of honour and worship. . . . *Culture* in all its early uses was a noun of process: the tending *of* something, basically crops or animals. . . . At various points in this development two crucial changes occurred: first, a degree of habituation to the metaphor, which made the sense of human tending direct; second, an extension of particular processes to a general process, which the word could abstractly carry."[14]

The term *culture,* according to Williams, was not significant as an independent noun before the eighteenth century and was not common before the nineteenth century. But even before the nineteenth century the term was already beset by the etherealizing tendencies of ethnocentric universalism, so that Johann Herder could state that "nothing is more indeterminate than this word, and nothing more deceptive than its application to all nations and periods." *Colonize* and *culture* are both derived from the same root, and Herder was well aware of how the Enlightenment dream of "universal reason" could also be used as an expression of European Power. He complained of the treatment of human histories and diversities as mere manurance for European culture: "Men of all the quarters of the globe, who have perished over the ages, you have not lived solely to manure the earth with your ashes, so that at the end of time your posterity should be made happy by European culture. The very thought of a superior European culture is a blatant insult to the majesty of Nature."[15]

Cultural anthropology has in many ways taken Herder's words to heart, admitting—to use the title from one of Clifford Geertz's books—"the interpretation of cultures" in the plural as its central task. Yet in the long history and vicissitudes of the term *culture,* there has remained a broader sense of culture as meaning in general, which remains a central problematic of social theory even if it has lost its earthy origins. We cosmopolitans do not like the smell of Bacon's conception of "the culture and manurance of minds," preferring the intellectualistic "systems of symbols and meanings." Now I am not simply calling for an anti-intellectual, nostalgic return to farmer's wisdom, such as expressed in the following German saying: "Die Quantität der Potate ist indirekt proportional zur Intelligenskapazität ihres Kultivators!" (Or, as it is put in the south: "Der Dümmste Bauer hat die grösste' Kartoffel'!").[16] I am simply saying that we must revitalize the concept of culture and free it from the abstractionist grip of our time: we must put the *cult* back into *culture.*

We have come a long way from the earthy conception of culture as a living process of furrowing and cultivating nature within and without, of the organic admixture of growth and decay that such a conception implies, of the springing forth of tendrils of belief needing active cultivation for survival. One of the glaring holes in most contemporary conceptions of culture is the lack of attention to the birth of meanings, a lack that applies equally to the term *conception.* In intellectual discourse conception connotes, almost without exception, rational beliefs and not the gestation of something new, the birth of meaning. Likewise, *culture* has come to mean systematized meaning for most culture theorists and has lost the fertile, seminal, and gestational meanings it once carried: "the culture and manurance of minds." The urge to issue forth meaning, emanating from the culture and from within the individual, is more essential to human nature than the need to comprehend, and therein lies human genius and therein lies our penchant for depravity. Both the living source and the final aim of culture, I claim, is *cultus.* Yet it is precisely the cultic that is so frequently occulted by contemporary culture theory.

The word *cult,* despite its obvious relation to culture, seems worlds apart from its meaning in everyday language. Nowadays cults are often associated with pathologically disturbed or ideologically brainwashed groups—satanists, the suicidal followers of Jim Jones at Jonestown, Moonies, and the lunatic fringe in general—but the term also applies to emerging religious sects, such as the early Christian cults. In the anthropological sense the word *cult* is strongly associated with ritual, as in the "cargo cults" that appeared in the South Pacific after World War II or the various rituals to Afro-Christian "saints" in the Umbanda cults of Brazil. The ethnographic record, Freud, and Durkheim have sensitized us to how certain objects become endowed with sacred or obsessional significance as fetishes—such as a wooden sculpture of a human form studded with nails by the Bakongo people of West Africa. We see in these examples how deep human needs and desires seek objectified, and often fantastic or perverse, form.

One of the most insightful accounts of the cultic roots of culture is to be found in the work of Victor Turner. His masterful ethnography reveals the fundamental reality of the subjunctive mood in human affairs: the ritual process. In Turner's analyses of the *Isoma* and *Wubwang'u* rituals of the Ndembu of northwestern Zambia, one sees the fantastic interplay between human affliction and symbolic renewal, between human communities and a natural environment teeming with signification. The Ndembu are revealed to be a people with a deep appreciation of the complexity of existence and endowed with a sophisticated technics of meaning, a vast architectonic of felt, expressive forms through which they journey to those borderlands beyond human comprehensibility: death, the dead, the call of the motherline, fecundity, transformation, the interstices of social structure. Systematizers who seek an airtight scheme with absolute closure will not find it in Turner's work. His theories are open-ended, ever acknowledging the greater richness and potentiality and not-yet-decipherable and perhaps not systematizable richness inherent in experience and culture. He continually directs our gaze instead to those social "openings" through which the ferment of culture erupts. Cultures are not simply inert structures or bloodless "systems" but form a processual dialectic between structure and liminality.

In his well-known essay, "Betwixt and Between: The Liminal Period in Rites of Passage,"[17] Turner attempted to grasp that virtually ungraspable mercurial element in human affairs in which normal social structure and mores of conduct are temporarily eclipsed. Liminality was that which dismembered structure in order to transform, renew, and re-member it. Turner went on to show, in this essay and in other works, how liminality provides a time of visceral or meditative (or both together) reflection, a time of reflective speculation: "Liminality here breaks, as it were, the cake of custom and enfranchises speculation. . . . Liminality is the realm of primitive hypothesis, where there is a certain freedom to juggle with the factors

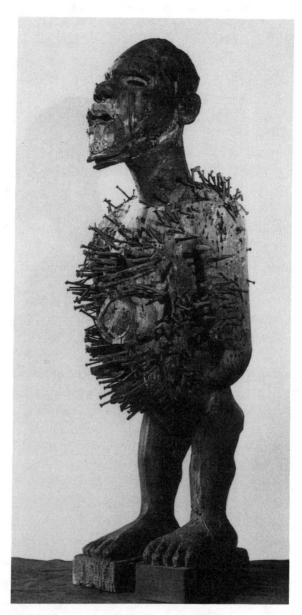

Figure 2. Large wooden figure studded with nails, Bak-ongo tribe, Angola, nineteenth century. The University Museum, University of Pennsylvania.

of existence. As in the works of Rabelais, there is a promiscuous intermingling and juxtaposing of the categories of event, experience, and knowledge, with a pedagogic intention."[18] Turner notes, however, that the liberty of liminality is ritually limited in tribal societies and must give way to traditional custom and law.

Structure and liminality are engaged in a ceaseless dialectic, and societies themselves are symbolic processes, engaged in dialectics between structure and communitas. By "communitas" Turner means a state of immediate, total, and egalitarian "confrontation of human identities," which is dialectically opposed to the normal interactions of people through the roles, statuses, and hierarchies of social structure. As Turner demonstrates so clearly, liminality tends to produce a powerful sense of communion among ritual participants, who are stripped naked of the normal accretions of status, prestige, and caste. Yet the dehabituated state of liminality and communion can only exist for so long before it too begins to take the shape of habituation: the problem is not so much what to do during the revolution but what to do the day after the revolution.

In Turner's work one continually confronts the drama and mystery of life itself in its humanly perceivable forms. The live human creature, not the dead abstract system, is the source of what he termed *processual anthropology.* Throughout his book, *The Ritual Process,* he engages Claude Lévi-Strauss in a dialectical contrast, posing his processual anthropology against Lévi-Strauss's structuralism, while yet drawing from Lévi-Strauss's analyses that which he finds useful. In Turner one sees that meaning is much more than a "logical structure," because it involves powerful emotions not reducible to logic, a purposiveness not reducible to binary oppositions, "a material integument shaped by . . . life experience." In short, a processual approach views structure as a slow process, sometimes very slow indeed. Or as Turner puts it, "Structure is always ancillary to, dependent on, secreted from process."[19]

Turner is very much concerned with systemic or structural questions, but he continually reminds us of the human face behind the social roles, status hierarchies, and social structures. That human face may be painted with the red and white clays of *Wubwang'u,* or it may be adorned with the phantasms of carnival, or it may be soberly dressed in ritual poverty, but Turner's theories, as well as the body of his work, never let us forget those deep human needs for fantastic symboling to express the fullness of being. He avoided, in other words, the abstractionist vacuum cleaner into which many other symbolic anthropologists and semioticians were sucked.

Central to Turner's processual anthropology and comparative symbology is the ritual symbol, which he considered the "core" unit of analysis and which, in his hands, did not exclude social structure, human personality, or contingencies of experience from analysis. The symbol is the "blaze"—the mark or path—that directs us from the unknown to the known, both in the Ndembu sense of *ku-jikijila* (to blaze a trail by cutting marks or breaking or bending branches on trees) and in C. G. Jung's sense. Key to the indigenous hermeneutic of the Ndembu is the term *ku-solola*—"to make visible," or "to reveal"—which is the chief aim of Ndembu ritual, just as its equivalent concept of *aletheia* is for Hans-Georg Gadamer's hermeneutic. These Ndembu terms derive from the vocabulary of hunting cults and reveal their high ritual value. The idea of making a blaze or path through the forest also draws attention to the significance of trees for the Ndembu, not only as providing the texture of the physical environment but also as sources of spiritual power. The associations of substances derived from trees with properties of blood and milk, or of toughness with health, and fruitfulness with fertility, which Turner discusses in his description of the *Isoma* ritual, also reveal why he chose Baudelaire's phrase, "the forest of symbols," as the title for one of his books. In his ground-breaking discussions of color symbolism in Ndembu ritual, Turner shows how the social system of classification comes into play, but he roots the social meanings of red, white, and black symbols to the experiential level of bodily fluids and substances of blood, milk and sperm, and feces.

At the time of his death in 1983 Turner was fully engaged in the struggle to achieve a new synthesis—a theoretical rite of passage to a broadened vision of anthropology and social theory. A number of social theorists have been claiming to be transforming social theory—I am thinking here of Habermas, Luhmann, Giddens, and others—but for the most part they have been replaying tired variations on old themes without ever questioning the premises of modern social theory. But in Turner's synthesis of social dramas, liminality, communitas, Deweyan and Diltheyan understandings of "experience," and neurobiological semiotics, perhaps we see the unexpected outline of a new understanding of the human creature: one which reconnects biological life and meaning, which embraces the "subjunctive" as no less fundamental a reality of human existence than the "indicative," and which views the realm of the fantastic as a precious resource for continued human development rather than as a vestige of an archaic and obsolete past.

It might seem unlikely that Turner was so drawn to Dilthey while simultaneously investigating neurobiological brain processes as a means to understanding ritual processes. Dilthey, after all, wanted to keep the *Geisteswissenschaften* distinct from the *Naturwissenschaften,* and he developed an explicitly non-naturalistic *Lebensphilosophie.* It was Dilthey's concept of "structures of experience" which attracted Turner: "Long before I had read a word of Wilhelm Dilthey's I had shared his notion that "structures of experience" are fundamental units in the study of human action. Such structures are irrefrangibly threefold, being at once cognitive, conative, and affective. Each of these terms is itself, of course, a shorthand for a range of processes and capacities . . . persons will desire and feel as well as think, and their desires and feelings impregnate their thoughts and influence their intentions. . . . It became clear to me that an 'anthropology of experience' would have to take into account the psychological properties of individuals as well as the culture which, as Sapir insists, is *'never given'* to each individual, but, rather, 'gropingly discovered,' and, I would add, some parts of it quite late in life. We never cease to learn our *own* culture, let alone other cultures, and our own culture is always changing." Turner admired Dilthey's attempt to root meaning within human experience rather than in a conceptual apparatus superior to the human activities that form its object. For the same reasons he was attracted to Dewey's experientially rooted pragmatism. Although he acknowledged that Dewey's "process of experiencing cleaved closer to the biological," he did not, to my knowledge, explicitly take up the implication of Dilthey's antinaturalism, or, put inversely, of his own pronaturalism in contrast to Dilthey.[20]

Turner addressed the issue instead by plunging into neurobiological brain research, which can be seen as a radical continuation of his earlier attempts to root color symbolism in body processes. He asked whether we can escape "from something like animal ritualization without escaping from our own bodies and psyches, the rhythms and structures of which arise on their own." From the perspective of cultural anthropology and contemporary intellectual life, Turner became a heretic in admitting to the possibility of biology as having a formative influence on human action, and some of his closest colleagues seemed to be embarrassed by this aspect of his work, as though he were forsaking the challenge of the ritual process and its interpretation, as though he were becoming a reductionist. That the rigid division of a falsely mechanical nature from a de-natured culture might itself be the product of a reductionist ethos did not occur to these critics. Locked in by outdated dichotomies of nature and culture, the ethereal rational intellect of today seems unwilling or unable to confront its own material embodiment in organic life. At the beginning of his career Turner had to jettison the baggage of structural-functionalism because it proved inadequate to his needs. And at the end of his career he found that he had to discard his acquired prejudice against the biosemiotic sources of meaning. He saw the need for a "deep ecology" of human experience, perhaps to complement those "structures of experience" he found in Dilthey and Dewey. Referring to the model of the triune brain structure proposed by neurobiologist Paul MacLean, Turner rhapsodized, that

> if one considers the geology, so to speak, of the human brain and nervous system, we see represented in its strata—each layer still vitally alive—not dead like stone, the numerous pasts and presents of our planet. Like Walt Whitman, we "embrace multitudes." And even our reptilian and paleo-mammalian brains are human, linked in infinitely complex ways to the conditionable upper brain and kindling it with their powers. Each of us is a microcosm, related in the deepest ways to the whole life-history of that lovely deep blue globe swirled over with the white whorls first photographed by Edwin Aldrin and Neil Armstrong from their primitive space chariot, the work nevertheless of many collaborating human brains. The meaning of that living macrocosm may not only be found deep within us but also played from one mind to another as history goes on—with ever finer tuning—by the most sensitive and eloquent instrument of Gaea the Earth-spirit—the cerebral organ.[21]

Turner is regarded as an anthropologist in the Anglo-American sense, but his late work, like that of Lewis Mumford, reveals him to be a philosophical anthropologist in the German sense as well. Turner and Mumford are no throwbacks to biological reductionism. Quite the contrary: both are master interpreters of meaning, both are original contributors to the semiotic turn of the social sciences, both are exponents of a dramaturgical understanding of human action. Yet both felt compelled, *in the name of human meaning,* to delve into the biological sources of signification. The liminal processes revealed in lucid detail by Turner and the broad historical account of human development and sociocultural transformation given by Mumford complement each other and illustrate how both authors share a deep appreciation of the cultic roots of culture, of the human semiotic essence. Their work shows the ways toward undoing the devitalized specter that haunts the contemporary study of meaning and culture as well as its mechanico-materialist opposite in human ethology and sociobiology. They stand in stark contrast to the effete homophobia—fear of the human—which motivates postmodern antihumanism. At the heart of Turner's and Mumford's work is ever the incandescent human form.

To those who can no longer live within the frame of mythic rationality and its cultural nominalism, the artificial split between a mechanical nature devoid of generality and a culture reduced to human conventions devoid of tempered experience and organic roots seems a quaint relic from the bifurcated world of cultural nominalism, mythic modernity. This peculiar mindset took the rationalization of culture, the technicalization of society, and the mechanization of the universe to be a troubling, yet logical development in Occidental culture: *Disenchantment* is the name and cost of freedom.

Is *rationalization,* the term used by Weber to describe the spread of bureaucratic rational mind over the institutions of modern life, ultimately the proper term for Weber's project? Or does *rational maximization,* a concept possibly at odds with rationalization, better capture the processes that Weber thought he saw inherent in religion and in the peculiar developments of the Occident?

Rationalization ought to describe the normal development and context of rationality in human life, the place of rational capacities as organs of a mind deeper and broader than rationality alone. The human mind, in both its individual and collective manifestations, reveals the extrarational capacities of memory and invention, interpretative "sensing" and organic balancing, rich emotional communication—not at all limited to what words alone can say—and an obsessive need for the semblance of meaning which can lead to creative or destructive behavior.

The fullness of the human body also reveals dark, destructive impulses potentially active in all of the human capacities, impulses generated no doubt from our own animal depths but by no means excluded from our rational heights: for every Caliban there is also one of Kafka's devitalized rational apes. The rationalist too frequently places the blame for human evil and folly on the irrational, ignoring the great tendencies of decontextualized rationality toward self-destruction. The law courts know that someone who commits a "crime of passion" can be a murderer just as someone who commits a premeditated murder is. Only the latter is regarded as the more dangerous kind of murderer. We murderous half-Raskolnikovs tend to forget this fact when we think that the rational curbing and governance of the passions is the proper means to a just society. "The devil made me do it" alibi only works when one fully acknowledges the ever-present devil within: criticism must always invoke self-criticism, and the capacity to be self-critical depends on the availability of one's honest feelings to conscious evaluation, not on the repression of one's feelings by objective rules of rational validity. There is in pure rationality a profound aptitude for cold-blooded murderousness and its seeming opposite: *Weltschmaltz,* the self-beautifying lie of excessive sentimentalism. Albert Speer said that Hitler in his more manic moods and rages would discuss plans he did not necessarily mean to carry out. But when he was calm, cool, and collected—"rational"—his inner circle knew he fully intended to carry out his calculations, no matter how extreme. In Speer's account one sees what is perhaps the twentieth century's most notable "achievement": rational madness.

Refinding the Human Way

> *One of these days, perhaps, there will come a writer of opinions less humdrum than those of Dr. [Alfred Russel] Wallace, and less in awe of the learned and official world . . . who will argue, like a new Bernard Mandeville, that man is but a degenerate monkey, with a paranoic talent for self-satisfaction, no matter what scrapes he may get himself into, calling them 'civilization,' and who, in place of the unerring instincts of other races, has an unhappy faculty for occupying himself with words and abstractions, and for going wrong in a hundred ways before he is driven, willy-nilly, into the right one. Dr. Wallace would condemn such an extravagent paradoxer.*
>
> Charles Peirce, 1901.[22]

Though social theorists have drawn attention to the many distortions that entered into modern life through capitalism, rationalism, technicalism, and individualism, somehow the question of whether the mechanization of nature and denaturalization of culture since the seventeenth century was also part of this distorting process never gets posed. Because virtually all of social theory has grown out of the same processes of cultural nominalism, theorists tend to accept uncritically the reified split between thought and things, between culture and nature. Culture can then be assumed to be free from nature or to seek as its goal to escape from nature through the perfection of rationality. In both cases the underlying task is to divest the human creature of its organic, cultic, biosemiotic roots. Yet all the inner autonomous forms of culture, all the outer technical codes and know-how, and all the rational justifications for progressive, modernized, "communicative" culture remain insufficient for a truly vital culture when disconnected from the tissues of life, from human bodies and their social relations.

We need to find the means out of our posthuman world back to being human again. The modern age of "humanism" resulted, paradoxically enough, in an ever-growing dehumanization, which crystallized in the twentieth century. Today, postmodernists extoll antihumanism, in favor of "decentered" selves who are but instances of conventions. Hence the author is dead and the poet is but an ideologue and politician, and the qualitatively unique individual is merely a fiction. Such views can be seen as part of the quest to eradicate the human person, which was the underlying ethos of the mechanical worldview. Being human is something we have been all too easily surrendering. But being human in the modern humanist's sense is itself no longer adequate for a world undergoing ecological disaster because of the exercise of human power and will. Though it remains opaque to those still committed to the ghost in the machine, being human involves, among other things, being a living creature in continuity with organic life and with forms of reason we do not yet know, either because they are too deeply embedded in our consciousness, or because we have not yet brought them to life.

The human penchant for dream and play and ritual and myth and religion—and for what is now pejoratively called metaphysics—cannot be rationalized as a vestige of primitive, child-like creatures, now obsolete because they were insufficiently clear-sighted with the lights of rationality and postrationality as their guide. Instead, the urge for transcendence is basic to being human. We remain neotenic mammals, dream creatures fundamentally shaped by the mammalian characteristics of intense mother-infant bonding, play, and rapid eye movement dreaming. These ecstatic forms of communication remain deeply and unavoidably embedded in our biosemiotic nature, and it is through the meeting of these communicative capacities with the general laws of nature, out of which our brainy bodies are made, that we can enter into the ongoing creation of the universe. As "degenerate monkeys, with a paranoic talent for self-satisfaction," as Peirce put it, who must reason much of what other creatures do with unerring instinct, we have also achieved the power—and have too many times betrayed the will—to destroy our little portion of the universe. Would the world be a better place without humans? Perhaps. But if the world means more than dead matter and meaningless spawning, if the development of reason is a real, though not inevitable, process of the living world, then we must hope that our inescapable impulses to meaning can still find viable expression in that process.

The evolution of humans is marked by various anatomical changes, such as the development of the upright stance, the radical enlargement of the cranium and specifically, for anatomically modern homo sapiens sapiens, the forebrain, and the creation of a vocal cavity with lowered larynx and subtle tongue and lip movements capable of producing an enormous variety of utterances. Clearly speech is one achievement of this process that uniquely identifies us as humans. But so too, for that matter, is artistic expression. Both are sign-practices dependent on, and probably generative of, the achievement of symbolic representation, and both reveal how to be human is to be a living, communicative symbol. In the case of the symbolic sign, as distinguished from iconic or indexical signs, the process of interpretation comes to the foreground, and from a cultural perspective, this is to say that to be human is to be an interpreter. The very achievement of symbolic signification stands upon the vast capacities for pre- and protosymbolic communication developed by our forerunners and tempered into our physical organisms. Dreams, to give one example, may very well have provided the inner drama necessary to provoke us into interpretation by presenting our distant ancestors with images of a phantasmagoric "here and now" which break into and color the habits of everyday life. Dreams emanate from a liminal realm where social relations of the wildest sort are possible, where animals talk and dead relatives live, where the marvelous and horrific conspire to present a baffling inner landscape that must have seemed as real to early humans as the day world, if not more.

Perhaps the symbol itself, as the distinguishing medium of human consciousness, is so constituted, both in its freedom grounded in human conventions and in its mysterious relations to the central and autonomic nervous systems, that it *needs* to be connected to perceptive and critical, that is, lived, experience. Contrary to celebrated views of the symbol (or *sign* in Saussure's terminology) as completely "unmotivated" or arbitrary, I claim, the symbol is that sign most dependent on vital and critical experience for its continued development.

We live in signs and they live through us, in a reciprocal process of cultivation that I have elsewhere termed *critical animism*. If most tribal peoples and even many civilizational peoples have traditionally lived in a world of personified forces—or animism—and if this general outlook was evicted by the modern "enlightened" view of critical rationality and its "disenchanted" worldview, then I am proposing a new form of reenchantment, or marriage, of these opposites. Critical animism suggests that rational sign-practices, though necessary to contemporary complex culture and human freedom, do not exhaust the "critical" and that the human impulse to meaning springs from extrarational and acritical sources of bodily social intelligence.

The evolution of protohumans, though marked by the greater reliance on symbolic intelligence, did not necessarily mean the complete loss of instinctive intelligence as theorists such as Gehlen have implied. On the contrary, one key aspect of the emerging symbolic intelligence "in the dreamtime long ago" may very well have been an instinctive, yet highly plastic or generalized, ability to listen to and learn from the rich instinctual intelligence of the surrounding environment.

The close observation of birds, not only as prey for eating or ornament but also as sources of delight, could also help to inform one of an approaching cold spell or severe winter.

A better example might be the empathic relations to animals and natural phenomena shared by many tribal peoples. One frequently sees an identification with an animal or plant related to the practices of a people, such as the cult of the whale for fishing peoples, and a choice of an object that somehow symbolizes a central belief of a people, such as the white *mudyi* tree as a symbol of the milk of the matrilineally rooted Ndembu of Africa. There exists then a range from a practical, informing relationship to nature, or a fantastic elaboration of that relationship, to a purely symbolic relationship to the environment that either may be unrelated to the surrounding instinctual intelligence or that might even function as a kind of veil to obscure the informing properties of the environment. These relationships were crucial to the emergence of humankind: the deeply felt relationship to the organic, variegated biosphere, which was manifest in those natural signs or instincts of other species, and the corresponding pull away from the certainties of instinctual intelligence toward belief, toward humanly produced symbols that created a new order of reality and, in doing so, both amplified and layered over the voices of nature.

Through mimesis, emerging humankind could become a plant or bird or reindeer, and thereby attune itself to the cycles of nature through the perceptions of these beings. A mimetic understanding also involves the generalizing of nature into symbolic form. A man dressed as a raven or bear at the head of a Kwakiutl fishing boat and the lion-headed human figurine dating back thirty-two thousand years found in Germany (a very early find possibly suggesting interaction between Neanderthals and anatomically modern humans) signify the symbolic incorporation of animal qualities into human activities and provoke human reflection, through what William James called the "law of dissociation," on the meaning of human activities.

Dreaming is central to mimesis, and dreaming itself may be seen as an inbuilt form of "recombinant mimetics"—with all the power and danger of recombinant genetics—in which fantastic juxtapositions of neural pathways and cultural images and associations take place. Dreaming is perhaps the primal "rite of passage," through cult, to culture.

In the brain-mind dialogue of dreaming we see a domain that bridges nature and culture, which may have been essential to the emergence of human symbolic culture and may remain essential to its continued development. In that sense dreaming opens an unexpected window onto the cultic roots of culture: the spontaneous springing forth of belief. And if Mumford's idea that dreaming may have impelled us toward a technics of symbolism both to control the anxieties produced by the inner world and to be animated by its image-making powers is on the mark, then perhaps we can see another way of connecting body, brain, and culture with the ritual symbol and the drama of communication which emerged from it, one resonant with Turner.

In suggesting the semiotic line of evolution we big-brained apes must have followed in entering and establishing the human world, one conceivable consequence has, I hope, become somewhat clearer. The impulse to meaning is both original to our nature and ineradicable. The origins of culture are to be found in those communicative practices through which emergent humanity literally bodied itself forth, creating a forebrain with language, speech, and personality capacities, creating a tongue, larynx, and throat capable of articulate speech, creating forms of inward and outward expression, rituals of affliction and celebration, dramas of mythic, social, and personal communication, and stable institutions such as agriculture, villages, and later, cities, which have endured from Neolithic times to the present. The very expression "the culture and manurance of minds" may reflect the invention of manuring and its connection, through agriculture, to the development of permanent villages and protocities in the Neolithic Age. In other words, the very concept of culture may be an achievement and legacy of the Neolithic Age. Contemporary culture and culture theory seem to be intent on etherealizing these achievements out of existence and may very well succeed.

Modern deratiocination, termed "rationalization" by Max Weber, is that decontextualized form of rationality whose continued and unlimited growth involves the progressive elimination of the impulse to meaning. Its logical terminus is closed rational system *and* stochastic indeterminacy. This is what Jürgen Habermas euphemistically calls "a progressive unfettering of the rationality potential inherent in communicative action"[23]. Contrary to Habermas's unshakable Enlightenment optimism, the unfettering of the limits of rationality led to what Kundera aptly calls *The Unbearable Lightness of Being*, which no new and improved "communicative" rationality is sufficient to correct. Dressed in our little brief "rationalization," we become most ignorant of what we are most assured, our extrarational impulse to meaning, and cultural life withers, as do rationalistic theories of culture.

Relativists refuse to consider the meaning-generating nature of human biology, and objectivists refuse to consider that which cannot be formatted into the machine of scientism. No age proves more than ours what a dangerous thing a little knowledge can be. Overweening knowledge and technique have characterized the modern age, producing great and terrible ideas and powers. Modern culture, in all of its sociopolitical, psychological, artistic, and intellectual varieties created new possibilities for autonomy and human freedom, ideals which more often than not turned into their opposites, but which yet might remain compelling.

Despite the perversions of democracy in various "people's democratic" countries and in the seemingly more benign mass consumer societies, the ideals of human rights and self-critical institutions which grew out of modern culture remain worthy achievements to contribute to a world culture in the making. Yet the foundation of this nominalistic epoch has been a worldview which increasingly has displaced and devalued organic human purpose and the impulse to meaning. Human reason, when found in all its fullness, is in living continuity with the cultic roots of culture. When that continuity is broken or thwarted, as it was in the guiding ethos of modern culture and its quest to "enlighten" itself of its burdensome organic roots, the result is a "rational" civilization bereft of reason, split between cold rational madness and hot antirational eruptions. Hawthorne's dark short story of 1851, "Ethan Brand," captures that civilization with amazing prescience:

> Then ensued that vast intellectual development, which in its progress, disturbed the counterpoise between his mind and his heart. The Idea that possessed his life had operated as a means of education; it had gone on cultivating his powers to the highest point of which they were susceptible. . . . But where was the heart? That, indeed, had withered,—had contracted,—had hardened,—had perished! It had ceased to partake of the universal throb. He had lost hold of the magnetic chain of humanity. He was no longer a brotherman, opening the chambers or the dungeons of our common nature by the key of holy sympathy, which gave him a right to share in all its secrets; he was now a cold observer, looking on mankind as the subject of his experiment, and, at length, converting man and woman to be his puppets, and pulling the wires that moved them to such degrees of crime as were demanded by his study.
>
> Thus Ethan Brand became a fiend. He began to be so from the moment that his moral nature had ceased to keep the pace of improvement with his intellect. And now, as his highest effort and inevitable development,—as the bright and gorgeous flower, and rich, delicious fruit of his life's labor,—he had produced the Unpardonable Sin!"

Ethan Brand, prophet of modernity and soulmate of his contemporary, Captain Ahab, attained to the final perfection of Kafka's ape, Minsky's computers of the future, and the overwhelming bulk of contemporary theory: he became a fiend, blighted by the "Unpardonable Sin," "from the moment that his moral nature had ceased to keep the pace of improvement with his intellect."

Modern nominalistic culture may be characterized as seeking to escape its organic roots through spectral theories of mind and mechanistic theories of matter. The chief task of a theory of culture today is to rediscover those extrarational, incarnate sources of meaning that the cult of modernity has now reduced to insignificance and to create a new outlook that can encompass humanity incarnate, in all of its valuable diversity. This task is not a retreat into "irrationalism" or biological reductionism but is a frank recognition that the beliefs of modern progress and modern rationality were built on false nominalistic premisses: the reified view of nature as a mechanical system and the etherealized view of culture or mind as subjectivistic and set apart from nature. Human reason, in all its fullness, is in living continuity with the cultic roots of culture, and is much more than merely rational. The cultic roots of culture, expressed in mother-infant bonding and those playful, dream-like, inquisitive and ritualistic forms of conduct, gradually impelled our protohuman ancestors to humanity and, whether we like it or not, remain deeply embedded sources of human cultures and conduct.

4

Lewis Mumford's Organic Worldview

Virtue is not a chemical product, as Taine once described it: it is a historic product, like language and literature; and this means that if we cease to care about it, cease to cultivate it, cease to transmit its funded values, a large part of it will become meaningless, like a dead language to which we have lost the key. That, I submit, is what has happened in our own lifetime.

—Lewis Mumford[1]

If predictable order alone were uppermost, living creatures would have the static fixity and duration of shapeless stones, shells, or crystals. Fortunately for man's further development, life does not culminate in repetition and automation, but begins *there in the automatic (pre-organic) atom, before Nature manifested in living organisms. Unfortunately, until the nineteen-thirties, modern American and English dictionaries and encyclopedias did not mention Nature's earliest steps toward single cell organisms: repetition and "playfulness." Shells and crystals were in existence for billions of years before life, so to say, broke loose.*

—Lewis Mumford[2]

INTRODUCTION: PUBLIC INTELLECTUAL, INVISIBLE MAN

Lewis Mumford is world renowned, yet seldom considered as a social theorist with contemporary interest for social scientists, philosophers, or literary critics. Despite a renewal of interest in Mumford as a "public intellectual," the fact that he has written a sizable body of work that should be considered social theory seems to be a well-kept secret these days. Apart from the widespread ignorance about Mumford's diverse body of work, I find it most odd to see how quickly his reputation dropped out of the picture in the past two decades. He tends not to be considered a sociologist by sociologists, despite his work on cities, early connections to Patrick Geddes and Victor Branford (who also have been forgotten), a brief stint in London as editor of *The Sociological Review* in 1920, his even earlier meeting with Charles Horton Cooley, and acquaintance with Thorstein Veblen and John Dewey when they all worked on *The Dial.* Though he debated with Dewey in the 1920s and 1930s, and Santayana said of his book *The Golden Day: A Study of American Experience and Culture* that it was "the best book about America, if not the best American book" he had read, no philosopher today would think of Mumford as a philosopher. Literary philosophy and philosophical literary criticism may have become fashionable, but they tend to retain an academic cleverness and to draw heavily on legitimized academic sources. Similarly, despite his histories of technics, the city, and civilization, he is more often considered as a datum of history among historians rather than as himself a historian. Although he was among a group of writers who brought the American literary transcendentalists of the nineteenth century to light in the 1920s, and produced the first biography of Herman Melville, Mumford is virtually unknown by today's high-tech literary critics and theorists and would definitely be regarded as passé.

Mumford's original contributions to literary criticism, architectural criticism, American studies, technics, urban history and regional planning, and a number of other areas could each in themselves form significant contributions to twentieth-century scholarship. Some have questioned, however, whether Mumford was truly original or merely derivative—a mere synthesizer of others' ideas. In my view it is precisely his great openness to the thought and influence of others that is inseparable from his originality and that ultimately makes Mumford one of the most original voices of the twentieth century.

Our time celebrates originality as the unique and absolutely unprecedented, the idiosyncratic. Yet one of the peculiar marks of originality is not so much the radical departure from one's own time, as how original ideas seem so frequently to be expressed by multiple persons at the same time, perhaps as the expression of a *Zeitgeist.* Originality is, in this sense, not antithetical to the social, but the empathic sensing of the social milieu and the generation of new ideas out of it, ideas fitted to yet transcending their time. Mumford's work of the twenties, for example, was part of a rediscovery of literary transcendentalism, which included others such as Waldo Frank, Van Wyck Brooks, Paul Rosenfeld, and D. H. Lawrence. Yet Mumford also contributed to this movement his unique perspective on American culture. Or perhaps one could take the spate of books published on the city around 1961, including Jane Jacobs's *The Death and Life of Great American Cities,* Kevin Lynch's *Image of the City,* Gideon Sjoberg's *The Preindustrial City,* Anselm Strauss's *Images of the American City,* and Mumford's majestic *The City in History.* Mumford may have been part of a collective trend of works on the city but, in its historical scope and reconstructive realism, his own work easily transcends these other efforts in terms of originality.

Another example of Mumford's original, yet strangely invisible, contribution to social thought can be found in the explosion of interest in symbolism in the 1960s, expressed primarily in anthropology. Key works by Claude Lévi-Strauss, Victor Turner, Clifford Geertz, and others appeared at this time, which radically transformed the face not only of cultural anthropology but of the social sciences generally. Structuralism, semiotics, symbolic anthropology, symbolic interactionism, interpretative or *verstehende* sociology were some of the major movements that sprang forth from the barren ground of mid-twentieth century social science and have continued to exert growing interest. Many of these developments had roots going back to the "classical" figures of the turn of the century, but the earlier traditions had been displaced by the combination of Nazism in Europe and ideological scientism in America. The whole question of meaning itself, which had seemed to be in eclipse in the "dead zone" of the middle decades of the twentieth century, now sprang back with a vengeance. Yet something had happened in the interim, for the dominant feature of the new symbolism in the social sciences and semiotics was and remains a tendency to technicalism, a domination by the techniques and technical jargon of theory making and symbol interpretation, such as the "infernal culture machine" of Lévi-Strauss's binary structuralism or, more recently, the anarchistic semiological "fission" advocated by Derrida's poststructuralism. The question of meaning has become all the rage, but the question of meaningfulness has become all but lost.

With structuralism serving as perhaps the central preoccupation of anthropologists, literary critics, and social theorists in the 1960s and 1970s, before becoming displaced by poststructuralism, it is no wonder that Mumford's *Technics and Human Development* remained virtually invisible to the anthropological community. As we shall see, Mumford proposed a bold, historically informed, semiotic model of human development, one which cut against the grain of the dominant conceptualism. In my view it should be seen as contributing to symbolic anthropology and more broadly to the semiotic turn of the social sciences, though it was scarcely recognized as such at the time.

No social theorist, at least as far as I have been able to determine, would include Lewis Mumford among the "classics." I have asked sociologists and other social scientists informally over the past decade about Mumford, and their responses indicate that they tend to know him as a writer on cities (and "writer" sometimes carries a pejorative meaning, denoting an insufficiently specialized popularizer). Some know his architectural and cultural criticism. Indeed, his prescient critique of architectural modernism has been receiving renewed interest since the decline of modernism and again in the decline of its afterthought, postmodernism. Mumford's writings on cities is, with his architectural criticism, probably the most widely known aspect of his work. But because of the current prejudice for "situational" or particularistic thinking and against historically informed "big picture" thinking, his advocacy of large-scale urban and regional planning in the name of limited and decentralized cities is frequently rejected in favor of the kind of cultural laissez-faire of the street advocated by Jane Jacobs and, more recently, by Marshall Berman in his spirited book, *All That Is Solid Melts into Air*.[3]

Berman devotes a good amount of his book to the themes of the modern city, including a long and compelling chapter on the tragedy of Robert Moses's destructive development policies for New York City. Jacobs, who fought fiercely against Moses, is a major source of inspiration for Berman, while Mumford is conspicuously absent. This is an odd omission, given that both Jacobs and Mumford united against Moses in public debate, despite their marked intellectual differences. Moses was the archetypal grandiose planner, arrogantly imposing on the citizens of New York his big picture of how the city should be remade into a megatechnic, paved, promised land. Given such an imperial attitude toward urban planning in a Moses or, more recently, in a Communist tyrant such as Nicolae Ceaucescu of Romania, one can well understand the general antipathy to big picture planning today.[4] There was also something of the philosopher-king in Mumford's temperament and approach, but in attempting to root planning in organic needs of communities and regions, in paying close attention to the forms, functions, and social context of architecture and planning in their details while retaining the big picture of the city as a historical achievement and agent of the good life, he developed a perspective on city life at odds both with the Moses modernists and the Jacobs piecemeal street-centered account. There are clear signs that Mumford's outlook is again beginning to stir architects, planners, and critics, not the least because of its attention to ecological considerations. When one includes the ecological basis of New York City in city planning, both Moses and Jacobs appear overly anthropocentric. Yet one need not reject Jacobs's approach in toto, as Mumford did, in order to appreciate Mumford's contribution, nor vice versa.

It is puzzling how a public intellectual of the stature of Mumford has been so ignored by a variety of fields in which he wrote well-known books. This might be explained in part as a result of the ever shorter "shelf-life" of intellectuals in a postmodern era of increasingly commodified mind. Part of the answer might also be that Mumford was someone who bridled at the corraling of the American scholar by academic specialization in the twentieth century, a public intellectual who sought to develop a critical vision undeformed by the rationalization of reason. Because he "trespassed" on the different properties of various Professor Pigeonholes while avoiding institutional loyalties, it was difficult later for the academy to appropriate and institutionalize Lewis Mumford. Perhaps now that he is safely labeled as a "public intellectual" the appropriation process may be easier to undertake.

There may be other reasons for Mumford's apparent invisibility. First may be the matter of his writing style: the fact that he was a master of English prose would virtually disqualify him from serious consideration by purveyors of "sociologese" or "semi-idiotics." As one sociologist told me, "Mumford writes in a popular style, not a sociological one." Mumford's use of passionate reason instead of the ideal of dispassionate "value-free" inquiry would also be an obvious cause for disqualification. "His work may be good," as a colleague once told me, "but is it sociology?" This comment also highlights the problem of Mumford's unashamed generalism, his joining together in organic wholes what sociologists and their counterparts in other disciplines have carved into cleanly separated areas of inquiry.

There is also Mumford's seeming disregard for the perceived classics of social theory themselves. It is not so much that he is ignorant of the "classical" or critical traditions—his work reveals a working knowledge of German scholars that most Americans were ignorant of until recently—as that his writings do not have the "aura" of belief in the perceived tradition that one sees in mainstream sociology: the attribution to "classical" social theory of a canonical status. Similarly, those who consider themselves critical theorists seem to think that critical theory is a school emanating from Frankfort or Paris rather than a way of thinking, and so tend to ignore thinkers who do not conspicuously display their "critical theorist" tags.

Finally there is the stuff of Mumford's world picture itself, with its image of life and evolutionary love as *axis mundi*. Most contemporary thinkers, rigidly disdaining even the possibility of large-scale historical or evolutionary structures— "the Big Picture"—would find his ability to "think big" a wrong-headed vestige of the past. Yet Mumford's vision, expressed in varying ways throughout his work, but always with passionate eloquence, is, I submit, ultimately embarrassing to humanists, scientists and intellectuals in general, as presently constituted, because it invokes emotional depths and cosmic heights of the human creature that utterly shatter the procrustean bed of contemporary rationalism and conventionalism. Therefore Mumford is wisely avoided by contemporary intellectuals, or whittled down to size.

Mumford, more than any other social thinker of the twentieth century, has undercut the fundamental premises of modernity, and, by recalling Lewis Mumford from intellectual oblivion, I hope to show why this break and the alternative he proposes marks him as a central social theorist of the twentieth century.

RECALLING AMERICAN CRITICAL THEORY

Mumford's researches share concerns common to the so-called classic sociological tradition. Yet, unlike Marx, Weber, Durkheim, Georg Simmel, or Talcott Parsons, Mumford does not regard the developments of modern life as inevitable or, to a great extent, as progressive. Quite to the contrary, he shows in lucid detail how the modern ethos released a Pandora's box of mechanical marvels which eventually threatened to absorb all human purposes into "the myth of the machine." His inquiries in a variety of fields share a common concern with the ways that modernity as a whole, although providing possibilities for broader expression and development, simultaneously subverts those possibilities and actually ends up tending toward a more restrictive scope and diminution of purpose.

Lewis Mumford's work underwent a continuous series of transformations as he broadened and deepened his scope. From his American studies in the 1920s, which helped to place the accomplishments of the literary transcendentalists of the 1850s and the later architectural achievements of Richardson, Sullivan, and Frank Lloyd Wright before the public, through the four-volume "Renewal of Life" series published between 1934 and 1951, which outlined the place of technics, cities, and worldviews in the development of Western civilization, to his late studies of the emergence of civilizations and the place of signification in human development, he boldly denied the utilitarian view while evolving his own vision of imaginative realism.

These transformations, enlarging from the American studies of the 1920s, to the context of Western and Modern Civilization in the 1930s and '40s, to the yet larger context of human development and the making of world civilization in the '50s and '60s, revealed a continuously growing mind, and only the infirmities of old age and death cut short a final transformation of Mumford's work, the consideration of organic life itself as the source of human organic intelligence. This final transformation, though unfinished, remained continuous with the development of Mumford's thought and with the themes which occupied him throughout his life.

Though Mumford is most frequently associated with cities, architecture, and technics, one might say that a transformed understanding of the concept of life is the key to understanding his mature work and its critique of modern life, signified in the very title of his series, "the renewal of life." In rejecting both the natural determinism of the Darwinian and sociobiological traditions, and the cultural determinism which views nature's contribution to meaningful human conduct as inconsequential, Mumford was also rejecting the ghost in the machine metaphor of the modern world. In articulating a sociohistorical view of life as a biocosmic, transformative, emergent, and purposive process, he was both a unique embodiment and virtually the last keeper in the Anglo-American context of the project of organic philosophy which animated Whitehead, Patrick Geddes, Cooley, Dewey, and Mead, emergent evolutionists, and others. But his sources resonated back to the naturalism of Melville and Peirce as well, while developing these ideas within his own framework.

Mumford first outlined his renewal of life series in 1930, a time, as discussed in Chapter 2, in which the concept of life was on the verge of being perverted by Nazism in Germany, and of being reduced in America to social Darwinism (an active force throughout the previous period) or supplanted by environmental or more sophisticated sociological explanations of human behavior. The one great exception, perhaps, was Dewey, who retained and further refined his organic situationalism. But Dewey and pragmatism as a whole went into eclipse, and when pragmatism partially reemerged in the figure of George Herbert Mead and the discipline of sociology, it had been divested of its biosocial basis in favor of a one-sided "symbolic interactionism." Even now, despite a widespread renewal of interest in pragmatism, the socialized biology developed by the four major pragmatists remains a dormant secret.

These transitions represent an appropriation of the life-concept by the ghost in the machine away from organic contextuality and dynamic process to those more mechanical ideas of force, will, and like-minded submission to authority in the German context and, in the American context, to capitalistic struggle and maximization in the Chicago school of sociology, and to machine-rooted "systems" theory in the later dominant structural-functionalist school. The net result was either to repress the life-concept, pervert it to ideological dogma, or transform it to the principles of the inorganic machine.[5]

Given the marginalization of the concept of life as the twentieth century moved increasingly into the "dead zone" of rational-mechanical abstraction, one can well see how Mumford's rooting of his ideas in an organic conception of life would set him apart from the dominant drift of twentieth-century thought. It also might help to explain the eclipse of his body of work today, given an intense anti-naturalism in contemporary intellectual life. Despite the revival of interest in Nietzsche and Dewey and their philosophies of deconstruction and reconstruction, their concerns with life have been blocked from awareness.

Yet before one stresses the concept of life in Mumford's work too much, one can also point to another central underlying theme, that of the tension between autonomy and the automaton. One can find this theme near the very beginning of his career in his 1921 essay, "Machinery and the Modern Style." One of his most provocative claims is that the possibility of human autonomy is rooted in our biological constitution, that autonomy or freedom is not a human achievement in opposition to nature but is an aspect of human nature and emergent product of general nature. Mumford is in this sense diametrically opposed to the philosophical anthropology of Arnold Gehlen, who believed in the automaton model of instincts.

In Gehlen's model, as discussed earlier in Chapter 2, humans need to make up for an instinctual poverty by making institutions which can mimic the objective stability of instincts. Individual human autonomy, when expressed, for example, in the capacity to criticize and dissent from existing institutions, is viewed as a weakness by Gehlen rather than a virtue. Autonomy threatens to fragment and demoralize those societies without highly disciplined and virtually automatic institutions. Gehlen looked admiringly at the Third Reich as an exemplar of highly disciplined institutions which functioned to keep the corrosiveness of moral self-criticism in check. His theory of institutions, though clothed in more sophisticated scholarship, accurately reflected Hitler's statement in *Mein Kampf:* "The victory of an idea will be possible the sooner, the more comprehensively propaganda has prepared people as a whole and the more exclusive, rigid, and firm the organization which carries out the fight in practice."[6] Gehlen's Nazi social theory was more scholarly than Hitler's and is not without interesting critiques of modern life, such as the flight of modern art into an isolate conception of autonomy. But it is downright spooky how a number of social theorists, from right-leaning Peter Berger to neo-leftist Alan Wolfe, choose to downplay or ignore the totalitarian implications of Gehlen's institutionalism, such as his ideal of immunity from self-criticism.

A VASTLY DIFFERENT PHILOSOPHICAL ANTHROPOLOGY is depicted in Mumford's two-volume magnum opus, *The Myth of the Machine,* the culminating work of his life-long critique of the place of technics in human conduct and civilized life. The first volume, *Technics and Human Development,* was published in 1967 as a new cultural anthropology was emerging in the works of Lévi-Strauss, Geertz, Victor Turner, and others.

In that volume Mumford projects a view of human development as rooted in the communicative, signifying capacities of the organic body. In his view, the key to human evolution was *homo symbolicus,* man the self-signifying creature, not *homo faber.* He marshals a broad range of archaeological and anthropological data to claim that the transformation from animal to human was one involving powerful energies of feelingful communication: of dreams, gestures, utterances, and ritualized behaviors which projected an inner landscape whose possible significance transcended human understanding, rousing humans toward a ritual life capable of controlling inner anxieties and outer tensions, and comprehending fantastic scenarios bodied forth in the dream world. By this account, nonutilitarian activities such as dreaming, playing, and communicative forms of emotional bonding provided far more pivotal means to the emergence of humans than "tool-use."

Man's inner world, as Mumford says, "must often have been far more threatening and far less comprehensible than his outer world, as indeed it still is; and his first task was not to shape tools for controlling the environment, but to shape instruments even more powerful and compelling in order to control himself, above all, his unconscious. The invention and perfection of these instruments— rituals, symbols, words, images, standard modes of behavior (mores)—was, I hope to establish, the principal occupation of early man, more necessary to survival than tool-making, and far more essential to his later development."[7] We see here a deep resonance between Mumford and Victor Turner concerning the organic bodily depths in which human signification and ritual are embedded.

Sociologists may see in Durkheim's theory of *conscience collective* a more socially based understanding of dreams than the account given by Mumford, yet from my perspective Durkheim is the narrower of the two. In his late work Durkheim attempted to show how the faculties of knowing are social, as opposed to the individual faculty theory of knowledge deriving from Kant. Yet he remained tethered to the legacy of Kantian structuralism, in believing (1) that a fundamental duality between individual consciousness and collective consciousness exists; (2) that collective representations ultimately represent one fundamental, underlying, unchanging entity—society, and (3) that collective representations are essentially conventional. These beliefs reveal why Durkheim's approach remains inadequate not only for understanding the social reality of dreaming but also more generally for understanding human social life. In contrast with Durkheim, I would claim that (1) individual consciousness is a social precipitate continuous with the collective cultural and biosocial heritage rather than dualistically opposed to it, (2) both that which collective representations signify and the representations themselves may emerge, develop, die, and undergo genuine transformation in time, and finally, (3) as dream-symbols make abundantly clear, collective representations are not limited to purely conventional signification but draw from other modalities of signification, such as iconic and indexical signs. Despite an acknowledgment of the place of experience in social life, Durkheim remained too much the conceptualist.

Mumford implicitly rejected Durkheim's conceptualism when he took seriously the Australian aboriginal concept of "Alcheringa" or "the dreamtime of long ago." Like Durkheim, Mumford believed that aboriginal peoples are "almost as close as we can get in the flesh to early man." Mumford also used aborigines to reveal underlying connections between them and us, but he did not deny that real historical development and transformations have taken place, not reducible to underlying "elementary forms." He also denied the inevitability of progressive differentiation, and uses the terms "organic" and "mechanical" in roughly the opposite sense of Durkheim. Mumford charged the scientific community with ignoring or underrating valuable evidence, because of the seemingly intangible, imaginary nature of dreams. As facts of human and even mammalian physiology, however, rapid eye movement (REM) dreaming has been around longer than humans and suggests a potentially crucial element in the emergence of image-making, ritualizing, interpreting humans.[8]

Mumford's *Technics and Human Development* flatly rejects *homo faber,* man the tool-user, as an adequate standard for understanding the evolution of human beings. This view has dominated physical anthropology, leading, in Mumford's opinion, to an overvaluation of hard physical evidence—bones and stones—and an undervaluation of soft and impermanent physical artifacts, such as wood objects, clothing, and artistic expressions; and further, to a virtual ignoring of nontangible factors such as dreams, ritual, and speech. *homo faber,* the term popularized by Henri Bergson and associated earlier with Benjamin Franklin, is an artifact or by-product of the modern utilitarian age, the machine age which came to view human development as metallically passing from rocks to copper to bronze to iron, and finally to Weber's "steel casing" or "iron cage" of the twentieth century. This externalist view of technics is repeatedly rejected by Mumford as an insufficient explanation of human genesis and human technics. In its place is *homo symbolicus,* man the signifying and self-creating symbol, whose own body forms an infinitely more sophisticated instrument for the development of technics than hard functional tools. Mumford proposed a biosemiotic account of human evolution in which the human body itself is created out of the rich interplay of ritual action and symbolic communication with biology:

> By means of ritual, I suggest, early man first confronted and overcame his own strangeness, identified himself with cosmic events outside the animal pale, and allayed the uneasiness created by his huge but still largely unusable cerebral capacities. At a much later stage these inchoate impulses would come together under the rubric of religion. Actions still "speak louder than words," and the movements and gestures of ritual were the earliest foreshadowings of human speech. What could not yet be said in words or shaped in clay or stone, early man first danced or mimed;

if he flapped his arms he was a bird: if the group formed a circle and re-volved in measured steps they might be the moon. In short, what André Varagnac happily identified as the "technology of the body," expressed in dance and mimetic movements, was both the earliest form of any kind of technical order and the earliest manifestation of expressive and communicable meaning.[9]

By centering on the organic human body, Mumford developed a much broader semiotic than the conceptualist theories that now form the "leading edge" of social theory, including those "body as text" theories, and a much deeper theory of culture—one that roots purposive meaning in human biology. His organic world picture allows him to champion the technics of the body as both the means for our own transformation into humans and the first truly human achievement.

Mumford's semiotically based account of human development provides the anthropological grounding for his critique of the modern age. In the first two volumes of his "Renewal of Life" series, *Technics and Civilization* (1934) and *The Culture of Cities* (1938), Mumford proposed that the roots of modern life are to be found in destabilizing and deurbanizing processes emerging out of late Medieval Civilization. Although acknowledging the genuine achievements of the modern era, from its universal physical science to its intensification of the human personality in art and the development of political freedoms, he criticized its inherently destructive potentials, rooted in the rise of centralizing, quantifying, machine-like tendencies in capitalism, baroque political power, the city, and science and technics. Where the "Renewal of Life" series mapped out a critical vision of the development of Western Civilization, Mumford began in the 1950s to question the implications of civilizational structures themselves in human development. His relatively brief book, *The Transformations of Man,* projected this new terrain which would occupy him for the rest of his life.

The "renewal of life" books typically began with the origins of modern Western Civilization, but *The Transformations of Man* reaches back into the origins of humans. It was here that Mumford first fully articulated his mature philosophical anthropology of *homo symbolicus,* though he had been developing it for years. Following his usual chronological approach to history, he proposes an account of the stages or transformations of humankind leading up to contemporary civilization. The first two chapters deal with the origins of history, in the evolution into humankind and the development of "archaic man" in the paleolithic and neolithic ages. Mumford notes how the very term "neolithic" is prejudiced in favor of durable data, and suggests by contrast a feminist interpretation of neolithic culture, resting on "insight into living processes" rather than mechanical improvements: "This domestication of plants seems largely women's work: instead of taking life, like the hunter, she nurtured it in the earth, as she nurtured it in her own womb."[10] His feminist outlook on human development takes women and particularly the capacity for nurturance as pivotal in the evolutionary emergence of humans and culture. Later, in his 1961 lecture, "An Apology to Henry Adams," he would call for a feminization of public life and civilization. Taking a position aligned more with those strands of feminist theory which allow for temperamentally determined differences, he believed that the proclivities for empathic feeling and nurturance are not solely "social roles" but are probably biologically more pronounced in women on the average than men. Yet these are capacities obviously also available to men and must, in this view, be brought to the fore of social life and its institutions by women and men.

Hence the domestication of plants in archaic life is simultaneously a self-domesticating process. As human life becomes more "settled" and regularized around growing seasons, custom and ritual observance assume increasing importance. The land "becomes a repository of sentiment, swarming with memories and projects: the place where one's ancestors are buried, whose paths were worn by their feet, whose trees were planted by their hands, whose stones were formed into walls and buildings by their labors, the place whose perpetual renewal or restoration forms the best part of the present generation's labors."[11] The earthiness and communality which characterize archaic culture is counterbalanced, in Mumford's view, by the closedness of the community and its fear of novelty. But the very successes of domestication and the increase of population it made possible set the necessary, but by no means sufficient, conditions for the emergence of civilizations.

The emergence, in Mesopotamia, Egypt, India, China, and among the Incans of Peru, of cities, forms of literacy, bureaucracy, a division of labor, and powerful centralized government concentrated in a king, marked a new departure of humankind. Yet Mumford had no illusions about the negative effects of what Melville called "snivelization": "Economically, the new order was based largely on the forcible exploitation of cultivators and artisans by an armed and ever-threatening minority: mobile intruders or heavily entrenched lords of the land. For civilization brought about the equation of human life with property and power; indeed, property and power became more dear than life."[12] With civilization came the emergence of a centralized bureaucratic cult, which Mumford was later to term the "megamachine."

A strong case can be made that civilizational structures tended to reduce political and economic welfare for the bulk of people while focusing power in the hands of the elite. Studies of nutrition in the ancient Near East, for example, show a poorer diet for most inhabitants of cities over their preurban ancestors, and a correspondingly better-fed bureaucracy. One of the key questions for any theory of human development has to be not so much why vast regions of people accepted civilization—the force of the powerful to impose their will might explain that—but why humans evolved such seemingly inhuman, yet enduring, structures. Was Dostoevsky's Grand Inquisitor in *The Brothers Karamazov* right when he said that humankind lives by miracle, mystery, and authority, or is it possible for humans to "live in truth," as Vaclav Havel puts it, to construct enduring institutions which make a free life possible?

We shall return to Mumford's view of civilization and its significance for understanding modern life later. Here let me note that he sees the next transformation in human development, the axial age, which, beginning around 600 B.C. signaled an opposition to and compensation for the one-sidedness and impersonality of bureaucratic civilizational structures. As he put it in *The Transformations of Man:* "The central change brought in by axial religions is the redefinition —in fact the recasting—of the human personality. In that act, values that emerge only in the personality replace those that belonged to institutions and institutional roles. The new feelings, emotional attachments, sentiments are now incarnated in a living image, that of the prophet."

Archaic man, civilized man, and axial man together form three layers of what Mumford calls "Old World Man," whose successes held until the emergence of what he terms "New World Man." New World Man denotes a way of life not limited to the geographical new world but rather the emergent modern attitude or temper. In defining New World Man, Mumford returned to a polar tension he used early in his career, in his book *The Golden Day,* that between two poles of the human personality, the romantic and the mechanical. In his words, "During the last two centuries, these types flourished side by side, attracting and producing contrasting types of human character, one dominant, the other recessive. . . . What bound them together and made them temporary allies was the fact that they were both in revolt against Old World culture. But as the geographic New World filled with immigrants, indeed as population generally began to increase, the mechanical New World almost automatically became dominant."

Though New World culture promised a reconciliation of the subjective life with the power of the mechanical worldview, of civilized humanity with the natural environment, though it promised political and economic equality, these promises were thwarted by the very dynamics of New World culture itself. In Mumford's mordant words:

> The virgin lands, once penetrated, brought forth another kind of offspring. Vitality gave way before the uniformities of mechanized power, adventure was driven to more distant frontiers, and close behind the valiant conquistadors marched the capitalist enterprisers, girdling the continents with railroads and steamship lines and telegraphs. Instead of entering into reciprocal relations with the peoples he conquered, seeking to prolong and enhance the values that had been repressed by Old World Culture, New World man too often showed himself more savage than the most primitive groups whose cultures he despoiled. Imperialist competition and exploitation brought on a cycle of wars that culminated in the twentieth century, making that period the most bloody and brutal epoch in history. With the lands of the New World largely occupied and settled, with population pressing upon food supply throughout the planet, with an ever larger mass of people all over the world caught in the new industrial machine, the compensatory vitalities of New World man sought another, darker outlet. Not freedom and vitality, but power, regimentation, conformity, and absolutism have now become the dominant elements in the New World culture: not least in countries where totalitarian automatism is quaintly called "free enterprise" and generals and businessmen act in interchangeable roles.

Animating New World romantic and enlightenment culture was the dream of the perfection of humankind, but the dream resulted in a nightmare culture which threatened to perfect the machine and the spectral human consciousness projected into it at the cost of eliminating humanity. Mumford suggested in 1956 that the continued perfection of the New World dream, of the practices introduced by capitalism, the physical sciences and technology, bureaucratic administration, and totalitarian government, would constitute a further transformation in human development, which he called, using Roderick Seidenberg's term for his own purposes, "Post-Historic Man." Post-Historic Man, "governed by a deliberately depersonalized intelligence" which recognizes no desires which deviate from its own purposes, would be truly liberated from what Mumford elsewhere calls "the fibrous structure of history," the various strata of the past which remain stubbornly embedded in societies, and which human lives touch through organic and social memory. But such a liberation is merely an alienation from the fibrous structure of the human self.

The "end of history" idea which marked progressive thought from Hegel and Marx through revolutionary movements in twentieth-century politics, avant-garde art, and social thought, and more recently has been taken up by conservatives to signify the end of communism, has proven to be itself a dead-end concept. Human selves and human societies remain inextricably and fibrously interconnected to the histories which shape them, histories which can also prove deadly to an individual or society either gripped by the dead hand of the past or, as in the case of posthistoric man, gripped both by the denial of the past and the dead hand of the closed rational-mechanical system. The fibrous structure of history can also form the basis of a subtilized and enlarged consciousness and culture when allowed to be called forth and engaged.

Mumford deviated from Roderick Seidenberg's original definition of post-historic culture in allowing that it is not the inevitable future of human development but only a likely direction. Counterposed to Seidenberg's understanding of Post-Historic Man as the inevitable outcome of a human evolution of intelligence and eradication of instinct are both Mumford's claims for the fibrous structure of history and the continued emergence of human transformations. Therefore Mumford, who ended the book with a call for a further transformation, which he termed "World Culture," would seem the more optimistic of the two. Yet in a letter to Seidenberg, he noted, "As for the essential difference between us, about the possibility of Post-Historic Man's survival, my own view is, believe it or not, more pessimistic than yours. You see a long, slow development ahead over the eons: I foresee catastrophe & extinction within a limited time, if present trends continue. The escape from this would be as much a miracle for Post-Historic Man as for his more benign alternate!"[13]

The term "Post-Historic," as Mumford used it in 1956, captures both the mechanomania of postwar modern culture and the more recent worship of the "virtual reality" which postmodern culture represents. Both cultures are motivated by the same modern impulse: to displace the feeling, spontaneous, experiencing, and purposive human being with the nonspontaneous purposes of the machine and an exaggerated conception of the nonpurposive contingencies of existence—the residues of mechanical order.

Against the dismal prospects of posthistoric culture, Mumford proposes an outline for World Culture, one which attempts to acknowledge and utilize both the fibrous structure of history and genuine emergence of new directions in human affairs, from the self to civilizations. The concept of "the fibrous structure of history" illustrates a fundamental difference between Mumford's developmental view of history and those of Hegel, Marx, and other believers in linear progress, because it acknowledges that history can sometimes take wrong detours and that the past is not necessarily overcome by, and therefore made obsolete by, present developments. From a "fibrous" view of historical development, past modes of life reveal a valuable legacy which can critically counterbalance unacknowledged prejudices in contemporary life. World Culture represents the opening up of contemporary life to the past, while simultaneously recognizing limits to being which are disguised by the culture of mechanical power. In his words, "[T]he New World ideology must itself undergo a change that will rescue it from the shallowness of its original vision and technique. Not expansion and conquest but intensive cultivation, not 'freedom from' but 'freedom for,' not wholesale mechanization for the sake of power, profit, productivity, or prestige, but a mechanization measured by human need and limited by vital norms. . . . This means a general change from a money economy to a life economy . . . a survey of the possibilities of human existence, in a new ecological pattern, region by region, is the necessary basis for the resettlement and recultivation of the planet. That will be more than a reversal of New World habits: it will be a moral atonement for four centuries of ruthless exploitation and desecration."

Mumford's description of World Culture, written in 1956, suggests a prescient alternative to postwar power culture and its postmodern refinements which time has only proven to be more necessary today. Yet one wonders what the negative side of World Culture might be, given that all the other transformations of human history contained shortcomings. Did Mumford, despite his appreciation for the fibrous structure of history, fall prey to Hegelian/Marxian tendencies to idealize a future freed from human frailties? The world today, almost forty years after Mumford's description of World Culture, is coming to recognize the necessity for "a new ecological pattern," but it has also renewed ethnic hatred and blinded religious fundamentalism. In short, I agree with Mumford's call for a new global civilizational structure, but surely such a development would also call forth its own emergent destructive forces as well.

RATIONALIZATION AS MEGAMACHINE

Further implications of how Mumford's thought provides an alternative to codified theory and most understandings of modern culture are revealed by comparing his views of modern life with that of Max Weber. Weber assumed throughout his varied researches a radical and unprecedented uniqueness in modern Western civilization, and here emerges one of the major differences between Weber and Mumford. Weber saw that the development of modern rationality was not a necessary consequence of progress, since other directions could have been taken. Yet where Weber sees the "rationalization" of the West as a progressive, logical development, even if deeply problematic or tragic, Mumford interprets the same processes to represent a fatally flawed worldview leading ultimately to derationalization. What Weber describes as the spirit of capitalism is set by Mumford within a broader concept of the megamachine. Mumford views modernity, with Weber, as an idiosyncratic development, but, unlike Weber, he does not see it as unprecedented.

Developing further the ideas he articulated in *The Transformations of Man,* Mumford boldly claimed in both volumes of *The Myth of the Machine* that the achievement of civilizational structures also brought with them the rise of the megamachine, which provides the underlying myth of the modern world. In describing the power complexes of early civilizations as a megamachine, Mumford used the term "machine" literally, following the classic formulation of Franz Reuleaux. If a machine be defined, as Mumford says, "as a combination of resistant parts, each specialized in function, operating under human control, to utilize energy and to perform work, then the great labor machine was in every aspect a genuine machine: all the more because its components, though made of human bone, nerve, and muscle, were reduced to their bare mechanical elements and rigidly standardized for the performance of their limited tasks. The taskmaster's lash ensured conformity. Such machines had already been assembled if not invented by kings in the early part of the Pyramid Age, from the end of the fourth Millennium on."[14]

Hence, though the modern epoch in many ways marks a stark departure from the ways of the past, Mumford sought to show how it also represents the rebuilding of the megamachine of ancient civilization. In the earliest river civilizations of Mesopotamia, Egypt, India, and China, new configurations of human relations arose involving the centralization of power: large-scale military and bureaucratic organizations centered in cities and subject to kings regarded as divine, as in Egypt, or rulers surrounded with the aura of divine power. The transition from village-centered cultures to city-centered civilizations is marked by the gradual emergence of power-minded, mechanically regimented institutions, symbolized, especially in Egypt and Mesopotamia, by the displacement of earthly deities by more rational celestial ones, and personified by the king, who impersonated earthly power and cosmic order. The regimentation of the mass of men by a select elite, who lived in a grandiose style through appropriating the labor of the whole community, signifies the first megamachine in Mumford's perspective, a megamachine whose parts were almost entirely human.

With the rise of these civilizational structures, new energies crystallized in the establishment of centrally organized power, ranging from economic, political, and religious bureaucracies to the harnessing of large-scale organized human labor. Civilized man discovered and made conscious the secret of the ants and bees: how a division of labor could produce a populous and efficient social life. The great dream of civilizational life might be expressed as how an increase in forms of automata could create living conditions which might enlarge autonomy. Thus was born the specter of human reason, the emanation to outward institutional form of the rational capacity, which increasingly displaced the nonrational but reasonable sources of institutions. And thus too, if we listen to William Blake and Lewis Mumford, was born the power of the human machine world, of mechanized order and stochastic contingency, which is completing itself—realizing its entelechy or perfection—in our time.

As Blake said almost two hundred years ago in his poem *Jerusalem,* "The Spectre is the Reasoning Power in Man, and when separated from Imagination and closing itself as in steel in a Ratio of the things of Memory, It thence frames Laws & Moralities to destroy Imagination, the Divine Body, by Martyrdoms & Wars." Those who live by conceptual reason alone often devalue Blake by consigning him to the category of a "romantic," meaning by romanticism some combination of excessive sentimentalism, individualism, or nature mysticism. Yet he poses a serious critique of *homo sapiens* in the previous quotation and throughout his work. He is saying that Imagination is a deeper human capacity—poetically expressed as "the Divine Body"—than rational reasoning—poetically expressed as a secondary emanation or "Spectre"—and that rational reasoning depends upon a living continuity with Imagination.

The separation of rational reasoning from Imagination—"closing itself as in steel in a Ratio of the Things of Memory"—is expressed in a way similar to the metaphor used by Weber to describe the developmental logic of instrumental rationality in modern culture: a steel-hard casing or "iron cage." But where Weber's negative metaphor served to depict the consequences of what he took to be the inherent closed-ended logic of modern rationality, Blake's poetic expression explicitly denies that rationality is a fully autonomous capacity, and shows the way to conceive of rationality as an open-ended capacity which depends upon something greater than itself—Imagination—in order to function reasonably. To a modern or even postmodern rationalist, however, the idea that something as wispy sounding as "Poetic Imagination" can be foundational to rationality must seem like a fanciful delusion. Perhaps it is. And yet I beg the reader's patience, for I am claiming that Blake's words derive from an anthropology that resonates with the scientific philosophy of Peirce and the social philosophy of Mumford, one which could contribute to a transformation of social theory today. It is an anthropology which allows that intelligence is projective before it is reflective, and that conjecturing remains a more basic capacity than criticism, a capacity which is the very ground on which criticism stands. In the anthropology suggested here, emergent humanity would be better described as a conjecturing creature rather than as *homo faber* or *homo sapiens,* though all three characterizations remain partial. Protohumans didn't critique their way into culture, they dreamed and played and desired and nurtured and hunted their way into big brains and symbolic communication.

If we consider the conceivable influences of dreaming and ritual life as creating a movement toward interpretative meaning and order, we can see how those processes could also lead to an excess of order. When stretched beyond organic limits, such as life-purposes, local habitat, local social organization, the tendency toward interpretation could take on a life of its own. Perhaps the reified centralized order of the megamachine was not only a product of civilization, as Mumford claims, but also a latent possibility already built-in to the human creature as a negative consequence of the dream-induced body technics.

Is it possible that the idea of the megamachine goes back much further again, back to the emergence of *homo sapiens sapiens* itself? If protohumans evolved the tools of ritual, speech, artistic expression, and mores of conduct as means of controlling the inner anxieties, anxieties related to our big brains, perhaps there was also embedded in the central nervous system the tendency to automaton-like order. Hence we would be creatures biologically impelled toward autonomy and meaning, as Mumford says—or toward the inborn necessity of freedom—yet also biologically tending to take the quest for meaning too far, thereby substituting order for meaning. The acquisition of meaning and autonomy may have been achieved at the cost of repetition compulsions—or even the removal of biological inhibitions against overcentralization. Though cultural reductionists claim that human culture helped free us entirely from instincts, this view overlooks the possibility that human instincts continue to operate in vague and suggestive, yet vitally important, ways. Largely liberated from the genius of instinctive determination, we may be creatures neurologically constituted to walk the knife-edge between autonomy and the automaton, our task being not to escape biology but to make human autonomy instinctive.

Biological evolution and cultural development are not simply a progressive casting off of shackles toward a greater and ultimately unrestrained freedom: they involve trade-offs of one kind of limitation for another. The achievement of human symbolic consciousness may have cost us a somewhat diminished perceptual or emotional life: Who is to say that the forms of feeling produced by Neanderthal burial rituals, and the dawning significance of death and mortality for *homo erectus* and even earlier creatures, may not have more to do with the real essence of human symbolic consciousness than a modern rationalist treatise on culture produced by a human product of that consciousness? On the other hand, the Mozart or Verdi *Requiem* provide ample evidence that the achievement of symbolic consciousness also makes possible an enlargement and enhancement of perceptive and emotional capacities. There may have been a trade-off of emotive brain power in the overall reduction of brain size from earlier humans such as Neanderthal to *homo sapiens sapiens,* but the subtilizing of brain through the enlargement of the forebrain may have provided compensation. One is reminded of Herman Melville's dictum: "Why then do you try to 'enlarge' your mind? Subtilize it."

Mumford and only a very few other social theorists point to the unusual fact that our big brains seem possessed of excess energies and that this may explain a number of peculiar features of human existence. But there is an even more fundamental question which seems to me to be ignored by most social theorists, even though it goes to the crux of the evolutionary debate going back to Darwin and Wallace: How did our big brains come about? It is not simply that we had big brains which we then had to control, but also that we evolved big brains, presumably through an evolutionary increase of brain use and adaptiveness. What was it that made big brains adaptive? Increasingly complex social organization? Increasingly complex dreaming? Or both? Did the human brain evolve in the context of an evolving mind? Did mind, and not simply chance variation or adaptiveness, need more brain power? Did the emergent symbolic consciousness need more forebrain to articulate its emotional and grammatical communicative needs and therefore "select" for the growth of this region? If so, it would suggest that mind may have bootstrapped itself not only into consciousness but into the regulative principles of evolution as well, infusing purposes into processes of chance.

LET US RETURN NOW from these anthropological conjectures to the significance of the megamachine of modernity. Where the original megamachine used mostly human parts, seeking to mold the human to the mechanical, the modern one devoted itself to its own mechanization, progressively replacing human parts with mechanical ones. The cult of the king and the myth of the machine reemerged in the modern West transformed as the ghost in the mechanical machine: the true spirit of capitalism, communism, and modern technology. In Mumford's perspective, the appearance of virtually deified Great Dictators in the twentieth century—from Hitler, Stalin, Mussolini, Franco, and Attaturk to Mao, Ceaucescu, and Saddam Hussein—is no accident or antimodern throwback but a vital component of the megamachine of modernity, the visible appearance of an avatar of the god in the machine. Saddam Hussein, with his socialist fundamentalism, his admiration for both Hitler and Stalin, his nuclear, biological, and chemical weapons, even provided a sort of literal support for Mumford's thesis of a link between the ancient king cult and the modern megamachine, when he inscribed a dedication before the Gulf War to himself and his fierce powers on an ancient Assyrian relief in Iraq on which were similar boasts from ancient Assyrian tyrants.

Although Mumford agreed with Weber's linking of the Calvinist ethic with the machine-like spirit of capitalism, he believed that Weber overemphasized the gap between the otherworldly asceticism of the Catholic monestaries and the this-worldly asceticism of Protestantism. From Mumford's perspective, Weber undervalued the prime part played by Medieval Catholic culture: "In view of the patent facts of history, this belief is as strange as it is indefensible: for it assumes that modern capitalism did not take form until the sixteenth century; whereas it existed as a mutation at least three centuries earlier and by the fourteenth century it pervaded Italy: a country where Protestantism has never been able to gain a hold. Capitalism was, in fact, the great heresy of the Middle Ages . . . the heresy had been nourished in the very bosom of the church, and almost from the first had the protection of the Papacy. It was not Calvin in the sixteenth century, but Vincent of Beauvais in the thirteenth who first admonished people to work, not just for a living, but for the sake of accumulation, which would lead to the further production of wealth."[15] In other words, Mumford claims that Weber did not adequately acknowledge the extent to which capitalism grew out of Medieval Catholic culture in general, and not only within the ascetic discipline of the monasteries or in opposition to Catholicism.

In his discussions of the elective affinities of the Benedictine monastery, Mumford details how those distinguishing features of regularity, renunciation of personal autonomy, scrutiny of one's and others' conduct, and especially the performance of daily work as a Christian duty led to a highly rationalized existence characteristic of the spirit of capitalism and the megamachine. Devotional order proved applicable to generalized economic order: regularized time, record keeping, exact measurement, and the increasing invention of and reliance on mechanical devices not only helped the soul to prosper but caused greater economic success. The vow of poverty, or rather the economic value of a methodically ordered life, produced a great wealth in the Benedictine monasteries, so that "[b]y the twelfth century the efficient rationalization that had been achieved in the monastery was ready to be transferred to secular occupations. For the Benedictines had proved what the English evangelist, John Wesley, was to point out many centuries later: that Christian thrift, sobriety, and regularity would inevitably lead to worldly success. Most of the habits that Max Weber erroneously treated as the special property of sixteenth-century Calvinist Protestantism were in effective operation in the medieval Cistercian monastery."[16] Mumford may be overstating his case here, since Weber did acknowledge the rational order of the monastery. The main point of Mumford's critique is that capitalism and its rationalized order were emergent properties of Medieval Culture. From my perspective, Weber undervalues the role of emergent nominalism in fashioning a rational-mechanical worldview and culture of which science, capitalism, *and* Protestantism were elements.

In many ways Weber is regarded as the "ideal type" of sociologist by academic sociologists, and in many ways Mumford is Weber's complete antithesis. Weber believed that professional training of a scholar should be specialistic and should avoid consciously inculcating values; Mumford not only scorned this "value-free" specialism but the toady professionalism it spawned in universities as well. Yet despite what Weber preached about specialized scholarship, in practice he was one of the most broadly ranging scholars of the twentieth century. So in practice, if not in theory, Weber and Mumford resonate as scholars unconstrained by disciplinary boundaries.

Weber preserved the rigid neo-Kantian divide between facts and values, claiming that values are relative in their foundations, subjectively chosen, and that one's own values must never interfere with analysis. Mumford denied the split between facts and values and rejected the idea that values are purely subjective and relative. Values are rooted in their relation to life and social milieu and objectively tempered through experience. Furthermore, Mumford viewed the "disinterested" model of scholarship and research as an abdication of the responsibility of a scholar or scientist. This is particularly clear in his response to the development of nuclear weapons, in which "scientific objectivity" was a smokescreen for disinterest in the uses and social consequences of the weapons produced and an alibi for continued research funding. Objectivity remained for Mumford a public responsibility, not a means to privatize knowledge through secrecy or specialization.

From the beginning of his career, Lewis Mumford was what is nowadays called a critical theorist. His late work, for example, might be regarded as a critical theory of civilizations, and his book *The Pentagon of Power,* volume two of *The Myth of the Machine,* gives the lie to the idea that American thinkers ignore the place of power in social life. Yet Mumford's vision might also be taken as a critique of those critical theories which ignore or undervalue those aspects of human conduct and institutions which are noncritical.

Let us consider further in this context Mumford's organic and critical alternative to the codification of critical theory. The very term "critical theory," although it connotes images of radical thought at the margins of intellectual life, actually denotes a well-established tradition deeply entrenched in the academy, whose roots are usually associated with Europe and specifically Frankfurt and Paris. Critical theory in America is probably most closely associated with the New School for Social Research in New York, which not only welcomed many European theorists displaced by the Nazis but which today explicitly supports a broad program of critical social thought. Yet the idea that critical theory, even critical theory at the New School, is a specifically European tradition reflects both an amnesia regarding American intellectual history and a nostalgia for a particular European intellectual history. This becomes particularly evident when we put Mumford back into the picture.

Mumford attended a course given by Thorstein Veblen at the New School just after World War I and, shortly after, in 1920, was a colleague of Veblen's on the New York journal *The Dial.* Veblen himself was the founder of what could be called the first school of Chicago economics, having taught at the University of Chicago during most of its first decade. "The Chicago school of economics" is usually associated with Milton Friedman, a school which purports to be "value-free" in the interests of science. One could see just how value-free the school was when it freely gave of its political-economic values in the form of advice to the CIA in helping to overthrow the democratically elected government of Allende in Chile and maintaining the repressive regime of Pinochet by "counselling" former students from Chile who held high positions in government. When the history of the American Age is written, perhaps the term "value-free," championed by the Friedmans and the Parsonses, will be shown to have functioned as a synonym for "national security."

Veblen proposed a quite different economics from that of the second Chicago school, a critical-symbolic economics, which acknowledged that markets serve values—conspicuous consumption and "pecuniary standards"—and are not some natural reality on which values perch. He wrote *The Theory of the Leisure Class* (1899) in Chicago, and transposed the Northwest Coast Native American potlatch feast of ritual waste to the economic practices of the Chicago of the turn-of-the-century "Gilded Age." Veblen's views were not without limitations, such as his tendency to overvalue technical efficiency as an economic standard capable of correcting the abuses of "invidious comparison," in which the engineer rather than the business man served as a model. He nevertheless unmasked the fantastic underpinnings of socioeconomic life, just as Freud was simultaneously doing for the psyche. Much of the interest today in the work of French poststructuralist Jean Baudrillard relates to ideas traceable back to Veblen.

In 1923 Mumford was invited by Alvin Johnson, the director of the New School, to give a course on the history of architecture. Mumford spent six months reading for his lectures only to have the course canceled when only six students showed up. But Johnson invited him to give the course the following autumn, and thanks to a librarian at the New York Public Library who took it upon herself to promote Mumford's course to her colleagues, Mumford was able to offer the course, probably the first general course offered on the development of American architecture. Those lectures ended up forming the basis of his second book, *Sticks and Stones,* which is still widely regarded as a classic in architectural criticism.[17]

Hence well before the European immigrant scholars of the thirties—including the Frankfurters, Horkheimer, Adorno, Lowenthal, and others as well as Claude Lévi Strauss—two key American critical thinkers, Veblen and Mumford, had already taught there. But the kind of critical view of human development Mumford would develop diverged in numerous ways from the Frankfurt school: most crucially, in Mumford's critique of the presumed centrality of critical consciousness itself in human affairs.

Against those theorists who view that which is "noncritical" as suspect, Mumford insisted on the pivotal significance of reasonable, yet not critical, human capacities. His critique of the megamachine can also be taken as an argument against the modern dream of achieving rationally grounded societies. Critical intelligence, although an essential ingredient in Mumford's world picture, neither provides the underpinnings for a society nor is a capacity limited to the realm of the rational.

Emotions may provide a critical standard of judgment, although not rational, and may provide a commonsense basis for conduct transcending the critical. "Common sense" has taken a beating in intellectual life in recent years, yet Mumford's approach seems to me rather uncommon by contemporary standards, perhaps closest in spirit to Charles Peirce's too little-known marriage of opposites, "critical common-sensism." Although conventionalists discount common sense as merely conventional knowledge, one can view common sense as the bringing to bear of one's feeling and experience to a situation, as allowing the emotional promptings of the heart a voice in conduct. Hence common sense is the ability to "sense" a situation, using feelings, perceptions, cultural tradition, and even knowledge to make a judgment, even though such a judgment may not appear at first as rationally or critically grounded.

Mumford's concern with the potentially debilitating effects of living from critical consciousness alone came to a head in the late 1930s, as liberals pleaded for a "rational" response to Hitler's emergent terror. Mumford excoriated what he termed "pragmatic liberalism" and its "dread of the emotions," and the debate between Dewey and Mumford throws light on the problematic nature of rationality and critical consciousness as guides for the conduct of life.

MUMFORD AND THE FAILURE OF LIBERALISM

Mumford had two notable encounters with John Dewey and pragmatism. The first came about through Dewey's response to Mumford's chapter on "the pragmatic acquiescence" in *The Golden Day,* where Mumford claimed that the period from the Civil War to the 1920s in America was a virtual capitulation to industrialism and utilitarianism, signified intellectually by pragmatism. Mumford indicted William James and John Dewey as key players in the descent to expedient practicality, although he did except the founder of pragmatism, Charles Peirce, as someone who preserved the integrity of his vision against the grain of his time.

William James characterized the split between art and science which opened in the decades after "Golden Day" of the literary transcendentalists—Emerson, Hawthorne, Thoreau, Melville and Whitman. James had wanted to be a painter, but after a period of black depression decided on scientific psychology. In Mumford's view both James's repressed artistic longings, as well as his version of pragmatism, which James once unfortunately expressed as "the cash value of an act," typified a "pragmatic acquiescence" to the forces of utility and technical scientism. He criticized Dewey for his stress on "instrumental" intelligence—which, it should be noted, was something broader than Weber's category of *Zweckrationalität,* purposive or instrumental rationality, denoting inherently social and correctible means and ends—at the expense of imaginative and aesthetic reason. Dewey's critical reply to Mumford's characterization of pragmatism in 1927 correctly pointed out that "instrumental" was a phase in human conduct, which also included "consummation" or aesthetic quality.

In Dewey's view Mumford had falsely caricatured his position as utilitarian, and in my view Dewey was technically correct, but only technically correct. While Dewey had just begun to develop his theory of aesthetic quality as the ground of experience in his *Experience and Nature* (1926), and was on the way toward his fullest expression of aesthetic quality and art, which he would publish in *Art as Experience* (1931), the writings Mumford criticized are imbued with that optimistic progressivism that society can be reconstructed through the model of scientific inquiry. Dewey was no "bread and butter" practicalist—of the sort one hears about nowadays when politicians and fashionable academics such as Richard Rorty claim to be "pragmatists" because they follow what is expedient for an immediate purpose, apart from any consideration of the long-term consequences which transcend immediate situations. Dewey held a broad vision of scientific inquiry indeed. Yet in my view Mumford's critique still holds: the model of scientific inquiry, including humane social sciences, may be necessary in the modern world, but it remains utterly insufficient to provide a basis for a society or civilization.

As far back as 1927, Mumford saw the dangers not only of scientism, of which Dewey too was somewhat aware, but of making a method of deliberate conduct the basis of all conduct. It is true that Dewey had described a dialectic of impulse and habit in his *Human Nature and Conduct* (1924), which become regulated in the practice of human conduct. But in Mumford's view, Dewey seemed to pay too much attention to the means of conduct and to assume that the ends or ideals of conduct would almost come about on their own. Dewey, in other words, undervalued the imaginative life in favor of the regulative life, and in his optimism ignored the "desiccation and sterilization of the imaginative life" over the past few centuries, as the scientific worldview came to power.

The second confrontation with Dewey and pragmatism occurred on the eve of World War II and concerned what Mumford termed "The Corruption of Liberalism." Mumford believed that fascism would not listen to reasonable talk and could not be appeased, and he urged strong measures as early as 1935 against Hitler and in support of European nations which might be attacked by Hitler. By 1938 he urged in *The New Republic* that the United States "[s]trike first against fascism; and strike hard, but strike." His militant position was widely attacked by the Left, and he lost a number of friends in the process, including Frank Lloyd Wright, Van Wyck Brooks, Charles Beard, and Malcolm Cowley among others.

To give an idea of the opinions and climate of the prewar debate, just consider the titles of commentaries published in the March 1939 issue of *Common Sense* on the question "If War Comes—Shall We Participate or be Neutral?": Bertrand Russell, "The Case for U.S. Neutrality"; Max Lerner, " 'Economic Force' May Be Enough"; Charles A. Beard, "America Cannot 'Save' Europe"; John T. Flynn, "Nothing Less than a Crime"; and Harry Elmer Barnes, "A War for 'Tory Finance'?" Dewey's contribution was titled, "No Matter What Happens—Stay Out," and it could not have been more opposed to Mumford's piece, "Fascism Is Worse than War."

Mumford believed that the inability of the Left to see that rational persuasion and appeasement were inadequate to stem Hitler's hell-bound ambition indicated a corruption in the tradition of what Mumford called "pragmatic liberalism." The fatal error of pragmatic liberalism was its gutless intellectualism, its endorsement of emotional neutrality as a basis for objectivity, which he characterized as "the dread of the emotions." He illustrated why the emotions ought to play a significant part in rational decisions with an example of encountering a poisonous snake: "If one meets a poisonous snake on one's path, two things are important for a *rational* reaction. One is to identify it, and not make the error of assuming that a copperhead is a harmless adder. The other is to have a prompt emotion of fear, if the snake *is* poisonous; for fear starts the flow of adren[al]in into the blood-stream, and that will not merely put the organism as a whole on the alert, but it will give it the extra strength needed either to run away or to attack. Merely to look at the snake abstractedly, without identifying it and without sensing danger and experiencing fear, may lead to the highly irrational step of permitting the snake to draw near without being on one's guard against his bite."[18] Emotions, as this example makes clear, are not the opposite of the rational in the conduct of life, and therefore should not be neutralized in order for rational judgments to be made. The emotion of fear in this example is a nonrational inference which provides a means for feeling one's way in a problematic situation to a rational reaction before the rationale becomes conscious.

An encounter with a liberal friend concerning the possibility of war crystallized Mumford's feelings that liberalism had been corrupted, had lost its moral moorings through living by an idealized conception of life. The friend said he could not in any way condone the killing of people in war. The postponing of an inevitable war, even if it meant possibly aggravating the situation, seemed preferable to this friend of Mumford, because "any extra time spared for the private enjoyment of life seemed that much gained." Such an endorsement of living at the cost of all the aims of living seemed to Mumford a spineless attitude, precisely the kind of attitude Hitler was counting on in the Western democracies in order to spread his terror.

In my opinion Dewey's concept that the "context of situation" should provide the ground for social inquiries remains an important antidote to empty formalism and blind empiricism. Yet the clearest evidence of its shortcomings in the practice of life was Dewey's belief on the eve of World War II that the United States should stay out of the impending war against Nazi Germany, because it did not involve the American situation. As he said in 1939, "If we but made up our minds that it is not inevitable, and if we now set ourselves deliberately to seeing that no matter what happens we stay out, we shall save this country from the greatest social catastrophe that could overtake us, the destruction of all the foundations upon which to erect a socialized democracy."[19] Dewey criticized the idea that American involvement was "inevitable" while simultaneously assuming such participation would somehow produce inevitable results.

Perhaps American involvement did lead to the military-industrial-academic complex and McCarthyism after the war—though the former would likely have emerged in any case—but Dewey's localism blinded him to the fact that Western and World Civilization were being subjected to a barbaric assault, an assault from fascism and from within, which would not listen to verbal reasoning. By ignoring the question of civilization as a legitimate broader context of the situation and the possibility that the unreasonable forces unleashed in Hitler's totalitarian ambitions could not be avoided indefinitely, Dewey was unable to see the larger unfolding dynamic of the twentieth century, and was led to a false conclusion concerning American intervention which only the brute facts of Pearl Harbor could change.

Was Mumford the reactionary that the prewar Left attacked him for being? Consider that by the end of World War II Mumford was attacking the allies' adoption of Nazi saturation bombing, both in the firebombing of Dresden and in the nuclear bombing of Hiroshima and Nagasaki. He decried the fall of military standards and limits in the deliberate targeting of civilians. Mumford was among the earliest proponents of nuclear disarmament, having written an essay on the nuclear bomb within a month of the bombing of Hiroshima and a book within a year, as well as helping to organize the first nuclear disarmament movement. He was an early critic of the Vietnam War, expressing opinions publicly in 1965 which again cost him friendships. Mumford's last scholarly book, *The Pentagon of Power* (1970) was, among other things, a fierce attack on the antidemocratic military-industrial-academic establishment.

The concern with the conditions of continuing humane social life in the face of the nuclear war golem and the modern cult of antilife in general becomes central to Mumford's writings after War War II and differentiates him from earlier theorists. In my opinion the emergence of the nuclear age posed new and unavoidable problems for social theory which earlier theorists could not foresee and which most theorists have continued to avoid: the preservation, not only of Western Civilization but of human life and of organic life itself. It is intriguing then, especially given recent discussions of the decline of public intellectuals in America, to consider three unusually sensitive intellectuals who have not avoided this problem. All three came to maturity before the Second World War. They are not usually associated with the academy or with the publicized New York intellectuals of the *Partisan Review*, although they all lived within reach of New York City. These three chose to devote their late work in the 1960s and 1970s to developing "philosophical anthropologies" of the biological and interpretative capacities and limits of the human creature: Mumford, Arthur Koestler, and Suzanne Langer. Mumford's *The Myth of the Machine,* Koestler's *The Ghost in the Machine* and *Janus,* and Langer's three volume *Mind: An Essay on Human Feeling* mark not only breaks with contemporary ethereal conceptions of human conduct and meaning, and with the machine-like reductionism of Darwinian biology, but also provide an outline for the transformation of social theory. In my opinion these three have engaged the basic questions of the life-threatening nuclear age—even if their answers are not always satisfying.[20]

While debating the appropriate response to fascism and developing his critique of pragmatic liberalism in the late 1930s and early 1940s, Mumford was preparing *The Condition of Man,* which was a "usable history" of Western Civilization. His concerns at that time cast an unexpected light on the contemporary debate regarding multiculturalism and Western Civilization.

Stanford University has acted as a focal point in the past few years for the heated controversy regarding multiculturalism and the curriculum of Western Civilization. Stanford multiculturalists attacked the "Eurocentrism" of the Western Civilization curriculum, with the basic claims that a Western-based curriculum was biased in favor of the existing power structure, the legacy of imperialism, racism, class privilege, and patriarchy, that it was too narrow in the context of world culture, that it was in fact an elitist "canon" and ignored the values of a number of minority groups in America, and that the claims to universality of Western Civilization are specious, simply the relative values of a particular culture. The revised curriculum of the late 1980s deleted the term "Western" and changed the name of the eight track course to "Culture, Ideas, and Values," or CIV for short.

As philosopher John Searle, one of the few clear-headed participants in the debate, has noted, the new version retained the Bible, Marx, and Freud in all eight tracks for the course and required readings of "a classical Greek philosopher, an early Christian thinker, a Renaissance dramatist, an Enlightenment thinker," at least one non-European work, including Confucius and the Koran in most of the tracks, and "substantial attention" each quarter to "the issues of *race, gender, and class.*" The eighth track of the course, "Europe and the Americas," was the one most significantly revised, including works by American minority groups alongside European classics, and it was this track which excited the most criticism by neoconservatives.

Searle, despite his strong aversion to the heavy-handed leftist rhetoric of relativist multiculturals, sees the broadened content of the revised curriculum as an improvement over the earlier one, if not the ideologies of its most outspoken promoters.[21] Though the actual curriculum at Stanford has not seemed to change that much, the relativistic reading of the materials used in teaching Western Civilization still holds great import. In my opinion it represents the cultural fragmentation which is characteristic of our time, and specifically a debate rigidly split between fragmatists and foundationalists. Hence, in criticizing the relativism of Stanford multiculturalists, I also must criticize their neoconservative opponents, such as Roger Kimball, for holding on to an ideological concept of a "canon" which must be defended because it upholds the values of Western Civilization.

The source for my critique comes from Stanford's own seemingly forgotten past. About fifty years ago, in 1942, Lewis Mumford went to Stanford, in one of his few connections to university life, as a founding member of the new School of Humanities. As his critiques of fascism and pragmatic liberalism made clear, he was consumed during this period of the thirties and forties with preserving the values of a Western Civilization crumbling into rational barbarism. Remember the Mumford, who in his 1938 book, *The Culture of Cities,* suggested that Western cities were on their way to necropolis, the city of the dead, an outrageous claim in the "Century of Progress," when, as the motto of the 1933 Chicago World's Fair put it: "Science Finds, Industry Applies, Man Conforms." Yet at the end of the Second World War in 1945, a mere seven years after the publication of *The Culture of Cities,* most of the major cities of Europe were necropolises, to be followed, in another few decades, by the self-destruction of many American cities.

Given Mumford's beliefs at the time that Western Civilization was unraveling, that totalitarianism was one of its chief symptoms but by no means the cause, and that what was valuable in the West needed to be cherished and renewed, consider what he had to say about Western Civilization in teaching the basic three-term humanities course. Mumford required the acquisition of six books over the three quarters, chosen, he said, "because they are the most essential expressions of their culture; because they furnish an indispensable key to the understanding of the ultimate beliefs and the daily practices of the peoples who have been closely affected by these books, and because they offer an approach to fundamental tasks of worldwide intercourse and spiritual traffic upon which the future development of our whole civilization depends." Now perhaps the relativist, multiculturalist reader may have noticed that Mumford invoked ideas of essentialism and a grand narrative of history, ideas which are strictly verboten in postmodern times.

Consider the first two books on Mumford's list: the Bible and Plato's *Republic,* works as canonical as one can get.[22] Yet consider what Mumford had to say about the Bible: "The bible not merely contains the history and literature of the Jews, through the formative stages of their existence; but it connects the Christian culture that grew out of it with the more ancient civilizations of Egypt and Babylonia, and it is an indispensable aid to the understanding of Moslem thought, which followed so close on the Christian dispensation that it was at first regarded as a mere heresy."

Now consider the third book, which Mumford saw as having universal value and as a particularly important source for a world at war. This basic Stanford humanities book from fifty years ago is the *Bhagavad Gita,* and as Mumford describes it, "It arises out of the conflict that goes on in the soul of Arjuna on the eve of battle, as he finds himself confronted with the odious task of fighting with intent to kill against his relatives and against enemies who had once been friends. The conflict is brought out in a debate with Krishna, one of the ultimate forms of Hindu Godhood; and the morality of selfless action, mindful of immediate duties but unconcerned as to results, which is upheld by Krishna, is among other things an answer to the pacifist's problem of how to live in a world where force plays a part, without submitting to brute power—and therefore to inhumanity and injustice—or being forced to surrender all one's own values in resisting it."

In addition to the *Bhagavad Gita,* Mumford's list of six books included Lucretius's *On the Nature of Things,* a standard work of the Western tradition, and also two classics from the East, *The Analects of Confucius,* and Lao-Tse, *The Tao Teh Ching.* To top off the list, Mumford included Emerson's *Essays,* a work which clearly exemplifies the American perspective on the humanistic tradition. But read how Mumford describes this American source and its import for the School of Humanities: "Emerson is the Representative Man of humanism in America; and his essays, with their sudden flashes of wisdom and prophetic insight, have not merely stirred successive generations of Americans, beginning with his own younger contemporaries, Thoreau and Whitman, but they have a special meaning for us in the New World, in that they add the precious fruits of our pioneer experience to the older wisdom that Emerson had absorbed. Plato and Plutarch were among Emerson's most prized treasures; but in reaching out toward the poetry of the Persians and the Hindus—that of the Chinese was not available in his day—Emerson set the example for that wider humanism, embracing the East no less than the West, which the School of Humanities stands for today." That "wider humanism, embracing the East no less than the West," seems strangely near to and distant from the Stanford School of Humanities and the multiculturalism debate of today.

Listen to Mumford's Memorandum on the General Education Plan for Stanford University, where he says, "I would suggest that the precedent set by the present course on Western Civilization be carried farther, as follows. Three quarters on primitive civilizations: Amerindian, African, and Eastern. These courses would lay the necessary factual background for the systematic course on anthropology which would follow. The next three quarters should be devoted to the ancient civilizations of the west: Babylonia, Egypt, Greece and Rome. The third three quarters would deal with a survey of Eastern civilizations, and in the final year modern Western civilization from the fall of Rome down to the present day should be the object of study. The most serious lack at the present time is a survey of Eastern civilizations comparable to that which we have devoted to the west. This is an unpardonable provinciality in a world which has invented the cable, the airplane and the radio."

In his 1942–43 description for a course on "The Nature of Man" Mumford further stated his position on the necessity of multiculturalism as a means to understanding "the universal nature of man's higher culture." One sees too his organic vision of human culture and the self as continuous with biology and emergent evolution:

> This course will attempt to describe the whole nature of man: it will therefore not merely utilize all the material made available in the humanities, but will also include the more definite and stable conclusions of the sciences. The standpoint will be that of an "organic humanism." Unlike the humanists of the renaissance, we will not dissociate literature and the arts from the practical life of society, nor will we ascribe an exaggerated value to the literature of Greece and Rome alone. On the contrary: we will treat the humanities as part of the natural history of man, will show how the higher activities emerge from man's biological and social nature, and we will emphasize, whenever possible, the universal nature of man's higher culture. To this end, we will introduce as soon as possible some of the poetry and philosophy of the non-European cultures, Hindu and Chinese in particular. Unlike the New Humanism of Babbitt and his followers, we shall not hold to the assumption of a dualism between man's original nature and his values: Morgan's doctrine of "emergence" provides a sounder approach to the series of ascending relations which begin with brute matter and culminate in the personality. The first half of the course will be largely a reinterpretation of the commonplaces of biology, anthropology, and sociology, for which the student will, in varying degrees, be prepared. The second part will deal more specifically with the nature and function of the humanities, taken in their widest sense, in the life of man. At this point, I believe, original texts in the humanities should serve to focus the student's thinking and give it concrete illustration. The selection of these texts will require further reflection and experiment.

One half of a century ago Mumford was at Stanford calling for an inclusiveness quite similar to that demanded by many multiculturalists today. But his reason for including non-Western sources at Stanford, namely, that these were works which transcended the cultures and civilizations in which they arose, were diametrically opposed to the relativistic premises of many contemporary multiculturalists.[23] One possibly legitimate critique of Mumford by contemporary multiculturalists might be an underemphasis on ethnic, class, and gender diversities in portraying American culture and history in general. Here the crucial question is what role do these factors play within the *civilizational* context.

Mumford was calling for a general education which would make a big picture of the varieties and continuities of humanity available to students, because he believed that a deep sense of history, cultural diversity, *and* common humanity was essential both to a humanistic education, and to a world culture in the making, and that a humanistic education must address the whole person, not simply the intellectual portion. His outlook could not be more at odds with the postmodern temper and its view that everything is a question of ideology.

Again the emotions, as well as aesthetic and moral standards of discrimination and judgment, weighed heavily in Mumford's view of education:

> If we are to create balanced human beings, capable of entering into world-wide co-operation with all other men of good will—and that is the supreme task of our generation, and the foundation of all its other potential achievements—we must give as much weight to the arousal of the emotions and to the expression of moral and esthetic values as we now give to science, to invention, to practical organization. One without the other is impotent. And values do not come ready-made: they are achieved by a resolute attempt to square the facts of one's own experience with the historic patterns formed in the past by those who devoted their whole lives to achieving and expressing values. If we are to express the love in our own hearts, we must also understand what love meant to Socrates and Saint Francis, to Dante and Shakespeare, to Emily Dickinson and Christina Rossetti, to the explorer Shackleton and to the intrepid physicians who deliberately exposed themselves to yellow fever. These historic manifestations of love are not recorded in the day's newspaper or the current radio program: they are hidden to people who possess only fashionable minds. Virtue is not a chemical product, as Taine once described it: it is a historic product, like language and literature; and this means that if we cease to care about it, cease to cultivate it, cease to transmit its funded values, a large part of it will become meaningless, like a dead language to which we have lost the key. That, I submit, is what has happened in our own lifetime.[24]

The cultivation of moral and aesthetic values and emotions became a hot potato in twentieth-century educational life in America. Public schools, from kindergarten through college, absorbed many of the tasks formerly centered in the church and family. But the cultivation of values and virtues in universities was taken to be primarily an intellectual task rather than also moral and aesthetic. Hence the cultivation of passions and standards of discrimination and discipline requisite for passionate living were too often relegated to "physical education," or worse, to collegiate spectator sport. Values and emotions were either etherealized into abstract mind, whether modern or postmodern, or materialized into gladiatorial spectacle, into Ariel or Caliban. There is little place for a Prospero, the agent and mediator of values and emotional life, in such an educational system.

Mumford's lament in 1946 that virtue has become meaningless, "like a dead language to which we have lost the key," resonates with the recent work of philosopher Alasdair MacIntyre in his 1981 book *After Virtue* and subsequent works. MacIntyre's critique of the fragmentation of moral reasoning and language and his defense of the virtues as real components of the human self so grates against contemporary intellectual life that he begins *After Virtue* using the metaphor of a catastrophe which has gone virtually unrecognized. He shows how the conception of morality as involving a whole self, that is, one embedded within a variety of social groups and a cultural tradition and also capable of acting from, while cultivating, the goal of a good life, "is something that ceases to be generally available at some point in the progress—if we can call it such—towards and into modernity."[25] In place of a whole self oriented by the goal of a good life, contemporary social life in MacIntyre's view is the realization of the bifurcated modern world depicted earlier by Max Weber, characterized by an organizational realm whose depersonalized rational ends are taken for granted and a personal realm of the "emotivist self," whose subjectivist ends are ultimately criterionless.

MacIntyre believes that this modern worldview must be rejected through a renewal of local community and the practices which contribute to making the good life in Aristotle's sense. He urges a retreat from "the new dark ages" we have entered similar to that undertaken at the end of the Roman imperium, and in this echoes Mumford's call in 1970 to withdraw from "the pentagon of power." Yet Mumford, despite his pessimism concerning the power complex, hoped for more than the endurance of the tradition of the virtues:

> How long, those who are now awake must ask themselves, how long can the physical structure of an advanced technology hold together when all its human foundations are crumbling away? . . . the human institutions and moral convictions that have taken thousands of years to achieve even minimal efficacy have disappeared before our eyes: so completely that the next generation will scarcely believe they ever existed. . . . The Roman empire in the East won a new lease on life by coming to terms with Christian-

ity. . . . But it must be remembered that this intermixture of Roman and Christian institutions was achieved at the expense of creativity. So until the disintegration of our own society has gone even further, there is reason to look for a more vigorous life-promoting solution. Whether such a response is possible depends upon an unknown factor: how viable are the formative ideas that are now in the air, and how ready are our contemporaries to undertake the efforts and sacrifices that are essential for human renewal? . . . Has Western civilization reached the point in etherialization where detachment and withdrawal will lead to the assemblage of an organic world picture, in which the human personality in all its dimensions will have primacy over its biological needs and technological pressures? . . . When the moment comes to replace power with plenitude, compulsive external rituals with internal, self-imposed discipline, depersonalization with individuation, automation with autonomy, we shall find that the necessary change of attitude has been going on beneath the surface during the last century, and the long buried seeds of a richer human culture are now ready to strike root and grow, as soon as the ice breaks up and the sun reaches them. If that growth is to prosper, it will draw freely on the compost from many previous cultures.[26]

IMPLICATIONS OF MUMFORDIAN SOCIAL THEORY: IMAGINATIVE REALISM

Mumford's indictment of the consequences of the "myth of the megamachine" in modern life is indeed broad in scope but by no means indiscriminate, as a number of his critics claimed. Throughout his work he was ever the advocate of the broader possibilities inherent, if insufficiently realized, in modernity, and of the genuine and enduring achievements in political, cultural, and scientific life the modern world has produced. Yet throughout his career, his criticism of many aspects of modern culture as forms of regression rather than truly modern or progressive led many critics to call him a reactionary antimodernist, a Luddite, a dreamer. In the first volume of the new journal of reviews of the American Sociological Association, for example, Lewis Coser reviewed *The Pentagon of Power*.[27] His review illustrates the typical inability of the sociological academy to deal with thought that upsets established canon. Instead of seriously confronting Mumford's reconstructive critique of modernity, Coser caricatures him as a prophet of gloom who "hates almost all modern ideas and modern accomplishments without discrimination." Unfortunately Coser misses Mumford's tempered praise of Marx's critique of specialization, or his acknowledgment of the many positive goods modern technology has produced and which remain important ingredients for an organic world culture. In Mumford's words, "The only effective way to overcome the power system is to transfer its more helpful agents to an organic complex. And it is in and through the human person that the invitation to plenitude begins and ends.[28]

Others have challenged Mumford's appeals for the remaking of cities, selves, and civilization as antidemocratic. His call for organic planning as an antidote for unplanned, megamechanical sprawl makes him into a "philosopher-king" in the eyes of many, such as Jane Jacobs, who believe that a deliberate planning approach toward a city as a whole is a direct challenge to democratic pluralism. As mentioned earlier, both Mumford and Jacobs were allies against Robert Moses and his style of deliberate planning for the city of New York, which served the needs of automobiles for hegemony but which had devastating effects on citizens and their neighborhoods. In Mumford's view, neither the megalomania of Moses's authoritarian planning nor what he saw as the dogmatic localism of Jacobs, which seemed to base itself largely on the avoidance of crime, were sufficiently broad to serve the interests of democratic pluralism. I agree in the main with Mumford's criticism of Jacobs, but perhaps he undervalued the place of spontaneous unplanned events in neighborhood and city life to which her work sought to draw attention.

Mumford decried the destructive, monopolizing effects of the automobile, "the chief architect of the American city," but he also believed that it should have its place within a varied system of transportation. The common prejudice of American individualism is that any intervention on the "free market" of the automobile industry leads to increased government coercion, as though the history of the rise to power of the American autombile and oil companies after World War II is free from government and big industry power plays, quite removed from the "vox populi." Such a view cheerfully ignores the evisceration and malling of the American city which auto-culture has helped bring about: the ultimate auto-da-fé. Mumford's main concern was to advocate the planning of cities, regions and transportation systems which would place some restrictions on the use of the auto in order to preserve a livable city.

Mumford proposed the outlines of a new epoch, but that large-scale vision or "big picture" is anathema to a time in which the Right has celebrated capitalistic minimalism in government and socialistic maximalism in that portion of the government which is the military machine, while the Left celebrates "neopragmatist" situationalism: both allow the underlying premisses of modernity to go uncriticized and disallow any such large-scale criticisms—as long as people can drive their cars in and out of their unlivable cities. The deepest American thinkers—Melville, Charles Peirce, Lewis Mumford—held dark visions concerning the direction of the modern era, visions which have been too easily buried by the glib American optimism, and by that rationalism which must lampoon that which falls outside of its delimited domain. Mumford's *The Pentagon of Power* is such a dark vision, a critique of that systematized mechanization in modern culture which would divest the world of human purposes, as well as a passionate call for a rehumanized technology.

Although generally sympathetic to Mumford's outlook, even his biographer, Donald Miller, echoes the dread of passionate critique which is so pervasive of academic intellectuals, and which explains in part perhaps why Mumford's writings have held only marginal significance thus far in professional intellectual life, when he says of *The Pentagon of Power:* "Later that summer he resumed work on his book, which, not surprisingly, turned into an all-out attack on the culture that he considered responsible for his failure to gain wider influence as a writer. *The Pentagon of Power* is belligerent in tone and piercingly polemical. Analysis turns too often to assertion, considered criticism to sweeping condemnation. The enemy is misapplied science and technology—nothing new here; but it is the culture that Mumford believes they have brought about, whose corruptions run from television to LSD, that comes under the heaviest fire."[29] Miller suggests that Mumford's motive in writing *The Pentagon of Power* had a strong tinge of revenge against the culture which ignored him. Note that the word "polemical" is assumed by Miller, as for many academics (and for many Americans), to be negative, as, elsewhere, "moralizing" is as well. In my opinion Miller's commitment as a historian to details and particulars causes him to lose sight of the larger vision which informed Mumford's critique—or perhaps of the philosophical temperament in general—and of the possibility that impassioned critique need not conform to the dispassionate standards of the academy in order to hit its targets accurately.

Another type of thinker temperamentally opposed to, and perhaps threatened by, Mumford's work is the apologist for science. In his review of Mumford's book *The Pentagon of Power,* featured in *The New York Times Sunday Book Review,* the historian of science Gerald Holton, a committed defender of the rational scientific faith, revealed the fear and loathing of the rational ego and of established science when confronted with impassioned reason. Mumford, after all, had not only dared to hit hard against the scientific establishment, and to claim that it was destructive of human life, but also argued that modern science is based on a falsely mechanical worldview which provides an inadequate conception of science. In criticizing Mumford, Holton said,

> We have no one to blame but ourselves for the fact that the image Mumford paints of science and technology is so monstrously distorted and may be so widely believed. . . . For before anyone dismisses science as the bad habits of inhuman robots rather than seeing it as a successful method— within its limits—for understanding the world we live in, including our minds, bodies and societies, he had better realize that at the center of every major problem upsetting us these days there sits, among other ignorances, also ignorance of scientific facts. . . . Ironically Mumford does not touch, let alone name and expose, the actual technocratic barons and baboons who are responsible for many of the excesses of uncontrolled technology. Instead—and this is a harbinger of consequences to come from the book—Mumford falls into his own trap and turns on those with whom he should forge an alliance against common enemies.[30]

In Holton's assumption that science has proven itself a "successful method" whose misuse is really due to "technocratic barons and baboons" rather than to scientists themselves and the premises which have underlain science thus far, and in suggesting that Mumford should have recognized scientists as allies against the bad misusers rather than as themselves implicated in the evils which science has wrought, we see an excellent example of the very insulated mentality of established science which Mumford criticized in the book, a mentality that sees clearly how outsiders may be ignorant of it, but which is blind to the possibility that it may be ignorant of realities which fall outside of its own rationality.

Mumford's criticism might lend itself, in Holton's judgment, to an irrational reaction against science, and this was automatically assumed by Holton to be worse than the pristine, morally untouchable world of science and technology. At a time when physicists worked on the dole at the Los Alamos secret military nuclear weapons laboratories (I personally remember a conversation with one Los Alamos lab director who said, "It's all right, they [the military] let you do what you want), when former Nazi S.S. Officer and V-2 terror rocket specialist Wernher von Braun directed the American space rocket program, when the overwhelming source of money for basic computer research came from the Pentagon, when tons of napalm bombs were routinely dropped on Vietnamese villages, when the nuclear bomb pimp Herman Kahn advocated detonating scores of underground explosions in Pennsylvania to provide natural gas—which would have been lethally radioactive and unusable—in short, at a time when the cult of Big Science and technology in

America and elsewhere was thoroughly corrupted and fit for the looney bin, the good Professor Holton sought to defend it from severe criticism and to immunize it from the "irrational" and to place all burdens on outsiders, whose chief task is to assimilate scientific knowledge.

Even today Holton's faith in benevolent rational science has hardly diminished. In his book *The Advancement of Science and Its Burdens,* published in 1986, he said, "The marriage of science and technology is undoubtedly permanent and beneficial to each," and went on to cite as an example that "the design of industrial products of biotechnology follows by only a few years or even months the latest results of basic research in genetics and molecular biology."[31] Holton's cheerful optimism that commerce can capitalize so quickly on basic research in biotechnology gives a chill to anyone concerned with the public nature of science and the problem of biotechnology outracing the limits of ethical and safety standards, not to mention the whole Pandora's box that marriage also opened up in the twentieth century. His moral blindness to the fact that actually existing science itself is deeply implicated in the destructive forces unleashed in our time reminds one of those Western intellectuals, who when confronted with the brutalities of Stalinism defended them as necessary evils in order for progress to occur. "Big science," practiced by scientists in institutions which are typically receiving moneys from the Pentagon and which freely allow the Pentagon's military priorities to receive increased attention, deserves the closest public scrutiny, not lickspittle apologetics.

If we turn to the man who has emerged as the chief spokesman for the humane spirit in the last decade of the twentieth century, Vaclav Havel, we see a deep resonance with the organic worldview developed by Mumford. Havel's key essay of 1978, "The Power of the Powerless," depicts a "post-totalitarian system" in which the preservation of power by a dictator or ruling clique is no longer the inner aim of the system but rather, he says, "the social phenomenon of self-preservation is subordinated to something higher, to a kind of blind *automatism* which drives the system. . . . Part of the essence of the post-totalitarian system is that it draws everyone into its sphere of power, not so they may realize themselves as human beings, but so they may surrender their human identity in favour of the identity of the system, that is, so they may become agents of the system's general automatism and servants of its self-determined goals, so they may participate in the common responsibility for it, so they may be pulled into and ensnared by it, like Faust with Mephistopheles."[32] Such a system, in Havel's view, promotes "living within a lie" as against "living in truth," and in doing so subverts the very means to an identity.

The conditions for a humane life are to be found in the conditions of life itself, as Havel sees it, and, in taking life itself as a starting point for human freedom, he reveals both his resonance with Mumford and his opposition to the cult of antilife which dominates the systematizers and "post-systematizers" of social theory today:

> Between the aims of the post-totalitarian system and the aims of life there is a yawning abyss: while life, in its essence, moves towards plurality, diversity, independent self-constitution and self organization, in short, towards the fulfillment of its own freedom, the post-totalitarian system demands conformity, uniformity, and discipline. While life ever strives to create new and "improbable" structures, the post-totalitarian system contrives to force life into its most probable states. . . . The essential aims of life are present naturally in every person. In everyone there is some longing for humanity's rightful dignity, for moral integrity, for free expression of being and a sense of transcendence over the world of existence. Yet, at the same time, each person is capable of coming to terms with living within the lie. Each person somehow succumbs to a profane trivialization of his or her inherent humanity, and to utilitarianism."[33]

To suggest that there might be an inherent humanity, that the aims of life—of "rightful dignity," moral integrity, or free expression of being—might be present naturally in people, as well as the tendency to deny and destroy life-aims by living within the lie, these are utter blasphemies to the ideological bent which now dominates social theory.

In the great tradition of modern social thought, Mumford questions those modern patterns of thought and conduct that have tended to diminish rather than enhance human capacities and possibilities, that have raised the mechanical worldview to an unquestioned centrality in the conduct of life—even though its scientific significance has long since been exploded—and that have, to an extent no department of the academy is willing to admit, led to destructive, life-denying, self-annulling consequences. Whether in its reified or etherealized manifestations, the megamachine of modernity tends to treat the human part as the whole human, as though either critical rational intelligence or brute force alone were independently sufficient to direct social life. His critique of modern life calls for a renewal, a fundamental transformation of the entrenched patterns of thought and conduct peculiar to the modern era in particular and to civilization in general. There are hopeful signs of a renewal of interest in Mumford's project today among architectural critics and urban planners, social theorists and historians. Yet it seems to me that the larger vision he proposed, that of a transformation not only of modern civilization but of the dynamics which have thus far motivated civilizational humankind, has remained as a blind spot even to many of those interested in his work, including his own biographer Donald Miller, when not actively denigrated as a mere "jeremiad."

The idea that critical rational intelligence can by itself bring about the conditions for a free and vital social life is simply insufficient, as is the alternative idea that the blind power and will of *Realpolitik* can by force create the good life. Perhaps the ultimate meaning of modernity has been to develop critical, rational capacities while simultaneously showing how self-destructive and world-destructive they can be when uprooted from the deeper sources of tempered bodily and imaginative intelligence.

The great attempt by modern thinkers such as Hegel and Marx, and by the political legacies of their ideas, to equate the rational with the actual in the name of freedom has failed, as those "psychic seismographs" of the twentieth century, Henry Adams or Mumford, long ago sensed, and as anyone not benumbed by the megamachine or beguiled by its avatars can now see. The Holocaust and the German State which produced it were both actual and highly rationalized: Should we call them reasonable? The rational may be actual, but both the actual, existence itself, and the reasonable are extrarational. The confusion of the actual with the rational has produced massive unfreedom in the world: whether in the guise of the grim face of totalitarianism, Left or Right, or the great guffaw of Americanism, the cardinal rule seems to be to deny reality in the name of some rational ideology.

Henry Adams and the architect Louis Sullivan saw in the Chicago Columbian Exhibition of 1893 the ominous signs of the twentieth century, clothed in electric dynamos and Greek temples. Sullivan felt the effect of the Greco-Roman revivalism to be disastrous for American democracy, claiming that millions of people "departed joyously, carriers of contagion, unaware that what they had beheld and believed to be truth was to prove, in historic fact, an appalling calamity . . . a naked exhibitionism of charlantry in the higher feudal and domineering culture, conjoined with expert salesmanship of the materials of decay." Sullivan, like Adams, sensed the coming antidemocratic culture of mass consumerism, the remaking of life as an entertainment. Today, when the high nostalgia of neoclassic architecture has fused itself with its seeming opposite, ascetic modernism, to produce the titillating pasties of postmodern architecture, as found, say, in the works of Phillip Johnson and John Burgee or of Michael Graves, Sullivan's and Adams's prophetic intuitions have a renewed significance. But the contemporary rational mind is embarrassed by the human capacity *to sense* and passionately interpret the deeper import of things, and so belittles this interpretive sensitivity by labeling it "prophecy," as though it were hocus pocus. Or it derides it as a mere "jeremiad," as though critique must be synonymous with weak tea in order to appear objective. I submit that it was precisely the passion which infused Mumford's work which allowed him to react quickly and objectively to the unavoidable threat of fascism while most intellectuals remained fogbound. It enabled him to write the anti-nuclear weapon essays immediately after Hiroshima and Nagasaki, it enabled him to see the futility and wrongheadedness of the Vietnam War in 1965, before many intellectuals reached a measured position. Passion is simply not the opposite of reason, though it can be, just as rationality can be.

Throughout his work, Lewis Mumford intuitively sensed the signs of the times, manifest as architecture, cities, technics, personalities, and the very fabric of twentieth-century life. If we attempt to fathom the present in that same spirit, and sense, however darkly, its possible purport, omens abound. Our cities and intellectual life are rife with postmodernism, a movement that claimed to break out of modern architecture and its dominant rational box by lopping off the corners or pasting on an ornament, or to break out of "logocentrism" in intellectual life by a freewheeling irrationalism or "anti-" or "post-humanism." Aside from the problem that so-called postmodernism simply inverts or varies the premisses of modernism rather than creating genuinely new ones, it is also instructive to place the positive valuation of "post-" in postmodernism next to the negative valuation of "post-" in Mumford's discussions of "Posthistorical Man." Instead of transcending history, posthistorical man is deprived of it, whereas postmodern man and woman, whether neoconservative or neoanarchist, are deprived not only of living history but also of those positive impulses of modernity. In this perspective, postmodernism becomes the ultimate form of self-alienation, reduced to scavenging an unfelt past or ravaging an unfelt present.

Or let us turn to one of the great mythic rituals of our time, the Olympics. Every four years there opens up a ritual "sacred space" as mortals and the gods touch through the immortal Olympic Flame. The ceremony of the Olympic torch is actually modern, having begun with the 1936 Berlin Olympics and therefore conceivably tainted by the Nazi penchant for pseudoancient spectacle. Nevertheless, the lighting of the Olympic Flame with a torch taken from the site of the ancient Games and passed hand-to-hand over great distances has become a powerful symbol of human continuity and transcendence. Yet those who saw the opening of the 1984 Los Angeles Olympic Games know that no human hand touched the gods. Instead, an athlete ignited a machine of fire, in the form of the Olympic Rings, which raced upward to a chimney tower beyond human reach. There the machine of fiery rings automatically brought the Olympic Torch to flame in a literal chain reaction. The sacred flame had already been pimped from coast to coast to anyone who would pay money to run with it, itself a sign of the professionalization of the games, but the capitalization of the sacred was merely a prelude to the mechanization of the sacred: the great flaming metallic chain towered above the human form, the ceremonial performance of Beethoven's ode "To Joy" gave way to the great guffaw of American rock-and-roll entertainment; a Hollywood actor disguised as an American president presided over a thoroughly unspontaneous script of Yahooism. The date, the city, the president, the nation, the ritual symbolism all signify our time as the dynamos did for Henry Adams.

Given the ritual celebration of technical, disembodied automatism in the lighting of the Olympic Fire, is it any wonder that the misbegotten dreams of the *Challenger* space shuttle or Chernobyl should have exploded in our faces soon after? We, who have lost the ability to touch the gods of our fates and to accept the limits of our biological being, gave birth to dreams of throwing a "star wars" military machine to the heavens and sacrificing to it human politics, with all its uncertainties. We commodified the human body, separated it from humane relations and its own organic mysteries through multiple anonymous sex and dirty drug needles, commercially motivated blood and plasma banks, and reaped the firestorm beginnings of the AIDS epidemic in the 1980s, a firestorm fueled by the Reagan administration's delay and discouragement tactics for research and public health information based purely on ideological grounds of political correctness. We race ever faster in our "inevitable" progress toward ecological disaster. We perfect a machine-world "virtual reality" while denying the possibility that being human involves the deepest natural needs. Posthistoric man, postbiological genderless person, postmodernity: we are in reality perhaps the first posthumans. To my mind, the world is fast unraveling, and Bhopal, Chernobyl, the rapid initial spread of AIDS in the early 1980s from commodified body exchanges, *Challenger* and its defective "O" rings, the realization of a growing hole in the ozone layer of the atmosphere, and the fiery Olympic rings of 1984 were but the "opening ceremonies" to the next phase of human self-sacrifice and megamechanical madness. Did democracy really defeat communism at the conclusion of the 1980s, or was it defeated by the smoother running electronic machines of the West?

IN LEWIS MUMFORD'S TWO-VOLUME INTERPRETATION of *The Myth of the Machine* and earlier works, and in his organic, biocosmic alternative, new foundations are laid which can begin to renew social theory. His work forms a "speculative grammar," to borrow an expression from Duns Scotus, for a new social philosophy and truly nonmodern world picture. This new world picture, as I see it in Mumford and in a few others, such as Charles Peirce, rejects rationality's grandiose claim to be equated with actuality or reality. Instead of Hegel's maxim that the rational is actual and the actual is rational, it holds that the fantastic is involved in the real and that the real is fantastic, and that both are greater than the actual or rational. We live in a fantastic reality, whose purport we can but dimly perceive. Those beliefs that can most fully capture and convey the wonder of things—of creation, of organic growth and decay, of the drama and tragedy of human existence, of its unending follies, its brutalizations of truth and decency, and of its deepest motivations to participate in and question the incarnate cosmos—those beliefs are what are needed to animate a renewed world culture and civilization today. Such beliefs cannot be solely rationally founded, for the rational alone is too meager and rootless to act as inspiration for enduring belief. Such beliefs cannot be arbitrary, for the same reasons. Such beliefs have to be organically rooted in life itself, with its capacity for transformation, growth, and renewal, and in a realization that rationality, necessary though it is, remains a limited organ of a greater reasonableness.

Lewis Mumford created a body of work in which the human form stands in its wholeness, transilluminated. Although he draws from the guiding ideas of modern social theory, his work fundamentally challenges its premises and, in so doing, shows the way to a transformation of social theory and an outline for a new human epoch. Such an outline is but a suggestive, and necessarily incomplete, understanding of the prospects we face. But it gets to the root of the problem of modern life, in my opinion, whereas much in contemporary thought is merely an example of the problem itself. The outlines of a transformed social theory are also suggested by the philosophy of Charles Peirce, to which I now turn.

5

The Transilluminated Vision of Charles Peirce

The agility of the tongue is shown in its insisting that the world depends upon it.

Charles Peirce[1]

Most, if not all of you, are, I doubt not, Nominalists; and I beg you will not take offence at a truth which is just as plain and undeniable to me as is the truth that children do not understand human life. To be a nominalist consists in the undeveloped state in one's mind of the apprehension of Thirdness as Thirdness. The remedy for it consists in allowing ideas of human life to play a greater part in one's philosophy. Metaphysics is the science of Reality. Reality consists in regularity. Real regularity is active law. Active law is efficient reasonableness, or in other words is truly reasonable reasonableness. Reasonable reasonableness is Thirdness as Thirdness.

Charles Peirce[2]

The 1930s were a terrible decade for book burnings in Europe, but one of the most deadly and least noticed occurred in America in 1939. In that year the bulk of Charles Peirce's book collection and perhaps also his two hundred thousand or so note cards were burned by the people who had purchased his home after the death of his wife, Juliette Froissy. Apparently the new owners tried to sell the books in good American fashion, and finding no buyers simply consigned them to the flames as worthless. Peirce believed that one should converse with one's books through annotation, and his books were filled with his marginal comments. Philosophy and American culture lost a treasure with that burning, just as they had earlier come within a hairsbreadth of losing all of Peirce's papers after his death in 1914 (until Harvard paid the vast and magnanimous fee of five hundred dollars to Peirce's widow, for what amounted to seventy or more volumes of manuscripts).

That cremation of Peirce's books in 1939 was a sardonic scenario which marked the centenary of his birth and the twenty-fifth anniversary of his death. It symbolized as starkly as possible the decline of American philosophy and the eclipse of pragmatism.

Peirce is generally regarded as the founder of philosophical pragmatism, and, with Saussure, of modern semeiotic, and also as one of the founders of mathematical or symbolic logic. An original contributor to a number of natural sciences, he was also deeply absorbed by linguistic researches throughout his life, learning languages in remote areas while travelling on geodetic surveys. His first published paper was on Shakespearean pronunciation. A natural scientist by training and the son of the eminent mathematician Benjamin Peirce, he developed the philosophical basis of semeiotic in a series of articles in the late 1860s ("Questions Concerning Certain Capacities Claimed for Man," "Some Consequences of Four Incapacities"). There Peirce leveled a devastating critique of Cartesian philosophy and foundationalism, arguing that all cognition is irreducibly triadic (whence comes "Thirdness"), of the nature of a sign, fallible, and thoroughly immersed in a continuing process of interpretation. He considered his semeiotic (as he spelled it, in contrast with current usage of "semiotics" as an inclusive term for all the various studies of signs) as a general theory of logic, and saw language as but a portion of semeiosis. Some of Peirce's letters to Lady Welby were included in the appendix to Ogden and Richards's *The Meaning of Meaning,* and, with Charles Morris's largely unacknowledged appropriation of Peirce's ideas in his influential monograph *Foundations of the Theory of Signs* (1938), Peirce's ideas were problematically introduced to a broader community.[3] His semeiotic, though systematically distorted by Charles Morris's positivism and the unthinking acceptance of Morris's pseudo-Peircean, pseudo-Meadian "pragmatics," nevertheless revealed a more supple understanding of signification than that provided by Saussurean semiology.

Peirce's writings are pervaded by triadic divisions, which, given that he felt himself to be at heart a mathematician, he expressed most basically in numerical form as Firstness, Secondness, and Thirdness. While still in his twenties Peirce first began to formulate these divisions using personal pronouns: I (Firstness), IT (Secondness), and THOU (Thirdness). Firstness means a quality considered by itself, Secondness indicates brute reaction, and Thirdness signifies thought, representation, triadic relation, or mediation. The three categories are irreducible, but Firstness is involved in Secondness, and Firstness and Secondness are involved in Thirdness.

In Peirce's evolutionary cosmology, Thirdness, or triadic relation, or semeiosis, is considered to be a fact of the universe and not simply limited to the human mind, and therein lies the difference between Peirce and Kant, and between Peirce and much of modern linguistics and language theory. By Peirce's semeiotic realism language does not simply refer to things outside of signs. Though largely of a conventional nature, language is a mode of conduct and, as such, produces conceivable consequences and is normatively bounded.

In its abilities to body forth new possibilities for conduct, to determine and be determined by further experience, and to communicate valid generals bearing conceivable consequences, language is *real,* in Peirce's nonmodern version of semeiotic realism. Note that reality is a conditional in Peirce's view, a would-be rather than an existent, of the nature of a general sign rather than of material particulars. Both his realism and pragmatism are theoretically at odds with the positivism and behaviorism of Charles Morris, and to the nominalist conventionalism of Saussure and more recent neopragmatists and poststructuralists. Though linguists and semioticians have been most fascinated by Peirce's elaborate triadic technical divisions of signs, such as icon, index, and symbol and type, token and (usually ignored) tone, the larger philosophical outlook and anthropology underlying those divisions have yet to be incorporated into linguistic studies, and yet to be fully appreciated and utilized in the human studies.

Just the year before the burning of Peirce's books, the *International Encyclopedia of Unified Science* made its debut and served as a sort of manifesto for the positivist movement, which was in the process of taking over American philosophy. The introductory volume, with programmatic contributions by Otto Neurath, Niels Bohr, John Dewey, Bertrand Russell, Rudolph Carnap, and Charles Morris, was to serve as a background to the "International Congress for the Unity of Science" at Harvard University from September 5–10, 1939. By Reason's fantastic cunning, the Peirce Sesquicentennial International Congress met exactly fifty years later at exactly the same place where pragmatism was to have been buried by positivism.

Dewey was a reluctant participant in the volume, and from the fervor of some of its positivist contributors one can see why. Positivism was to be the wave of the future, and pragmatism was merely the somewhat fuzzy "preparation" for positivism. As Neurath put it in the introductory essay: "The fact that Peirce was a logician and simultaneously interested in empiricism was in turn important for the preparation of modern scientific empiricism in the United States."[4] Peirce was not exactly forgotten but simply treated as a "forerunner" to positivism, as is also evident in Charles Morris's words: "Logic thus rests, as Peirce maintained, on a general theory of signs, formal logic tracing the relations between signs within a language. So conceived, logic deals with the language in which statements about nature are made, and does not itself make statements about the nonlinguistic world. . . . The clear development of this view and the utilization of the methods of the new logic within the framework of empiricism are the significant achievements of logical empiricism as represented by the Vienna Circle (Carnap, Frank, Hahn, Neurath, Schlick) and by Russell, Wittgenstein, and Reichenbach."[5] Morris held a linear modernist's view of progress—what is happening now must be better than what went before—and was a true believer in the positivist/Cartesian quest to construct an infallible, scientific foundation for philosophy.

Not only did Morris contribute to the view that pragmatism was a vague anticipation of positivism, which would exhibit "the clear development of this view," but in his statement that logic is limited to a linguistic world we see that fundamental misinterpretation of Peirce's semeiotic which was to run wild in Morris's monograph *Foundations of the Theory of Signs,* which also appeared in 1938 as the first monograph in the unified science series. Perhaps it is no exaggeration to say that Morris did for Peirce's semeiotic what the new owners of Peirce's house in Milford did for his books. But general ideas are not as easily extinguished as particular books, and are, like the Phoenix, capable of being reborn from the ashes of systematic ideological distortion.

The severe ascetic face of modernism, in its guise as logical positivism, and later as language analysis, assumed a virtual hegemony in postwar Anglo-American academic philosophy. Imbued with the quest to overcome history and open-ended interpretation, so-called logical empiricism seemed to show how philosophical foundations could be secured. But this movement, based on an apparent misunderstanding of Wittgenstein's distinction between the limits of knowledge and that which can only be directly shown, was scarcely established in America before Wittgenstein's "second school," rooted in the use-context of language, began to displace it. Ironically, the logical positivists helped to displace pragmatism in its home turf, at the University of Chicago. Morris helped Carnap to escape Nazi Europe in the thirties by bringing him to the University of Chicago. There Morris, who had been a student of George Herbert Mead, sought to "improve" pragmatism by linking it with Carnap's logical empiricism. Chicago became the beachhead for European positivism, which claimed to provide the firm and final foundations for scientific philosophy.

When language analysis grew in opposition to positivism, it was seen as overcoming the limitations of positivism. If one accepted those blinding limits imposed on human thought by the now solidly institutionalized professional philosophy departments as valid, then perhaps language analysis was broadening. Even the great "breakthrough" of Wittgenstein himself (who possessed too much integrity to be a mere formalist), the idea of context of use as key to meaning, was an explicit aspect of Dewey and Mead's earlier "situational" pragmatism. It was also the central theme of Malinowski's essay on the "context of situation" in ethnography, published as "The Problem of Meaning in Primitive Languages," in a supplement of Ogden and Richards's influential 1923 book *The Meaning of Meaning.* This essay itself very well could have influenced Wittgenstein's shift from a closed picture theory of meaning to an open "language game" theory, just as it also inspired an essay by Dewey.[6] But the times had changed, and Dewey's works lacked the modernist glamor of Wittgenstein's nonnarrative *Philosophical Investigations.*

In retrospect it is clear that institutionalized language analysis was only a variation on the ascetic modernism which also characterized positivism, its chief Anglo-American exponents speaking but a different dialect of empty Formalism. Analytic philosophy fitted well with the needs of the "Ph.D. Octopus," as William James derisively termed academicism, to produce a hyperspecialized priestly class with its own private canon. The major intellectual and cultural movements of the postwar years in America were dominated by the priests of abstractionism: by scholastic language analysts in philosophy, by the technotalk of a Parsons in sociology or Charles Morris in semiotics, by the true believers in the rationalist grid in "international style" architecture and serial chromatic composition, by those champions of cybernetics who wanted to make the machine the helmsman of society. Even such a seeming opposite to mid-century abstractionism such as Abstract Expressionism in painting, an antiformalist process approach to making art, ossified by the mid-1950s into a school of "one-idea artists," whose highly limited range of expression actually enhanced the rational market value of their works as easily identifiable commodities.

No wonder postmodernism seemed at first to be a breath of fresh air after such sterile ideas. But in tending only to invert the premises of severe, mid–twentieth century modernism instead of truly challenging them, postmodernists remain part of the very problems they oppose. There are, however, other directions taken by contemporary philosophers. Alisdair MacIntyre's recent writings signal a renewed interest in developing public philosophy rooted in the Aristotelian tradition and in critically understanding the historical narrative of the philosophical tradition itself. Despite his departure from the dominant schools of philosophy MacIntyre does seem to share the common tendency of contemporary thought to stress the local as against the universal, more specifically the local community. In this regard he may be at odds with Peirce's "big picture" philosophy, but on many other points, including the appreciation of Aristotle and Medieval Realism, the centrality of a community of interpretation as basic to the development of the self, and the good life as the chief end of human conduct, he resonates with Peirce. It should be interesting to see if the growing influence of MacIntyre's work opens up possibilities for philosophers to reconsider Peirce in the context of public philosophy instead of the predominant view of him as a logician and philosopher of science.

Given the "progress" of twentieth-century philosophy into a cul-de-sac of its own making, it is no wonder that Peirce's general philosophy has only recently begun to attract increasing attention. Peirce's writing is difficult, though in my opinion always clear, but this only partly explains the marginal status he had until recently. The deeper reason why Peirce has remained obscured in the thought of the twentieth century, I claim, is that he represented a new and nonmodern mind struggling to form, one in which Rational mind, the motive source and aim of the modern era, is transilluminated by Instinctive mind: a new configuration of reason occulted by and contrary to the twentieth century and its excessive rationalism.

From the standpoint of the contemporary mind of the late modern era, Peirce's concepts and forms of expression often seem contradictory or baffling. He chooses his words with a mathematician's precision and an etymologist's passion, retaining meanings to words such as "reality," "observation," and "pragmatism" that clash with current use. His semeiotic is frequently cited as a forerunner of language philosophy, and when he says, "Thus my language is the sum total of myself; for the man is the thought," one can see why Peirce might be identified with Wittgenstein's "language game" perspective. Yet Peirce also insisted that language does not exhaust intelligent signification, and that interpretation, including scientific interpretation, involves modes of signification transcending language conventions and rationality.

In a revealing critique of Hume's empiricism and concept of "balancing likelihoods," Peirce showed why *both* conjecture and experience are necessary yet not alone independently sufficient for science: Against Hume's arguments for experience as the sole source of knowledge and induction as the only way to pass from the "known to the unknown," Peirce said, "Not only is our knowledge not exclusively derived from experience, but every item of science came originally from conjecture, which has only been pruned down by experience. . . . The entire matter of our works of solid science consists of conjectures checked by experience. The entire matter of those works which have been written upon the method of judging of testimony by balancing likelihoods consists of conjecture running rough-shod over the pertinent facts."[7] Or as William Blake put it at the beginning of the nineteenth century in one of his Proverbs of Hell: "What is now proved was once only imagined."[8] As simple as Blake's proverb is, it nevertheless expresses the reality of imagination as a vital source of intelligence that is neither rational or critical, nor empirical. What Blake termed the "Poetic Imagination" is as crucial to Blake's romantic worldview as it is to Peirce's logic of science. It is precisely this generative modality of intelligence which was increasingly devalued and denied by the rise of Western nominalistic science and culture, because no place could be found for it within the ghost in the machine. Consider too Peirce's appreciation for the conjecture-like power of memory: "Memory would be nothing but a dream if it were not that predictions are based on it that get verified. When we think how slight and entangled must be the ultimate bits of feeling out of which memory constructs her mosaic, we are compelled to liken it to conjecture. It is a wonderful power of contructing quasi-conjectures or dreams that will get borne out by future experience. The power of performing this feat, which is the power of the past, is a gentle compulsiveness."[9]

Peirce also claimed that interpretation is guided by the *summum bonum,* Beauty, Goodness, and Truth, which are utterly unfashionable today, even in uncapitalized form. In his classification of the normative sciences logic is conceived not as rational calculation but as self-controlled thought, which is a subspecies of self-controlled conduct, or ethics, which in turn is dependent upon the intrinsically admirable, or aesthetics. Though himself a master logician, Peirce's classification reverses the tendency in modern thought to make ethics and esthetics separate from or subsidiary to logic.

Peirce sounds at other times like a positivist, for example, in his use of the term "observational," or in describing semeiotic as an observational science. And Peirce himself admitted he was a realist. But what is one to make of Peirce's realism in the light of modern science when he says things such as, "I will not trouble you with any disquisition on the extreme form of realism which I myself entertain that every true universal, every continuum, is a living and conscious being"? Peirce begins to sound more like an unscientific animist rather than a "laboratory philosopher," and yet he saw such semeiotic animism as requisite to the maturation and further development of science.

Peirce was one of the creators of modern symbolic logic, and his mathematical logic now appears far in advance of its day, linking him with the advance guard of the twentieth century. Logicians are beginning to appreciate the greater subtlety of Peirce's mathematical logic in comparison with Frege and Russell and Whitehead. The question that is endemic to much of Peirce's work is how he could have been ignored for so long.

Peirce was saturated with the history of philosophy and logic in a way that seems contradictory to the antihistorical tendencies characteristic of many twentieth-century philosophers. He uncovered the fallacious foundations of modern philosophy in his criticism of Descartes's foundationalism in the 1860s, and yet he seemed to agree with Descartes that we are possessed of indubitable ideas, but in the form of common sense. In his development of "critical common sensism,"

Peirce argued that there are original, and in that sense, indubitable, ideas, but that they are also fallible. Peirce was a practicing physicist, steeped in nineteenth-century physical science, yet he came to see the eviction of real qualitative possibility and final causality from the natural world as a temporary mistake due to the dominance of nominalism in the modern mind. Against the whole grand march of modern positivism and conceptualism, he claimed that science depends upon the reality of the general laws it investigates, upon a reasonableness in the very nature of things. Despite a growing appreciation of Peirce, these ideas remain intolerable to contemporary scientists and social thinkers.

PRAGMATISM AND THE PRAGMATIC ACQUIESCENCE

To understand why pragmatism went into eclipse by mid-century, one needs to consider both the spirit of scientistic modernism in the twentieth century and the rigidifying effects of newly institutionalized academic disciplines in America. Scientistic modernism shared with many of its artistic counterparts the urge to break through the mediating veil of history by discovering fundamental principles or forms of expression, to finalize what the nineteenth century had reached toward. Scientistic modernists believed (and some still do today) that the past could be forgotten because of the revolutionary progress of science. In its extreme versions it held that all that is not immediately present as fact or phenomenon is extraneous metaphysical figment. The practice of science and philosophy was to be based on universal foundational principles rather than self-correcting inquiry, and science, so conceived, was to provide the rational foundations for all human conduct and institutions. All of these ideas mark the scientistic modernists as unscientific.

As Peirce pointed out so clearly, every scientific inquiry must stand upon an as yet unquestioned ground of preconceptions, which is to say that interpretation requires a "past" simply in order to interpret. All human knowledge, especially scientific, is inescapably fallible. Science itself includes more than rationality, as Peirce's discussions of abduction showed so well, so that the misguided attempt to reduce human institutions and conduct to so-called rational foundations or standards reveals a grave mistake in disallowing the deeper basis of human reason. Both conjecture and experience are ingredients in the logic of science, and both are extrarational. Scientistic modernism sought to finalize the machine image of science which pragmatism had rejected and a scientistic worldview which was the logical endpoint of cultural nominalism.

The pragmatists had developed a view of science as a mode of conduct, as living inquiry, as what Peirce called the living, inferential metaboly of signs. One could see why the empirical temper of pragmatism and the stress it gave to inquiry might appeal to the positivists, and also why they needed to replace open-ended interpretation with a closed system: they were avatars of the great machine of modernity itself. The positivists helped to finalize the view that science had no passion, no subjectivity, no morals, no humanity. And as they were helping to finalize that machine-made myth the world saw its practical consequences in Nazi "medical" murders and death camps based on extremely rational means, in American nuclear warfare conducted on civilian populations, and in a postwar world where science unashamedly prostituted itself to the purely technical interests of the military-industrial-academic complex.

Compared to scientistic modernism, pragmatism has recently begun to be rehabilitated as a more scientific and humane view. But in the context of American culture, it is important to remember the great tension between the romantic and the technical which characterized the exploration, conquest, and settlement of the New World, and America in particular. Those vast visions of nature one reads in a Melville, Thoreau, Emerson, or Whitman powerfully reveal the quest to grow a new kind of civilization in the New World, one which would place man in communion with nature and cosmos, which could draw from the positive achievements of civilization while stripping them of its corrupting brutalities, greed, insensate poverty, and craving for human domination. As Thomas Paine said on the eve of the American Revolution in 1776, "We have it in our power to begin the world over again. . . . The birthday of a new world is at hand." But already by the time of the American Revolution the ills of the Old World had emerged in the new—genocide had been practiced against native Americans and against Africans being transported to America, slavery was an established institution. Yet in that brief flowering of American culture between about 1850 and 1856 the dream of a new world was at least partially realized. American industrialism and capitalism mushroomed after the Civil War, marking the emerging hegemony of the technical and mechanical over the romantic, and by the turn of the century those with eyes to see saw the decline of what Whitman had called "Democratic Vistas."

The end of the nineteenth century saw the visions of the literary transcendentalists transformed to the scientific philosophies of the pragmatists, and in this process one can see the successful rise of the modern cult of science. William James was an immensely warm and humane writer, but he was besieged by a scientistic conception of science with which he never quite came to terms. Dewey and Mead developed broad social philosophies which also sought to reform science, yet unquestioningly assumed the centrality of science as the basis for reconstructing modern life. Peirce too, who considered himself a "laboratory philosopher," was an ardent champion of science. He harbored some wrongheaded ideas that drew from the culture of nominalistic scientism, for example, he believed that poetry would eventually become transformed into science. Yet Peirce alone, I claim, continued the broad cosmic vision of the transcendentalists in his philosophy, while the other pragmatists unnecessarily narrowed themselves to realize their views of science.

Although Dewey and Mead in particular were powerful critics of the ills of industrial capitalism, their buoyant assumption of progress and deep suspicion of long-term stabilities paradoxically resonated with the cultural dynamism of industrial capitalism and its "short term," or situational, or market, outlook. Peirce struggled to the end against the cultural and scientistic nominalism that dominated his age. In his later work, he realized the very nonmodern implications of his three modes of being—Firstness, Secondness, and Thirdness—and brought forth a new kind of mind which could encompass the tensions between the romantic and mechanical, the inner and outer, the indubitable and the fallible.

IN MY BOOK *Meaning and Modernity* and an earlier book, *The Meaning of Things,* I proposed three levels of self—the personal self, the social self, and the cosmic self—influenced, in part, by Peirce. Modern culture whittled away at the cosmic dimension, the traditional province of religions, and particularly evident in Medieval philosophy and cathedrals, and tended increasingly to favor a subjectivist self and a mechanical universe in its place. Peirce's philosophy resonates closely with the generation of American literary transcendentalists who preceded him in reestablishing the cosmic dimension as a valid ingredient in human affairs, particularly his writings of the early 1890s. This tendency toward "Concord transcendentalism," especially in his earlier work, though crucial in cutting through the ghost in the machine outlook of modernity, also seems to me to undervalue the place of the delimited, concrete self. From my point of view Peirce did not fully appreciate the value of the qualitative uniqueness and autonomy of the personal self, even though his later philosophy implicitly supports such a view. Consider, for example, the following discussion of "synechism," Peirce's theory of continuity, which was written in 1892, so eloquent concerning his view of the living cosmos and the cosmic self, so inadequate concerning the personal self:

> Synechism, even in its less stalwart forms, can never abide dualism, properly so called . . . dualism in its broadest legitimate meaning as the

philosophy which performs its analyses with an axe, leaving as the ultimate elements, unrelated chunks of being, this is most hostile to synechism. In particular, the synechist will not admit that physical and psychical phenomena are entirely distinct,—whether as belonging to different categories of substance, or as entirely separate sides of one shield,—but will insist that all phenomena are of one character, though some are more mental and spontaneous, others more material and regular. Still, all alike present that mixture of freedom and constraint, which allows them to be, nay, makes them to be teleological, or purposive.

Nor must any synechist say, "I am altogether myself, and not at all you." If you embrace synechism, you must abjure this metaphysics of wickedness. In the first place, your neighbors are, in a measure, yourself, and in far greater measure than, without deep studies in psychology, you would believe. Really, the selfhood you like to attribute to yourself is, for the most part, the vulgarist delusion of vanity. In the second place, all men who resemble you and are in analogous circumstances are, in a measure, yourself, though not quite in the same way in which your neighbors are you.

There is still another direction in which the barbaric conception of personal identity must be broadened. A brahmanical hymn begins as follows: "I am that pure and infinite Self, who am bliss, eternal, manifest, all-pervading, and who am the substrate of all that owns name and form." This expresses more than humiliation,—the utter swallowing up of the poor individual self in the Spirit of prayer. All communication from mind to mind is through the continuity of being. A man is capable of having assigned to him a *role* in the drama of creation, and so far as he loses himself in that *role,*—no matter how humble it may be,—so far he identifies himself with its Author.[10]

In saying that "your neighbors are, in a measure, yourself," Peirce states a dialogical view of the self similar to what Mead would later articulate as the internalization of the "generalized other." He also seems to be saying that the higher development of the self requires the negation of personal identity through "losing" oneself in one's role in the drama of creation. Peirce struggled against the rampant individualism of his time, and such a recommendation would make a good recipe for fending off such individualism, but the drama of creation is, more than anything, a drama of spontaneous development, and the deepest development of the self involves more than losing oneself in a role, no matter how noble that role. It involves as well the infusion of the spontaneous in oneself, of the open or undetermined sensing of a situation, into the practice of life. For the fully mature self is an ongoing drama of self-creation as well as being involved in the drama of cosmic creation. Perhaps I am being too picky here, perhaps Peirce meant to indicate that losing oneself in the drama of creation means being an active participant in the creation and not only an empty vessel. But one finds the theme of self-effacement in a number of places in Peirce. For example, in 1891 he remarked, "Everybody will admit a personal self exists in the same sense in which a snark exists; that is, there is a phenomenon to which that name is given. It is an illusory phenomenon; but still it is a phenomenon. It is not quite *purely* illusory, but only *mainly* so. It is true, for instance, that men are *selfish,* that is, that they are really deluded into supposing themselves to have some isolated existence; and in so far, they *have* it. To deny the reality of the personality is not anti-spiritualistic; it is only anti-nominalistic."[11]

I claim, against Peirce, that to deny the reality of the personality is both nominalistic and wrong and contradicts Peirce's own version of realism. The real, as I understand Peirce, is not at all depersonalized, especially since Peirce himself claimed elsewhere that "every true universal, every continuum, is a living and conscious being" and that reality is of the nature of a sign. To claim that the personality is real by no means entails "some isolated existence," for that version of Isolatoism, or what Robert Bellah and the coauthors of *The Good Society* have depicted as "Lockean man," is a truly nominalistic interpretation of what constitutes the self. The development of a healthy self necessarily involves the development of the personal dimension as part of the whole person. Modern culture may have over-stressed the personal self, but one need not deny the qualitative uniqueness of the individual and its significance in human conduct in order to stress the continuity of social being.

Though himself a Christian, and though I am not, Peirce does not in my opinion sufficiently acknowledge the valuable legacy of Christian personalism in his view of the self, a legacy which also includes the deepening of the subjective realm in modern culture, and therefore fails to recognize fully the possibilities inherent in what he elsewhere calls the "Buddhisto-Christian religion." Peirce's view of the personal self suffers from narcissism: it is all swallowed up in a cosmic fusion of the sort described so well in the writings of psychoanalysts Heinz Kohut and D. W. Winnicott and in Christopher Lasch's book, *The Minimal Self.* Peirce sees the fallacy of nominalistic individualism, which supposes acting individuals apart from the communicative medium of conduct. But in its place he would swallow up the personal within the transpersonal.

Both alternatives fit the pattern of exaggerated separation or symbiotic union which form the polarities of the narcissistic self. Narcissistic disturbance, according to psychoanalytic theories, results from deficient mothering, either from an unempathic mother, from abuse or trauma, or from overprotection, around the age of two to three. This is the crucial time for the development of autonomy in the child, when the child learns how to be separate from its mother and begins to develop a sense of itself as an "I." Such development is essential for a self that can recognize its relation to and embeddedness in its significant environment as well as its difference from it, and for what it is as a delimited person in a social milieu. Thwarting the development of autonomy results in a hollow self, a false self that masks its lack of autonomy through fantasies of merger or absolute separateness.

In my opinion the neo-Freudian approaches to narcissistic disturbance and developmental studies of autonomy in early childhood illustrate that there are "essences" involved in the self. The self, from this point of view, is not simply a conventional social construct but is something more like a biosocial construction in its emergence, a biosocial construction involving communicative essentials, such as the development of empathy and autonomy. My principal divergence from the Freudians, however, is that they operate on nominalistic premises which go back at least to Hobbes, and deny reality to the possibility of an evolutionary reasonableness in nature, treating the possibility of a cosmic dimension to human affairs solely as fantasy, rather than considering the possibility that it is the nature of our relation to such a dimension which determines whether it is a narcissistic fantasy. My own inclination is to regard evolution in general and human development in particular as both real and fantastic: as an evolutionary and developmental fantasia.

An adequate view of the self, in my opinion, recognizes cosmic embeddedness *and* the difference of the personal self from its surrounds. And an adequate philosophy today must, in my opinion, recognize the dual materialistic-etherealistic depersonalizing tendencies which came to full expression in the twentieth century, and the decline of public life, not to mention the destruction and terror they wrought. Hence I believe Peirce failed to realize the positive value of the personal self, though his late philosophy implicitly moves in that direction.

Consider the following discussion of pragmatism, where Peirce stresses the nonexpedient, nonutilitarian nature of pragmatism, which regards the ultimate aim of conduct as aesthetic:

> For if the meaning of a symbol consists in *how* it might cause us to act, it is plain that this "how" cannot refer to the description of mechanical motions that it might cause, but must intend to refer to a description of the action as having this or that *aim*. In order to understand pragmatism,

therefore, well enough to subject it to intelligent criticism, it is incumbent upon us to inquire what an ultimate aim, capable of being pursued in an indefinitely prolonged course of action, can be. . . . In order that the aim should be immutable under all circumstances, without which it will not be an ultimate aim, it is requisite that it should accord with a free development of the agent's own esthetic quality. At the same time it is requisite that it should not ultimately tend to be disturbed by the reactions upon the agent of that outward world which is supposed in the very idea of action. It is plain that these two conditions can be fulfilled at once only if it happens that the esthetic quality toward which the agent's free development tends and that of the ultimate action of experience upon him are parts of one esthetic total. . . . If it is *not* so, the aim is essentially *unattainable* . . . so the rule of ethics will be to adhere to the only possible absolute aim, and to hope that it will prove attainable. Meantime it is comforting to know that all experience is favorable to that assumption.[12]

This statement is crucial to understanding Peirce's late formulation of the doctrine of pragmatism. The ultimate aim of conduct is not utility or expedience but aesthetic harmony between the spontaneous development of the agent and the continuing experience of the world. The conduct of the person or institution then requires an agent possessed of a qualitative uniqueness, who can develop his or her proclivities freely, not merely ideally or conventionally, and a patient who can continue to undergo the otherness of events, which is what is meant by the term "experience," with the aim "undisturbed." Peirce's proposal of an ultimate aim does not say that people actually attain such an aim, but only that such an ultimate aim would constitute the equivalent of "Enlightenment." It is hard indeed to know what an aim "immutable under all circumstances" would be like in the face of life's contingencies and human frailties.

Peirce is claiming, against the idealist and materialist traditions, that an ultimate aim of life "should accord with a free development of the agent's own esthetic quality," and therefore that aesthetic development is basic to the development of the person, reducible neither to "cognitive development" nor "moral development." His statement is a direct outgrowth of his reasoning concerning the normative sciences that logic, as self-controlled thought, is dependent upon ethics, as self-controlled conduct, which in turn is dependent upon aesthetics, or the intrinsically admirable. Such a view is contrary to most modern understandings of logic, as well as the logocentric developmental theories of Piaget and Kohlberg. It is a view completely resonant with Winnicott's stress on the "true self" as that self capable of openly engaging in the spontaneous conduct of life, in empathic relation and autonomy. Yet the basis of Winnicott's model of self rests on the relation between the young child and the "good enough mother," as he puts it, who can provide a "holding environment," literally, that can support the development of the child. How different a basis this is from Peirce's logical argumentation. And yet both present a model of a spontaneous, self-developing self as a goal of human development.

Peirce, of all the pragmatists the most deeply saturated with the practice and study of science, was and perhaps remains the least known. And the scientifically oriented philosophies of the other pragmatists were in turn buried by positivists with a brasher scientistic macho. In my opinion much of the story of twentieth-century philosophy, including continental philosophy, is an ever-narrowing path guided by scientist modernism and its antitheses, and it is precisely Peirce's evolving philosophy of semeiotic realism freed from the limitations of nominalism that forms a critical alternative to the dead end reached by the late modern era.

After the nineteen-sixties, new influences from continental philosophy began to be felt, and in the rediscovery of semiotics it became increasingly clearer that Peirce could no longer be virtually ignored. Because of its concern with the dialogical and sign nature of thought, pragmatism is now viewed by philosophers and social theorists as potentially contributing to a restructuring of the intellectual landscape. Yet this contemporary appropriation of pragmatism is highly selective: the deconstructionist Dewey of Richard Rorty and the structuralist, positivist, and poststructuralist Peirce of contemporary semiotics have been metamorphosed from pragmatists into contemporary rationalists.

LAW AS A REASONABLENESS ENERGIZING IN THE WORLD

> *The one intelligible theory of the universe is that of objective idealism, that matter is effete mind, inveterate habits becoming physical laws.*

> *Peirce*[13]

Peirce effected a marriage of opposites in his philosophic vision which speaks directly to the greatest needs of our time today. Yet this vision is occulted, because it undercuts the common nominalistic premises on which the modern era is founded. It is easy enough to find references to Peirce's semiotic or theory of the unlimited community of inquirers in the general literature, but only rarely does one see the broader implications of Peirce's vision discussed. Most of the discussions of Peirce's semeiotic reveal fundamental distortions now embedded in semiotics, and a tendency toward empty technicalism. Even Peirce scholars themselves seem much more interested in the technical aspects of his philosophy than in the live implications it holds for contemporary thought.

If we take Peirce's claim seriously that the modern era can be characterized as dominated by nominalism, then we are seeing the terminal product of that nominalism today. Modernism claimed to transcend history by finally deciphering the fundamentals, and postmodernism claims to transcend modernism, by assembling the shards of history into an ever-shifting, arbitrary eclecticism. Modern humanism broke down the cosmic vision of the Medieval time, fixed as it was on the uplifting image of a comprehensive religious cosmology which swallowed the individual. By celebrating the human perspective, the modern era brought into existence new forms of subjective consciousness, of cultural, political, religious, and economic individualism. From Luther's conceptions of a personal calling and *sola fide* as the new basis of religious authority to the growing concern with individual political rights—regardless of how often they were violated—the West collectively brought forth a new conception of the human individual. Yet one of the chief ironies of this development was that the modern West was building a worldview in its science and technics which had no place for the human person. That growing Objectivism, which Peirce called the Mechanical Philosophy, led to the worldview I have been calling "the ghost in the machine," a world of spectral subjectivity and mindless materialism.

Such is the world of the positivists, for whom truth is a devitalized sentence, pointing to, but never touching, a "fact." Such is the world of the fragmatists, who wish to decenter the self and view the living, passionate human being as a disembodied "text," while yet frequently assuming that nature really is a machine. Cultural nominalism involves the reification of the object and the etherealization of the subject, and it is the underlying principle of the modern world. Modern varieties of materialism, whether scientific realism or dialectical materialism, deny the irreducible reality of mind or, as Peirce put it, a reasonableness energizing in the world, and so agree with the nominalist assumption that all reality is to be rooted in the particulars. Modern conventionalism, which assumes mind to be either an epiphenomenal characteristic of matter, or a product of human language and culture totally transcending material conditions, agrees with the nominalist assumption that all generals are but "names" or mere conventions. In this split-brained view of the world, all that is real must be soulless and mindless, and all that can be loved or admired must be unreal.

Peirce's transilluminative vision rejects the opposing claims of the modern era that the rational ego, either individual or collective, is at the center of the universe, and that the natural universe is a mindless machine. His Critical Common-Sensism rejects the foundationalism of scholastic realists and scientistic realists, the modified universal Kantian transcendentalism of Habermas, and also the relativism of neopragmatist fragmatists, while yet restoring the cosmic dimension in human affairs in a way which would also allow the valid achievements of the modern era. Peirce proposed that there are ideas so deeply embedded in the human body over the course of natural and cultural evolution as to be indubitable, ideas so imbued with the general laws of nature and tempered through experience as likely to be instinctively true, yet which nevertheless remain fallible.

Peirce claims that there is a reasonableness in nature and not apart from it, that nature has soul—or live aesthetic quality (Firstness)—and mind—or generality (Thirdness)—as well as body (or Secondness). Such a view undercuts the whole nominalistic worldview and its ghost-like view of mind, culture, and purport, and machine-like view of nature. Peirce's semeiotic naturalism, his view that there is a reasonableness energizing in the universe, that signs can be viewed as living beings, that instinct continues to animate human conduct vaguely, as conjecture, and that the genius of the human mind is its ability to hit on truth without the rigid determination of instinct, probably strikes the contemporary modern or postmodern thinker as unfathomable or eccentric. Yet it is precisely such ideas, I claim, which show the way beyond the impasse of the ghost in the machine.

This view directly challenges the Enlightenment legacy by claiming that human rational capacities are grounded by and ultimately serve extrarational reasonableness. In other words, what Enlightenment humans possess is possible because the plastic nature of human practices remain potentially transilluminated by extrarational forms such as dream-conjecture, sentiment, and perhaps ritual-like habits deeply embedded in the human brain, patterns tempered over long-term evolutionary development. Our social constructions are themselves potentially real because we humans are social constructions of nature, beings for whom the real development of imagination, emotion, autonomy, experience, and reasoning was crucial in our physical evolution and for whom these capacities remain as deep sources for further development. Peirce's understanding of rationality as the most immature of human capacities, as both our unique blight and glory, offers a new philosophical anthropology in pragmatic perspective. Critical consciousness, which it was the virtual task of the modern era to cultivate—and perhaps the axial age up to the present—is fused with those deeper, tempered forms of reasonableness, the biosemiotic capacities through which we became human in the first place.

Peirce's claim that there are influences and limitations upon human conduct which transcend current norms and local traditions does not lend itself to the contemporary atmosphere of rampant relativism and social constructionism. By arguing for the reality of generals, Peirce is linked with the philosophy of scholastic realism which was rejected by the modern era, including the other pragmatists. Yet his philosophy, despite his love of that tradition, is no throwback to scholastic realism but is, in my opinion, an outline of a new kind of mind and blueprint for a new kind of civilization. In this view rationality is no longer the "invisible dictator" of human destiny which the modern era assumed it to be, but is regained as but one of the valuable organs of human reason, what he called "the capacity for blundering." Other evolutionary and anthropological authors have dealt with the idea of human evolutionary plasticity, but none have projected the vision of human development in quite the way that Peirce did in 1902:

> I doubt very much whether the Instinctive mind could ever develop into a Rational mind. I should expect the reverse process sooner. The Rational mind is the Progressive mind, and as such, by its very capacity for growth, seems more infantile than the Instinctive mind. Still, it would seem that Progressive minds must have, in some mysterious way, probably by arrested development, grown from Instinctive minds; and they are certainly enormously higher. The Deity of the Théodicée of Leibniz is as high an Instinctive mind as can well be imagined; but it impresses a scientific reader as distinctly inferior to the human mind. It reminds one of the views of the Greeks that Infinitude is a defect; for although Leibniz imagines that he is making the Divine Mind infinite, by making its knowledge Perfect and Complete, he fails to see that in thus refusing it the powers of thought and the possibility of improvement he is in fact taking away something far higher than knowledge. It is the human mind that is infinite. One of the most remarkable distinctions between the Instinctive mind of animals and the Rational mind of man is that animals rarely make mistakes, while the human mind almost invariably blunders at first, and repeatedly, where it is really exercised in the manner that is distinctive of it. If you look upon this as a defect, you ought to find an Instinctive mind higher than a Rational one, and probably, if you cross-examine yourself, you will find you do. The greatness of the human mind lies in its ability to discover truth notwithstanding its not having Instincts strong enough to exempt it from error. This is the marvel and admirable in it; and this essentially supposes a generous portion of the capacity for blundering. . . .
>
> The conception of the Rational Mind as an Unmatured Instinctive Mind which takes another development precisely because of its childlike character is confirmed, not only by the prolonged childhood of men, but

also by the fact that all systems of rational performances have had instinct for their first germ. Not only has instinct been the first germ, but every step in the development of those systems of performances comes from instinct. It is precisely because this Instinct is a weak, uncertain Instinct that it becomes infinitely plastic, and never reaches an ultimate state beyond which it cannot progress. Uncertain tendencies, unstable states of equilibrium are conditions *sine qua non* for the manifestation of Mind.[14]

Peirce reverses the major tenets of the modern era by claiming that rationality is immature and that the "primitive" aspects of human nature, such as sentiments, dreaming, memory, and instinctive impulses, are the most mature. He acknowledges that the mature aspects of Instinctive mind tend to operate on us vaguely or suggestively rather than rigidly. His view implies that Instinctive mind by itself would reach a harmony or dynamic equilibrium with its environment which would preclude further development. By contrast Rational mind is capable of continuous development through its plastic connection to Instinctive mind and the informed "blundering" it makes possible. Rational mind alone would be unable to get its bearings, unable to receive the "first germs" of its own further development. Such a rationalized mind or culture would quickly become unhinged, unable to rest in archaic habit yet also unable to draw from its nonrational wellsprings the imaginative energies needed for continued renewal. I take contemporary postmodern culture and the great tendency today to despise the possible organic basis of human meaning to be such a state, what H. G. Wells titled his last book: *Mind at the End of Its Tether.* Peirce is proposing that the combination of Rational and Instinctive mind—the transillumination of rationality by suggestive and mostly unconscious instinctual and emotional promptings—is what makes the human mind truly infinite. He suggests, here and elsewhere, that the future of human development lies not in a more rational culture but in the instinctualization of Rational mind.

Consider Peirce's words in 1901, which at first suggest a confirmed Darwinian evolutionist but then turn in a surprisingly different direction:

> Today, the idea uppermost in most minds is evolution. In their genuine nature, no two things could be more hostile than the idea of evolution and that individualism upon which Ockham erected his philosophy. But this hostility has not yet made itself obvious; so that the lion cub and the lamb still lie down together in one mind, until a certain one of them shall have become more mature. Whatever in the philosophies of our day (as far as we need consider them) is not Ockhamism is evolutionism of one kind

or another; and every evolutionism must in its evolution eventually restore that rejected idea of law as a reasonableness energizing in the world (no matter through what mechanism of natural selection or otherwise) which belonged to the essentially evolutionary metaphysics of Aristotle, as well as to the scholastic modifications of it by Aquinas and Scotus.[15]

To today's Darwinians and neo-Darwinians, indeed to today's intellectual in general, Peirce's words surely must seem as outdated as Aristotle's biological theories. Peirce was well aware of the rudimentary nature of Aristotle's biological ideas, while still supporting a modified view of his understanding of final causality. Aristotle was supposed to be the antievolutionary philosopher whose concept of final causality was evicted by modern natural science. Yet Peirce, as thoroughly a natural scientist as ever there was, and who deeply appreciated Darwin, is saying that Darwin was insufficiently evolutionary and that "every evolutionism must in its evolution eventually restore that rejected idea of law as a reasonableness energizing in the world."

Peirce could not have been aware of the tremendous advances that would be made in twentieth-century quantum physics and biology, yet those discoveries thus far seem to support his claim that there is real chance and Firstness in nature. But the natural sciences have yet to confront Peirce's other great challenge, that there is an evolutionary reasonableness in nature. Not only does Peirce's transilluminated vision pose a challenge to the materialistic basis of evolutionary biology, but what physicist today, even with the radically enlarged understanding of the self-organizing properties of matter—let alone what social philosopher—might be prepared to take seriously Peirce's view that Thirdness is real, that matter is mind, hidebound with habits, that there is a "reasonableness energizing in the world?"

Those who see pragmatism as a reflection of American self-interest, expediency, and crass commercialism should remember what Peirce had to say in 1898: "To pursue 'topics of vital importance' as the first and best can lead only to one or other of two terminations—either on the one hand in what is called, I hope not justly, Americanism, the worship of business, the life in which the fertilizing stream of genial sentiment dries up or shrinks to a rill of comic tit-bits, or else on the other hand, to monasticism, sleepwalking in this world with no eye nor heart except for the other. Take for the lantern of your footsteps the cold light of reason and regard your business, your duty, as the highest thing, and you can only rest in one of those goals or the other."[16] From these and other words, it is quite clear that Peirce saw pragmatism as opposed to crass practicalism and cold rationalism, and rationality itself as subordinate to sentiment in the conduct of life.

What are the consequences of Peirce's vision in the context of the modern era and contemporary intellectual life? His concept of a "final interpretant" as the logical terminus of the process of interpretation, unlike Hegel's concept of the Absolute as the unifying completion of all history and unlike positivists' scientistic modernism and Rorty's "final vocabulary," is not the cessation of all that has gone before but living incarnation: the birth of "*ceaselessly prolific ideas.*" As Mumford, who is perhaps closer in spirit to Peirce than any other twentieth-century writer, expressed it in a conversation with me a few years ago: "Beginnings, that's what it's all about! Otherwise the whole thing would just keep going round and round."

Peirce did not see the modern era as a culmination of human development so much as a continuation of its beginnings: "One thing, as it seems to me, the history of science renders abundantly clear, it is that man's nature, or natural and apparently innate ideas, are in the early stages of intellectual development."[17] As we will see in the next chapter, Peirce's vision in the contemporary context is approximately opposite to that of the well-known social theorist Jürgen Habermas, who believes that the life-world should be progressively subject to what he terms "communicative rationality." Peirce's transilluminated vision leads instead to an appreciation for the reality of imaginative projection—or what Peirce elsewhere termed Musement or Pure Play—as an aspect of all "higher" human activities and not only the lower ones, and the greater reason of a limited rationality continuous with, rather than raised above, its largely unconscious, nonverbal, and instinctive promptings.[18]

The renewal of interest in pragmatism poses a question for social thought that goes beyond pragmatism: Can the cold light of reason which has thus far served as the lantern for social theory's footsteps give way to that brighter transilluminated light of warm sentiment? To those who believe in the supremacy of rationality the very question is embarrassing. But to those who suspect that reasonableness is more than rationality, the renewal of meaning in contemporary life involves reconceiving human intelligence and reclaiming critical, organic human purpose. It means reattuning ourselves to the cosmic dimension of human affairs which was largely eclipsed by the mechanical worldview, acknowledging our part in the ongoing drama of creation, while cultivating the personal and societal or public dimensions of the self as requisite to the whole person. Classic pragmatism may not always provide clear or adequate answers, but in raising the very question of the grounding of rationality in suprarational biocosmic resources of the human body, pragmatism attempted to reassert the wholeness of intelligent life against the all too frequently inhumane intelligence of rational life.

A renewal of social theory, however, will involve going beyond the limitations of classic pragmatism. I submit that in the deepest workings of pragmatism, in the thought of Peirce, there were signs of a new and non-modern mind beginning to body forth. A reconstituted "pragmatic attitude," drawing from these ideas, offers what much of contemporary social theory rejects: against contemporary objectivists it claims that the denigrated human capacities to muse, marvel, imagine, and body forth meaning are our chief claim as humans to objectivity. Against contemporary subjectivists it claims that the repressed or despised biological roots of human existence form the living source for meaning, subjectivity, and transformation. Against those who would etherealize human meaning or reduce it to an epiphenomenon of a mechanical universe, the Peircean transilluminative vision presents strong counterclaims for concrete reasonableness: the incarnation of bodied intelligence, and indeed the reincarnation of that intelligence through the varieties of human communication. But it is not enough to draw from these ideas without filtering them through the tragic lessons of the twentieth century, when the would-be new Adams of political, intellectual, and cultural life, fed on the apples of the modern knowledge-complex, sought to end history, tradition, and metaphysics, and instead have nearly succeeded in ending humanity.

6

Jürgen Habermas's Theory of Communicative Etherealization

We are starved to death, fed on the eternal sodom-apples of thought-forms. What we want is complete *imaginative experience, which goes through the whole soul and body. Even at the expense of reason we want imaginative experience. For reason is certainly not the final judge of life.*

Though, if we pause to think about it, we shall realize that it is not Reason herself whom we have to defy, it is her myrmidons, our accepted ideas and thought-forms. Reason can adjust herself to almost anything, if we will only free her from her crinoline and powdered wig, with which she was invested in the eighteenth and nineteenth centuries. Reason is a supple nymph, and slippery as a fish.

—D. H. Lawrence

PROJECT HABERMAS

Jürgen Habermas is one of the most prominent social theorists today, a central figure in debates about postmodernism, relativism versus universal reason, and the nature of modern rationality. He has written highly technical and complicated works which nevertheless have a wide readership, and also has spoken out forcefully as a public intellectual in Germany on many significant issues, ranging from the role of universities in the sixties to his well-targeted criticisms of German revisionist historian Ernst Nolte, who claims that the Holocaust did not occur.

Habermas fervently believes that through rational argumentation a just society can be created and sustained, and his two-volume magnum opus, *The Theory of Communicative Action* (*TCA*) is a massive compendium which explicates these beliefs by squeezing a vast array of high-powered theories into its "brief" one thousand or so pages. Habermas's intentions are grand: his theory of communicative action is at once an attempt to develop a socially based theory of action as an alternative to the subjectivist and individualist underpinnings of much of social theory, a "two-level concept of society that connects the 'lifeworld' and 'system' paradigms," a critical theory of modernity which retains the enlightenment ideal of rationally grounded societies, and a theory of meaning rooted in a developmental logic of world-historical rationality.

Habermas seeks to find a *via media* between totalitarian closure and relativism, to show why the modernist project of a universal reason is still viable, and to propose a "public" discourse of rationally grounded argumentative speech—or communicative action—as his answer. Despite the widespread attention Habermas's work has received, and despite my sympathy for issues Habermas has raised,

I hope to show why his project is fundamentally flawed because of its uncritical assumption that only rationality can provide a legitimate standard for communicative reason. These flaws become particularly evident in examining his analyses of myth, action, the "lifeworld," his relation to Mead and pragmatism, and the "three spheres" of modernity. In examining Habermas's attempt to build a model of universal reason in this chapter and contrasting his model with Rorty's postmodern theory in the next, one can see, I believe, a key indicator of the diminution of reason which the overenlargement of rationality has brought about.[1]

Like Talcott Parsons's *The Structure of Social Action,* Habermas's book draws from a selection of sociological theorists in order to arrive at a grand synthesis: one which includes Parsons's grand system of systems as a component. In fact this book, originally published in German in 1981, was part of a virtual genre of early 1980s books which made "grand theory" seem respectable again and which summarized and synthesized the so-called classics in the manner of Parsons while including Parsons as a "classic." C. Wright Mills originally applied the term "grand theory" to Parsons because Parsons shaped the world of ideas to fit his one-size-fits-all system: a jargon-ridden, grandiose theory in which all competing models could be subsumed. The good news for Parsons is that these books of the early 1980s have enshrined him among the "classics." The bad news is that these very same books have swallowed him up within even bigger Ukrainian Matreshka doll-within-doll systems.

In examining the numerous social theorists and philosophers who appear in *TCA,* it becomes obvious that Habermas relies most heavily on those deriving from the Kantian world, including Max Weber, Emile Durkheim, Parsons, Jean Piaget, Lawrence Kohlberg, and Claude Lévi-Strauss (whose structuralism Paul Ricouer has characterized as Kantianism without a transcendental ego). In his explicit appropriation of the mainstream sociological tradition of Weber, Durkheim, and Parsons, Habermas reaffirms the frequently unacknowledged grip of Kant over the sociological tradition. Parsons, for example, thought he saw a great synthesis in the work of Durkheim and Weber, but this "synthesis" is more accurately described as their shared foundations in Kant, which the two theorists put to very different uses. And the great synthesis Habermas seeks from his use of Weber, Durkheim, and Parsons is, like that of Parsons, more accurately described as a case of seeing the world through Kantian-tinted glasses, the effect of which is to presume artificial dichotomies as given.

Although he criticizes Weber's subjectivist theory of action as inadequate, Habermas accepts his theory of the "disenchantment" of the world through rationalization as not only a historical fact but also as a logical necessity for the development of communicative action. The term "communicative" is used by Habermas in a technical sense to mean "rationally grounded convictions" produced by the intersubjective "validity claims" of propositional, argumentative speech. Against Weber's purposive-instrumental rationality (*Zweckrationalität*) he proposes communicative rationality: "[T]his concept of *communicative rationality* carries with it connotations based ultimately on the central experience of the unconstrained, unifying, consensus-bringing force of argumentative speech, in which different participants overcome their merely subjective views and, owing to the mutuality of rationally motivated convictions, assure themselves of both the unity of the objective world and the intersubjectivity of their lifeworld."[2]

Habermas does not allow the possibility that "disenchantment" may reflect the peculiar distortions inherent in the modern epoch, distortions due to a nominalized, split worldview of materialism and conventionalism. He cannot conceive that a "communicative re-enchantment" may be possible should the modern epoch be replaced by one that substitutes a more humble "caretaking" attitude toward the great mystery of organic life and our place in its drama for the arrogant claims of rationality to be the chief or sole arbiter of human conduct. Habermas not only does not conceive of this possibility, he leaves no room for it, for his rationalistic theory of communicative action provides the sole measuring stick and vantage point for self-criticism: "In an extensively rationalized lifeworld, reification can be measured only against the conditions of communicative sociation, and not against the nostalgically loaded, frequently romanticized past of premodern forms of life."[3] Apparently premodern forms of life lack the rational basis required for "communicative sociation," and so attempts to introduce what virtues as premodern cultures might have, such as the concept of virtue itself, can be dismissed as "nostalgically loaded." Historical development involves a Hegelian "overcoming" of prior phases in Habermas's critical progressivist theory, a view completely at odds with that of the "fibrous structure of history" advocated by Mumford.

If we apply Habermas's theory of communicative action to the method of his book itself, we might see an apparent conversation between the principal figures of social theory, based on dialogical principles of rational argumentation and striving toward intersubjective consensus. Or do we? The major place given to Marx, Weber, Durkheim, G. H. Mead, and Parsons as a group might instead signify an uncritical acceptance of the legitimacy of institutionalized academic sociology and its canonical theorists. Mead students may like the fact that Mead provides a basis for the theory of communicative action, but they may be disappointed that Habermas needs to tether Mead to Durkheim's Kantian-based theory of collective consciousness in order to provide the genesis of the generalized other. In *TCA* the canonical theorists appear to have their say, but, as I hope to show, Habermas's Kantian and Hegelian filters only allow through that which fits his rationalist presuppositions. This suggests that the structure informing his work is that of a projection of, and attraction to, his own unexamined assumptions rather than a genuine communicative dialogue in which a genuinely other view might be allowed its say against Habermas's wishes. Could it be that his own arguments are not rooted in the process of communicative action he calls for, that the apparent dialogue of theories masks an underlying "merely subjective" Kantian quest for synthetic system rather than objective consensus? Does Habermas preserve in his own thought an element of the assumed correctness of one's inner feelings, consciousness, and values usually associated with the traditional German romanticism he otherwise rejects?

TCA represents Habermas's move away from his earlier stress on a "consciousness" based-theory in *Knowledge and Human Interests* to a broader model of intersubjective understanding influenced by the "linguistic turn" of philosophy. One might quibble, perhaps, that the transition from subjective to intersubjective is insufficient, in the sense that "intersubjective" still carries a sense of isolate subjects in communication rather than the centrality of communication itself, intrinsically involving, not subjects, but persons, produced out of the communication process. More fundamentally, though, communicative reason is far more than the restrictive linguistic domain in which Habermas sees it. Human communication is a sign-process involving the varied human capacities and touching the deepest *extrarational* sources of intelligence built into and grown out of the human body. These resources of reason, as I hope to show, are systematically rejected by Habermas's rationalistic worldview. Hence, despite his attempt to frame a version of rationality which is user friendly, his project is an ideal document of how excessive rationality will mistake its part for the whole.

Mythical Worldviews and the Structuralist Myth

In the first chapter of his Volume One, Habermas attempts to come to terms with the concept of rationality in a number of ways, including extended sections on myth and action. He turns to "mythical world-views" because they represent, in his view, an antithesis to the modern understanding of the world, and thereby provide a mirror of otherness through which we can reflect upon the modern world. Habermas claims that this way of proceeding has the advantage of forcing him to turn from conceptual to empirical analysis, by which he means that, as he puts it, "for the sake of simplicity," he confines himself to the results of two structuralists, Claude Lévi-Strauss and Maurice Godelier. He uses these two exemplars of twentieth-century French rationalism as the sole representatives of mythic thought, and assiduously avoids any concrete discussion of a single myth in his "empirical" review. At least Lévi-Strauss, the "cerebral savage," as Clifford Geertz termed him, spent time studying specific myths, even if he did then divest them of their specific qualities in attempting to reveal an abstract universal structure of binary logic. But here and throughout *TCA* Habermas never engages in specific analyses of ethnographic, historical, or empirical data and never goes back to the source materials used by Lévi-Strauss, Piaget, Weber, or others that he draws on.

Habermas relies in particular on Maurice Godelier, a structuralist Marxist who appropriates the side of Marxism in which determining conditions of social life are "invisible," not consciously known in experience. As a structuralist, Godelier must deny what is essential to Marx: that there can be meaning in praxis. Structuralism denies meaning to "surface" phenomena, such as *parole* or speech, because it views meaning as a "faculty" of *langue* or deep structure not susceptible to modification through experience. From a structuralist perspective, myth is only interesting as a manifestation of the underlying logic of the system, not as a voicing and bodying forth of the inner life of humanity, of its achievements and tragedies, of recurrent experiences with wondrous and terrifying forces and movements of nature, and, least of all, of the drama inherent in human communication.

Structuralism denies meaning to praxis, and hence it is rather odd, to say the least, for someone like Habermas, concerned with a broad-based theory of "communicative action" as means to a free social life, to limit himself "for the sake of simplicity" to structuralist technicians who deny meaning at the level of action and who represent perhaps the most intellectualistic and abstracted approach to myth within the much broader spectrum of schools of thought. Strange also is his reliance on what I will call a totalitarian way of thinking: structuralism denies that flesh and blood human beings embody and body forth meaning and can criticize and revise the "code" of meaning, because it holds meaning and structure to be purely "skeletal," merely the property of a single underlying universal and unchanging code of binary opposition, to be found in all human endeavor regardless of time, place, or circumstance. There is a myth to be found here, but it is the myth of twentieth-century binary thinking, itself the legacy of cultural nominalism.

Structuralism reproduces the nominalist tendency to begin with a false dichotomy requiring synthesis. It projects this view on to the world as an "objective" theory: nature and culture are clear and distinct categories, surface phenomena and deep structure are clear and distinct categories, individual versus social are clear and distinct categories, logic is a rational, binary system.

One gets the impression in Habermas's discussion of myth that those who live within mythic belief are extremely limited by our standards, that myth is a fuzzy and backward form of thought. Habermas uses the dichotomous premisses of modern thought as found in structuralism and semantics to criticize myth as merely vague, as having "a deficient differentiation between *language and world.*"[4]

That the primary purpose of myths might be precisely to express intensely felt relationships to the world—meaning "felt relationship" as that quality that literally lives in the transaction between person and world and not in system or logic or brain—escapes Habermas's single-visioned view. The entire discussion of myth can be read as an example of how rationalism denigrates those "divine deep waters," as the Babylonians said, in which living myth swims: modalities of intelligence not reducible to the thin filmy surface of rationality. Habermas's two primary criticisms of mythical worldviews are that they are marked by "insufficient differentiation among fundamental attitudes to the objective, social, and subjective worlds; and the lack of reflexivity in worldviews that cannot be identified *as* worldviews, as cultural traditions. Mythical worldviews are not understood by members as interpretive systems that are attached to cultural traditions, constituted by internal interrelations of meaning, symbolically related to reality, and connected with validity claims—and thus exposed to criticism and open to revision."[5]

Both of these criticisms reveal a shallow ethnocentrism which disallows the voice of mythical worldviews as dialogical "other" in communicative debate. But even if one were to concede Habermas's criticisms, they still reveal the superiority of mythic to rational "communicative" thought. Mythic "thought" indeed does not view objective, social, and subjective worlds as autonomous in Habermas's sense but rather as fluid and continuous. And there is no reason why mythic thought should radically differentiate these three spheres, because these spheres, as I will argue later, have their existence within the cultural nominalism of modernity and are mere distortions, mentally skewed forms of communicative action rather than constituent features of it or the world.

Habermas's second criticism is that mythical understanding acts as a form of reification and one not subject to criticism: How can one criticize the myth one believes in when one believes in it as reality itself? Although the possibility of critical perspective and of criticism itself is undeniably an important consideration in modern society, Habermas neglects the ways in which even a single mythic world-view allows for critical conflict and ambiguity of interpretation, as almost any of the Greek myths attest and as a close look at traditional village life will reveal.[6] More fundamentally, he neglects the facts that belief comes first and doubt comes after belief, and that myth and ritual involve more than just belief.

We should remember that myth and ritual are living forms which transformed us into humans, a fundamental fact which never penetrates Habermas's rationalistic armor. In Habermas's evolutionary perspective, earlier embodiments of human communication are absolutely *"aufgehoben,"* that is, overcome or superseded by a seemingly ever-expanding rationality. Ritually based societies did and do place severe limitations on personal autonomy, but ritual, contra Habermas, was perhaps the original means of "reflexivity." This was not the dispassionate reflexivity of rational communicators who know what their validity claims are about, but the humble reflexivity of humans confronted with a baffling world and a deeply felt need to give it voice. By their very restricted and repetitive natures ritual action and myth gradually peeled emergent humankind from pure participation and impelled us toward belief, toward the good and bad aspects of human belief. This process not only brought about the enlargement of imagination but also the encasing of human perception within new webs constructed by these imaginings.

If emerging humankind had only possessed Habermas's communicative action instead of ritual and mythic action, it could never have coped with the enormous anxieties produced by its surplus brain energy, it could never have un–self-consciously formed the artistic expressions of the human psyche, the utterances of speech, the structures of language: it could never have become human. Rather than characterizing mythic-bound cultures as having "deficient differentiation," Habermas should have considered how they could have been so extraordinarily efficient, creating vital societies that often endured for millenia, creating art and language in paleolithic culture, developing the basis of virtually all modern grains in the neolithic age, inventing mathematics and astronomy in Babylonian civilization, giving birth to philosophy in ancient Greece. The real question Habermas never asks is whether and in what ways myth might enhance rather than hinder communicative reason.

Habermas does not allow the possibility of a noncritical yet perceptive and self-illuminating narrative. Because he makes propositional argumentation based on the ability to respond yes or no foundational for communicative action, he unnecessarily disallows other modalities of communicative action, such as myth. D. H. Lawrence held a much more "evolved" view of myth and human conduct than does Habermas. In contrast to allegory,

> Myth likewise is descriptive narrative using images. But myth is never an argument, it never has a didactic nor a moral purpose, you can draw no conclusion from it. Myth is an attempt to narrate a whole human experience, of which the purpose is too deep, going too deep in the blood and soul, for mental explanation or description. We *can* expound the myth of Chronos very easily. We can explain it, we can even draw the moral conclusion. But we only look a little silly. The myth of Chronos lives on beyond explanation, for it describes a profound experience of the human body and soul, an experience which is never exhausted and never will be exhausted, for it is being felt and suffered now, and it will be felt and suffered while man remains man. You may explain the myths away: but it only means you go on suffering blindly, stupidly, "in the unconscious," instead of healthily and with the imaginative comprehension playing upon the suffering.[7]

"With the imaginative comprehension playing upon the suffering": this idea—virtually a definition of art—falls utterly outside the neat system Habermas has constructed, where "imaginative comprehension" would be reduced to so-called aesthetic-practical, subjective expressions. Because emerging humankind could not absolutely differentiate itself from the cosmos, from the sun and moon and birds and beasts and trees and stones, from the wondrous and terrifying passage of seasons, forces of weather, cycles of birth and decay and death, it is judged inferior to Habermas's modern rational communicator and barred from entry to the denatured kingdom of communicative action, with its ultrarationalized, autonomous individuals and logically airtight spheres of action: the world of the talking heads.

ACTION AND COMMUNICATIVE RATIONALIZATION

Habermas's discussion of myth in his Volume One is followed by a section on four sociological concepts of action. There he maps out the following progressive differentiation in relations of actor and world:

1. Teleological action. This conception of action is defined by the actor's choice of successful means to realize his or her goal: "The central concept is that of

a *decision* among alternative courses of action, with a view to the realization of an end, guided by maxims, and based on an interpretation of the situation."[8] Instrumental action, rational or economic choice, game theory models, and strategic action are all varieties of this category. Habermas claims this model has been at the center of action theory since Aristotle, but this seems to me to individualize Aristotle's conception of teleology. It derives from the spirit of the modern solitary individual of Weber's *Zweckrationalität,* not the socially rooted ancient Greek citizen contextualized within the public sphere of the polis.

2. Normatively regulated action. This model deals with "members of a social group who orient their action to common values," and is the model of action informing role theory in the tradition of Durkheim and Parsons.[9]

3. Dramaturgical action. If teleological action is excessively individualized and normatively regulated action is excessively socialized, dramaturgical action seems to include both sides, referring "to participants in interaction constituting a public for one another, before whom they present themselves."[10] Central to this model is, of course, Erving Goffman's conception of the "presentation of self" in social situations. Or stated differently, Habermas's conception of dramaturgical action is entirely limited to Goffman's conception of presentation of self, ignoring other, less rationally calculating aspects of Goffman's work, such as the "framing" of situations. Much more significantly though, Habermas has ignored other potentially broader dramaturgical accounts of action, such as those of Kenneth Burke or Victor Turner. In Burke and Turner, dramaturgical action may include strategic self-presentation as one aspect, but it also involves broader dimensions such as specific scene and wider context, and especially in Turner, a critical relationship of actor, enacted, and "audience" which, in the case of ritual action, completely transcends the intentions of the individual actor to include those of competing factions, of the dead, of genders, of stages of life, and of the ongoing problems of a society as a whole.

Sociologists have been quite willing to cannibalize stock terms from drama, such as role, actor, or script, but sociology has fairly consistently shied away from taking on the full implications of the dramaturgical perspective, which involves a deep feel for and appreciation of the fundamental significance of signs and symbols, the fantastic, and the "per-forming" or actual forming of meaning through communication and communion involved in the enactment of human action and the drama of life. Habermas unimaginatively reduces the diversity of dramaturgical action to the monopoly of rationalistic individuals presenting themselves, making life in all its fullness to be but a scrim behind which operates the Great Calculator.

What is Goffman's "dramaturgical" presentation of self seen from the perspective of drama? It seems to me that Goffman is better seen as an antidramaturgist, in the same way, perhaps, that many of the dominant playwrights of the same time period, such as Samuel Becket or Harold Pinter, have been antidramatists. Aristotle believed that drama produced catharsis, yet what one finds in plays such as Becket's *Waiting for Godot* or Pinter's *The Birthday Party* is the denial of catharsis, the exact antithesis of Aristotle's conception of drama. If one thinks also of drama as producing un–self-conscious absorption of the audience into the action of the play—a loss of self—then these and many other avant-garde plays also produce the opposite: the continuing breaking of action through self-consciousness. I am not saying that such works are not truly artistic: some powerfully capture the alienated and starved spirit of our time. But they do represent a peculiar moment in the history of drama and are by no means representative of drama as a whole.

Similarly, Goffman's theory is constantly focused on those moments of the eruption of self-consciousness, on those self-presentations of calculating individuals strategically creating facades, ever mindful of potential blockages. Goffman's "actors" seem more concerned with avoiding exposure of their true feelings and intentions than with attaining the catharsis of consummated human actions. His model of the self resembles D. W. Winnicott's description of the "false self" which performs its actions for an effect as opposed to the spontaneous, engaged self.

As we saw with Habermas's treatment of myth, un–self-conscious belief does not meet the legitimacy claims that rationally chosen belief does. Similarly, drama in the sense of un–self-conscious action would not have the legitimacy that rationally chosen strategic action does, let alone "communicative action." Perhaps this is why Habermas could rely on one narrow conception of drama, just as he relies on one narrow structuralist conception of myth: his rationalist predilections lead him to rationalist theories and away from considering contrary approaches or concrete experience.

Before going on to Habermas's own fourth type of action—communicative action—I want to consider briefly his use of Karl Popper's concept of "three worlds" as it relates to his types of action, since this distinction is central to Habermas's theories of communication and modernity. Early in his chapter on types of sociological action, Habermas quotes from Karl Popper's 1967 address, "Epistemology without a Knowing Subject," where Popper states: "We may distinguish the following three worlds or universes: first, the world of physical objects or of physical states; secondly, the world of states of consciousness, or of mental states, or perhaps of behavioral dispositions to act; and thirdly, the world of *objective contents of thought,* especially of scientific and poetic thoughts and of works of art.[11]

Although expressing strong reservations about Popper's ontological grounding of these categories, Habermas finds ways to "soften" them, and ends up using them in a way much more congruent with Max Weber's distinctions of several cultural spheres of value: science and technology, law and morality, and art and criticism. I will return to the problem of the three spheres later, but for the moment I want to indicate that Habermas considers teleological and strategic action as presupposing only the first world, the objective world, since actors coordinate their actions only on the basis of an egocentric calculus of utility. Normatively regulated action, because it involves not only "the objective world of existing states of affairs" but also "the social world to which the actor belongs as a role-playing subject," presupposes two worlds. This level is more inclusive, but still does not include "the actor *himself* as a world toward which he can behave reflectively"[12] as the next stage, dramaturgical action, does.

Still, because Goffman's dramaturgical action is seen by Habermas as concerned with the coordination of inner and outer worlds, self and audience, it remains at the two-world level. Only with the "additional presupposition of a *linguistic medium* that reflects the actor's relations to the world as such" do we advance to the third world: "Only the communicative model of action presupposes language as a medium of uncurtailed communication whereby speakers and hearers, out of the context of their preinterpreted lifeworld, refer simultaneously to things in the objective, social, and subjective worlds in order to negotiate common definitions of the situation."[13]

Habermas is clearly seeking a theory of action that can do justice to the intrinsically dialogical nature of human communication, and so it remains odd to me that dramatic expression would be considered uncommunicative. Because of an excessive regard for rational justification Habermas's theory of action divests living speech of its intrinsic quality. Yet from my perspective there is quite clearly a capacity of human passions to utter living, yet noncritical, truth, just as there is a capacity for linguistically valid, intersubjective, argumentative speech to make falsehoods. Communication need not be critical or reflective to be true. In this sense Romeo, Juliet, Hamlet, Prospero, and Lear may be among the most communicative "actors" the world has known, even if they could not give fully rational justifications for their actions—or any justification whatsoever. By contrast, those priests of secrecy at the Pentagon and Kremlin may have some of the most rational justifications ever devised regarding their plans to cremate the earth. Habermas shows the way to avoid the Scylla of unjustified action through communicative intersubjectivity, yet he does so at the cost of plunging into the Charybdis of verbal rationalizations: a legalistic "post-action" theory where explanation counts for more than the living act itself. Although communicative action theory denies it, "actions speak louder than words," and both actions and words can speak truer than rational afterthoughts.

LIFE-WORLD VERSUS CRITICAL COMMUNICATION

Through his inclusion of the life-world, Habermas seeks to redress an undervaluing by rationalization theories of the everyday practices which contextualize meaning. Critically drawing from a variety of sources in the phenomenological tradition, especially Alfred Schutz, Habermas develops a conception of the life-world as that unquestioned, unproblematic background which stands in contrast to communicative action. Although providing the context for communicative action, as common knowledge, the life-world is "the conservative counterweight to the risk of disagreement," and is "immune from critique." As Habermas says in introducing the concept in Volume One, "Subjects acting communicatively always come to an understanding in the horizon of a lifeworld. . . . The lifeworld also stores the interpretive work of preceding generations. It is the conservative counterweight to the risk of disagreement that arises with every actual process of reaching understanding; for communicative actors can achieve an understanding only by way of taking yes/no positions on criticizable validity claims. *The relation between these weights changes with the decentration of worldviews.* The more the worldview that furnishes the cultural stock of knowledge is decentered, the less the need for understanding is covered *in advance* by an interpreted lifeworld immune from critique, and the more this need has to be met by the interpretive accomplishments of the participants themselves."[14]

One sees in this statement Habermas's belief that human development is a process of progressive rationalization. The traditional life-world placed fetters on "rationality potentials," which Habermas sees as progressively released in the "decentering" transformations from traditional mythic worldviews through religious-metaphysical worldviews to modern worldviews. In this evolutionary process, there occurs a separation of systemic "steering mechanisms" from life-world as well as an increasing complexity in systems and rationalization of the life-world.

Habermas points to the "colonization of the lifeworld" by "autonomous subsystems" as a key problem of uncontrolled instrumental rationality, and he sees his theory of communicative action as providing a medium of rationality for balancing life-world and system, and for coordinating relations of the life-world to the three autonomous objective, social, and subjective spheres. He is not against the rationalization of the life-world per se, but wants to place his good kind of communicative rationalization against the "colonization of the lifeworld" by instrumental rationalization. Yet he never considers whether a culture based on achieving understanding "only by way of taking yes/no positions on criticizable validity claims" could remain viable and vital. Could its members always wait for the communicative question to be validly posed, let alone answered, before acting? Could painters paint, carpenters hammer, scientists hypothesize, if they had to wait for the problem to be self-consciously posed as a criticizable validity claim on which they had to take a yes/no position within a consensual community? If actor A saw actor B about to be run over by a speeding train and sought to communicate the problem linguistically through propositional argumentation, resulting in actor B achieving a consensual understanding of the problem at the last moment before being splattered by the train, would that be communicative action? If actor A instinctively ran and tackled actor B out of the way of the train with brute force, would that be merely a "power claim" and therefore not communicative action?[15] Or if it could be regarded as communicative action, would the brute act itself be so regarded, or merely its rational "criticizable validity claim" which would function as the logical afterthought to the act? If actor B did not want to be rescued, would that invalidate the act, since a participant rejected its validity claim?

One of the problems is that Habermas has conceived the life-world as a passive reservoir of knowledge with no capacities for reasonable activity. His life-world is drawn from the antinaturalist tradition of Dilthey, Schutz, Husserl, and Wittgenstein: biology plays no part in his conception, he conceives life solely from the rationalist's viewpoint as "tacit knowledge." He could have broadened his conception of the life-world, even while safely drawing from the Kantian domain by incorporating the life-concepts of Georg Simmel or Max Scheler, who held life to be an active force, dialectically opposed to rational form or Geist. In Simmel's *Lebensphilosophie,* as described in Chapter 2, life is virtually pure activity or energy, a formless volcanic magma which breaks through old cultural forms and generates new ones.

Habermas claims system and life-world exist in opposition to one another. He seems to deny the many systemic and critical capacities that mark the life-world, although not necessarily rational: the long-term tempering of beliefs through experience, the development of instinctual proclivities such as the capacity for speech, the development of habits of belief providing common sense prejudices, wisdom, traditions, and crafts. Because of Habermas's commitment to the bifurcated world of Kant and its rigid tendency toward dichotomy, he is incapable of seeing that his system and life-world distinction may be a false abstraction, a legacy of cultural nominalism. If he were to use the concept of living habit developed by the pragmatists, he might see the possibility of a continuum between the unreflective habit that is the life-world and the reflective habit of critical rationality or system. He might take more seriously the problem of how the life-world generated "communicative action" out of itself without recourse to the principles of communicative action: by definition the life-world cannot explain its actions.

The peculiar passivity and inertness of the life-world is revealed when Habermas contrasts it, as a "complementary concept," to communicative action as the locus of the problematic: the life-world "cannot become problematic, it can at most fall apart. The elements of the lifeworld with which we are naively familiar do not have the status of facts or norms or experiences concerning which speakers and hearers could, if necessary, come to some understanding."[16] Were Habermas ever to climb down from his lofty meta-meta-theoretical perch to examine the substance of myths, rituals, and religious practices, he might see that they form living archives of humanity's attempts to deal with the problems of affliction, life-transitions, death and suffering as well as the celebration of life and community. Were he seriously to draw from Dewey and Mead's pragmatic philosophy of experience, he would see that problem finding, though reasonable, is not a fundamentally rational process, and that the finding and resolving of problems through reasonable, communicative means is not restricted to rationally linguistic validity claims but is an in-built facet and potential of human experience. Were he to go yet further, he would see that the purpose of communicative rationality is to give itself to and be absorbed by the life-world, not the reverse.

The life-world itself is the incorporation of prior experience in human traditions and practices, yet Habermas's life-world seems to be formed out of pure innocence rather than experience. When he defines it as "immune from critique," he neglects the possibility that the life-world, as the product of a vast span of experience, may itself be a form of implicit critique or subliminal, criticizable interpretation. Consider John Dewey's way of putting it, "There exists at any period a body of beliefs and of institutions and practices allied to them. In these beliefs there are implicit broad interpretations of life and the world. These interpretations have consequences, often profoundly important. In their actual currency, however, the implications of origin, nature, and consequences are not examined and formulated. The beliefs and their associated practices express attitudes and responses which have operated under conditions of direct and often accidental stress. They constitute, as it seems to me, the immediate primary material of philosophical reflection."[17] Dewey's "life-world," unlike Habermas's, is forged out of problematic life-experience and is not necessarily arbitrary. In Dewey's view both individual human conduct and institutions represent a dramatic dialogue of impulse and habit. System or social structure, in other words, is regarded as open-ended habit. Common human experience, localized in situational contexts rather than rational linguistic validity claims, provides the yardstick for both individual conduct and systemic norms. Dewey's whole notion of inquiry as rooted in an indeterminate or problematic situation, which is *felt* as such and is progressively transformed to a determinate solution, shows qualitative feeling to be essential to scientific inquiry—science is not limited to rational verbal discourse. Similarly Peirce's concept of abduction illustrates that science is not limited to language or rationality.

As the incorporation of prior experience, the life-world may possess more reason in a given situation than communicative action. How many times have rational decisions, fortified by linguistic validity claims and consensual agreement, been shown to be inferior to traditional practices which could not be rationally justified by their practitioners? One can cite modern attempts to make "perfect" symmetrical violins which lacked the beautiful sound of an asymmetrical Stradivarius, Maoist attempts to utilize land on mountains and high hills for agriculture which resulted in ruining irrigation systems, or "functionalist" urban and architectural design which ignored the informal rules of neighborhood interaction. In these examples it is usually the case that the traditional practice incorporated a broader experience and interpretation of the problem than could be available to communicative rationality, even if this information could not be articulated. In short, the life-world should be conceived as more than simply as a form of inadequate rationality or as a passive data-base for critical rationality.

Habermas believes that an impassable gulf exists between life-world and discursive thought: "Members of a social collective normally share a life-world. In communication, but also in processes of cognition, this only exists in the distinctive, pre-reflexive form of background assumptions, background receptivities or background relations. The life-world is that remarkable thing which dissolves and disappears before our eyes as soon as we try to take it up piece by piece . . . one can label as a life-world only those resources that are not thematized, not criticized. The moment one of its elements is taken out and criticized, made accessible to discussion, that element no longer belongs to the life-world. I also think it is impossible to create new forms of living by talking and talking about things."[18]

Critical communication, in other words, nullifies the contents of the life-world by raising them to self-consciousness. Conversely, rationality cannot become a part of the life-world. Surely this dichotomy proposed by Habermas is not necessary, for it denies both the possibility that life-worlds can grow through human cultivation (or, for that matter, that they can atrophy or self-destruct from lack of it), and that the highest critical capacities may serve the life-world rather than pulverize it. Perhaps a much more fruitful way of viewing what Habermas sees as a dichotomy between the critical (or system) and the life-world is to view the two as linked polarities of human existence: polarities marked by potentially creative tensions as well as potentially destructive tendencies when the polar relation is severed. From this perspective it would be by no means "impossible," as Habermas says, "to create new forms of living by talking and talking about things"—as long as one acknowledges that talk is experientially rather than rationally based.

Idle talk is, of course, nothing next to creative human conduct. Yet there are forms of "talking" essential to the creation of "new forms of living," as myths and sagas, poetry, religious and literary writings, political speeches and manifestos, and even scientific papers have shown so many times in human history. Stranger though, for Habermas's denial that talk can create new forms of living, are the implications for his theory of consensual communicative action. His theory of communicative action is, if nothing else, a "talking cure." Are members of a society supposed simply to nod to "create new forms of living?" Or more broadly, does this mean that new forms of living arise solely from the life-world and apart from critical capacities? If this were true it would simply reassert the uncontrolled subjectivity typical of traditional German romanticism in the guise of a life-world concept, thereby undermining Habermas's claim to have moved away from a philosophy of consciousness or subjectivity.

MEAD, DURKHEIM, AND THE SPECTER OF KANT

Habermas's Volume Two opens with a description of how the philosophy of consciousness was attacked early in the twentieth century by both analytic philosophy of language and behaviorism. He mentions three times that these two separate traditions had common origins in the pragmatism of Peirce, despite going off in their own directions. Yet oddly enough, he ignores Peirce's critique. He notes that Mead also provides a point of common intersection between the two traditions, and therefore that he will examine Mead's theory as providing a "communication-theoretic foundation of sociology," yet one with certain gaps needing to be filled by Durkheim's "theory of social solidarity connecting social integration to system integration."[19] Since Habermas relies heavily on linguistic philosophy and speech act theory—which Mead did not—it is strange that he here totally ignores Peirce, who Habermas surely knows developed explicit linguistic analyses and a conception of logic as semeiotic. As with his discussion of myth, Habermas never makes validity claims for his selection of one theorist over another, despite the centrality of rationally and explicitly grounded argumentation to his own theory of communicative action, but seems to rely on tradition in selecting well-known social scientists and philosophers.

Habermas traces Mead's "logical genesis" of meaning, passing from gestural through symbolically mediated interaction to normatively guided interaction. He believes that in the transition from symbolically mediated to normatively guided interaction "there is a gap in the phylogenetic line of development which can be filled in with Durkheim's assumptions concerning the sacred foundations of morality, the ritually preserved fund of social solidarity."[20] Another way of interpreting this "gap" is that Mead's continuous theory of the emergence and evolution of human symbolic communication, rooted in a theory of social experience, does not satisfy Habermas's Kantian predilections for discontinuous evolution requiring an idealized, antinaturalistic conception of norms as a means of artificially "synthesizing" subject and object worlds. This is apparent in the following statement: "Human cognitions and expressions, however shaped by language they may be, can also be traced back to the natural history of intelligent performances and expressive gestures in animals. Norm consciousness, on the other hand, has no equally trivial extralinguistic reference; for obligations there are no unambiguous natural-historical correlates, as there are for sense impressions and needs."[21] The first sentence can be read as Mead's theory, the second one as Durkheim's. Both are then "synthesized" through Habermas's discussion of the differentiated speech requirements of communicative action.

It seems puzzling when one knows of Mead's and Dewey's participation in the American genetic epistemology movement (which later moved to Switzerland with James Mark Baldwin and was taken over by Jean Piaget), and especially of Mead's interest in "emergent evolutionism," that Habermas sees Mead as ignoring a phylogenetic account of human development in favor of an ontogenetic account of socialization. Mead does draw most of his examples from individual interactions, but it seems to me that these discussions are always framed within a phylogenetic context of the natural emergence of human symbolic communication and rationality. Perhaps because Habermas ignores the crucial place of experience in Mead's thought, he does not see that Mead's account of human development is an experiential phylogenesis—evolution discussed from the perspective of the social act. Habermas's linguistic conceptualism consistently causes him to avoid the place of social experience in the shaping of myth, ritual, action, and the life-world, and the genesis of Mead's "generalized other." He fails to see that Mead sought to account for an evolving process of social cooperation and signification which generated an increasingly self-interpreting sign-world. This organ of interpretation not only could give body and voice to the otherness of death, affliction, the animals and plants of the surrounding environment and the place of humans in that environment, but in so doing it helped to shape the emerging inner landscape of human consciousness and symbolic communication and the outer landscape of social practices and institutions.

In coming to generalize the otherness of experience, emerging humankind radically broadened the possibilities of its participation in the environment. Mead may have outlined this process in overly bland and otherwise limited ways in his discussion of the generalized other, but it seems to me that his account is theoretically more satisfactory than Durkheim's sociological Kantianism. Habermas finds in Durkheim's theory of *conscience collective* the equivalent of a quasi-transcendental grounding for norm consciousness: he reintroduces the element of idealistic foundationalism which Mead's theory makes unnecessary.

This becomes clearer in Habermas's interpretation of Durkheim's view of truth as an ideal added to and above experience and deriving from collective identity: "The idea of truth can get from the concept of normative validity only the impersonality—supratemporal—of an idealized agreement, of an intersubjectivity related to an ideal communication community. This moment of a 'harmony of minds' is *added* to that of a 'harmony with the nature of things.' The authority standing behind knowledge does not coincide with moral authority. Rather, the concept of truth combines the objectivity of experience with a claim to the intersubjective validity of a corresponding descriptive statement, the idea of the correspondence of sentences to facts with the concept of an idealized consensus. It is only from this *combination* that we get the concept of a criticizable validity claim."[22] Habermas remarks in a footnote that this dualistic conception comes close to Peirce's conception of truth, but Peirce does not hold to the nominalistic divide between thought or representation and reality which Durkheim and Habermas do. Defining truth as the last result to which the community of inquirers would be led, and of the nature of a sign or representation, Peirce goes on to say that the object of that representation, "that to which the representation should conform, is itself something in the nature of a representation, or sign—something noumenal, intelligible, conceivable, and utterly unlike a thing-in-itself."[23] Peirce's thoroughly semeiotic conception of truth denies the materialized conception of experience and idealized conception of intersubjective representation *added* to experience. Similarly Mead's naturalistic account roots symbolic communication in experience and not in a conceptualistic realm superimposed upon it. Human evolution is marked by the progressive incorporation of otherness into sign-habits: internalized dispositions and externalized cults and practices.

Cults and social groups are in Mead's view means of engaging in communicative, though not necessarily self-reflective or rational, dialogue with the external and internal environment. The core of the generalized other in this sense can be characterized as a habitual representation of conceivable experience produced by experience and carrying consequences for future experience.

Habermas does see how the generalized other as a dialogue of "me" and "I" provides a critique of the subjectivist philosophy of consciousness inherent in Durkheim's thought, yet because of his neat separation of objective, social, and subjective worlds, he again infuses his dichotomous view into Mead's distinction, seeing it in terms of an external world of norm-conforming actions versus an inner world of spontaneous experiences.[24] He ignores Mead's pragmatic perspective, in which there is an emergent or novel aspect to nature itself, just as the inner world is largely an internalization of experience. The inner world is not only "spontaneous experiences" but includes long-term tempered experiences grown into the body, biological experience as well as traditional and historical experience.

In what seems to me a fundamental misreading of the generalized other, perhaps based in part on a lack of clarity in Mead, Habermas says that the generalized other "is supposed to have arisen by way of the internalization of group sanctions. However, this explanation can only hold for ontogenesis, for groups must have first been constituted as units capable of acting before sanctions could be imposed in their name. Participants in symbolically mediated interaction can transform themselves, so to speak, from exemplars of an animal species with an inborn, species-specific environment into members of a collective with a lifeworld only to the degree that a generalized other—we might also say: a collective consciousness or a group identity—has taken shape."[25] Habermas fails to see that groups arise in the same way as individuals for Mead—as habituated practices which incorporate prior experiences and are in communicative dialogue with the internal and external environment. He introduces the idea of collective representations as a collective social glue providing the basis of "norm conformity." Religious symbolism and the sacred form a netherland of "paleosymbols" in which behavior is no longer guided by instincts and not yet governed by the properties of propositional linguistic speech. Hence religious symbolism simply represents the transformation from nature to culture. The import of Habermas's use of Durkheim is to reintroduce the Kantian dichotomy, undercut by Mead's philosophy, of a nature incapable of signification and a culture incapable of natural experience. He must then limit "communicative action" to rationally grounded linguistic argumentation instead of the much broader category of dialogical significatory experience which Mead could have provided. As with the treatment of myth, practice is subsumed under the requirements of rational structure.

The Three Spheres of Modernity

If we start from the view that modern structures of consciousness condense to the three complexes of rationality [i. e., cognitive-instrumental, moral-practical, aesthetic-practical] then we can think of the structurally possible rationalization of society as a combination of the corresponding ideas (from the domains of science and technology, law and morality, art and eroticism) with interests, and their embodiment in correspondingly differentiated orders of life. This (rather risky) model would enable us to state the necessary conditions for a nonselective pattern of rationalization: The three cultural value spheres have to be connected with corresponding action systems in such a way that the production and transmission of knowledge that is specialized according to validity claims is secured; the cognitive potential developed by expert cultures has, in turn, to be passed on to the communicative practice of everyday life and to be made fruitful for social action systems; finally, the cultural value spheres have to be institutionalized in such a balanced way that the life-orders corresponding to them are sufficiently autonomous to avoid being subordinated to laws intrinsic to heterogenous orders of life.[26]

Habermas believes that modernity can be characterized by the differentiation of three autonomous and logically valid spheres of rationality possessed of their own inner logics: cognitive-instrumental rationality, moral-practical rationality, and aesthetic-practical rationality. Triadic divisions of reason are not new, but Habermas is appropriating the modern tradition of Max Weber and Immanuel Kant and not the trifold beauty, goodness, and truth of the scholastic *summum bonum*.

For a truly communicative rationality to develop, Habermas claims that a balance between the three spheres is needed, one which will ensure undistorted communication and institutional legitimation. But the problem is much more fundamental. The very spheres themselves, as he has defined them, are products of an uncritical application of nominalized rationality, and reproduce the old Cartesian/Kantian problem of how to relate a primal object and its mechanics with an isolate subject and its values (and with a society whose inner logic is "norm conformity").

One of the dangerous, and I would say mythic, implications of Habermas's argument for the rational autonomy of the three worlds is the subjectivism which underlies his definition of each. Technicalism underlies the objective world, so that "cognitive-instrumental" rationality and science and technology are pictured as intrinsically technical and strategic, and any moral or aesthetic considerations have to be "brought in" by communicative coordination from the outside, from the other "spheres." "Moral-practical" rationality and law and morality are intrinsically about norm following, regardless of objective conditions or subjective perspective, suggesting that within this sphere is an image of the social world constituted by the faceless herd. The subjective world is the sphere of "aesthetic-practical" rationality, art and eroticism: a view which strikes me as an unintended parody of subjective idealism and romanticism, a world lacking inherent objective or moral tempering except insofar as it coordinates itself with these separate spheres. In the term "aesthetic-practical," the "-practical" addition to aesthetic is as needless as the "rationality" addition to "aesthetic-practical" is wrong. Surely even if post-Enlightenment culture carved the world up into the three clear and distinct spheres, it does not follow that the conduct indigenous to each sphere must be characterized as a rationality complex.

Habermas seeks to acknowledge the genuine achievement of different spheres of conduct in the modern world, the ways in which art and morality, for example, broke free from their traditional religious moorings and developed autonomous secular standards. But in the place of a medieval religious civilization which prevented the emergence of differentiated spheres of conduct, he would shrink the three domains of science and technology, law and morality, and art and eroticism to a modern equivalent by viewing them as "complexes of rationality." The reader should examine figure 3 below, taken from Volume One of *TCA*, to see how Habermas fits these categories into neat systematic boxes, as if art and eroticism fit neatly into different aspects of one box, and as if erotic life is cleanly separable from moral life and can only be associated with "aesthetic-practical rationality."

Worlds / Basic Attitudes	1 Objective	2 Social	3 Subjective	1 Objective
3 Expressive	Art			
1 Objectivating	↑ Cognitive-instrumental rationality Science Technology ¦ Social ¦technologies↓		X	
2 Norm-conformative	X	↑ Moral-practical rationality Law ¦ ¦Morality↓		
3 Expressive		X	↑ Aesthetic-practical rationality Eroticism ¦ Art	

Figure 3. Rationalization complexes. From Theory of Communicative Reason, *by Jürgen Habermas.*
Copyright © 1984 by Beacon Press/orig. pub. Verlag Suhrkamp.
Reprinted by permission of Beacon Press.

The development of modern art has much more to do with the expansion and articulation of human feeling than it has to do with mere rationality, unless one adopts a purely technical and external approach, as Habermas does. And the linking of science and technology as if they were synonymous, and as if they could be characterized by "cognitive-instrumental rationality," reveals a fundamental misunderstanding of the nature of modern science. Science is a method of inquiry intrinsically incorporating "intersubjective" inquirers into the very notion of objectivity, as well as extrarational tempering—learning by experience and extrarational conjecturing or hypothesis—what Peirce termed "abduction." Science, conceived from a truly "communicative action" perspective, as opposed to Habermas's, includes rationality but is by no means limited to it, and a rationality intrinsically subject to criticism by all other inquirers rather than an individualistic "cognitive-instrumental rationality" unbounded internally by the critical community. Habermas has constructed his three spheres to be internally deficient and requiring rescue from the outside by a communicative rationality balancing act.

Yet the possibility of communicative action is built into these spheres of conduct internally, and not merely in an external coordinating action of linguistically based intersubjectivity.

Against Habermas's theory that the three spheres are "complexes of rationality" whose balancing results in "good" rationalization, I would juxtapose Peirce's view that rationality is but an aspect of one sphere, the logical, itself defined differently from Habermas, and that the logical sphere is dependent on the ethical sphere, which in turn is itself dependent upon the aesthetic sphere. Even logic, in Peirce's conception, involves more than rationality, as illustrated by Peirce's incorporation of abductive inference within logic.[27] Peirce's approach provides a much broader basis for the *relative* autonomy or irreducibility of the three modalities of being than does Habermas's Kantian-based three forms of rationality. Instead of three separate spheres externally connected by communicative rationality, Peirce's conception would have the sphere of logic within the larger one of ethics, and ethics in turn within the larger sphere of aesthetics. The *Summum Bonum* of Peirce's approach can be expressed in the traditional words of Native Americans: "to walk in Beauty," in other words, it is conduct harmonious with Being and its development. This argument amounts to overturning the dominant categories of modern thought and their prime avatar, rationality.

As opposed to a view of humanity becoming matured by becoming better rationalized, it is more accurate to see modern life as a historical era in which humanity becomes increasingly denatured, dematured, and etherealized through its overreliance on decontextualized rationality. What probably began in the prolonged physical immaturity of the human species, which allowed a plasticity requiring the institutions of culture and brain capacities for elaborate symbolic communication, may have culminated in creatures overly dependent on, and dominated by, their ability to be abstract. Being abstract, being "critical," is and will ever remain but one of the means to being whole, and never by itself the goal of human development.

RATIONALITY'S MYRMIDON

It is clear from a number of his writings that Habermas has the frightful image of the totalitarian Nazi Germany of his youth as a key element of his own life-world. He is rightly concerned with designing a theory that can prevent such irrational forces from dominating and destroying, and that can provide the basis for a just society. Yet for all of his just concerns, he seems to me to have taken an insufficiently critical examination of the place of rationality in human communication and modern life: he thinks that we only need to "improve" our conception of rationality, but he neglects to ask whether we need to question more fundamentally the place of rationality in the general scheme of things. The forces of twentieth-century totalitarianism did not simply represent irrationality but involved the most advanced forms of rationality as well: our century can well be described as a time of rational madness.

Habermas's theory of "communicative rationality" only increases the role which modernity assigned to rationality as the be-all and end-all of life. The task of social thought today should be instead to find the means to reactivate the fullness of human reason while carefully reharnessing rationality to serve reason. Nostalgic sentimentalism will not do, but neither will nostalgic rationalism.

What is perhaps most strange in this complex work is that Habermas never critically examines his presupposition that critical rationality, rooted in linguistic validity claims, provides the only possible basis for a communicative action society. Because of Habermas's limited understanding of Peirce's, Dewey's, and Mead's theories of signs and communication, he fails to see the ways in which these theories show rational linguistic symbols to form only a portion of rational symbols and rational symbols to form only a portion of symbols, and symbols to form only a portion of those signs which constitute reasonableness—in other words, socially based communicative reason circumscribes communicative rationality. Habermas is handicapped by a blindingly thin view of signification and a bloated conception of the place of propositional rational language within semeiosis.

Habermas's *TCA* may involve "subjects," but it says nothing about *persons*. The irreducible person, "intersubjective" but qualitatively unique, says with Walt Whitman, "I and mine do not convince by arguments: we convince by our presence." The very notion of "presence" in communicative action is virtually absent in Habermas's rationalistic account. Yet the bodying forth of new ideas through the person does not come about simply through parliamentary rules of debate. Rather, as Mumford observed, "men become susceptible to ideas, not by discussion and argument, but by seeing them personified and by loving the person who so personifies them."[28] But love plays no real part in Habermas's version of the evolution of reason, as it does for Mumford. Love is, after all, a human passion neither logical nor "differentiated": communicative rationality, not love, is the engine of historical development. Habermas would probably discount Mumford as illogical, but what would he say to Peirce, the bone-dry arch logician who included agapasm—evolutionary love—as an indispensable aspect of evolution and partic-ularly human evolution: "In genuine agapasm . . . advance takes place by virtue of a positive sympathy among the created springing from continuity of mind. . . . The agapastic development of thought is the adoption of certain mental tenden-cies, not altogether heedlessly, as in tychism [Darwinian], nor quite blindly by the mere force of circumstances or of logic, as in anancasm [which would include Hegelianism], but by an immediate attraction for the idea itself, whose nature is divined before the mind possesses it, by the power of sympathy, that is, by virtue of the continuity of mind; and this mental tendency may be of three varieties, as fol-lows. First, it may affect a whole people or community in its collective personality, and be thence communicated to such individuals as are in powerful sympathetic connection with the collective people, although they may be intellectually incap-able of attaining the idea by their private understandings or even perhaps of con-sciously apprehending it. Second, it may affect a private person directly, yet so that he is only enabled to apprehend the idea, or to appreciate its attractiveness, by virtue of his sympathy with his neighbors, under the influence of a striking experi-ence or development of thought. . . . Third, it may affect an individual, independ-ently of his human affections, by virtue of an attraction it exercises upon his mind, even before he has comprehended it. This is the phenomenon which has been called the *divination* of genius; for it is due to the continuity between man's mind and the Most High."[29]

Social theorists will likely cringe at the wording "Most High," which the religions have called God, and which signified for Peirce the evolutionary creation and growth of reason in the universe. Habermas, of course, thinks the whole busi-ness to be some archaic remnant, dressed up as the "sacred," a self-image formed out of collective narcissism and having no contemporary value other than having started the ball of human consciousness rolling. Yet Peirce's idea implies some-thing quite different from Habermas—and from religion. The implication is that there is a living continuity between the human mind in its cosmic, social, and per-sonal aspects and the general laws of nature and that because of this sympathy or continuity, human minds can become touched by, while co-creating, purposive evolution. This view is radically opposed to the Kantian view of a human mind set apart from a mechanistic universe—expressed in Weber's ideas on culture and so-called purposive or instrumental rationality, in Durkheim's "collective faculty" theory of mind added to nature but fundamentally different, and in Habermas's all-pervasive rationalism.

What is most important here—and one need not accept Peirce's semeiotic realist understanding of the continuity between the human mind and the living cosmos—is that there is a mode of evolution by love or sympathetic communication, which need not involve self-conscious understanding, rational argumentation through linguistically based validity claims, or any rationality at all: a thoroughly social form of communicative reason rooted in the unconscious, extrarational, biosemiotic temperament of the human animal. Far from being "*aufgehoben*" or surpassed by the civilization of rationality, sympathetic communication or evolutionary love remains the "supple nymph" on which the "powdered wig" of modern rationality sits.

Habermas presents us with a vision of society which would discount the sympathetic impulse to meaning by making it a mere *conscience collective,* not touched by experience and continuity with nature. The condition of a communicative action society would, in my opinion, literally destroy the living impulse to meaning, and eventually itself, through its disallowance of ideas which cannot yet be rationally justified. Far from being an antidote to the self-destructive tendencies in modern life, *The Theory of Communicative Action* is an ideal document of the escape from life in the late twentieth century under the dead hand of ethereal rationality.

What Habermas has done is to complete the construction of his infernal communicative rationality machine. All that remains left to do, theoretically speaking, is to apply it where he and his followers will. His communicative rationality machine can digest all hitherto existing theories, and functions as a vast immune system against the threat of the extrarational, and against a thoroughgoing critique of the nominalist premises of the modern era. It invokes the valid modern achievements of "intersubjectively" based formal, juridical, and otherwise institutional, argumentative, and self-critical procedures as rights of human conduct, while unfortunately preserving the dictatorial claims of rationality to be the universal arbiter of reason. This becomes even more apparent if we consider Habermas as a key figure in the phenomenon of "neopragmatism."

7

The Neopragmatic Acquiescence: Between Habermas and Rorty

*[The democratic ideal] bases its faith upon the heart in
preference to the intellect, though knowing well the power of
the latter when controlled. It knows that the intellect, alone,
runs amuck, and performs unspeakable cruelties; that the heart
alone is divine. For it is the heart that welcomes Life and would
cherish it, would shield it against the cannibalism of the
intellect.*

—*Louis Sullivan*[1]

*What is really "in" experience extends much further than that
which at any time is* known. . . . *By "intellectualism" as an
indictment is meant the theory that all experiencing is a mode
of knowing, and that all subject-matter, all nature, is, in
principle, to be reduced and transformed till it is defined in
terms identical with the characteristics presented by refined
objects of science as such. The assumption of "intellectualism"
goes contrary to the facts of what is primarily experienced. For
things are objects to be treated, used, acted upon and with,
enjoyed and endured, even more than things to be known. They
are things* had *before they are things cognized.*

—*John Dewey*[2]

The history of pragmatism is a history of misunderstanding. Many Europeans of the early twentieth century, including, for example, Simmel and Durkheim, looked down on pragmatism as merely a crude expression of Americanism, or as a philosophy which blurred the fundamental dichotomies of subject and object laid down in the Cartesian/Kantian tradition. Other Europeans and Americans embraced pragmatism as a philosophy of life, primarily identified with William James. Although he was an intensely vivid writer, James's philosophical ideas frequently lend themselves to misinterpretation or caricature—his idea of meaning as the "cash value of an act" certainly does not help to distinguish pragmatism from crass Americanism, even though he is also the author of the phrase "the bitch-goddess Success"—and they illustrate why the many misunderstandings of pragmatism are not limited to entrenched philosophical chauvinism but also stem from the pragmatists themselves.

Yet one should not discount the chauvinism. Consider the crude uncritical cant of Frankfurt School exponent Max Horkheimer, who said, "If it were not for the founder of the school, Charles S. Peirce, who has told us that he 'learned philosophy out of Kant,' one might be tempted to deny any philosophical pedigree to a doctrine that holds not that our expectations are fulfilled and our actions successful because our ideas are true, but rather that our ideas are true because our expectations are fulfilled and our actions successful."[3] Sly Max Horkheimer attempts here to ridicule pragmatism by saying that a reference to Kant, that is, a German, is pragmatism's only claim to a "pedigree." Or take this howler: "Pragmatism reflects a society that has no time to remember and meditate. . . . Both

Peirce and James wrote at a period when prosperity and harmony between social groups as well as nations seemed at hand, and no major catastrophes were expected. Their philosophy reflects with an almost disarming candor the spirit of the prevailing business culture, the very same attitude of 'being practical' as a counter to which philosophical meditation as such was conceived."[4]

It is simply an exaggeration to deny "philosophical meditation" to James, even while admitting his optimism. One can also read James's warnings concerning German and Japanese militarism in his essay on the theme of "the moral equivalent of war." But it requires sheer uncritical ignorance to reduce Peirce's philosophy to "business culture," given Peirce's distinctions between the pragmatic and the practical, and his prophetic remarks in 1893 that the "Philosophy of Greed" inherent in modern capitalism would result in catastrophe: "The twentieth century, in its latter half, shall surely see the deluge-tempest burst upon the social order—to clear upon a world as deep in ruin as that greed philosophy has long plunged it into guilt."[5] When Horkheimer published his words in 1947, Europe was plunged deep in physical ruin thanks to a prevailing German Nazi culture Horkheimer would undoubtedly not want his philosophy reduced to, Stalinism was greedily extending the Russo-Communist slave state in the name of anticapitalism, and America was cheerfully beginning its deadly cult of nuclear masturbation—bomb testing—with its newly acquired Nazi rocket scientists, forgetful of its barbaric targeting of civilian populations in Hiroshima and Nagasaki. The positivism which Horkheimer held in such contempt was indeed endemic in the American academy, but some of its chief spokesmen were fellow German speaking Europeans, such as Carnap.

James and Dewey, the chief public spokesmen for pragmatism, were also powerful manifestations of the modernist impulse in the early twentieth century. Their ardent optimism, pluralism, and situationalism showed new ways to reconceive mind as vitally continuous with nature, experience, and conduct. Yet these strengths also blinded them to the possibility that the modern era and its science and technics were producing ultimately self-destructive consequences. By midcentury these destructive forces had assumed control, not only burying pragmatism under the banner of scientistic modernism—which appeared in the various guises of logical positivism, behaviorism, Charles Morris's "pragmatics," and Parsonian structural functionalism—but in the process showing the inadequacies of James, Dewey, and Mead's progressivist optimism. Paradoxically it was Peirce, the practicing experimental scientist, who in his late writings saw deepest into the dangers of nominalistic scientism and the mechanistic worldview, while proposing a science based on a reanimated universe and the organic human inquirer. James and Dewey both acknowledged the power of Charles Peirce's thought, yet were simply unable to comprehend the extent to which it surpassed the modern impulse even while drawing from it.

Philosophical pragmatism has resurfaced as a significant part of intellectual life in the past decade. What had been a body of thought reduced largely to the influence of Mead in academic sociology, and passing references to James, Dewey, and Peirce, has reemerged with significance for semiotics, philosophy, literary criticism, and other disciplines.

James's and Dewey's situationally based philosophies have seemed to provide a vital alternative to the narrowly positivist/language analysis world in which academic philosophy had become enclosed in the Anglo-American context. Strangely enough, Mead's fortunes rose in the 1940s and 1950s in sociology just as his work and that of the other pragmatists were being eclipsed in philosophy. Symbolic interactionism functioned in mid-century to keep the Meadian stream of pragmatic thought flowing, perhaps as the Irish monasteries in the dark ages preserved the texts of Western Civilization. Now Mead has begun to be taken seriously by philosophers again, though, symbolic interactionism, in my opinion, remains overly bound by the Meadian monastery.

Habermas and Rorty are two widely discussed theorists closely associated with this renewal of interest in pragmatism. Both are heavily influenced by the "linguistic turn"—by the dominant postwar Anglo-American "language analysis" (out of which Rorty in particular derives)—and both are contributors to attempts to link Anglo-American and continental philosophies.

Influenced both by his colleague Karl-Otto Apel's inquiry into Peirce and the tendency of supposedly critical theorists, such as Horkheimer, to view pragmatism as positivism, Habermas depicted the pragmatisms of Charles Peirce and John Dewey in his early work as having critical potential, yet as ultimately ingredients in the development of modern positivism. In his *Knowledge and Human Interests* he devotes himself to a dazzlingly complex discussion of Peirce, and through his Kant-tinted glasses claims that "the intention of what Peirce called pragmatism and then, in order to set it off from psychologistic interpretations, pragmaticism, has a more far-reaching aim. The issue is not the derivation of a criterion of meaning but rather the central question of a logic of inquiry that is guided by reflection on the basic experience of positivism: *how is scientific progress possible?* Pragmatism answers this question by legitimating the validity of synthetic modes of inference on the basis of the transcendental structure of instrumental action."[6] Now Peirce is not the easiest philosopher in the world to comprehend. Still, Habermas missed Peirce's crucial transformation of Kant's problem: to put it tersely in Kantian terms, science is not the "synthesis" of the immediate, as Kant thought, but rather the "analysis" of the mediate. Habermas also imposed a Weberian concept of strategic, "instrumental action" that was alien to Peirce's framework and that of the other pragmatists as well, including Dewey's "instrumentalism."

Such interpretations ultimately decapitated pragmatism in order to fit the interests of Habermas's system. Nevertheless, the explosion of interest in Habermas, in connection with Apel's inquiries, also sparked interest in pragmatism both in Europe and America. Apel, who translated Peirce into German, helped to show how Peirce's rejection of foundationalism had, in effect, transformed Kant's transcendental subject into a "transcendental" unlimited community of inquirers as the limit of knowledge. Apel's reintroduction of the term "transcendental," in its technical sense, to Peirce's philosophy is problematic, since Peirce believed that the pragmatic maxim denied Kant's concept of incognizable things-in-themselves, and thereby the concept of transcendental underpinnings.

Habermas's appreciation of pragmatism has grown since those early works, and more recently he has attempted to develop his theory of communicative action, based on a concept of "linguistically generated intersubjectivity" influenced in part by Mead. Although Habermas has sought to come to terms with the body of pragmatism as a whole, I claim that his work is fundamentally opposed to the spirit of pragmatism, even if it does incorporate some of its technical concepts.

Rorty, for his part, claims to be a pragmatist influenced by Dewey, not to mention such seemingly distant sources as Martin Heidegger and Wittgenstein. The pragmatic vision Rorty extols is that of philosophy as conversation or, rather, as a form of *kibitzing* instead of a quest for truth or wisdom. In his book *Consequences of Pragmatism,* Rorty depicts pragmatism as "the doctrine that there are no constraints on inquiry save conversational ones—no wholesale constraints derived from the nature of the objects, or of the mind, or of language, but only those retail constraints provided by the remarks of our fellow-inquirers . . . the pragmatist tells us that it is useless to hope that objects will constrain us to believe the truth about them, if only they are approached with an unclouded mental eye, or a rigorous method, or a perspicuous language. He wants us to give up the notion that God, or evolution, or some other underwriter of our present world-picture, has programmed us as machines for accurate verbal picturing, and that philosophy brings self-knowledge by letting us read our own program."[7]

Rorty's pragmatist bears an uncanny resemblance to the late Wittgenstein of language game fame rejecting the early Wittgenstein "picture theory of knowledge." The pragmatists also rejected such foundationalism, beginning with Peirce's bold anti-Cartesian articles of the late 1860s and culminating with Dewey and Bentley's *Knowing and the Known* in 1949, but they did so by articulating a fallibilist, experiential model of inquiry which showed, in contrast to Rorty's statement, how the "nature of objects" and the evolutionary genius of the human mind tempered or constrained inquiry toward truth and "self-knowledge." In other words, Rorty's "pragmatism" is no pragmatism at all, but a form of conceptualism which abstracts certain concepts associated with pragmatism, such as fallibilism and situationalism, while denying or ignoring others, such as nondiscursive experience, aesthetic quality, the "Outward Clash" of brute, compulsive facts (or what Mead described as "contact experiences"), the social basis of human biological nature and its place in conduct, the continuum between self and community, and perhaps even the basic concept of pragmatism that acts produce actual or conceivable consequences (which in Rorty are transformed into "redescriptions"). Rorty shares with Habermas a much narrower understanding of the modalities of signification than that of the pragmatists, and instead views meaning in the manner of a poststructuralist as based on a dichotomy of dead convention versus contingent difference. Hence Rorty, for all of his self-description as a pragmatist, also violates the spirit of pragmatism while claiming to appropriate it, but for reasons quite different from those of Habermas.

When Rorty, who is perhaps most closely identified with the so-called neopragmatism, says that Peirce's only contribution to pragmatism was to give it a name, he reveals that the difficulties Peirce faced a century ago in having his philosophical doctrines understood, even by fellow pragmatists James and Dewey, have by no means diminished. In Rorty's case one sees a good example of the contemporary "postmodern" academician, bound by a contempt for large-scale historical or transhistorical norms, for reasonable argumentation, and limited by an extremely bookish understanding of what comprises human beings.

PRAGMATISM VERSUS FRAGMATISM

Peirce distinguished his pragmatism from what he considered distortions of the doctrine in James and others, by renaming it "pragmaticism," as a more specialized doctrine. In order to avoid further confusion of Rorty's and Habermas's positions with that of the spirit of pragmatism, I shall announce the birth of a new term, *fragmatism,* which, like Peirce's term, is not without its rhyme or reason. The term denotes in particular the relativism of Rorty (and like-minded so-called neo-pragmatists), expressed in his idealization of contingency and unquestioning belief in the incommensurability of belief communities. Fragmatism is the reason why Rorty can see nothing of value in Peirce's pragmatism except that he gave it its name, and fragmatism is the more proper name for Rorty's own brand of "pluralism." In a broader context fragmatism is a synonym for late twentieth-century "postmodernism," and therefore includes those poststructuralists, such as Jacques Derrida, who react against the totalistic outlook of French structuralism with a seemingly antithetical view of the continual "fissioning" and "creativity" of arbitrary signs. This outlook continues the antinaturalistic, antipersonal, and binary view of meaning characteristic of structuralism, but merely swings the pendulum from a single, all-encompassing standard—the deep code—to the opposite view that one standard is as good as any other. Habermas's clear-headed critiques of this position—Rorty's as well as poststructuralists—would seem to put him at odds with fragmatism.[8] Yet in Habermas's tendencies toward Kantian compartmentalization we see what I will venture to call *transcendental fragmatism.*

Both Habermas and Rorty, in their opposing ways, make language to be the basis for public life as well as the medium of science and human belief. Though Rorty claims to be against the Enlightenment view of reason, he and Habermas share the Enlightenment endorsement for the "disenchantment" of the world, for the progressive unfettering of human institutions and habits of conduct from overarching religious or metaphysical worldviews. Yet between their common enthusiasm for modern disenchantment lies a vast difference of opinion and even of temperament. Habermas seeks to overcome the tendencies toward a subjectivist, consciousness-based outlook in modern social theory by building a truly intersubjective theory of "communicative action/rationality." His aims are grand: to rescue the modern project of establishing universal norms for rational conduct, and thereby to further the goal of emancipating human societies from unreasonable practices and institutions.

Rorty's postmodern fragmatism is quite different from Habermas's transcendental fragmatism. Rorty is skeptical of tight divisions between forms of rationality, or of distinct disciplinary boundaries, but he thinks that the disenchantment of the world in the sense of a release from fixed foundational moorings is part of the progressive development of any free society. "Disenchantment" thus works in opposite directions to enable the rational foundations of Habermas's ideal society to be established, and to make possible the destruction of rational foundations in Rorty's ideal society. Rorty believes that the very idea of a universal reason—the whole idea that there are logically valid, universal norms—is the great fallacy of modern thought. He repeatedly states that norms are made, not discovered, and therefore would consign the very attempt to discover universal norms to the dungheap of historical contingency. He believes further that human creativity is revealed in original acts of private consciousness, which distinguish the creative ones—the "poets" and "revolutionaries"—from socially binding conventions and the hoi polloi.

Where Habermas is earnest and heavy in temperament, Rorty is frequently casual and light. Who could be further apart: Habermas, the arch defender of rationality, Rorty, the carefree attacker of rationality? Yet between their opposed positions are some common assumptions which perhaps help to explain why they have held such a fascination for contemporary philosophers and social theorists. Though both thinkers seek justice and freedom in their theories of public life, their conceptualist premises frustrate the conditions for a flourishing contemporary culture and remain inadequate to meet the needs for contemporary theory. In their overreliance on conventionalist theories of language and meaning, I claim that one sees the desiccating effects in the late twentieth century of what William James termed "vicious intellectualism."

The Unbearable Enlightenment of Being

> *Within their own narrower ambit, primitive peoples had usually preserved, better than those who had submitted to civilisation, their contact with the central modes of life: respect for sexuality and for the phases of bodily growth, communication with their own unconscious resources, welling up in dream and myth, not least the innate joy of being, in a harmonious relationship to nature. Had [Enlightenment] man shown more understanding of the whole range of primitive gifts, too often despised and cast aside, he would have left mankind as a whole both wiser and richer.*
>
> Lewis Mumford[9]

Despite the catastrophic destruction witnessed in the twentieth century, Habermas remains convinced that the modern project of rational enlightenment remains a valid goal of contemporary life. While admitting with Weber that the project produced a loss of ultimate meaning and many unanticipated forms of alienation, he believes that the problems of the twentieth century are the result of an insufficient realization of the challenge of modernity to create rationally grounded societies, a challenge which can only be met by a systematic reformation of the concept of rationality. In Habermas's Hegel-like view of the grand march of history, humanity develops from "mythic thought" through "religious-metaphysical thought" to "enlightened thought" through the progressive growth of rationality, which makes possible a "decentering of world view" in Piaget's sense.

Piaget's psychological theory of cognitive development involves a progression from concrete operational thinking to full abstract thought, and from an egocentric to a "decentered" self. Although widely believed to be an adequate theory of development today, Piaget transformed James Mark Baldwin's now virtually forgotten aesthetically based genetic epistemology to a narrower logically based theory, while assuming the key terms of Baldwin's system. In my opinion Piaget's theory undervalues or completely ignores the central place of emotional development and aesthetic experience in childhood while falsely idealizing an abstracted model of rational intelligence as the goal of development. With Kohlberg he maintains that the more rational stage of development will be the more mature moral outlook. Still, Piaget provides Habermas with a potential model of human development, which he needs in order to develop a universally valid model of enlightenment. Drawing from Piaget and Kohlberg, as well as Weber's discussions of the rationalization of worldviews, Habermas extends this model from individuals to societies, to show how only the modern Western tradition bore the conditions for a fully free social life: "Piaget distinguishes among stages of cognitive development that are characterized not in terms of new contents but in terms of structurally described levels of learning ability. It might be a matter of something similar in the case of the emergence of new structures of worldviews. The caesurae between the mythical, religious-metaphysical, and modern modes of thought are characterized by changes in the system of basic concepts. With the transition to a new stage the interpretations of the superseded stage are, no matter what their content, *categorially devalued. . . .* These *devaluative shifts* appear to be connected with socio-evolutionary transitions to new levels of learning, with which the conditions of possible learning processes in the dimensions of objectivating thought, moral-practical insight, and aesthetic-expressive capacity are altered"[10]

In this perspective the mythic worldview falsely blurs together that which the modern world separates. Again, Habermas's method is to assume uncritically that the differentiations and dichotomies of the modern world are correct, and then to show how traditional or mythic worldviews deviate from the true modern world-picture. This is as pure an example as one can expect to see of what anthropologists call ethnocentrism. He wishes to draw attention to the development of critical consciousness in modern society, but does so by falsely assuming that mythic consciousness must be *aufgehoben* or jettisoned in order for critical consciousness to develop. Yet such a basic "sphere" of the modern world as science did not require the differentiation of cleanly separated "validity relations" for sophisticated work to be accomplished. The ancient Babylonian astronomers, for example, were fully immersed in mythic consciousness and seemed to lack the critical-reflective attitude of the Greeks, yet created a mathematical astronomy far surpassing that of the Greeks in predictive capacity. Even though the Greeks were interested in "saving the appearances," that is, in prediction, their qualitative geometric theories were simply not successful at predicting celestial phenomena until they adopted Babylonian quantitative parameters. The less "differentiated" of the two cultures, in other words, produced the more efficacious science, which seems to cast doubt on Habermas's "purity law" of *absolutely* differentiated spheres as a developmental requirement of communicative action.

Or let us take the example of a modern physical scientist and originator of the "communicative" philosophies of pragmatism and fallibilism, Charles Peirce, for whom the very idea of an absolute differentiation of mind from world or of critical consciousness from acritical consciousness would make science impossible. As Peirce put it: "It may be answered, very truly, that experience has taught us that astrology, correspondences, magic, and many hypotheses formerly considered reasonable are to be put aside. Yes, but if primitive man had not had, at the very outset, some decided tendency toward preferring truthful hypotheses, no length of time,—absolutely none,—would have been sufficient to educate him. . . . It seems to me that the only admissible view is that the reasonableness, or idea of law, in a man's mind, being an idea by which objective predictions are effected,—for all physical theories originate in human conjectures, and experiment only lops off what is erroneous and determines exact values,—must be in the mind as a consequence of its being in the real world. Then the reasonableness of the mind and that of nature being essentially the same, it is not surprising that the mind, after a limited number of guesses, should be able to conjecture what the law of any natural phenomenon is. How far this power of conjecture may go we certainly do not know. We do know that it goes far enough to have enabled men to make already considerable progress in science."[11]

Peirce transformed Kant's faculty theory of knowledge by showing how the human mind itself is adapted to *general,* not simply mechanical, laws of nature. He rejected the nominalist assumption of a denaturalized mind and a mechanical nature as illogical, and instead articulated the logic of *abduction,* based on the continuity of human mind with the reasonableness of nature, as the ground of the possibility of science. Indeed science "would be impossible if man did not possess a tendency to conjecture rightly," and pragmaticism itself "implies faith in common sense and in instinct, though only as they issue from the cupel-furnace of measured criticism."[12]

Peirce and Dewey would have no trouble understanding why a character of Polish writer Stanislaw Lem's novel *His Master's Voice* (1968), a mathematician named Hogarth, described the heart of living scientific inquiry as nonlinguistic "surfacing." Following a brief but devastating criticism of positivism, Hogarth launches into an attack on language analysis, and on the underlying rationalism which has framed so many philosophical accounts of science in the twentieth century:

> I had to laugh, for instance, at the assurance of those who determined that all thought was linguistic. Those philosophers did not know that they were creating a subset of the species, i.e., the group of those not gifted mathematically. How many times in my life, after the revelation of a new discovery, having formulated it so solidly that it was quite indelible, unforgettable, was I obliged to wrestle for hours to find for it some verbal suit of clothes, because the thing had been born, in me, beyond the pale of all language, natural or formal?
>
> I call this phenomenon surfacing. It defies description, because what emerges from the unconscious with difficulty, slowly, finds nests of words for itself; it exists as an entity before it settles inside those nests; yet I can give no indication, no hint, to explain in precisely what form that non- and preverbalness appears; it is heralded only by a keen presentiment that the expectation of it will not be in vain.

Habermas and Rorty, who limit science to linguistic concepts, would have to treat "surfacing" as illogical and unscientific. Rorty would probably view it as creative contingency, but Hogarth's statement is an excellent example of what Peirce means by logically valid, abductive inference.

Habermas sees the differentiation of spheres of rationality—the scientific-technical, the moral-practical, and the aesthetic-practical—as a necessary precondition to a free society. In the following passage, which I quote at length, Habermas states his general viewpoint quite concisely:

Myth owes the totalizing power with which it integrates all superficially perceived phenomena into a network of correspondences, similarities, and contrasts to basic concepts that render consistent with one another categories that are no longer compatible in the modern world. For example, language, the medium of presentation, is not yet abstracted from reality to such an extent that the conventional sign is completely separate from its semantic contents and its referents; the linguistic world view remains interwoven with the order of the world. Mythic traditions cannot be revised without danger to the order of things and to the identity of the tribe set within it. . . . Only demythologization dispels this enchantment, which appears to *us* to be a confusion between nature and culture. The process of enlightenment leads to the desocialization of nature and the denaturalization of the human world; we can conceive of this with Piaget as a *decentering of world view*.

The traditional world view ultimately gets temporalized and can itself be distinguished as a variable interpretation from the world itself. This external world is differentiated into the objective world of entities and the social world of norms (or normatively regulated interpersonal relations); they both stand in contrast to each person's own internal world of subjective experiences. As Max Weber has shown, this process proceeds by the rationalization of world views that, as religion and metaphysics, are themselves the result of demythologization. Where (as in the Western tradition) rationalization does not stop at basic theological and metaphysical concepts, the sphere of validity relations is not only purified of empirical admixtures but also gets internally differentiated in terms of the viewpoints proper to truth, normative rightness, and subjective truthfulness or authenticity.[13]

Habermas adopts the antipragmatic perspective of the modern structuralist that myth is really about underlying "basic concepts," and that language is "the medium of presentation," neglecting how most myths were traditionally expressed in the multi-media of dramatic ritual, in which grammatical structure per se is trivial in comparison with the live ritual process. In the totalitarian world of French structuralism, as I mentioned in the previous chapter, a single underlying code, incorrectible by critical conduct, determines meaning regardless of time, place, and circumstance, regardless even of whether the subject happens to be myth or modern communicative action. Oddly enough for Habermas's developmental theory, there is no true *development* in the French structuralist model but only variations on the theme, homologies rather than evolution or growth. I suspect that Habermas's Kantian predelictions led him to what Clifford Geertz has called the "infernal culture machine" of Levi-Strauss's structuralism, just as it led him to Piaget's biostructuralism.

Habermas says that the mythic view must be destroyed for a rational fallibilist view to emerge. He ignores the possibility that the mechanical worldview which the Enlightenment inherited and on which the "differentiation of validity spheres" is based is a disguised religious phenomenon, literally a secularized deus ex machina, or what Mumford has depicted as *The Myth of the Machine*. He ignores the possibility that mythic comprehension may outreach critical rational understanding, as a form of collective abductive inference. By itself, such a faculty would be inadequate to meet the conditions of contemporary life, and on this point I agree with Habermas. But without it, modernity has proven inadequate to meet the conditions of life in general: to generate believable and sustainable modes of living in harmony with experience and nature. The experience of twentieth-century communism is a case in point: apart from the raw use of terror, much of its seeming viability depended on forms of being—such as customary morality and social rituals of everyday life, habituated ways of farming and trading—which were formally declared obsolete but which provided an unseen "fuel" of social energies beneath the egalitarian enthusiasms of the early years. As Communist societies increasingly rationalized these ways of living out of existence, they reaped deadened systems in which nobody could believe. The devastation of the inner world by dehumanizing, bureaucratic Communist and capitalist societies in the twentieth century, which Habermas's phrase "the colonization of the lifeworld" captures nicely, and the devastation of the biosphere and its miraculous variescence by technological hubris, will not be remedied by a new, improved rationality but by an imaginative realignment of humanity's place in the cosmos.

One would expect a truly critical theorist to be critical of the positivist conception of language and signification that Habermas endorses in the previous quotation, in which the conventional sign is supposed to be completely separate from its "semantic content and its referents," as he puts it. In the positivist view, outlined by Carnap and formularized by Charles Morris, the referent or object of a sign was considered as separate from the sign and thereby outside of the sign process, as opposed to the pragmatic view of Peirce, who considered the object of a sign as within the sign process. Habermas wishes to describe the ability to discriminate between the fictional and the real, yet the complete separation of a sign from its "referent" renders a subjective theory of knowledge ultimately based upon the infallible, direct knowledge of things or of thought itself, precisely the position for which Peirce criticized Descartes and against which he proposed his "intersubjective" model of the conditional consensus of an unlimited community of interpretation. A similar objection can be made against Charles Morris's term "pragmatics" and his entire semiotics as a form of positivism which utterly violates the spirit of pragmatism and the terminology of Peirce's semeiotic, as indeed was made by Dewey and Bentley in *Knowing and the Known*.[14]

Habermas, in his quest for synthetic system, seems not to see that his language theory is rooted in nominalistic presuppositions which are ultimately foundationalist rather than fallibilist, and subjectivist rather than "intersubjective." His turn to Mead is understandable, but merely gluing a patch of Mead over a faulty language theory is insufficient. Because Habermas does not question the nominalistic premises of a chasm between language and world, he is trapped by the "creation myth" which haunts modern thought: the incognizable "first thought" Descartes claimed to uncover, the problem of the "first man" in Hobbes and Freud, the question of where structure comes from in the first place. Habermas's response is to assume the Kantian pose by "grounding" Mead's intrinsically developmental theory through Durkheim's sociological transcendentalism: in the beginning there was collective consciousness. Were Habermas to draw from Peirce's logic, he would see the fallacy in assuming that conventional language is utterly separate from world.

When Habermas says enthusiastically: "The process of enlightenment leads to the desocialization of nature and the denaturalization of the human world" in the previous quotation, he again reveals himself to be a conventionalist theorist rather than a critical theorist or any sort of pragmatist: a true believer in the modern myth of cultural nominalism. The same mechanical worldview which separated thought from things, manifested in the Cartesian inorganic mechnical body versus *res cogitans,* in the Hobbesian "state of nature," in the development of capitalism with its personification of things and reification of people, produced the "ghost in the machine" world which functions as the presupposition of Habermas's thought.

A more critical approach would be to consider whether the desocialization of nature—the removal of generality and social purposiveness or final causality—and the "denaturalization of the human world"—the view that an unbridgeable gulf exists between the workings of nature and the faculties of mind or culture—might represent the unwarranted assumptions of modern nominalism. Such a critical view of nature would lead to a socialized conception of nature—contra Hobbes and Darwin and Spencer—and to a naturalistic view of the emergence of meaning and culture, contra critical theorists. Such a critical view of the received myth of the Enlightenment was developed by pragmatism and provides the basis of Peirce, Dewey, and Mead's community and ontologically based models of "communicative" reason, as opposed to Habermas's dichotomized, epistemological view.

The pragmatists claimed that reason is a way of being, to be found in actual or conceivable consequences of conduct, but Habermas claims that reason is a valid way of knowing, to be found in validity claims of speech acts. I pose the question to Habermas: How is it, despite the differences between James, Dewey, and Mead's situationalism and Peirce's semeiotic realism, that the pragmatists could reject the mythic ghost in the machine legacy of the Enlightenment which Habermas assumes—of etherealized subjectivity and reified objectivity, of a humanity alienated from organic nature and a nature divested of generality—in order to create a more encompassing "communicative" reason than that of Habermas? The biosemiotic view of human conduct one finds in the pragmatists—whether in Dewey's discussions in *Experience and Nature* (which, late in his career, he wished to retitle as *Nature and Culture*) of the place of qualitative immediacy, aesthetic experience, and the situation of inquiry, or in Mead's naturalistic account of the act, or in Peirce's doctrine of "Critical Common-Sensism"—avoids the reductionism of language analysis, structuralism, and Arnold Gehlen's noncontinuous nature-culture parallelism. Such an "undifferentiated" worldview did not lead the pragmatists to the kind of antirationalism Habermas rightly fears, whether fascist anthropology or Rortyan ironic privatism, but to a subtle understanding of the proper limited context of critical rationality within extrarational conduct. In short, pragmatism rejects those dichotomizing tendencies of modern thought which remain so essential to Habermas, as a hindrance to the development of what Peirce termed "concrete reasonableness."

Habermas's fear of "undifferentiated" spheres of culture is simply an endorsement of enlightenment prejudices—an endorsement that is blind to the many ways that the baroque age and its centralized, rationalized precepts represented a diminution of human freedom and human reason. In his underestimation of the negative side of the Enlightenment, he falls into the same trap as those neoconservative theorists who are blind to the positive achievements of the Enlightenment.

Habermas repeatedly returns to the ideal of the eighteenth century as his foundation for a rationally rooted society. In order to do so, he must ignore the fact that rational mind unnecessarily destroyed precious moral inhibitions and traditional mores in the process, without replacing them with deeply grounded alternatives. Habermas neglects the "polytechnic tradition" as Lewis Mumford calls it, that legacy of Medieval variegated life and form and city building that underlies the modern experience. More generally, he does not sufficiently appreciate how the achievements and debris of previous cultures may remain as reasonable correctives to limitations in contemporary cultures, especially in the age of centralization when one system guarantees the answer to the diverse and conflicting experience of life. Habermas's passive conceptualization of the life-world leaves its habitualized intelligence little or no possibility to act as a source of reasonable conduct in its own right, merely because it is not sufficiently "rationalized."

One could also characterize the age of the Enlightenment as the time in which the political absolutism of the baroque and the mechanical worldview became solidified. The Enlightenment, it should not be forgotten, sought to discredit its own "unenlightened" past. It sought a new image of man, freed from the constrictions of history, but in so doing also unloosed a potential reign of terror of far greater consequence than the actual bloody events in the short-lived Paris revolution.

We cannot ignore the Reign of Terror of the French Revolution as the dark side of "Enlightenment." The Reign of Terror, which replaced despotism with rational despotism and the Medieval executioner with the automatic killing machine "Madame Guillotine," was a foreshadowing of twentieth-century "Enlightenment," with its "scientific-technical" despotism, its Hitler and Stalin and rational gas warfare and unlimited submarine warfare and total warfare and nuclear warfare and its hyper-rational fusion of a military-industrial-academic complex, a community of inquisitors devoted to the pursuit of power in the name of a debased "pragmatism." Although neither Habermas nor Rorty would be willing to admit it, the legacy of the Enlightenment, despite the vision of liberty it helped to set free, may have ultimately served darker human forces instead of enlightening ones, and for reasons quite different from the standard conservative critiques.

THE CORRUPTION OF NEOPRAGMATIC LIBERALISM

> *Unconscious . . . of the sources of their ethical ideas, these*
> *pragmatic liberals pick up more or less what happens to be lying*
> *around them, without any effort at consistency or clarity, still*
> *less at effectiveness: here a scrap left over from childhood, there*
> *a fragment of Kant or Bentham, or again a dash of Machiavelli,*
> *pacifist Quakers one moment and quaking Nietzscheans the*
> *next.*
>
> Lewis Mumford[15]

> *We have to take as a starting point the world Orwell*
> *showed us in 1948. . . . We liberals have no plausible large-*

scale scenario for changing that world so as to realize the
"technical possibility of human equality." . . . This inability to
imagine how to get from here to there is a matter neither of loss
of moral resolve nor of theoretical superficiality, self-deception,
or self-betrayal. It is not something we can remedy by a firmer
resolve, or more transparent prose, or better philosophical
accounts of man, truth, or history. It is just the way things
happen to have fallen out. . . . What our future rulers will be
like will not be determined by any large necessary truths about
human nature and its relation to truth and justice, but by a lot
of small contingent facts.

Richard Rorty[16]

Rorty's recent book, *Contingency, Irony, and Solidarity* (1989), is a splendid illustration of contemporary postmodern intellectual life, embodying the beliefs of pluralism, postmodernism, and neo-Nietzscheanism, under the banner of a purported "neopragmatism." Yet beneath the glamour of "postmodern chic," I claim, lies the dead end of modern nominalism: a dehumanized world reduced to unreal language conventions where all that one can love or die for is a fiction, a thoroughly conventional world yet depending on a sensationalistic psychology of idiosyncratic self-creation, of pleasures and pains, "shivers and tingles." As Rorty expresses it: "[T]here is nothing deep inside each of us, no common human nature, no built-in human solidarity, to use as a moral reference point. There is nothing to people except what has been socialized into them—their ability to use language, and thereby to exchange beliefs and desires with other people. . . . Simply by being human we do not have a common bond. For all we share with all other humans is the same thing we share with all other animals—the ability to feel pain."[17]

Rorty sets up a utopian ideal of a liberal society whose heroes are "liberal ironists," a society of "people who are more afraid of being cruel than of anything else,"[18] a society liberated from objective, yet fallible, truth, moral moorings, or aesthetic qualities. In some ways Rorty's liberal position can be characterized as a more nominalized version of Jeremy Bentham, who sought both "the greatest good for the greatest number" and believed that humankind was ultimately under the governance of physiological pleasure and pain. Underlying Rorty's idea that human meaning is but a language game, one which through art or poesis sometimes imparts or receives physiological novelties, is the old familiar dichotomy of the ghost in the machine. Rorty professes his skepticism of the received dichotomies of modern philosophy, such as fact versus value, mind versus world, or subject versus object, yet he tends to reproduce them in even more extreme forms: contingencies versus conventions, language versus nonlanguage, private versus public. Human meaning is either an ethereal word game or a question of mechanical physiology, either a lifeless convention or "novel stimuli to action."

Despite his skepticism of the scientific worldview, he gladly endorses the evisceration of human purpose implied by the mechanical worldview and realized in the Darwinian account of evolution: "A nonteleological view of intellectual history, including the history of science, does for the theory of culture what the Mendelian, mechanistic, account of natural selection did for evolutionary theory. Mendel let us see mind as something which just happened rather than as something which was the point of the whole process. . . . This analogy lets us think of 'our language' —that is, of the science and culture of twentieth-century Europe—as something that took shape as a result of a great number of sheer contingencies."[19]

In this straitjacket dichotomy, only contingent novelty can renew deadened convention, revealing how the nominalist must ultimately throw all that is genuinely human overboard, while preserving the mechanical—contingency instead of living spontaneity, inert system instead of living habit. The denial of qualitative human feeling, along with organic human purpose, is one of the great tasks of "the project of modernity"—the ghost in the machine—and not simply a new achievement of postmodernism. And the renewal of qualitative human feeling (or aesthetic quality) and organic human purpose was one of the great tasks of pragmatism. Yet aesthetic or intrinsic quality is reduced from an irreducible mode of being to mechanical physiology in Rorty and to a subjective, "aesthetic-practical rationality" in Habermas, further revealing both their distance from pragmatism and fealty to the ghost in the machine.

Rorty inverts the Greek conceptions of oikos and polis, or private household and public realm, and asserts an unbridgeable disjuncture between them. Where the ancient Greeks saw the mastering of private necessities—food, clothing, shelter, and so forth—as a prerequisite to a free and autonomous public life, Rorty turns the relationship around so that the public becomes a mere means to private "expressiveness." His private realm is an isolate place of "autonomy" and "creativity," utterly lacking in the emotional warmth of family and loved ones, not to mention the necessities of life, as essential to "self-creation." Rorty's public is defined solely negatively as "becoming less cruel," not in Aristotle's positive sense as living well, or any other. His unpragmatic dichotomy between public and private endorses a libertine public realm and a narrowly elitist private realm—one that could only exist by assuming a comfortable economic level. Yet the lack of control over one's affairs which is endemic to poverty is a legitimate public concern, though not necessarily a question of "cruelty": even life's contingencies are not always evenly distributed. Passive indifference is one of the great public vices of twentieth-century Communist and capitalist bureaucracies, though it may not be as measurable as active cruelty and the shared "ability to feel pain" in Rorty's underlying Benthamite psychology of pleasure and pain.

Because he believes that there is no human nature, no inherent potentials within human beings generally, "autonomy," which to Rorty means "self-creation" or idiosyncratic difference from what has gone before, is reserved for the special few: "Autonomy is not something which all human beings have within them and which society can release by ceasing to repress them. It is something which certain particular human beings hope to attain by self-creation, and which a few actually do."[20] Rorty desires to undo Plato, but merely substitutes a "poet-king" for Plato's "philosopher-king." Had he taken even a cursory scan of human history, instead of professing it all obsolete, he might have seen that the varieties of human autonomy are not always limited to a tiny few, as they are in the antidemocratic American mass culture which seems to act as Rorty's assumed model.

Consider Rorty's vision of the liberal society as that which will tolerate virtually anything: "It is central to the idea of a liberal society that, in respect to words as opposed to deeds, persuasion as opposed to force, anything goes. This openmindedness should not be fostered because, as Scripture teaches, Truth is great and will prevail, nor because, as Milton suggests, Truth will always win in a free and open encounter. It should be fostered for its own sake. *A liberal society is one which is content to call "true" whatever the upshot of such encounters turns out to be.*"[21]

It is difficult to know what Rorty means by openmindedness for "its own sake," since he has denied intrinsic quality. But more disturbing is his breezy endorsement of "anything goes." He suggests that only "deeds" and "force" need have any limits, as though verbal communication is not itself a form of conduct or "deed." A Rortyan society would presumably allow Nazi rhetoric endorsing racism, genocide, and the abolition of free speech and human rights, but then be cruelly surprised when this rhetoric assumed power and consistently practiced what it had preached, obliterating the Rorty society in the process.

Yet Rorty believes that he is capable of moral fervor, even if he disallows moral goodness transcending particular "contingent" groups:

Nobody is convinced when we fuzzies say that we can be just as morally indignant as the next philosopher. We are suspected of being contritely fallibilist when righteous fury is called for. . . . When we suggest that one of the few things we know (or need to know) about truth is that it is what wins in a free and open encounter [cf. Rorty's apparent counterstatement in the previous quotation from him], we are told that we have defined "true" as "satisfies the standards of our community." But we pragmatists do not hold this relativist view. We do not infer from "there is no way to step outside communities to a neutral standpoint" that "there is no rational way to justify liberal communities over totalitarian communities." For that inference involves just the notion of "rationality" as a set of ahistorical principles which pragmatists abjure. What we in fact infer is that there is no way to beat totalitarians in argument by appealing to shared common premises, and no point in pretending that a common human nature makes the totalitarians hold such premises. . . . Suppose that for the last three hundred years . . . we had the sort of "weapons" against fascists which Dewey was said to deprive us—firm, unrevisable, moral principles which were not merely "ours" but "universal" and "objective." How could we avoid having these weapons turn in our hands and bash all the genial tolerance out of our own heads?[22]

Rorty's question is answered by noting how he assumes that firm and universal principles must be unrevisable, and that there are no central human values which falsify totalitarianism. He assumes that a rational way of justifying liberal communities over totalitarian communities would involve an "ahistorical" concept of rationality, when in fact historical reason—revealed in the deadly cruelties of totalitarian regimes—would suffice to show why totalitarian regimes are morally and politically bankrupt.

Like most contemporary critics of universals, Rorty confuses the universal with uniformity, not realizing that universals can be both various and locally diverse. Spoken language is a human universal, yet there are thousands of different languages, the diverse products of history, local culture, civilizational and language family influences. Because he confuses the universal with the uniform, Rorty does not even consider whether there might be some human values which might be universally worth living and dying for, regardless of whether some people might pervert these precarious ideals and turn them into "weapons." Lewis Mumford's critique of the failure of "pragmatic liberalism" to stand up against fascism in the 1930s as a form of "passive barbarism" holds just as true today for the "anything goes" society of Rorty. Contrast Mumford's view in 1944 with Rorty's: "Thus the active barbarians in our society were aided by the passive barbarians, who had lost their hold on central human values and who saw no reason to risk pain or death in behalf of human ideals—for ideals had become empty words. Disguising itself too often as Christian pacificism, as humanitarianism, as scientific dispassionateness, passive barbarism opened the gates to active barbarism. This moral cowardice, this inner corruption, this unwillingness to recognize fascism's brutal ways as evil or to accept evil itself as real—all this was not unexpected. The leaders of fascism had predicted it and counted upon it. Hitler had prophetically poured contempt on the democratic escapists in *Mein Kampf.*"[23]

"[T]his unwillingness . . . to accept evil itself as real": herein lies the failure of neopragmatic liberalism as well. Evil is not regarded by Rorty as an ineradicable part of the human condition but simply another language game, a portion of which, cruelty, is something which a liberal ironist should not do in public. If left to their own idiosyncratic fantasies, liberal ironist poets and revolutionaries are not evil but rather, creative, just as the less autonomous masses are conventional. Heidegger may have been a Nazi in public, but was "an immensely sympathetic" ironic poet in private, "as magnificent as Proust."[24] It is all a matter of language games, just as, for Habermas, it is all a matter of intersubjective agreement in a communicatively differentiated modern society which will have made human evil procedurally obsolete. To Habermas's credit, however, he has developed his theory of communicative rationality as a means of confronting the moral failures of our time, and his concerns can be seen quite clearly in his critiques of Heidegger and the contemporary apologist for the Nazis, historian Ernst Nolte.[25]

By contrast with the intellectualism of Rorty and Habermas, consider Mumford's example, which I cited in Chapter 4, of encountering a poisonous snake on one's path to illustrate why rational conduct depends upon nonrational capacities. Mumford called attention to "the dread of the emotions" as one of the reasons "pragmatic liberalism" failed to appreciate the deadly intentions of the Fascists to wage war. Neither Habermas's nor Rorty's theories allow the human ability to sense danger as reasonable in its own right but only as some sort of mind game.

In Rorty's "pragmatic" utilitarianism, emotions are only so much physiological "shivers and tingles" and the reasoning self only a language game. In Habermas's debating society, one would have to engage in intersubjective communication with those human equivalents of the snake in order to develop reasons to suspect or condemn them. Neither theorist would allow the emotion of fear or revulsion as a valid, nonlinguistic inference or hypothesis which determines a rational reaction. Yet a pragmatist would be able to understand such an example as an instance of Peirce's concept of abduction or of Dewey's notion that inquiry begins with a situation *felt* to be problematic.

Although he draws from the legacy of Peirce's antifoundationalism and fallibilism (while denying Peirce's significance), Rorty reduces the idea that no knowledge is certain to a view in which there are no real truths or errors but only "redescriptions." Once one accepts Rorty's "anything goes" view, it is difficult to make any mistakes, since all knowledge is simply a conventional "description" which may be "redescribed." Hence Rorty's extreme antifoundationalism undermines the possibility of fallibilism. There are no brute facts which might bruise one's description and determine the redescription. There is no experience one must suffer or undergo. In effect Rorty says that there is no genuine Other. If such a narcissistic view were more than a childish fantasy, then we could all be the isolate, autonomous gods Rorty wishes for, unbound by necessities, responsibilities, and by the commitments of love. Consider, by contrast, Peirce's view of truth as inescapably public:

> I now return to my abhorence of the doctrine that any proposition whatever is infallibly true. Unless truth be recognized as *public*—as that which *any* person would come if he carried his inquiry, his sincere search for immovable belief, far enough—then there will be nothing to prevent each one of us from adopting an utterly futile belief of his own which all the rest will disbelieve. Each one of us will set himself up as a little prophet; that is, a little "crank," a half-witted victim of his own narrowness.
>
> But if truth be something public, it must mean that to the acceptance of which as a basis of conduct any person you please would ultimately come if he pursued his inquiries far enough—yes, every rational being, however prejudiced he might be at the outset. For Truth has that compulsive nature which Pope well expressed: "The eternal years of God are hers."
>
> But, you will say, I am setting up this very proposition as infallible truth. Not at all; it is a mere definition. I do not say that it is infallibly true that there is any belief to which a person would come if he were to carry his inquiries far enough. I only say that that alone is what I call truth. I cannot infallibly know that there *is* any Truth.[26]

Rorty's "pluralist" relativism radically amplifies the problem in Dewey's situationalism which I criticized earlier, namely, to deny transituational or transhistorical norms, and thereby to assume them uncritically. But it would be a fundamental mistake to think that Rorty's outlook is Deweyan. Rorty's whole dichotomy of a "public" realm of convention, whose only rule seems to be anything goes except cruelty, in order to allow private anticonventional "difference" and idiosyncratic expressiveness, is a far cry from Dewey's social vision. It is the stuff of traditional American rugged individualism and contemporary Libertarianism, of what Robert Bellah, William Sullivan, and the other coauthors of *The Good Society* have depicted as anti-institutional "Lockean Man." Consider Dewey's statement in *Human Nature and Conduct:* "To view institutions as enemies of freedom, and all conventions as slaveries, is to deny the only means by which positive freedom in action can be secured. . . . Convention and custom are necessary to carrying forward impulse to any happy conclusion. . . . Not convention but stupid and rigid convention is the foe."[27] Rorty's dichotomy between rigid convention and contingent difference is typical of the kind of dichotomizing of experience Dewey used to criticize. In his unbuttoned postmodern enthusiasm, Rorty conveniently forgets the concept of *living habit,* so crucial to Dewey and the other pragmatists, which combines both habituated convention and spontaneous, habit-breaking impulse in a unified theory of human conduct.

Dewey's liberalism possessed an integrity which Rorty's lacks, yet was still inadequate to face the rational madness unfolding in the twentieth century. In our time, not only is such integrity scarce but rational madness has assumed a respectable appearance in intellectual life. Flatly denying reasonable argumentation, Rorty claims that even Nazism cannot be refuted: "This would mean giving up the idea that liberalism could be justified, and Nazi or Marxist enemies of liberalism refuted, by driving the latter up against an argumentative wall—forcing them to admit that liberal freedom has a "moral privilege" which their own values lacked."[28] In effect, there are no standards in the postmodern fragmentary world, that "best of all possible worlds," where "everything is permitted."

Rorty's liberal philosophy is, in my opinion, synonymous with twentieth-century rational madness, disavowing rational argumentation while disallowing modalities of signification other than those of rational relativism. Its radical denials of organic social experience and the continuum between private self and public realm, its belief that only irony can provide a critical perspective—as though the antidemocratic dangers of a culture predicated on cynical irony and kitsch are not already crystal clear in America—reveal this "neopragmatism" to be an exemplar of fragmatism. I was fortunate enough to hear an example of Rorty's ironical perspective at a conference on Heidegger at Yale University a few years ago, where Rorty fantasized a story which had Heidegger becoming a member of the German resistance, marrying a Jewish woman, and giving a eulogy for his son killed on the Golan Heights as a member of the Israeli military. Rorty finished his tasteless fantasy by flatly asserting that Heidegger's philosophical writings would have been unchanged. He did not trouble himself to give reasons for his belief, it was enough to be "ironical" and produce chuckles among the callow, black-clad graduate students in the audience. Yet even they stopped chuckling at the comic tidbits when Rorty fantasized the Nazi Heidegger giving a eulogy for his Israeli son.

Rorty's work has attracted widespread attention and is actually believed by the gullible, including Rorty himself, to be a continuation of Deweyan pragmatism. Rorty shrewdly uses elements of pragmatism, but he is no pragmatist. In denying the reality of emotional communication, the validity of rational argumentation, the irreducible element of Otherness in experience, and the ability to find fallible truth or goodness through socially purposeful conduct which transcends contingency, Rorty gives voice, instead, to what Christopher Lasch has aptly described as "the culture of Narcissism," a culture which sees its own empty image in everything it touches.

Beyond the Ghost in the Machine

Habermas's modernist rationalism and Rorty's "postmodernist" antirationalism both uncritically assume the underlying nominalist premises of the modern age rather than subjecting them to critical examination. Both Dewey and Weber, in their different ways, reflected the problem in modern culture of assuming a cultural ground while excluding it from the inquiry. In Dewey's case, trans-situational norms were excluded from situational inquiry, even though they might function as the ground of that inquiry. In Weber's case "values" are subjective, and, though they may provide the ground for an inquiry, they are excluded as much as possible from the inquiry itself. Weber assumed that inquirers would possess a richly endowed cultural value ground. But the course of development in twentieth-century social science was toward "value-poor" inquiry rather than "value-free": toward those specialists without spirit whose lack of connection to the assumed traditions and values of Western Civilization limited their possibilities for "value-free" interpretation. In other words, the tendency of the modern era has been to feed on the common values of Western Civilization, using them, in effect, as fuel for new ways of living from which those same values are excluded. Thus Habermas and Rorty can treat tradition as mere dross, while ignoring the extrarational forms of reasonableness undone by the Enlightenment dream. The twentieth century, the "century of progress," has now exhausted the modern project, not because there are not new ideas to be invented—just look at electronics—but because it has sufficiently devitalized those resources of meaning on which the modern experience depended but had to deny. The name of that exhaustion is postmodernism or, perhaps, fragmatism.

Neither brute force nor rational calculation alone can provide the basis for enduring cultures. Nor can communicative rationality or complacent contingency. The foundations of truly vital societies must always remain the fountain of organic life, which pours forth the energies and forms which animate the routine and transilluminate the calculable and rational. Vital cultures start with life and remain vital so long as their energies remain oriented toward life-enhancing forms of conduct. When power and rational calculation, which should be the means to life, usurp their limited context as means and become ends in themselves, as they have in our time, human purpose and autonomy give way to mechanism and automatism, to a world where uniformity and contingency, rather than pattern and purpose, determine human conduct.

Key to the theories of Habermas and Rorty is the modern myth of the ghost in the machine, the dual conception that the rational intellect, either in its individual "autonomous" manifestation, or its collective or "intersubjective" one, is at the figurative center of the universe, and that the natural universe is a mindless machine. This general outlook was described and criticized by Peirce in 1893:

> In the last chapter I assumed the reader would occupy the position of Common Sense, which makes the real things in this world blind unconscious objects working by mechanical laws together with a consciousness as idle spectator. I pointed out that this spectator cannot have part or lot even in the intelligence and purpose of the business; for intelligence does not consist in feeling intelligently but in acting so that one's deeds are concentrated upon a result.
>
> This makes the universe a muddle. According to it consciousness is perfectly impotent and is not the original of the material world; nor on the other hand can material forces ever have given birth to feeling, for all they do is accelerate the motions of particles. Nay, that they should so much as give rise to sensations in that consciousness is more than incomprehensible, it is manifestly impossible. There is no room for reaction between mind and matter. . . .
>
> The whole of this suicide of Common Sense results from its incautious assumption that it is one thing to look red or green and another to see red or green. . . . Grant that that assumption is somehow wrong, though we may not, at first, see how exactly, and the muddle begins to clarify itself. The spectator is no longer on the side of the footlights, and the

world on the other. He is, in so far as he sees, at one with the poet of the piece. To act intelligently and to see intelligently become at bottom one. And in the matter of auditing the account of the universe, its wealth and its government, we gain the liberty of drawing on the bank of thought.[29]

Though Habermas and Rorty both repudiate common sensism because of their different forms of intellectualism, and would make consciousness potent rather than impotent, the gist of Peirce's comments still hold: both theorists deny that human intelligence is natural and that nature is reasonable in any way more than a mere mechanical sense. Though Habermas seeks to trace out the grand narrative of reason as a human project, and Rorty seeks to deny the grand narrative altogether as mistaken, in favor of a "poeticized culture" of liberal ironists creatively breaking conventions, both would reject the "poetic cosmos" of Peirce's metaphor, in which human reason is an evolutionary development of the reason of the universe. Admittedly, however, Dewey and Mead would also differ with Peirce's poetic cosmos. Yet because they too sought to develop naturalistic and nonreductionist organic philosophies of human reason, they would, in my opinion, be much more sympathetic to Peirce's alternative to the ghost in the machine than to Habermas's or Rorty's positions.

The effusion of "neopragmatic" perspectives today tend to assume uncritically that human conduct is divorced from nature. Both Habermas's universal rationalism and Rorty's antirationalistic rationalism lead, in my opinion, to rational infantilism, to the empty formalism of Habermas's "differentiated spheres of modernity" or to the fragmatism of Rorty's laissez-faire relativism, whose only rule for public life is the negative injunction, "don't be cruel." These seeming antagonists both proudly endorse the liberation of human reason from organic nature, believing that such an alienation is necessary for a good society and represents the mature state of intellectual development. Such assumptions bespeak the general alienation of the intellect from its organic sources in the late twentieth century, under the domination of the ghost in the machine. They remain uncritically shackled to an obsolete mechanical view of nature and ignorant of our "glassy essence," the human biological proclivities for making meaning. Neither a mechanical conception of nature nor a supernatural conceptualism nor a mysterious "vitalism" will any longer suffice. The time has come to exorcise the ghost and scrap the machine.

PEIRCE'S AND MUMFORD'S CLAIMS THAT THERE ARE both organic and normative influences and limitations upon human conduct which transcend current norms, local traditions and institutions, and even human history do not find much favor in the contemporary atmosphere of rampant relativism, with its Rortys and Lyotards. And one will certainly not find such views, which see instinctive promptings as crucial to the spontaneity of the self, in the Fascist anthropology of Arnold Gehlen, whom Habermas rightly criticizes for his view that humans require rigid institutional order as a means of mimicking lost instincts. Peirce's view that rationality remains an immature capacity whose further development involves its dependence upon, and ultimately its coalescence into, the extrarational biosemiotic sources of concrete reasonableness is utterly at odds with Habermas's vision of human development as the perfection of rationality.

Habermas is one avatar of modern rationality's egocentric understanding of the world. He has tried to give rationality a human face through his concept of intersubjective, communicative action. But it has never occurred to him to question the underlying premiss of modern life which makes rationality the sovereign of reason.

Rorty is another avatar of modern rationality's egocentric understanding of the world. Against the cheery outlook of Rorty's contingent world where irony alone gives the intellectual elite a way of continually "redescribing" the world, a means of rationalizing anything it wishes through "contingent language games" as long as it isn't cruel, a world where valid inference and aesthetic quality are declared obsolete, where human feeling is only dehabitualizing "shivers and tingles," where black is white and up is down if one wishes it so, Habermas's earnest quest for rational justice is preferable. Though I am more sympathetic to the questions Habermas raises and the seriousness of his project in comparison with Rorty's complacent world of contingency, the alternatives proposed by both Habermas and Rorty contradict the spirit of pragmatism. Ultimately even Habermas's transcendental fragmatism, his earnest yet optimistic rationalism, is but another way of spelling shipwreck.

So-called neopragmatism, or what I have derisively termed "fragmatism," simply repeats the blunders of modern nominalism. Between the Scylla of Habermas's universal rationality machine and the Charybdis of Rorty's happy-go-lucky contingency machine there remains, however, a viable route for pragmatic thought. But it involves acknowledging what so much of contemporary intellectual life despises: that there are fallible forms of universal reason realized in local ways, that in the conduct of life personal and institutional rationality is dependent on deeper and nonrational forms of reason—of sentiment and instinctual promptings, conjecture, imagination, and experience—and that the human person is not simply a form of knowledge, social construction, or contingent difference, though these are all involved in what a person is, but that the human self is ultimately an organic social being infused with the spontaneity of life, capable of feeling, experiencing, empathically responding to the communicative environment, *and* rationally judging him or herself and the world, rightly and wrongly.

8

The Modern Error and the Renewal of Social Thought

> *And what passes for wisdom is not;*
> *unwise are those who aspire,*
> *who outrange the limits of man.*
> *Briefly, we die. Wherefore, I say,*
> *he who hunts a glory, he who tracks*
> *some boundless, superhuman dream,*
> *may lose his harvest here and now*
> *and garner death. Such men are mad,*
>   *their counsel evil.*
>
>   *—Euripides*[1]
>
> *All worthwhile theorizing is tentative, probing, provisional—*
> *contains an element of playfulness.*
>
>   *—Heinz Kohut*[2]

In his wide-ranging and provocative book, *All That Is Solid Melts into Air,* Marshall Berman favors a view of modern life as endless ferment, and interprets the great devastation which has accompanied twentieth-century social, political, and cultural life as the downside of an otherwise incompleted project worth continuing. He notes, for example, that the arts and sciences of our century have produced "an amazing plenitude of works and ideas of the highest quality. The twentieth century may well be the most brilliantly creative in the history of the world, not least because its creative energies have burst out in every part of the world. . . . And yet . . . we have missed or broken the connection between our culture and our lives. Our century has nourished a spectacular modern art; but we seem to have forgotten how to grasp the modern life from which this art springs. In many ways, modern thought since Marx and Nietzsche has grown and developed; yet our thinking about modernity seems to have stagnated and regressed."[3]

Surely the broken connection between our culture and our lives, as Berman points out, is one of the tragedies of the twentieth century. We can take, for example, the frequent failures to realize the many potentials of modern culture, such as using the material abundance made possible by technology to achieve economic equality and to enrich human autonomy and public life. Yet Berman chooses to keep the modern project immune from the problems it caused by saying that it is *we* who have simply failed to realize that project, not that the project itself failed. When he says, for example, "It is modernist culture that keeps critical thought and free imagination alive in much of the non-Western world today," using Chinese dissidents as one of his examples, he ignores the simple fact that it is also twentieth-century modernist culture which perfected the totalitarian Communist regime which is compelled to exterminate both tradition and the "critical thought and free imagination" of those dissidents.[4]

The final downfall of most of the European Marxist-Leninist regimes at the close of 1989 signaled the death knell of the nineteenth-century modernist dream of communism. Though Stalinism and its predecessor, Leninism, represent crucial breaks from Marx's critical program—most fundamentally in their ruthless repression of Marx's call for "relentless criticism of all existing institutions"—Marx himself is by no means immune from the failures of Marxism. His view of an inevitable grand march of history, his allowance of a transitional "dictatorship of the proletariat" phase, his relatively uncritical attitude toward centralized state power and machinery, all left great gaps through which gross tyranny could and did march.

If Marx had been able to rid himself of an inevitable conception of history and an overly materialized conception of human conduct, "historical materialism" might have provided a much needed corrective to the reified views of nature and etherealized views of mind which characterize the Kant-dominated tradition of social theory, including Weber, Durkheim, Simmel, Parsons, Habermas, and others. Yet its faith in inevitable and revolutionary progress appears as a quaint utopian fantasy after the catastrophic destruction of lives, cities, and the moral fabric of Western Civilization and world culture witnessed in the revolutionary twentieth century. For we have witnessed what Henry Adams sensed so accurately in his remarkable letter to Henry Osborn Taylor in 1905. Note that this letter was written within about a year in which Einstein discovered relativity, Picasso and Braque invented cubism, and Stravinsky released the demonic energies of *The Rites of Spring*. This historian and humanist and descendent of American Presidents said: "The assumption of unity which was the mark of human thought in the middle-ages has yielded very slowly to the proofs of complexity. The stupor of science before radium is a proof of it. Yet it is quite sure, according to my score of ratios and curves, that, at the accelerated rate of progression shown since 1600, it will not need another century or half century to tip thought upside down. Law, in that case, would disappear as theory or *a priori* principle, and give place to force. Morality would become police. Explosives would reach cosmic violence. Disintegration would overcome integration."[5]

Adams sensed the revolutionary social implications of the increasing release of power brought about by modern materialism. In the course of the "century of progress," law did give way to force, in the name of "realpolitik" and technological progress. Morality did become police as police states proliferated throughout the world, employing huge armies and centralized secret police institutions, and ever more sophisticated weaponry, all done frequently behind the facade of a "democratic" republic. Explosives did reach cosmic violence, with all the implications that "dreamers" such as Adams or H. G. Wells predicted and that "realistic" scientists and politicians were not prepared to meet. Disintegration did overcome integration, as the very "successes" of modern societies created disastrous consequences which we have yet fully to face. Consider the denial involved in Mikhail Gorbachev's statement in 1992 after the Soviet Union was dissolved—"I am entirely certain that its death [Stalinism] does not affect socialism itself. The idea of socialism lives on, and it is my feeling that the quest—the desire to experiment and to find a new form for putting the socialist idea into practice—is ongoing . . . this quest affects not only our country (where a phase of history well known to us all took its start and ran its course) but the entire world, including the capitalist countries."[6] A "phase of history," which "ran its course": what bloodless euphemism. Communism was a deadly phase of the era of dehumanizing materialism in which we are still living, and it was that materialism and its tendency to elevate power over purpose which was the root of the problem, not simply bad Stalinism versus good socialism.

In America alone, the birth of the atomic age coincided with the creation of an arrogant military welfare state whose relentless test detonations of "bombs of cosmic violence" up through the early 1960s will have killed more Americans— current estimates are at least 300,000 deaths due to radioactive fallout—than the Korean and Vietnam wars combined, not counting the scores of thousands of contaminated military personnel, uranium miners, and American families who lived near the bomb-making plants. Deliberate deception was employed by the U.S. government against the American public and any scientists courageous enough to release information showing the deadly probabilities.

A flood of materials was released around 1990, corresponding to the end of the Cold War, which demonstrated conclusively the ways American Cold War policy, in the name of "national security," subverted the requirements of public criticism for a viable democracy. Thousands of American families living near bomb-making factories and reactors, such as those in Fernald, Ohio, and Hanford, Washington, were exposed to appallingly high levels of radiation. Other unwitting individuals were dosed with radioactive substances, including deadly plutonium, as part of secret government-sponsored research. Meanwhile the government of the United States officially employed deception by claiming that there was no health hazard—even though it very well knew the dangers.[7] Likewise, the USSR probably killed at least as many of its citizens before Chernobyl through infantile handling of cosmic energies as the U.S. military-industrial-academic complex did, not even counting its lethal attitude toward other forms of environmental pollution.

In his remarkable New Year's Day 1990 speech, Vaclav Havel, who went from being a prisoner to becoming the president of Czechoslovakia in a matter of months, decried the way that communism had turned people into "the means of production." He went on to say that "we," the Czech people, are not simply victims but have also participated in the little lies which allowed the "monstrous, smelly machine" of communism to keep on rolling. In other words, it is not sufficient to point the finger at the other; one must also include the possibility of self-criticism. Clearly the Communist machine was a slave state in contrast to America. Yet the evil Communist machine did not exhaust the evil of machine-like ways of thinking, despite the gloating of those in the West who celebrated the "victory" of democracy and capitalism over communism. Havel's words also carry a universal significance beyond their immediate context which are directly applicable to America and its arrogant national security military machine.

Despite the end of the Cold War, there has been little serious consideration of the proper limited context of what Dwight Eisenhower called the "military-industrial complex" in a democratic republic. The irresponsible little Dr. Strangeloves and their minions continue to dictate vital decisions affecting public life, immunized from public criticism. The reification and deification of nuclear power by the United States and the USSR in the Cold War era, as well as the specific targeting of whole civilian populations by all of the great "enlightened" modern superpowers, are key symbols of the descent into rational barbarism which Adams forewarned. As Nietzsche said, "We moderns, we half-barbarians. We are in the midst of our bliss only when we are most in danger. The only stimulus that tickles us is the infinite, the immeasurable." What better symbol of immeasurable power, what better materialization of the infinite has the modern world produced than the cult of nuclear bombs. In the bowels of the deadly military bureaucracies of the superpowers, under pure and total rational control, sat the tens of thousands of mechanical nuclear Calibans, ready at the push of a button to wreak the extermination of the biosphere if "rationality" required it of them. "We moderns, we half-barbarians."

Though I remain deeply sympathetic to Berman's complex picture of modernity as both creative and destructive, and as having produced institutions of political and cultural freedom well worth preserving, it seems to me that his ardent enthusiasm for the twentieth century is excessive, when weighed against both the great works and ideas of the past and the dreadful cultural, political, personal, and ecological consequences those same twentieth-century ideas also produced. Something was terribly wrong in the very premises of the modern vision, and surely one can admit that today without having to reject all of those modern ideas worth preserving, and without having to be branded a reactionary or luddite. It is time to give up the ghost in the machine mythos of modernity. It is time, in short, for making a new civilization, with new interior landscapes of the mind and new exterior landscapes of cities and dwellings in harmony with the biosphere.

THE NEW WORLD MULTICULTURAL ORDER: AGAIN WITH THE CANON?

The greatest American minds, I submit, would have detested the relativism on which much of contemporary multiculturalism is based, while simultaneously embodying that diversity of world culture beyond Western Civilization toward which the best of multiculturalists aim. I submit that Herman Melville in literature, Charles Peirce in philosophy, and Lewis Mumford in social thought represent the inner meeting of the West with world culture, which is the tragic underlying reality of the dream of the New World. Now, as Americanism has smothered the world in its grinning embrace, with its military-industrial-entertainment-academic establishment riding high, and its cities, families, schools, and politics spinning out of control, the concerns of these three seem rather remote. All three—Melville, Peirce, Mumford—were driven by passions to embrace reality as fully as possible, and as they gradually succeeded their deeper probings were ignored by an America only too content to dream the optimistic "American dream."

They were not nourished by the relevant institutions of their time, not in any real sense, that is, by direct influence upon their inner development or viable means of existence. Melville could not make a living from his writing as he probed ever deeper into himself from *Moby Dick* on. Though whaling was his "Harvard and Yale," as he put it, his years as a customs inspector in New York City marked his exile from literary life. Peirce too, though genuinely enthusiastic about his five or so years at Johns Hopkins University, was blackballed from a regular university life and scholarly employment. His longer term work with the U.S. Coast and Geodetic Survey came to an end as bureaucratic motives assumed greater weight in the power structure and discouraged Peirce's researches. Peirce's employments, like

Melville's, not only do not account for the original work he produced but were, in fact, resistant against it. I think it is fair to say that friends—Hawthorne for Melville and William James for Peirce—provided the sustenance which institutions did not. In Mumford's case, his employment at *The New Yorker* and occasional positions in academic life did provide the material means for his writing, but I do not think they were essential for the inner development of his work, and the same is true of Melville and Peirce.

Melville did not go to college, Mumford did not graduate college, and Peirce received a master's degree in chemistry but received no graduate "training" in philosophy. So much, one might conclude from these examples, for the institutions of higher education!

Europeans since the time of Tocqueville have loved to treat American thought as a shallow declaration of independence from European traditions. Yet in *Moby Dick* the deep feeling Melville had for Shakespeare and the range of his philosophical learning is remarkable. So too, for that matter, is Melville's appreciation of the deadly fissures of racism in American and New World society and of the Western Civilization which begat it. Similarly, the pragmatisms of William James and John Dewey have been criticized throughout this century as representative of an American bias against history and nonuseful intellectual endeavor. Yet consider Peirce, the founder of pragmatism and modern semeiotic, in this context. Peirce claimed to have read all of the major treatises on logic in their original languages. He was an ardent student of history, and his entire philosophy bespeaks a careful sense of the etymological history of the terms he uses. One cannot read Peirce without a sense of philosophical history, and by today's standards Peirce would probably be called "European." Yet the deep feel for history in a Peirce or a Mumford—or for that matter, Melville—is essential for the development of their work. In a land where the proper institutions are wanting, a personal relationship to history is obligatory.

In reading *Moby Dick,* one of the greatest products of Western Civilization, how can one believe that Western Civilization alone ought to be the universal guide for contemporary life and education, as Roger Kimble does in his feeble appendix to his otherwise spirited attack on the ideology of leftist political correctness in his book, *Tenured Radicals. Moby Dick* points us to Queequeg and "the common continent of men," and one of the chief achievements of Western Civilization is precisely that it leads us toward the possibility of world culture. American intellectuals can ignore the ongoing making of a world culture, as the defenders of the "canon" of Western Civilization want to do, or can reify and then negate the abstraction known as "the canon" by advocating a relativistic multiculturalism, as so-called postmodern pluralists want to do. These multiculturalists refuse to consider that certain sentiments and ideals in Western Civilization articulated new possibilities for living which have enduring and universal value which transcend the civilization which produced them, such as the traditions and works of art—of perspective and abstraction in painting, of tonality and the Western orchestra, the novel, the plays of Shakespeare, and so forth—principles of human rights or the uniqueness of the individual. Canonical conservatives refuse to consider that certain destructive realities which are undeniably the legacy of Western Civilization, its obliteration of native peoples of the New World and enslavement of the rest of the world, first through raw imperialism and later through the "liberating" ideals of capitalism and communism, its universalization of destructive technologies of industry and war, its swallowing of the uniqueness of the individual into mass consumer materialism, its mad obsession to make the world rational, and finally, all-too-finally perhaps, its ongoing destruction of the biosphere. No relativist multiculturalist will deny the destructiveness of Western Civilization, yet few are willing to admit the valid universal excellence of some of its artists and scientists, and yes, even of some of its social and political theories and practices.

Both extremes ignore the fact that the best in a civilization—and even in the ways of local cultures—speaks to the human condition in general, and that all civilizations and cultures, except perhaps that of multicultural postmodernism, inculcate into their participants the capacity to discriminate, to distinguish better from worse, and to perceive the real thing hidden amidst the appearances. Against the multiculturalist, who sees only the diversity of things and cultures, the *Bhagavad Gita* says, "When one sees Eternity in things that pass away and Infinity in finite things, then one has pure knowledge. But if one merely sees the diversity of things, with their divisions and limitations, then one has impure knowledge." Stated in Western terms, this means that seeing the universe in a grain of sand is a clean, while seeing things only in terms of pluralistic difference is a dirty. Against the upholder of the "canon," who sees only the unity of the Western tradition—reified as the canon—instead of the diversity of its works, the words of Chuang Tzu hold: "Fish live in water and thrive, but if men tried to live in water they would die. Creatures differ because they have different likes and dislikes. Therefore the former sages never required the same ability from all creatures or made them all do the same thing. Names should stop when they have expressed reality, concepts of right should be founded on what is suitable. This is what it means to have command of reason, and good fortune to support you."

If the point of an education, including a professional education as a philosopher or theorist, is to have "command of reason" as Chuang Tzu puts it, rather than to have learned a great tradition or a pluralism of traditions, or to have learned what one's ethnic background is, then we must seek those works which will best give us a command of reason, that is, of the richness of qualities of feeling and perception, of standards of discrimination and of the abilities to interpret and generalize.

The typical multiculturalist assumes the culture is convention view, the "doughnut" theory of culture, with its obligatory, uncritical "antiessentialism." Thus the integrity of works of art or philosophy is denied at the outset, and they are hollowed out of their qualitative uniqueness and subsumed to a social convention. The reduced aggregate result can be called a "canon" or "Western Civilization" or "dead white males." Shakespeare can then be safely criticized from the outside for some political agenda, and the fact that he has deeply touched the souls of those whose souls have not been immunized by ideology from being touched, and that he will continue to touch the souls of those who honestly confront his work, can be ignored. If I may use the ideas of another playwright, Havel, again, the open engagement with the masterworks of Shakespeare, as with any intense reality, holds the possibility of "living in truth," of an experience of human passion before which all ideologies evaporate. Of course Shakespeare can be used for ideological purposes, and has been many times, but the living reality of his master works will speak to the perceptive listener regardless of those purposes.

In 1990, Maya Angelou, in one of the most passionate public addresses or performances I have been fortunate to witness, spoke of her deep love for Shakespeare, of how he spoke directly to her troubled soul at a time when she was unable to speak at all in public—after she was raped as a child, of how she had to try to hide the fact that he happened to be white from her grandmother. Living in racially segregated Arkansas, this budding adolescent memorized Shakespeare sonnets in secret, in the private world into which she was forced to retreat. Speaking to a large audience in public as an adult, she recited those sonnets from her heart with the love of language they helped to instill in her, while simultaneously celebrating the tradition of African American poetry. Shakespeare spoke so directly to her that she playfully fantasized that he must have been black, "passing" for white. She recited the well-known Sonnet 29,

> When, in disgrace with fortune and men's eyes,
> I all alone beweep my outcast state

and trouble deaf heaven with my bootless cries
And look upon myself and curse my fate,
Wishing me like to one more rich in hope,
Featured like him, like him with friends possess'd,
Desiring this man's art and that man's scope,
With what I most enjoy contented least;
Yet in these thoughts myself almost despising,
Haply I think on thee, and then my state,
Like to the lark at break of day arising
From sullen earth, sings hymns at heaven's gate;
For thy sweet love remember'd such wealth brings
That then I scorn to change my state with kings.

Angelou's title to her novel, *I know Why the Caged Bird Sings,* is a marvelous coelescence of images from this sonnet of Shakespeare and a line from the poem *Sympathy* by the nineteenth-century African-American poet, Paul Lawrence Dunbar, the stanza of which reads:

I know why the caged bird sings, ah me.
    When his wing is bruised and his bosom sore,—
When he beats his bars and he would be free;
It is not a carol of joy or glee.
    But a prayer that he sends from his heart's deep core,
But a plea, that upward to heaven he flings—
I know why the caged bird sings!

Experiencing Maya Angelou reciting Shakespeare and Dunbar and a host of works from memory and with passion, mixing her deep love of and feel for these works with a direct engagement with the shameful problems of race, gender, and class she experienced personally and America reproduces institutionally, gives the lie to pallid, multicultural relativists and their canonical race, gender, and class externalism. There is a legitimate place to criticize the social contexts of works of art, but it must ever remain external to the compelling nature of a real work of art. One can do a bibliographical survey of titles of books on Shakespeare over time and the majority of titles are likely to be good indicators of societal trends, of "social mediations," as Stanley Fish and many postmodern lit critters like to point out. But this is simply a sociological technique for viewing the narcissist at work, inflicting his or her obsessions onto Shakespeare, and does not really touch the living reality of Shakespeare.

In retrospect we can see how the modern age set out to build a rational science, society, and individual. It undertook a transformation of humankind into *homo sapiens,* man the knower, the rational creature, and as its successes multiplied and its powers grew with a seeming inevitability, powerful works and ideas were wrought. Developing out of the rationalized order of the Medieval monastery, to the rationalized orders of science, technics, and capitalism, the latent powers of rationality were increasingly institutionalized with world-transforming success. European civilization discovered a universe of mechanical laws in nature and of subjective dimensions of the human person without precedent. The achievement of perspective in painting and of tonality in music opened new inner worlds for artists to explore, and the masterworks of Florentine painting, of Bach, Haydn, Mozart, and Beethoven, radically intensified, enlarged, and subtilized the expressive capacities of Europeans, and of humankind in general. For the legacy of these great artists and their masterworks is indeed of universal significance, and is already contributing to the world culture in the making in ways which most multicultural ideologues of today, bounded as they are by narrow relativism and even narrower feelings, can little suspect. But as it opened up an inner landscape of subjective life and feeling, it was also creating a colonization of the new inner world, through the idealization of sentiments.

To the vaunted utilitarian ideal of a *homo faber,* fabricating humankind through stones and bones, his hard tools gradually evolving through the bronze and iron ages into our steel and plutonium world of the modern machine, and to the glorious ideal of *homo sapiens,* discoursing, rationalizing, and writing his manly way toward modern science, we need to add the creature *homo sentimentalis.* This creature has been singled out by Kundera in his book *Immortality,* and also by Doris Lessing, in her marvelous space fiction work, *The Sentimental Agents.* Kundera says of *homo sentimentalis:*

> Europe has the reputation of a civilization based on reason. But one can say equally well that it is a civilization of sentiment; it created a human type whom I call sentimental man. . . . *Homo sentimentalis* cannot be defined as a man with feelings (for we all have feelings) but as a man who has raised feelings to a category of value. . . .
>
> The transformation of feelings into a value had already occurred in Europe sometime around the twelfth century: the troubadors who sang with such great passion to their beloved, the unattainable princess, seemed

so admirable and beautiful to all who heard them that everyone wished to follow their example by falling prey to some wild upheaval of the heart. . . .

It is part of the definition of feeling that it is born in us without our will, often against our will. As soon as we *want* to feel (*decide* to feel, just as Don Quixote decided to love Dulcinea), feeling is no longer feeling but an imitation of feeling, a show of feeling. This is commonly called hysteria. That's why *homo sentimentalis* (a person who has raised feeling to a value) is in reality identical to *homo hystericus*. . . .

No civilization has ever created such a miracle out of musical sounds as European music, with its thousand-year-old history and its wealth of forms and styles! Europe: great music and *homo sentimentalis*. Twins nurtured side by side in the same cradle. Music taught the European not only a richness of feeling, but also the worship of his feelings and his feeling self.[8]

Lessing's *The Sentimental Agents* is part of a series of works dealing with the struggle between advanced beings from competing civilizations incarnated as natives on various planets in order to further evolutionary development. The agents of an evil civilization, Shammat, enslave their victims through rhetoric: "What Shammat does, in short, is to allow 'life itself' to throw up its material, encourage 'life itself' to develop it, and then, when these people are already well accustomed to assaults of Rhetoric, both from others and as used by themselves, they are taken into Krolgul's school, where they have to learn to become immune to it, so that they may control crowds by the most passionate, violent, emotional language possible, without ever being affected by it."[9] In other words, rhetoric serves as a means of idealizing the sentiments, and thereby producing the equivalent of Kundera's *homo sentimentalis*.

In their respective novels, Kundera and Lessing depict with pathos and lucidity the usually unacknowledged side of modern rational culture, namely, the tendency of overly rationalized beings simultaneously to become overly sentimentalized. They do not merely attack the emotional side of life, as typical postmodern theorists do, as reducible to forms of social legitimation or convention. Indeed, Lessing's rhetoricians seem, in many ways, like avatars of postmodern rhetoricians, who view rhetoric not as reasonable argumentation but as mere indoctrination to ideology and strategic persuasion.

Yet in their very terminology, Kundera and Lessing seem to surrender to the devaluation of the sentiments undertaken with virulence since the enlightenment. If I say that I am a rationalist, or a postmodernist, or a modernist, I will likely be taken as holding a conceivably legitimate position, even if wrong. But if I say that I am a sentimentalist, the word would evoke someone overly emotional or gushy. The possibility that sentimentalism could be a doctrine that human emotions are the chief vehicles for the practice of everyday life—or, in semiotic lingo—emotions are a principle mode of semeiosis or communicative practices in the conduct of life, operating at a level significantly different from that of rational discourse, a level more basic than rational or linguistic discourse or critical thought, and one which provides the tonal ground of rational discourse—the very possibility that sentimentalism could be the name of such a doctrine would fly in the face of our ingrained Enlightenment, modern and postmodern prejudices.

Kundera skewers modern *homo sentimentalis,* while not succumbing to misanthropism. Or perhaps I should say while not completely succumbing to misanthropism, because I am not convinced that his caustic view allows for the evolutionary *homo sentimentalis,* the one whose evolving capacity to feel the world and transmute those feelings into personal and institutional ways of living remains our best hope to offset the false *sentimentalis,* who idealizes the emotions. The real *homo sentimentalis* involves both types, both the human ability to feel one's way in the world and with others empathically, as well as the human ability to idealize the emotions, to make them servants of ideas. Perhaps Kundera believes so too, but his recurrent corrosive view of the family, particularly children, and of intimate relations as inescapably locked into a more existentialist version of what the Freudians call narcissistic "object relations"—the projection of primitive and idealized inner feelings onto outer loved ones—and perhaps also his apparent belief about the utter futility of politics, seem to me an overly jaded view of the world.

In the real world of politics, Kundera's cynicism lost to the hopeful "living in truth" politics of Vaclav Havel, which is why Kundera has been viewed negatively by many Czechs while Havel went from being a prisoner to becoming the president of Czechoslovakia within two months, in a drama that no dramatist or writer could have ever gotten away with. Havel may have only been able to hold Czechoslovakia together for a couple of years before routine power politics reasserted itself, but even his liminal presidency testifies to what he called "the power of the powerless," and the possibility of "living in truth." Living in truth is a conditional or subjunctive reality of being human, even if, to paraphrase Mark Twain, we humans only seem able to take truth in small doses.

Yet what may make for cynical politics in Kundera's case can make for powerfully moving and compelling art, when one sets out, as he does in his book *Immortality,* to slash the tires of human vanity on which we travel in delirious oblivion. Curiously similar for me are the sometimes unconvincing political views Doris Lessing holds in real life, compared to the Swiftian certainty of political critique found in *The Sentimental Agents.*

Kundera's view of *homo sentimentalis,* as creating an ideal inner mirror through which we see our own idealized emotions instead of the world, reminds one of Melville's description of Ahab's soul as having been captured by "the characterizing mind":

> . . . crazy Ahab, the scheming, unappeasedly steadfast hunter of the white whale; this Ahab that had gone to his hammock, was not the agent that so caused him to burst from it in horror again. The latter was the eternal, living principle or soul in him; and in sleep, being for the time dissociated from the characterizing mind, which at other times employed it for its outer vehicle or agent, it spontaneously sought escape from the scorching contiguity of the frantic thing, of which, for the time, it was no longer an integral. But as the mind does not exist unless leagued with the soul, therefore it must have been that, in Ahab's case, yielding up all his thoughts and fancies to his own supreme purpose; that purpose, by its own sheer inveteracy of will, forced itself against gods and devils into a kind of self-assumed, independent being of its own. Nay, could grimly live and burn, while the common vitality to which it was conjoined, fled horror-stricken from the unbidden and unfathered birth. Therefore, the tormented spirit that glared out of bodily eyes, when what seemed Ahab rushed from his room, was for the time but a vacated thing, a formless somnambulistic being, a ray of living light, to be sure, but without an object to color, and therefore a blankness in itself. God help thee, old man, thy thoughts have created a creature in thee; and he whose intense thinking thus makes him a Prometheus; a vulture feeds upon that heart forever; that vulture the very creature he creates.

The characterizing mind of Ahab, or what William Blake called "The Spectre" or the "Reasoning Power in Man," had usurped its proper limited context as an organ of extrarational reason. In its hubris, idealizing rational mind set out to dominate and control the transcendent spontaneity of life itself, which appears to the rational in pathologically distorted form as what Melville calls the "ultimate blankness in itself," whether the soul within or the whale and world without. In the making of itself, modern civilization dissociated its "characterizing mind" from the soul of the living world and simultaneously created *homo rationalis* and *homo sentimentalis.* The ultimate object of this fevered rationality is the destructively irrational appropriation of the soul of the world itself, as misperceived by the scheming self-mirror of rationalized sentiment.

Ahab, the very personification of narcissistic rage, becomes increasingly isolated as he approaches his ideal object, "the phantom of life" itself. In the moment of realizing his mad quest, his total isolation as a pure subject collapses into total merger with the object, as he is entangled in his harpoon line with the whale. His final moment is pure rage and pure dependence, quite the opposite of the Enlightenment ideals of liberty, equality, and brotherhood, of Quaker peace, of American independence, of modern rationality.

D. H. Lawrence, himself one of the rediscoverers of Melville, resonated with these ideas in his book, *Psychoanalysis and the Unconscious:* "This motivizing of the passional sphere from the ideal is the final peril of human consciousness. It is the death of all spontaneous, creative life, and the substituting of the mechanical principle. It is obvious that the ideal becomes a mechanical principal, if it be applied to the affective soul as a fixed motive. An ideal established in control of the passional soul is no more and no less than a supreme machine-principle. And a machine, as we know, is the active unit of the material world. Thus we see how it is that in the end pure idealism is identical with pure materialism, and the most ideal peoples are the most completely material. Ideal and material are identical. The ideal is but the god in the machine—-the little, fixed machine-principle which works the human psyche automatically."[10]

Lawrence distinguishes idealism by which he means "the motivizing of the great affective sources by means of ideas mentally derived," from the "true unconscious" (as opposed to Freud's), which is "not a shadow cast from the mind. It is the spontaneous life-motive in every organism." Lawrence's critique of Freud here and elsewhere in *Psychoanalysis and the Unconscious* anticipates by a couple of decades the turn toward a more relational view of early development and the spontaneous self as a therapeutic goal by psychoanalytic object relations theorists, such as D. W. Winnicott or Heinz Kohut.

Kundera, Lessing, Melville, and Lawrence all point to the paradoxical tragedies of modern life: the development of rational capacities oversteps boundaries and parasitically feeds on the emotional sources of rational life. Rationality is itself one capacity among others, which becomes destructive when taken to be the sovereign of reason.

Though we humans possess rationality, we are not rational beings and cannot become rational beings. Or let me modify that. The moment we truly become rational creatures is the moment when Ahab is lashed to the whale, when he, as the rational isolato subject, attains a final unity with the narcissistic object of his rationalization, his death. It is the moment of Raskolnikov's rational murder. That moment of the realization of the rational creature is the "interesting age" in which we now are living.

We humans are passionate beings, whether we are modern workers in a rationalized factory or computer terminal, or *Realpolitik* calculators planning how to maximize our individual strategic interests, or scientists inquiring into the origins of the physical universe, or philosophers inquiring into the sources and ends of public life. We are beings of passion currently possessed by a singular passion for being rational. This rational passion, having exalted itself above creation in the name of "God," "Science," "Reason," "Critical theory," "Modernity," and even, in unconscious self-alienation, "Postmodernity," has blinded its adherents to the inner community of passions which are necessary to human sanity, and to the passional relation to the outer world of nature and experience, mediated through an integrated self. In the quest to attain universal intellect at any expense, we have committed the "Unpardonable Sin," as Hawthorne put it, of rationally possessed hubris, and have become severed from the universal "heartthrob" of humanity. We moderns have become the fiendish Frankenstein monsters, Ethan Brands, Ahabs, Raskolnikovs, Mr. Kurtzs, and Adrian Leverkühns, presciently felt and imagined by those writers sensitive to the drift of modern culture.

The contemporary intellectual landscape is still dominated by those who believe that all we need to do is improve our critical rationality, science, or technology, or to include multiple "modes of authority" in our methods and theories. Yet, as Coleridge said, "[D]eep thinking is attainable only by a man of deep feeling"—today, of course, we would say "by a man or woman of deep feeling"— and those who, living from the head alone, have lost the capacity to feel deeply are not likely to point the way toward a renewal of thought and culture.

As the twilight of the twentieth century begins to set, neither a rationalist such as Habermas nor even a postmodern antirationalist such as Rorty—nor the majority of theorists, it is fair to say—face up to the fact that the dream of the modern age to create rationally grounded societies has long since revealed itself to be a nightmare, the hydraheaded nightmare of bureaucratic totalitarianism and bureaucratic capitalism, of mass Isolatoism. Human life, which developed through the enlargement and subtlization of the mammalian traits of REM dreaming, powerful mother-infant bonding and nurturance, and play, expressed in the development of ritual observances, emotionally rich linguistic communication, and the flourescence of fantastic symbolic forms in body decoration, painting, and even practical artifacts, is reduced to the rote, to lifeless formalism and its opposite: contingent sensationalism. The human person, who was the living incarnation of evolutionary reasonableness, was rendered into a cog of devitalized systems—whether politically as the mass man of brutal Communist and Nazi systems or of the control-by-reward consumer societies, or through general rational bureaucracy itself and various "systems" and behaviorist theories, or as psychological man—an isolate subject possessed of "subjective values" and incapable of touching the objective world. If modernity began with the celebration of the person in humanism, it ended in the twentieth century with a "posthuman" world from which the organic human person had been dispossessed.

The true utopia of the power mongers and rational calculators—not to mention the Arnold Gehlens and sociobiologists—is that of the beehive, one of the earliest manifestations of the megamachine. Sixty million years ago bees and ants achieved highly efficient societies that would be the envy of the leading economic powers and systems theorists of today.

Let me emphasize that I am not rejecting rationality per se, but simply the dominant tendencies of modern culture toward an ever more rational world. One of my basic premises is that the progressive development and release of rational capacities in modern culture and its institutions have been possible because of the legacy of the many forms of nonrational reasonableness embedded in Western Civilization, a legacy by no means obsolete. In its ever greater expansion the rational mind increasingly devalued that which was not rational, and claimed that reason was synonymous with the rational. It was only able to do so, in my opinion, because of the rich, hybrid compost of organic intelligence on which it was based and which fueled it, a reasonableness developed out of pre-Western, non-Western, and precivilizational, and even prehistoric sources. Emotions can develop or atrophy, both individually and institutionally, and can range from fleeting sensations to instinctive proclivities whose forms, however variously expressed, remain deeply engrained aspects of being human. Those patterns of ritual expression and forms of feeling in the human constitution, such as dreaming, play, and intense mother-infant bonding, reach back to deeply embedded biological sources—to prehuman and ecstatic mammalian sources—which were pivotal to the emergence of human beings and which continue to animate human conduct at the highest levels as well as the lowest.

The casting off of archaic culture, of traditional customs, mores, and beliefs, of localized community in the development of modern culture, not only produced positive energies in the development of the modern autonomous self but also had the unenlightening consequence of jettisoning the checks and balances of the human person, leaving the individual much more dependent on singular sources of socialization. "Enlightenment" was supposed to replace the chaotic dark regions of the mythologizing psyche with sober modern reason, a project which neglected the possibility that mythic narratives might be expressions of a deeper relatedness with the powers that move humans than rational consciousness can touch. As Havel has put it:

> Yes, when traditional myth was laid to rest, a kind of "order" in the dark region of our being was buried along with it. And what modern reason has attempted to substitute for this order, has consistently proved erroneous, false, and disastrous, because it is always in some way deceitful, artificial, rootless, lacking in both ontology and morality. It may even border on the ludicrous, like the cult of the "Supreme Being" during the French Revolution, the collectivist folklore of totalitarian systems, or their "realist," self-celebrating art. It seems to me that with the burial of myth, the barn in which the mysterious animals of the human unconscious were housed over thousands of years has been abandoned and the animals turned loose—or the tragically mistaken assumption that they were phantoms—and that now they are devastating the countryside. They devastate it, and at the same time they make themselves at home where we least expect them to— in the secretariats of modern political parties, for example. These sanctuaries of modern reason lend them their tools and their authority so that ultimately the plunder is sanctioned by the most scientific of world views.[11]

Consumer culture today is the chief socializing agent of the modern ghost in the machine, promising freedom and autonomy and immediate gratification while relentlessly colonizing both the civic community and the very structure of the self, from infancy on, like a retrovirus: a retrovirus which says, "Buy me, drink me, eat me, dream me, desire me, and you will be yourself." In the virtual reality of consumption culture anything goes if people will buy it, only the real cost for the delusion of endless possession is a loss of self-possession. The endless parade of consumptive fantasies becomes a way of life: the self can be endlessly redescribed, like new clothing. Between the Big System and pure chance contingencies stands the hollow self, with its glorious hypertrophied freedoms to choose and idealize, unburdened by its organic needs and limitations, by spontaneous empathy, or by purposes or commitments which transcend its singular existence. If, as Marshall Berman points out so well, Faust was the embodiment of the myth of development and modernization, postmodern Post-Faustian Person, driven by the irrational march of rational images and fantasies instead of the Grand March of history, is perhaps the logical terminus of the Faustian myth: the complete colonization of the inner life of humanity and the "wide world outside" by the ghost in the machine.

Berman has claimed that we need to live the modern project more fully to realize its potentials, but I disagree. People did not fail modernism, as Berman seems to imply, modernism failed people, because of its unbalanced premises. The modern era has indeed bequethed many valid potentials for human life, but to realize them a new civilizational context is required.

The future of human development at this point in history does not hinge on becoming more rational, or, in the name of pluralism, more arbitrary, or on the blank postmodern carnival of all-purpose contingency, but on reharnessing rationality to its humane and cosmic moorings. By cosmic I mean extrahistorical and even extrahuman, for example, certain deep primate feelings and capacities which we still carry and act from and certain late works of Beethoven speak from natural sources beyond what we normally assume to be human. The biological need of an infant to bond with its mother is one part of our primate heritage which is crucial for the emergence and development of the self. No matter how conventionally social and gender roles may be constructed, the stubborn fact remains that infants and toddlers require empathic mothering, however a mother may be defined. In contemporary society a father or caretaker can share or take on the role of the empathic mother as well, providing the needed supportive gaze and nurturing, because there is an open-endedness and adaptability to human needs. Still, we know that the processes of communicative attunement between mother and infant already begin in utero and run deep into unconscious habits. Yet again, we know that communicative reattunement between foster mother and infant is also a normal part of human adaptability. What remains unalterable, however, is the need for empathic communicative attunement, which is a basic requirement for the development of a healthy self and which is rooted in our prehuman primate heritage.

By contrast, I realize how strange it sounds to say that some of Beethoven's music speaks from natural sources beyond what we normally assume to be human. What I mean to suggest, however, is that he bodied forth imaginative possibilities in some of his late music which touch the deepest wellsprings of what it means to be human while simultaneously deepening the human experience. The most tangible example of this for me is the last movement of his last string quartet, *Opus No.*

135, which, as Kundera has discussed so well in his novel, *The Unbearable Lightness of Being,* involves a marvelous play between Beethoven's tragic and probing question "Muss es sein?" (Does it have to be?)—and his forceful answer—"Es muss sein!" (It has to be!).

Beethoven was owed money by a friend. When he asked for the money back, the friend wrote out for the stone-deaf Beethoven, "Muss es sein?" To which Beethoven replied, "Es muss sein! ja ja ja ja! Heraus mit dem Beutel" (It has to be! yes yes yes yes! Out with the moneybag). This joking interaction found its way into the last movement of the quartet, which Beethoven titled "Der schwer gefasste Entschluss," meaning the difficult or heavy resolution. What started out as a joke assumed cosmic weight in the question of being: "Must it be?"—and in the affirmation—"It must be!" Following the incredible sadness and longing of the third movement of the quartet, this question and its answer go back and forth, always with the affirmation. Kundera stresses the transformation of the light joking into the heaviness of ultimate being. He does not mention, however, what follows the Es muss sein dialogue, namely, what sounds very much like a light, dancing children's tune. Between the heaviness and weight of the questioning of existence, and the determined affirmation, is the lightness and innocence of a child's tune which also forms an essential part of the answer. To be able to unify a movement with such portentous weight and self-ironical play is fantastic, truly the difficult or weighty resolution ("Der schwer gefasste Entschluss").

We see in this last movement of Beethoven's music that the end of human experience is both complete mastery and affirmation of being, including the embrace of tragedy, but also the laughter of the child. Experience does not simply overcome and eradicate innocence, but the fullest experience is as open to the world and to the inner impulse to play as the play of a child. Even apart from the quartet in which it is embedded, Beethoven introduced into human culture in this one movement of the work a paradoxical resolution of the polarity between innocence and experience, potently illustrating that the most mature expressions of human wisdom so often involve a paradoxically playful *and* tragic relation to being. In the end we remain neotenic creatures, retaining characteristics of early childhood in transformed mature realization. Here play has become conscious, and in the complete mastery of the imagination, of technique, and of the bringing to musical consciousness the supreme questions of human "knowing," we see the complete unification of *homo ludens, homo faber,* and *homo sapiens;* the fullest realization of *homo symbolicus.* Must it be? It must be! And what is it that we affirm with such resolute earnestness: Why nothing other than the playful singing of experience.

At the end of human experience remains the neotenic essence: man's glassy essence, the mirror of our soul, is joyful play and dreadful suffering, mother's milk of human kindness and Beethoven's isolate deafness, the mammalian dream and variations.

The modern world thought it could attain rational maturity by eradicating cultural neoteny, but all it did was to institutionalize infantilism in its place. It did not realize that rational maturity means living in the gap between rational comprehension and the *sense of things* which never gets completely comprehended. Most of our brain feels, wills, and knows that which it cannot consciously formulate. Our greater powers of dreaming, playing, and loving reside in this vast complex, and, if we can find the means to grant them a real place in our dreamless, droning, loveless world of rational madness, they remain as our chief means of bringing the complex sum and potential of mind to consciousness.

Both the inherited mammalian tendencies for mother-infant bonding, play, and dreaming and the imaginative realizations of the gravity and inexhaustible exuberance of being are not simply human "texts" but involve, in the former case, capacities which derive from our evolutionary past and, in the example of Beethoven, possibilities which transcended the script of his time (and perhaps ours too). Their "becoming human" is one of the springs of culture, when we conceive of culture as rooted deeply in our biosemiotic temperament and open to genuine learning and embodying. The acknowledgment and institutionalization of the cosmic dimension, not in a mystical embrace of oceanic unity but in a realization of our rootedness in an inestimably sophisticated intelligence of nature, a realization which nevertheless requires our critical intelligence as well as our extracritical capacities, is part of what I conceive to be a necessary task of contemporary world culture, if we are to survive and flourish. The cosmic dimension of human existence has traditionally been the domain of religion, and the great world religions continue to nourish human needs to touch this dimension today. Still, I do not believe that the traditional religions have exhausted what is implied by the cosmic dimension of human affairs, nor do I think that the great world religions are prepared to meet the transvaluation required today. For this would require of a religion that it accept its own fallibility, in the hope that a fundamental deepening and transformation of its beliefs always remains a possibility in a universe still very much in the process of creation. By the same reasoning, I do not believe that the valid achievements of modern humanism need be tossed out as totally obsolete, because of antirational "posthumanism," as its standard bearers call it. The potential enhancements of the personal *and* public domains of life remain as valid legacies of the modern era, no matter how often the same modern impulses which promoted them also tended to thwart them.

The logic of modern "rationalization," as I see it, is sure and certain death, and we are perhaps already past the deadline—literally—for diverting the further descent into rational barbarism. Hence I see the need for a fundamental transformation of the modern outlook (including its postmodern variations) in which rationality is taken to be an essential but highly limited aspect of reason. That is to say, we hairless bipeds need to stop all the self-tickling and realize that it is our relation to something larger than ourselves that gives us our reason for being here. We neither "own" mind nor do we know it in its fullness, let alone entirety. The rational is and will ever remain the minority of the reasonable.

Placed in the context of contemporary social theory, these ideas undermine Jürgen Habermas's theory of communicative rationality, which claims that the modern project of instrumental or strategic rationality only needs to be improved with a better, brighter, "communicative rationality," which is inherently intersubjective. Habermas, supposedly a "critical theorist," never thinks to criticize the assumption that rationality must be preeminent in human development, which would require a thoroughgoing revision of his nominalist premises.

The dominant forms of philosophy and social theory today represent the conventionalist side of cultural nominalism. So-called postmodernism is itself, by my lights, one of the final degenerate stages of self-annulling modernity: if materialism said that only matter matters, postmodern etherealism says that nothing matters, everything goes. To be fair, postmoderns, with good reasons, have sought to discard the grand humanist narratives of history, which often tended to view the world ethnocentrically as culminating in modern Western Civilization. Yet not all modern historical narratives are Eurocentric, even when they hold that there are valid "big pictures" and valid historical universals. In dogmatically rejecting such possibilities because they do not fit "the postmodern condition," postmodern fragmatism merely echoes, by glorying in, the conventionalist half of modern cultural nominalism, only replacing universalist tendencies with radically relativist ones. It never denies the legacy of the modern nominalist era that all that can be loved must be unreal.

The acknowledgment of deep human passions, of the spontaneity of the human soul in its diverse expressions, flies in the face of most leading contemporary theories, with their effete disparagement of feelings, sentiments, and passions as reducible to conceptual forms of legitimation or convention. These theories reify the emotions as supposedly outside of mediation, and then recite the litany of how everything is socially mediated. These theorists refuse to consider the possibility that passions or emotions are themselves inherently social modalities of signification embedded in, but not reducible to, conventionalized signification. Thus, in postmodern dress, they mindlessly repeat the basic premises of cultural nominalism which are traceable to the rise of philosophical nominalism: all meaning is either a convention or a contingency. This neat dichotomy, with the extreme relativism which usually accompanies it, is simply too narrow.

When seen in this light, the seemingly benign postmodern, postfactual, postrational world where there are no truths or facts but only conventions and language games reveals its corrupt consequences. When a Stanley Fish or Richard Rorty says that everything, including truth and goodness and beauty, is a matter of "socialization," taking, I might add, the process of socialization in the most *banal* sense of automatic internalization of norms, when they or James Clifford or other postpeople say that experience is but a "mode of authority," the possibility of a public life, wherein fallible standards of discrimination, judgment, excellence, and justice form the fabric of the good life, must give way sooner or later to direct power: morality becomes police, and integration gives way to disintegration. Contemporary theory or philosophy provides the groundwork for such a postworld.

By contrast consider the playwright and president, Vaclav Havel, also the author of the essay, "The Power of the Powerless," as a social theorist. As Havel said recently, while still president of Czechoslovakia, in responding to a critic who claimed he did not see that politics is simply power:

> The idea that the world might actually be changed by the force of truth,
> the power of a truthful world, the strength of a free spirit, conscience, and
> responsibility—with no guns, no lust for power, no political wheeling and
> dealing—was quite beyond the horizon of his understanding. Naturally, if
> you understand decency as a mere "superstructure" of the forces of pro
> duction, then you can never understand political power in terms of
> decency. . . . Communism was overthrown by life, by thought, by human
> dignity. . . . Genuine politics—politics worthy of the name, and the only
> politics I am willing to devote myself to—is simply a matter of serving
> those around us: serving the community, and serving those who will come
> after us. Its deepest roots are moral because it is a responsibility, expressed
> through action, to and for the whole, a responsibility that is what it is—a
> "higher" responsibility—only because it has a metaphysical grounding:

that is, it grows out of a conscious or subconscious certainty that our death ends nothing, because everything is forever being recorded and evaluated somewhere else, somewhere "above us," in what I have called "the memory of being."[12]

Havel's idea of "the memory of being" may suggest some influence from Heidegger, whose politics and sense of decency were clearly opposite to those of Havel. Yet if one were to look around today for a thinker closest in spirit to the vision of Peirce or Mumford, it seems to me that Vaclav Havel is that person. Perhaps we could call his outlook "Prague-matism," and note that it is decidedly unacademic in squarely facing the problems of contemporary life and questions concerning "the big picture."

Between Havel and Mumford on one side and Habermas, Derrida, Rorty, and Bourdieu on the other side there is a yawning abyss: and I would suggest that the latter side is nothing less than the intellectual avatar of the posttotalitarian system which Havel describes, and which he makes quite explicit even in 1978 is not limited to the Communist system which dominated Eastern Europe but includes consumption societies as well. It is a well-oiled megamachine built on the narrow assumptions that the insurgent, interpreting human being can be comprehended on the basis of conventions and their oppositions, and that human signification is unnatural. This is simply old-time nominalism, the invisible hand of modern thought. It is far too restrictive a way of thinking, even for understanding human conventions, and is unconscious, it seems to me, of how much it unquestioningly enacts the myth of modernity.

The "severed head" of rationality is still busily universalizing itself in the name of "development" and "progress," and, like Faust, must face a reckoning for having sold its soul. The most obvious area where reckoning is coming due is perhaps the global attack on organic life at every level of land, sea, and, through ozone depletion, the air. It is also quite obvious that reversing this destruction means reconnecting ourselves globally with a felt and institutionalized sense of nature's limits and laws. Doing so requires a world politics and culture and not simply a piecemeal legislation of unlimited industrialism and capitalism.

Given the ways in which the enormous powers and poisons released by modern technology have pressed many natural and cultural environments to or beyond their limits, as seen, for example, in the effects of air pollution on some forests and in cities such as Los Angeles or Mexico City, the words of Edmund Burke, from his critical *Reflections on the Revolution in France,* speak with renewed meaning: Burke stated that if the state is to achieve its ends it should be adjusted, "not to human reasonings, but to human nature; of which reason is but a part, and by no means the greatest part." I would only revise Burke so that rationality is but a part, and by no means the greatest part, of human reason, and that human reason is a part of human nature, which includes human unreason, and that human nature is a part of an evolutionary reasonableness "energizing in the universe," to cite Peirce. The overcoming of rationality and "postrationality" involves reattuning our signifying, communicative human essence to nature's reasonableness, both within and without, and to the diverse ways in which traditional humans listened to and were nourished by nature's calls. Perhaps the dawning realization that the paleolithic diet is healthier than the typical postindustrial one—which is to say that it is more reasonable than that of the typical product of modern rationality—together with the recovery of Incan agriculture as a viable means of enhancing contemporary global agriculture, represent the beginnings of a reattunement after the estrangements of the modern mentality. Such a project amounts to more than a critique of rationality or modernity in the end, for in my view it involves the making of a new civilization.

The destructive consequences of the overextension of rationality need to be corrected by a renewal of other forms of reasonableness which it displaced and by certain institutions it discarded. But this renewal, though prompted by spontaneous need and by the mysterious processes of emergence, also requires *deliberation,* and here the positive fruition of the development of rational capacities and institutions in the modern era come to the fore. Deliberation requires rational planning. But rational planning, in this outlook, requires openness to the guiding emergent impulses, motives, and purposes, to the consideration of what patterns of conduct—individual and institutional—can sustain the richness and diversity of the biosphere on which we depend, and of the requirements of human life and the human self as well.

We need to remake ourselves before the world forces us, with catastrophic consequences, toward heeding limits, because the inner life of humans is just as endangered as the outer world. The de-localizing conditions of modern life may leave local "hybrid" cultures in its wake, but when one looks closely at these, there is great reason to suspect that the tendency may favor dissolution over integral culture. Shamans in Brazil, Australia, and Africa are today a dying breed, unable to impart their wisdom of ritual practices and herbal medicine, because their offspring have moved off to cities. The younger generations, continuing the global pattern of migration over the last century toward cities, leave to become modern material consumers but usually end up living in mass poverty. Those who remain are often warned against "deviltalk" by restless Christian missionaries, who spread "the good word" that the great and universal machine of Christianity does not tolerate local beliefs in their own terms. As Mark Plotkin, an ethnobiologist who works with Shamans in order to preserve valuable herbal medicines says, "Each time a medicine man dies, it is as if a library has burned down. We often talk about disappearing species, but the knowledge of how to use these species is disappearing much faster than the species themselves. The knowledge that's being lost most rapidly is information on healing plants. . . . To the peoples of the rain forest, plants are the source of myriad products, including latexes, essential oils and foods. Most every major commodity in the international marketplace was first discovered by native peoples. An American breakfast, from cornflakes and bananas, to coffee, sugar, and even hash brown potatoes, is all based on foods that originated in the tropics." Another ethnobiologist, Dr. Michael Balick, noted, "The 1990s may be the last chance to preserve what native healers know about the rain forest. We're in danger of losing this knowledge in the next generation. You frequently hear native healers say, 'My grandmother knew a lot, my mother knew less, and I know very little. There's already been a tremendous loss. We still find in many countries a very strong network of healers, but as the rain forest dies, so do their supplies—and so does their ability to use their knowledge."[13] The loss of organic wisdom entailed by the destruction of native peoples and their habitats is of a scope at least as large as the burning of the library of Alexandria. Yet even the ethnobiologists just quoted still are describing the utility of the forest and not what the loss of its intrinsically admirable qualities means.

The megamachine of modernity cares little for organic wisdom, whether rooted in local life or in universal aspects of human experience, and it has shown even less concern for organic life itself. That is why intellectuals tend to react to the terms "organic" and "wisdom" with embarrassment or contempt, and why abstract profits are valued as ultimate goals over the goal of a good life in harmony with community and nature.

The loss of native wisdom, dire as it is, can also be seen as analogous to the loss of civilizational wisdom underway today, when, gussied up in the names of deconstructionism, critical theory, new historicism, postmodernism, or relativistic multiculturalism, the received wisdom of the literary traditions is gutted in favor of social theory, of the most banal sort of sociology, conceived as automatic socialization into norms and conventions. No self-respecting, critical, hip-hopping postmodernist would want to be characterized as a Parsonian or mainstream sociologist, yet the underlying ideas are not so different, except that the postmodern version is far cruder in its "sociologocentrism."

THE FACT THAT HUMANS ARE ORGANICALLY OPEN-ENDED CREATURES, whose deepest instinctual impulses are embedded within cultural and personal habits of conduct involving contingencies, experiencing, and purposes, suggests why humans are also fallible creatures par excellence. The instinctive capacities of ants and bees so encompass the contingencies and experiences which the individuals and nests meet with as to provide a "purpose" to their existence which seldom errs. How different it is with us brain meisters! We must *guess* and fathom what other creatures *know* in their substance. We are instinctively conjecturing creatures. Conjecturing, dreaming, symboling, ritualizing, are all capacities which transcend the conventions in which they are embedded, and which spring forth from our biological, organic, incarnate being.

HOMO SYMBOLICUS

Although the achievement of symbolic signs seems to have occurred in a relatively brief span of time on a scale of biological evolution—the last twenty-five thousand years or so if we take the existence of cave paintings, or two hundred thousand years if we take the appearance of *homo sapiens sapiens*(the anthropological term for anatomically modern humans)—the symbol itself must have been the product of a vast span of time measured from the perspective of human experience. The evolving practice of symbolic communication required an evolving means of communication: a subtle tongue, vocal cavity, and vocal cords capable of producing a wide range of utterances, and a grammar of utterances, whether linguistic or gestural.

There is much debate about how and when these capabilities developed, yet one understandably neglected question is: What was humanity uttering as it emerged into symbolic vocalization? Evolutionary theorists tend to discuss the "survival value" of symbolic communication, which is, to my way of thinking, an ingredient, but only a partial one, in explaining the emergence of symbolic communication. Considering the emergence of speech and symbolic and artistic forms as a sudden efflorescence in biological time suggests to me that emerging humanity had *something to say* and that its needs to say it were so deep as to produce rapid biological and social transformations.

What did emergent humanity have to say? Doubtless there were functional utterances of warning or perhaps of the location of food, but if we can read into the kinds of experiences which find their way into ritual life in tribal societies, we might suppose that a crucial motive toward speech was to give voice to human suffering and celebration, and thereby to enrich existence through forms of symbolic expression. The existence in which protohumans found themselves was not a rational one, and, judging from the relative lack of scarcity in many hunting and gathering societies it was clearly not a Hobbesian "each-against-all" existence either, but a fantastic, mysterious, and transformative one, in which the great life-force seemed to wax and wane with the seasons or rains or passing generations, in which "the myriad vitalities in wild confusion," as D. H. Lawrence put it, were "held in some sort of array." That array, I would like to suggest, derived from a powerful ritual life which could give voice to our mammal nature. Considering the reality of ritual involves confronting the significance of repetition, of an exuberance of aesthetic expression, and of the dramatic play of chance and purpose.

Hominids have used tools for two million years, and we have seen, through Jane Goodall's studies, how chimpanzees are capable of using tools such as twigs to ferret out termites to eat. In comparison with the technics humans were creating themselves with, physical tools appear to be primitive. For humans, as Mumford noted, were evolving a technics of symbols, produced out of their own physical bodies and their enlarging capacities for communication. Life itself, as observed and as it revealed itself from within in emerging humankind's own physical constitution, provided the impulse to meaning. Through the creation of ritual symbols, the emergent impulse to meaning could clothe itself in the fantastic images, voices, and behaviors of life itself. I submit that the "elementary forms" of mammalian play, REM dreaming, and mother-infant bonding provided the ecstatic sources for the development of ritual communication and perhaps for the retardation of maturation. As emerging protorituals and ritual forms guided us toward humanity, they did so by favoring a more biologically neotenic and plastic creature. Let us call this the first mode of becoming human.

The second mode is experience and its incorporation into ritual life. Experience is the encounter with the otherness of life, with brutal facts and contingencies, and with those necessary course of events such as the life cycle. In this mode, key and common features of the life cycle, such as birth and death, puberty, mating, and seasonal shifts become causes for symbolic elaboration and ritualization, even as other species have instinctual guides for mating and changes of season. Experience is often contrasted with innocence, and in this sense of the term, acquired memory becomes significant. Experience involves the undergoing of certain qualities through engagement or attention. The first mode celebrates the moment and the potential, the second mode makes a past and marks the actual.

The third mode is purpose. In this mode ritual takes on the quality of directiveness, as emerging humans begin to meet the fantastic events of a dream-laden world and actualities of experience with a dawning sense of communicative intervention made possible by ritual. We tend to think of the purposive as the intentional and rational—something like Max Weber's *Zweckrational* category of strategic action, but this is far too narrow. Purpose is better conceived as habits of conduct, as dispositions toward conduct which remain modifiable through self-control, but which are embedded within cultural practices and traditions. This third mode marks the movement into the future through the habits of conduct we bring to given situations and the ways they may be modified through self-control. The emergence of purpose in human development brings with it the possibility of learning through self-control, and therefore genuine, consciously induced development. The development of mind is, from this perspective, truly a Lamarckian evolution through the "acquired characteristics" of culture.

Let me venture a conjecture here, using Charles Darwin for a very non-Darwinian purpose. In *The Descent of Man,* Darwin remarks:

> Rudimentary organs must be distinguished from those that are nascent; though in some cases the distinction is not easy. The former are either absolutely useless, such as the mammae of male quadrupeds, or the incisor teeth of ruminants which never cut through the gums; or they are of such slight service to their present possessors, that we can hardly suppose that they were developed under the conditions which now exist. Organs in this latter state are not strictly rudimentary, but they are tending in this direction. Nascent organs, on the other hand, though not fully developed, are of high service to their possessors, and are capable of further development.[14]

Now let us suppose rationality to be metaphorically a nascent organ, "not fully developed, . . . of high service" to humans, and "capable of further development." Suppose that human evolution, in its most recent *homo sapiens sapiens* phase, has been primarily devoted to the emergence of this nascent organ. Suppose that part of being a nascent, as opposed to a mature, organ involves the heightened centrality of the organ, and that its exercise in this case produces an overweening pride, possibly to the expense of the organism. If we think, for example, of modernity as a cultural template based ultimately on the maximal expansion of rationality, that overweening pride of nascent rationality may be expressed in its denigration of extrarational capacities—deeply embedded patterns of feeling found in those great mammalian achievements of play, REM dream sleep, and powerful mother-offspring attachment, literally incarnate in mother's milk—as "rudimentary organs" of no further usefulness to its further development. Such an attitude, taken to its logical endpoint, would deprive the organ of its own nourishment.

Suppose that the coming to maturity of an organ involves the integration of the organ's functioning within the greater organic whole. Then by my analogy the next phase of the development of rationality will not be the further enlargement of itself through its internal perfection (such as theories of communicative rationality), but the reintegration of rationality into the community of extrarational human capacities and into the reasonableness of nature from which it artificially severed itself. In Piagetian terms, I am suggesting that the next phase in the development of rationality is the *decentration of its egocentric understanding of the world*. I am suggesting further that the project of modernity, for better and for worse, has ended, though the corpse remains highly visible in postmodernism.

In the fallible big picture I am suggesting, critical consciousness, which it was the virtual task of the modern era to cultivate—and perhaps the axial age up to the present—is fused with those deeper, tempered forms of reasonableness, the biosemiotic capacities through which we became human in the first place. The seemingly scientific term *"homo sapiens"* becomes revealed as an artifact of the age of knowledge, for being human involves feeling, dreaming, experiencing, remembering and forgetting, and not simply knowing. Humans became human, in my view, by transmuting feeling into communicable form, by transforming those ancient biological mammal characteristics of mother-infant nurturance, play, and rapid eye movement (REM) dreaming into social forms. Through such forms— dramatic ritual, the art of language, the languages of art and myth—emerging humans learned to become humans by communicatively comprehending the joys and sufferings of life. The ritualized expression of these capacities not only helped turn us into humans, with all of our fantastic diversities, visions, and destructiveness, but remains, in personal, institutional, and civilizational forms the basis for the further development of the most sophisticated human endeavors.

The claim that there are both organic and normative influences and limitations upon human conduct which transcend current norms, local traditions, and even human history, is an idea which does not find much favor in the contemporary atmosphere of rampant relativism, with its Rortys and Lyotards, its deification of contingency, its narcissistic scorn for experience as an irreducible mode of being. Charles Peirce's view that rationality remains an immature capacity whose further development involves its dependence upon, and ultimately its coalescence into, the extrarational biosemiotic sources of concrete reasonableness, is utterly at odds with Habermas's vision of human development as the perfection of rationality, and with the pervasive, uncritical biophobia of contemporary thought. Why is it that supposedly critical thinkers fear critically reconstructing the received mechanical picture of nature, which remains inadequate to account for the rise of human purpose?

It is no exaggeration to say that the dominant contemporary theories of meaning advocate a thoroughly postbiological image of humankind (some, such as Derrida, even callowly terming themselves antihumanist, seemingly oblivious to the positive virtues of the humanist tradition). And in our "postrational," "postmodern," "post-" culture, postbiological is taken to be a positive achievement instead of the extreme form of self-alienation that it really is. Those who break the great taboo against mixing nature with culture tend to be looked upon with scorn and perhaps embarrassment by the majority of contemporary theorists. In this scorn and embarrassment, I claim, one sees the effete rational intellect, unwilling to confront critically its own extrarational context.

With shrunken hearts and swollen, talking heads, the weird parade of antinaturalists—the Stanley Fishes and Richard Rortys, Jürgen Habermases and Arnold Gehlens, radical feminists and conservative rational choice theorists, multiculturalists and defenders of the Western Civilizational Enlightenment—march in unquestioned lockstep unison. Because of these uncritical attitudes toward the received mechanical picture of nature by supposedly critical theorists, a social theory rooted in organic life and human passion, such as that which I am proposing, would undoubtedly be seen as obsolete by those leading theorists who have proudly and arrogantly severed the possibility of connections between their theories and biological life. Yet a biosemiotic social theory, capable of encompassing both the varieties and contingencies of human signification and the organic needs, limits, and transformative possibilities of the living human being in his and her social, political, and economic worlds, forms a profound critique of contemporary theory and contemporary life, and of the spirit of mechanized, depersonalized subjectivism which informs both.

We can pity poor modern man, who conceives the universe to be a machine or a cybernetic system, or an unreal convention, who conceives his or her own mind and brain to be a machine. The human personality *can* be reduced to a mechanical or material basis, only all that is most human must be denied or bleached. We can pity poor postmodern person, who can at best conceive of himself and herself as broken machines, or as "texts," or as electronic components of a "virtual reality." These postmodern versions bespeak the realization of a thoroughly dehumanized world, in which all human attributes, especially emotional warmth and empathy, have vanished. But more than pity is required, for we are all of us implicated in the tragedy of modern life. Without a deep empathy for fellow moderns and postmoderns, ranging from our immediate life-situations to the larger panorama of modern civilization in all of its diverse forms, and without self-empathy for our inescapable participation in this tragedy, we can too easily stand aloof while pretending simply to wipe the slate of history clean again. The myth of the machine, realizing its perfection in the electronic "virtual reality" that is contemporary life, resonates ominously with the description of the anxiety of the disintegration of the self given by psychoanalyst Heinz Kohut: "What leads to the human self's extinction . . . is its exposure to the coldness, the indifference of the nonhuman, the nonempathically responding world. It is in this sense, and in this sense only, that we may say that disintegration anxiety is closer to the fear of death than to what Freud designated the fear of loss of love. It is not physical extinction that is feared, however, but the ascendency of a nonhuman environment (e.g., of an inorganic surrounding) in which our humanness would permanently come to an end."[15]

The identification with animals and plants—mimesis—which helped make us human, was shattered in the modern mechanical worldview, to be replaced by the identification with or fetishism of, commodities and images today. We came to exterminate life. Now, as the marvelous variescence which characterizes life evaporates under human power, we forget that we too are an endangered species. Our souls remain animistic, and those living forms of extrarational reasonableness within us are dying under the continuing dictatorship of the ghost in the machine. It is time to begin to body forth a new worldview and world civilization, new ways of living both locally and globally in harmony both with outer nature and the nature within us, while preserving the genuine achievements of modern civilization, such as human rights, and private and public freedoms, as well as rediscovering the lost resources of the human past and new ways of joining them to the present.

A new attitude toward humankind's place in the wider world in general is urgently needed, but it must include the social and personal levels as well. We have to "pay attention," as Robert Bellah and his colleagues have put it so well, to the institutions of democracy if they are to thrive. This means cultivating the goal of a good life from the national and international levels, to the local institutions of one's city or neighborhood. And in a world of finite time, such good intentions require the wherewithal to pay attention. This is no mean task in a culture which promotes convenience and the automatic over fulfillment and autonomy, and cynicism over earnest enthusiasm.[16]

For these reasons the personal conduct of life has to be considered an essential ingredient in transforming the modern/postmodern world picture. Despite the greater significance to the subjective and personal spheres of life accorded by modern culture, the twentieth century has in many ways institutionalized a culture of depersonalization, ranging from totalitarianism to the narcissistic void of consumer culture, which would replace the autonomous and spontaneous self with ever-changing images of commodites as mirrors of the self.

We must find the means to correct the mistaken premises which form the modern error. In my view this task requires a fundamental transformation of the modern worldview rather than piecemeal change, because piecemeal change will amount to too little, too late. In the name of freedom and knowledge, the modern era gave birth precisely to the nonempathically responding world Kohut describes, the schizoid ghost in the machine which now threatens to dissolve our humanity and the natural world. Without the hope of such a thoroughgoing transformation, we are likely to continue to go the way of the earth's ozone shield into corrosive self-extinction.

No amount of tinkering with the modern ghost in the machine, whether through updated versions of ethereal rationality or through reified contingency, will be sufficient to come to terms with the bleak prospects of our time: a time when the organic human person and the nonhuman organic life-world shrivel in the face of an ever-expanding automatic culture. Neither an omnivorous communicative rationality machine nor an equally omnivorous "random number generating" contingency machine should be expected somehow to change the Enlightenment myth of a world without limits. Both Habermas and Rorty, two different types of public philosophers associated with "neopragmatism" would eradicate the requirements of humanity's organic "glassy essence," those communicative, extrarational capacities to feel, sense, and interpret the world, because they do not fit within the straightjacket of the modern "knowledge complex." Yet their theories are themselves avatars of the ghost in the machine: symptoms of the crisis of late modernity rather than means to its resolution.

The nominalistic premisses of the modern age, which remain uncritically assumed by both Habermas and Rorty, and by those who believe that human social life is solely a conventional construction, urgently need to be overhauled through an imaginative realignment of humanity's place in the cosmos. Such a realignment involves opening social theory and philosophy to the public dimension, but it also involves opening the public dimension of philosophy to the roots and limits of nature and world culture. Whether we will it or not, we are in the midst of making a world civilization, and the contemporary litany that theory can only be local, though not without its merit, is also a form of nearsightedness which remains blind to the significance of translocal norms and the bearing of those norms on local culture (not to mention that the assertion that theory must be local is itself not locally grounded and seems to claim the status of a universal).

The time has come to find a new way of renewing reason, a project requiring a transformation of values and outlook as vast as those which took place in the axial age or the modern age. The new range of feelings, perceptions, technical in-novations, and critical institutions developed in the modern era will contribute essential ingredients to the new outlook. But the underlying cultural nominalism, the very premises on which both the modern age and its postmodern burp were built, will have to be rejected as ultimately world destructive and self-destructive. Reason renewed will involve opening the gates to the entire historical and prehis-torical heritage of humankind, to renew the archaic values of family, household, neighborhood and local community, and the sympathetic relations they engender, to renew those organic and communicative essences of play, dreaming, and mother-infant nurturance which are our human-mammalian legacy and crucial for the development of the spontaneous self, and also making a life-sustaining world culture with vital and self-critical institutions capable of supporting and protect-ing the reasonableness of local ways. Actively cultivating such a "big picture" un-dercuts the one already in place, and provides a means to regain command of rationality and to reactivate the precious roots of reason which the modern age claimed to have outgrown. Despite the enormous destructiveness of our time the fact remains that we are alive in this dance of life once and once only.

Notes

Chapter One

1. Richard Rorty, *Contingency, Irony, and Solidarity* (New York: Cambridge University Press, 1989), 96–97.

2. As David Lehman has noted: "Literature, not criticism, is and always was the really dangerous activity; the death sentence on the author of *The Satanic Verses* is only the most violent reminder of that. But literature has received its walking papers in the age of theory—for the deconstructionist, it exists as something to be willfully misinterpreted if not ignored altogether. If our writers today operate largely in a critical void, surely some of the blame attaches to the academic theorists whose backs are turned to books other than their own" (*Signs of the Times: Deconstruction and the Fall of Paul de Man* [New York: Poseidon Press, 1991], 63),

3. Ibid., 75.

4. Stanley Fish, *Doing What Comes Naturally: Change, Rhetoric, and the Practice of Theory in Literary and Legal Studies* (Durham: Duke University Press, 1989), 256.

5. Ibid., 346.

6. Ibid., 298.

7. In Fred Siegel, "The Cult of Multiculturalism," *New Republic*, February 18, 1991:40.

8. The positivist desire to overcome metaphysics in the name of science was explicitly expressed in Auguste Comte's mid-nineteenth-century discussion of "the infantile state of social science," where he stated: "The scientific spirit is radically distinguished from the theological and metaphysical by the steady subordination of the imagination to observation; and though the positive philosophy offers the vastest and richest field to human imagination, it restricts it to discovering and perfecting the co-ordination of observed facts, and the means of effecting new researches: and it is this habit of subjecting scientific conceptions to the facts whose connection has to be disclosed, which it is above all necessary to introduce into social researches; for the observations hitherto made have been vague and ill-circumscribed, so as to afford no adequate foundation for scientific reasoning; and they are usually modified them-

selves at the pleasure of an imagination stimulated by the most fluctuating passions" (in *Varieties of Classic Social Theory,* edited by Hendrik Ruitenbeek [New York: E. P. Dutton, 1963], 33).

In the positivist outlook, from Comte through logical positivism and to the present, imaginative reasoning and human passion are dirties, while observation and "science" are cleans. Positivists normally assume that observation involves no interpretation and that imagination involves no observation. Both observation and imagination are usually taken to be noninferential: observation is the dyadic impression of sensations, imagination is the dydaic expression of the passions.

9. See Jacques Derrida, "Like the Sound of the Sea Deep within a Shell: Paul de Man's War," *Critical Inquiry* 14, no. 3 (Spring 1988): 590–652.

10. This statement comes from a newspaper interview with Derrida republished in the first edition of *The Heidegger Controversy: A Critical Reader,* edited by Richard Wolin (New York: Columbia University Press, 1991), which Derrida demanded be deleted from subsequent editions of the book. Apparently the possibility of criticism based on the evidence of his text proved too much even for Derrida, the master of fancy footwork, to bear.

11. Jacques Derrida, *Of Grammatology* (Baltimore: Johns Hopkins University Press, 1976), 314. Commenting on this neo-Nietzschean tendency of Derrida and similar statements from Jean Baudrillard and Michel Foucault, Dmitri Shalin notes, "I could not help wondering what a radical postmodernist unaided by moral labels tells a child who tortures a pet, uses a racial slur, or throws a tantrum? How does he manage to explain that this is not . . . altogether commendable conduct without committing a moral judgment. Things get still more confused when we grapple with actions considered criminal. If text writes itself and an author is but a vehicle for a linguistic code, then crime commits itself and no responsibility should be pinned on the perpetrator. All notions of justice, fairness, and plain decency are pointless unless there are moral subjects ready to answer for their deeds" ("Modernity, Postmodernism, and Pragmatist Inquiry: An Introduction," *Symbolic Interaction* 16, no. 4 [1993]: 303–31).

12. Cited in "Ph.D. Program Stirs a Debate on the Future of Black Studies," *Chronicle of Higher Education* 37, no. 40, June 19, 1991:A13.

13. Indeed, after writing this sentence, I discovered that E. C. Hirsch, whose book, *Cultural Literacy,* aired a dirty laundry list of common facts of which high school and college students were ignorant, himself stated that there is no difference between the knowledge gained from Shakespeare directly or from *Cliff's Notes.* See Roger Kimball, *Tenured Radicals: How Politics Has Corrupted Our Higher Education* (New York: Harper and Row, 1990).

14. Quoted in Joseph Berger, "U.S. Literature: Canon under Siege," *New York Times,* January 6, 1988.

15. See Houston A. Baker, Jr., "Hybridity, the Rap Race, and Pedagogy for the 1990s," in *Technoculture,* edited by Constance Penley and Andrew Ross (Minneapolis: University of Minnesota Press, 1991), 197–209.

16. Karl Marx, *Capital,* vol. 1, edited by Frederick Engels (New York: International Publishers, 1967 [1867]).

17. Emile Durkheim, *The Elementary Forms of the Religious Life,* translated from the French by Joseph Ward Swain (New York: Free Press, 1915 [1912]), 475.

18. Marx 1967, 1:380. International Publishers, 1967 [1867]), 1:380.

19. Lewis Mumford, *The Condition of Man* (New York: Harcourt, Brace and Co., 1944), 337, 332. Also see his *The Myth of the Machine, II: The Pentagon of Power* (New York: Harcourt, Brace, Jovanovich, 1970), 353.

20. As Alan Sica has put it, Weber "squeezed from human behavior—by weighting each type of social action in terms of its utility to science—the bulk of meaning-seeking activity, since irrational and nonrational motives remain, by their nature, largely unrationalizable. Although Weber decried the 'de-magicalization' of modern life and accepted the importance of the most irrational political force, charisma, his guidelines for social and political-economic analyses assert the paramount nature of *zweckrational* action," in Alan Sica, *Weber, Irrationality, and Social Order* (Berkeley: University of California Press, 1988).

21. Max Weber, "Objectivity in Social Science and Social Policy," in *The Methodology of the Social Sciences: Max Weber,* translated and edited by Edward A. Shils and Henry A. Finch (New York: Free Press, 1949 [1904]), 81; Georg Simmel, "On the Concept and the Tragedy of Culture," in *Georg Simmel: The Conflict in Modern Culture and Other Essays,* translated and edited by Peter Etzkorn (New York: Teacher's College Press, 1968), 33.

22. Georg Simmel, *The Philosophy of Money,* translated from the German by Tom Bottomore and David Frisby (London: Routledge and Kegan Paul, 1978 [1900]). See also Gianfranco Poggi's *Money and the Modern Mind: Simmel's Philosophy of Money* (Berkeley: University of California Press, 1993), where he argues that Simmel views modernity as an epiphany. Poggi quite accurately analyzes Simmel's Kantian idea that truth is relative, that is, is a relation of representations, and argues that this should be taken as another manifestation of the superiority of modern over premodern thinking. He ignores the dark side of the modern "epiphany," such as the simultaneous emergence of the absolutist state, from the baroque kings to the "Big Men" of twentieth-century totalitarianism. In celebrating the modern over the premodern, one must also ask how the modern police state is superior to the ancient Greek polis. Similarly, positivism is especially characteristic of the last century and must be reckoned with as a dubious modern achievement which punctures the presumed superiority of modern thought.

23. Eugene Rochberg-Halton, *Meaning and Modernity: Social Theory in the Pragmatic Attitude* (Chicago: University of Chicago Press, 1986).

24. Emile Durkheim, "The Dualism of Human Nature," in *Emile Durkheim: On Morality and Society,* edited and with an introduction by Robert N. Bellah (Chicago: University of Chicago Press, 1973), 161–62.

25. Eugene Halton, "The Reality of Dreaming," *Theory, Culture, and Society* 9 (Fall 1992): 119–39.

Chapter Two

1. Peter Kropotkin, *Mutual Aid: A Factor in Evolution* (Boston: Porter Sargent Publishers, n.d. [1902]), 5.

2. *Dilthey: Selected Writings,* edited and with an introduction by H. P. Rickman (Cambridge: Cambridge University Press, 1976), 232.

3. See Richard Hofstadter, *Social Darwinism in American Thought* (Boston: Beacon Press, 1955); also my "Life, Literature, and Sociology in Turn-of-the-Century

Chicago," in *Consuming Visions,* edited by Simon J. Bronner (New York: W. W. Norton, 1989).

4. D. Gasman, *The Scientific Origins of National Socialism* (New York: Science History Publications, 1971); Theo Kalikow, "Konrad Lorenz's 'Brown Past': A Reply to Alec Nisbett," *Journal of the History of the Behavioral Sciences* 14 (1978): 173–79; and "Konrad Lorenz's Ethological Theory: Explanation and Ideology, 1930–1943," *Journal of the History of Biology* 16 (1983): 39–73; J. Herf, *Reactionary Modernism. Technology, Culture, and Politics in Weimar and the Third Reich* (Cambridge: Cambridge University Press, 1984); R. J. Richards, *Darwin and the Emergence of Evolutionary Theories of Mind and Behavior* (Chicago: University of Chicago Press, 1987).

5. See Robert Jay Lifton, *The Nazi Doctors* (New York: Basic Books, 1986).

6. G. Neuweiler, "Evolution and Accountability," in *Alexander von Humboldt Stiftung Mitteilungen* 48 (December 1986): 1–14.

7. Quoted by Richards 1987:535–36, translated by Kalikow 1978, 1983.

8. Ibid.

9. Georg Simmel, "Über eine Beziehung der Selectionslehre zur Erkenntnistheorie," *Archiv für systematische Philosophie* 1 (1895): 34–45, cited in Richards 1987; *Schopenhauer and Nietzsche* (Amherst: University of Massachusetts Press, 1986 [1907]); *Lebensanschauung: Vier Metaphysische Kapitel* (Munich and Leipzig: Duncker and Humbolt, 1918). The first chapter of *Lebensanschauung* translated as "The Transcendent Character of Life," in *Georg Simmel on Individuality and Social Forms,* edited by Donald N. Levine (Chicago: University of Chicago Press, 1971); "The Conflict in Modern Life," also in Levine.

10. Simmel 1971:365–66, 375–76, 382.

11. Ibid., 367–68.

12. Ibid., 393.

13. Axel Honneth and Hans Joas, *Social Action and Human Nature,* translated from the German by Raymond Meyer (New York: Cambridge University Press, 1988 [1980]).

14. Scheler quotations are from *Man's Place in Nature,* translated with introduction by Hans Meyerhoff (Boston: Beacon Press, 1961 [1928]). Other related works by Scheler are "Versuche einer Philosophie des Lebens. Nietzsche—Dilthey—Bergson," in *Gesammelte Werke, Band 3: Vom Umsturz der Werte* (Bern: A. Francke A.G., 1955 [1913]); *Formalism in Ethics and Non-Formal Ethics of Values* (Evanston: Northwestern University Press, 1973 [1913–16]); and *Der Genius des Krieges und der Deutsche Krieg,* in *Gesammelte Werke, Band 4: Politische-Pädagogische Schriften* (Munich: A. Franke A.G., 1982 [1915]). See also A. F. Schneck, *Person and Polis: Max Scheler's Personalism as Political Theory* (Albany: State University of New York Press, 1987).

15. As Mumford says in his book, *The Transformations of Man* (New York: Collier Books, 1966 [1956]), 61: "The central change brought in by axial religions is the redefinition—in fact the recasting—of the human personality. In that act, values that emerge only in the personality replace those that belonged to institutions and institutional roles. The new feelings, emotional attachments, sentiments are now incarnated in a living image, that of the prophet."

16. In Levine, ed., 1971:386.

17. Quoted in Ralph Barton Perry, *The Thought and Character of William James, Vol. 2: Philosophy and Psychology* (Boston: Little, Brown, and Co., 1935), 424–25.

18. Quoted in ibid., 415–16.

19. Eugene Rochberg-Halton, *Meaning and Modernity;* Hans Joas, *George Herbert Mead: A Contemporary Re-examination of His Thought,* translated from the German by Raymond Meyer (Cambridge, Mass.: MIT Press, 1985 [1980]).

20. Eugene Rochberg-Halton, "Life, Literature, and Sociology in Turn-of-the-Century Chicago," in *Consuming Visions: Accumulation and Display in America, 1880–1920,* edited by Simon J. Bronner (New York: W. W. Norton, 1989), 311–38.

21. Hannah Arendt, *The Human Condition* (Chicago: University of Chicago Press, 1958), 47.

22. J. Arthur Thomson, *The System of Animate Nature, Volume 1* (New York: Henry Holt and Co., 1920), 202.

23. Arnold Gehlen, *Moral und Hypermoral* (Frankfurt am Main: Athenaum Verlag, 1969), 103, cited in Jürgen Habermas, *Philosophical-Political Profiles* (Cambridge, Mass.: MIT Press, 1983), 112. Though I remain highly skeptical of Habermas the theorist, his review of Gehlen is forceful and forthright.

24. Karl-Siegbert Rehberg, "Arnold Gehlen's Elementary Anthropology: An Introduction," in Arnold Gehlen, *Man: His Nature and Place in the World,* translated by Clare McMillan and Karl Pillemer (New York: Columbia University Press, 1988), xxix.

25. Gehlen 1969:154.

26. Johann Gottfried Herder, "On the Philosophy of History," in *Varieties of Classic Social Theory,* edited by Hendrik M. Ruitenbeek (New York: E. P. Dutton, 1963), 4–5.

27. Quoted in S. F. Mason, *A History of the Sciences* (New York: Collier Books, 1962), 349.

28. D. H. Lawrence. *Apocalypse* (New York: Viking Press, 1982 [1931]).

29. The charge that Lawrence had "proto-Fascist leanings" is one often heard, and so I should address it head-on. To me the claims that Lawrence was a proto-Fascist who died before the 1930s is on the same level as the claims made that Weber would have become Fascist if he had lived in the thirties. I have read most of Lawrence's nonfiction work, and my interpretation is that, like Weber, he was concerned with the problem of leadership in democracy after the First World War. But he states in various places a loathing of Italian Fascism, of the reduction of democracy to mass man, and senses a sinister *ressentiment* rising up in Germany in the mid-1920s. I think both Lawrence, who saw the First World War as largely senseless, and Weber would have gone in the direction taken by Thomas Mann, who was a pro-German nationalist in the First World War and became an ardent critic of the Nazi regime. What interests me most about Lawrence are his insights into the significance of the passions in the balance of conduct, and of how the modern West has overemphasized the ideal.

30. Stephen Jay Gould, *Wonderful Life: The Burgess Shale and the Nature of History* (New York: W. W. Norton, 1989).

31. Lewis Mumford, *The Myth of the Machine, Volume 1: Technics and Human Development* (New York: Harcourt, Brace, Jovanovich, 1967), 31.

Chapter Three

1. William Shakespeare, *Measure for Measure,* act 2, scene 2.

2. See Nancy Chodorow, *The Reproduction of Mothering: Psychoanalysis and the Sociology of Gender* (Berkeley: University of California Press, 1978); Carol Gilligan, *In a Different Voice: Psychological Theory and Women's Development* (Cambridge, Mass.: Harvard University Press, 1982); Edith Turner, *The Spirit and the Drum: A Memoir of Africa* (Tucson: University of Arizona Press, 1987); and "Encounter with Neurobiology: The Response of Ritual Studies," in *Zygon* 21, no.2 (June 1986): 219–32.

3. Howard Becker, *Art Worlds* (Berkeley: University of California Press, 1982); Peter Bürger, *Theory of the Avant-Garde,* translated from the German by Michael Shaw (Minneapolis: University of Minnesota Press, 1984); Wendy Griswold, "The Fabrication of Meaning," *American Journal of Sociology* 92, no. 5 (1987): 1077–1118; Ann Swidler, "Culture in Action: Symbols and Strategies," *American Sociological Review* 51 (1986): 273–86; J. Wolff, *The Social Production of Art* (New York: St. Martin's Press, 1981); Robert Wuthnow, *Meaning and Moral Order* (Berkeley: University of California Press, 1987).

4. See my *Meaning and Modernity* (Chicago: University of Chicago Press, 1986).

5. *The Collected Papers of Charles Sanders Peirce,* vol. 8 (Cambridge, Mass.: Harvard University Press, 1958), para. 335.

6. Cited in John Searle, *Minds, Brains, and Science* (Cambridge, Mass.: Harvard University Press, 1984).

7. Clifford Geertz, *The Interpretation of Cultures* (New York: Basic Books, 1973), 68.

8. Pierre Bourdieu, *Distinction: A Social Critique of the Judgement of Taste,* translated by Richard Nice (Cambridge, Mass.: Harvard University Press, 1984), 29–30.

9. James Clifford, *The Predicament of Culture: Twentieth-Century Ethnography, Literature, and Art* (Cambridge, Mass.: Harvard University Press, 1988), 15, 52, 145, 222, 229.

10. Victor Turner, *On the Edge of the Bush: Anthropology as Experience,* edited by Edith Turner (Tucson: University of Arizona Press, 1985).

11. Diana Fuss, *Essentially Speaking: Feminism, Nature, and Difference* (New York: Routledge, 1989), 114.

12. Oliver Sacks, *The Man Who Mistook His Wife for a Hat* (New York: Harper Perennial, 1987), 81.

13. H. S. Becker, *Art Worlds* (Berkeley: University of California Press, 1982); P. Bürger, *Theory of the Avant-Garde,* translated from the German by Michael Shaw (Minneapolis: University of Minnesota Press, 1984); Griswold 1987; J. Wolff, *The Social Production of Art* (New York: St. Martin's Press, 1981).

14. Raymond Williams, *Keywords* (New York: Oxford University Press, 1976), 77.

15. Johann Gottfried Herder 1784–91, cited in Williams 1976:79.

16. Loosely translated: "The size of the potato is indirectly proportional to the IQ of the farmer; or, the dumbest hick has the biggest spud."

17. Published in Victor Turner, *The Forest of Symbols: Aspects of Ndembu Rituals* (Ithaca: Cornell University Press, 1967).

18. Ibid., 106.

19. Victor Turner, *On the Edge of the Bush: Anthropology as Experience,* edited by Edith Turner (Tucson: University of Arizona Press, 1985), 190.

20. Quotations from Victor Turner, *From Ritual to Theater: The Human Seriousness of Play* (New York: Performing Arts Journal Publications, 1982): 63–64; *The Anthropology of Experience,* edited by Victor Turner and Edward Bruner (Champaign: University of Illinois Press, 1985), 39.

21. Turner, *On the Edge of the Bush,* 1985:252, 273.

22. *Charles Sanders Peirce: Contributions to the Nation, Part Three: 1901–1908,* edited by Kenneth Laine Ketner and James Edward Cook (Lubbock: Texas Tech Press, 1979), 17–18.

23. Jürgen Habermas, *The Theory of Communicative Action, Vol. 2: Lifeworld and System: A Critique of Functionalist Reason* (Boston: Beacon Press, 1987 [1981]), 191. Hereafter referred to as *TCA.*

Chapter Four

1. Lewis Mumford, *Values for Survival* (New York: Harcourt, Brace and Co., 1946).

2. Lewis Mumford (July 1979), unpublished.

3. Jane Jacobs, *The Death and Life of Great American Cities* (New York: Vintage Books, 1961).

4. Consider this account of reactionary modernism and its big picture approach to "city planning." Nicolae Ceausescu razed large portions of Bucharest to create a "people's" monument to himself. His "House of the Republic" was to be thirteen stories and have over 400,000 square feet. As a *New York Times* account detailed just after the tyrant was deposed, "The Rumania Hall—the central area for receptions—is almost as big as a football field, 240 feet long and 90 feet wide, with tower ceilings covered in gold leaf on pink gypsum. The marble columns are hand carved. Up to 50,000 people lost their homes, so that the site for it could be cleared when building started in 1984. Its outer dimensions are roughly 8,440 feet long, 720 feet wide, and 330 feet to the top of the soaring stone needle that acts as a flagpole. It is about two-thirds finished, and the cost has run into "tens of billions of lei," the local currency traded in the banks at nine to the dollar. Whole industries were set up to feed the palace's demand for marble and timber.

A colonel stationed at the palace told a reporter, "Ceausescu came every week, sometimes three times a week. First he wanted some of the floors to be all marble. Then when his wife came she said she wanted wood. So all the marble was torn up and destroyed. As a rule she agreed with his decisions. When there was an argument, they delayed and would come back with a common solution worked out in the family itself" (December 31, 1989:14).

5. Eugene Rochberg-Halton, "Life, Literature, and Sociology in Turn-of-the-Century Chicago," in *Consuming Visions: Accumulation and Display of Goods in America, 1880–1920,* edited by S. J. Bronner (New York: W. W. Norton, 1989).

6. Pointing out how Hitler's dictatorship differed from all preceding dictatorships because of its use of technical means of communication for total control,

Hitler's assistant Albert Speer noted, "Earlier dictators needed highly qualified assistants, even at the lowest level, men who could think and act independently. The totalitarian system in the period of modern technical development can dispense with them; the means of communication alone make it possible to mechanize the lower leadership. As a result of this there arises the new type of the uncritical recipient of orders," in Alan Bullock, *Hitler: A Study in Tyranny* (New York: Harper and Row, 1971 [1962]), 380. Speer spells out the modern mechanical recipe for Gehlen's anti-modern institutionalism.

7. Mumford, *Technics and Human Development,* 1967:51.

8. See Eugene Halton, "The Reality of Dreaming," *Theory, Culture, and Society* 9, no. 4 (November 1992).

9. Ibid., 62.

10. Lewis Mumford, *The Transformations of Man* (New York: Collier Books, 1966 [1956]), 29.

11. Ibid., 33–34.

12. Ibid., 40

13. Lewis Mumford, letter to Roderick Seidenberg, May 15, 1956. In another letter to Seidenberg on August 6 of the same year, Mumford said, "My intellect has told me since the late thirties that this society is as fatally doomed as Roman society was in the third century: not that its case is irremediable, but it is too sick to know that it needs a doctor; and since the sickness is of a mental nature, and is in fact a manifestation of insanity on the widest collective scale, no quick shot of anything is likely to cure us. . . . When I have said, as I have said repeatedly since 1950, that only a miracle would save us, I recorded my deep conviction. I have enough faith to believe a miracle may happen but neither the faith nor the intellectual arrogance to believe that any word of mine will bring it about" (reprinted with the permission of the University of Pennsylvania Special Collections, Van Pelt Library).

14. Mumford, *Technics and Human Development,* 1967:191.

15. Mumford, *The Condition of Man,* 1944:159–60.

16. Mumford, *Technics and Human Development,* 1967:272–73.

17. Donald Miller, *Lewis Mumford: A Life* (New York: Widenfeld and Nicolson, 1989), 171–72. In the *New York Times Book Review,* shortly before Mumford's death, Ada Louise Huxtable stated: "But he left the city in 1936 for a small upstate town . . . near Amenia . . . , where he has lived a structured, rural existence for most of his mature working years, increasingly out of touch with the urban condition and the forces of American creativity that he has understood and written so well about." For this facile and mistaken criticism—similar in spirit to sociological critiques—to have merit one must discount Mumford's *The City in History* (New York: Harcourt, Brace and World, 1961), and one must assume that only New Yorkers can understand "the forces of American creativity." One must discount Mumford's weekly visits to New York, his decades of architectural criticism for the *New Yorker,* his residence in other major cities, and his entire scholarly project.

18. Lewis Mumford, *Faith for Living* (New York: Harcourt, Brace and World, 1940), 113.

19. John Dewey. "No Matter What Happens—Stay Out," *Common Sense* (1939): 12.

20. Arthur Koestler, *The Ghost in the Machine* (Chicago: Henry Regnery,

1967); and *Janus: A Summing Up* (New York: Vintage Books, 1978); Susanne K. Langer, *Mind: An Essay on Human Feeling* (Baltimore: Johns Hopkins University Press, 1988 [abridged edition, original three volumes published 1967, 1972, 1982]).

21. John Searle, "The Storm over the University," *New York Review,* December 6, 1990.

22. Indeed, the Bible remains on the Stanford required reading list today, while Plato's *Republic* remained until the revision of the curriculum, when the requirement was broadened, as mentioned, to "a classic Greek philosopher."

23. I might add parenthetically that Mumford was also at Berkeley in 1961 to attack the scientific establishment for lending itself to military purposes while ignoring the need for moral limitations. In what I take to be one of the unknown beginnings of the free speech movement at Berkeley, Mumford also attacked academic historians for their bureaucratic formalism and denial of feeling, in his speech "An Apology to Henry Adams."

24. Lewis Mumford, *Values for Survival* (New York: Harcourt, Brace and Co., 1946), 183–84.

25. Alisdair MacIntyre, *After Virtue: A Study in Moral Theory* (Notre Dame, Ind.: University of Notre Dame Press, 1981), 34.

26. Lewis Mumford, *The Pentagon of Power* (New York: Harcourt, Brace, Jovanovich, 1970), 432–34.

27. Lewis Coser, review of ibid., in *Contemporary Sociology* 1, no. 1 (1972): 38–39.

28. Mumford, *The Pentagon of Power,* 404.

29. Miller 1989:533.

30. Gerald Holton, review of Mumford's *The Pentagon of Power,* in the *New York Times Book Review,* December 13, 1970.

31. Gerald Holton, *The Advancement of Science and Its Burdens* (New York: Cambridge University Press, 1986), 291.

32. Vaclav Havel, *Living in Truth,* edited by Jan Vladislav (Boston: Faber and Faber, 1989), 44, 52.

33. Ibid., 43–44, 54.

Chapter Five

1. *Collected Papers of Charles Sanders Peirce,* vol. 8 (1958 [1891]), par. 121. Henceforth references to the *Collected Papers* will be listed only with volume and paragraph numbers, and dates where original date is given, for example, *CP* 8.121 (1958 [1891]). Volumes 1–6 were published 1931–35; volumes 7–8 were published in 1958.

2. *CP* 5.121.

3. Major editions of Peirce's works include *The Collected Papers of Charles Sanders Peirce,* vols. 1–6, edited by Charles Hartshorne and Paul Weiss (1931–35), and vols. 7 and 8, edited by Arthur Burks (1958) (Cambridge, Mass.: Harvard University Press); *The New Elements of Mathematics by Charles S. Peirce,* edited by Carolyn Eisele (Atlantic Highlands, N.J.: Humanities Press, 1973–76); *Charles Sanders Peirce: Contributions to the Nation,* edited by Kenneth Laine Ketner and James Edward Cook, 4 vols. (Lubbock: Texas Tech Press, 1975, 1978, 1979, 1987); *Semiotic and Significs: The Correspondence between Charles S. Peirce and Victoria*

Lady Welby, edited by Charles S. Hardwick (Bloomington: Indiana University Press, 1977). A projected twenty-volume collection of Peirce's writings is currently underway: *Writings of Charles S. Peirce: A Chronological Edition* (Bloomington: Indiana University Press, 1982–). In addition, all of Peirce's published writings can be found on microfiche in *Charles Sanders Peirce: Complete Published Works, Including Secondary Materials. Microfiche Edition* (1977). His unpublished writings are collected on microfilm in *The Charles S. Peirce Papers, Microfilm Edition, Thirty Reels with Two Supplementary Reels Later Added* (1966).

4. Otto Neurath, *Encyclopedia and Unified Science, vol. 1, no. 1: Foundations of the Unity of Science,* edited by Otto Neurath et al. (Chicago: University of Chicago Press, 1938), 17.

5. Charles Morris, "Scientific Empiricism," in ibid., 67.

6. In "The Problem of Meaning in Primitive Languages," Malinowski states that "the meaning of the expression 'we arrive near the village (of our destination)' . . . is determined only by taking it in the context of the whole utterance. This later again becomes only intelligible when it is placed within its *context of situation,* if I may be allowed to coin an expression which indicates on the one hand that the conception of *context* has to be broadened and on the other that the *situation* in which words are uttered can never be passed over as irrelevant to the linguistic expression. We see how the conception of context must be substantially widened if it is to furnish us with its full utility. In fact it must burst the bonds of mere linguistics and be carried over into the analysis of the general conditions under which a language is spoken . . . the study of any language, spoken by a people who live under conditions different from our own and possess a different culture, must be carried out in conjunction with the study of their culture and their environment" (published as a supplement in C. K. Ogden and I. A. Richards, *The Meaning of Meaning* (New York: Harcourt, Brace and World, 1923), 306.

7. Peirce 1958:320

8. Blake 1946:253.

9. *CP* 7.667.

10. *CP* 7.570–72 (1958 [c. 1892]).

11. *CP* 8.83 (1958 [1891]).

12. *CP* 5.135, 136, from lectures on pragmatism of 1903.

13. *CP* 6.15.

14. *CP* 7.380, 381.

15. In *Charles S. Peirce: Selected Writings,* edited by Philip P. Wiener (New York: Dover, 1958), 299–300.

16. *CP* 1.673

17. *CP* 1:145.

18. From Peirce: "There is a certain occupation of mind which, from its having no distinctive name, I infer is not as commonly practiced as it deserves to be; for indulged in moderately—say through some five to six per cent of one's waking time, perhaps during a stroll—it is refreshing enough more than to repay the expenditure. Because it involves no purpose save that of casting aside all serious purpose, I have sometimes been half-inclined to call it reveries with some qualification; but for a frame of mind so antipodal to vacancy and dreaminess such a designation would be a misfit. In fact, it is Pure Play. Now, Play, as we all know, is a lively exercise of one's

powers. Pure Play has no rules, except this very law of liberty. It bloweth where it listeth. It has no purpose, unless recreation. The particular occupation I mean—a *petite bouchée* with the Universes—may take either the form of aesthetic contemplation, or that of distant castle building (whether in Spain or within one's own moral training), or that of considering some wonder in one of the Universes, or some connection between two of the three, with speculation concerning its cause. It is this last kind—I will call it 'Musement' on the whole—that I particularly recommend. . . . It begins passively enough with drinking in the impression of some nook in one of the three Universes. But impression soon passes into attentive observation, observation into musing, musing into a lively give and take of communion between self and self. If one's observations are allowed to specialize themselves too much, the Play will be converted into scientific study; and that cannot be pursued in odd half hours" (*CP* 6.458–59).

Chapter Six

1. A number of other key themes from *The Theory of Communicative Action*—his discussions of Weber, Parsons, Marx, Piaget, and Kohlberg, language analysis, or systems theory, for example—although significant, simply could not be addressed in any detail here. I would direct the interested reader toward the large number of reviews and critiques which have already appeared, including *Habermas and Modernity,* edited by Richard J. Bernstein (Cambridge, Mass.: MIT Press, 1985); *Kommunikatives Handeln,* edited by Alex Honneth and Hans Joas (Frankfurt: Suhrkamp Verlag, 1986); and "Life-World and Communicative Action," in Fred Dallmayr's *Critical Encounters* (Notre Dame, Ind.: University of Notre Dame Press, 1987); Moishe Postone, "History and Critical Social Theory," *Contemporary Sociology* 19, no. 2 (March 1990): 170–76; and the special issue of *Symbolic Interaction* on "Habermas, Pragmatism, and Critical Theory," edited by Dmitri N. Shalin, vol. 15, no. 3 (Fall 1992).

2. *TCA* 1:10.

3. *TCA* 2:342.

4. *TCA* 1:49.

5. *TCA* 1:53–54.

6. G. S. Kirk, *Greek Myths* (Middlesex: Penguin, 1974); Victor Turner, *The Forest of Symbols* (Ithaca: Cornell University Press, 1967); and *The Ritual Process* (Chicago: Aldine, 1969).

7. D. H. Lawrence, *Phoenix: The Posthumous Papers* (New York: Penguin Books, 1978 [1936]), 296.

8. *TCA* 1:85.

9. *TCA* 1:85.

10. *TCA* 1:86.

11. Karl Popper, *Objective Knowledge: An Evolutionary Approach* (Oxford: Clarendon Press, 1972), 106.

12. *TCA* 1:90.

13. *TCA* 1:94, 95.

14. *TCA* 1:70.

15. *TCA* 2:31.

16. *TCA* 2:130.

17. John Dewey, *On Experience, Nature, and Freedom* (Indianapolis: Bobbs-Merrill, 1960), 106.

18. In *Autonomy and Solidarity: Interviews with Jürgen Habermas,* edited by Peter Dews (London: Verso, 1986), 109.

19. *TCA* 2:1.

20. *TCA* 2:2.

21. *TCA* 2:61.

22. *TCA* 2:72.

23. *CP* 5:553.

24. *TCA* 2:42.

25. *TCA* 2:45.

26. *TCA* 1:239–40.

27. See my book, *Meaning and Modernity* (Chicago: University of Chicago Press. 1986).

28. Lewis Mumford, *The Conduct of Life* (New York: Harcourt, Brace and Co., 1951), 10.

29. *CP* 5.304, 307.

Chapter Seven

1. Louis Sullivan, *Autobiography of an Idea* (New York: Dover, 1956 [1924]), 324.

2. John Dewey, *Experience and Nature* (Chicago: Open Court, 1925), 21.

3. Max Horkheimer, *Eclipse of Reason* (New York: Continuum, 1974 [1947]).

4. Ibid., 44, 52. See also Hans Joas, "An Underestimated Alternative: America and the Limits of 'Critical Theory,' " *Symbolic Interaction* 15, no. 3 (Fall 1992): 261–75.

5. *CP* 6.292.

6. Habermas 1971:120–21.

7. Rorty, *Consequences of Pragmatism,* 1989:165.

8. Jürgen Habermas, *The Philosophical Discourse of Modernity,* translated from the German by Frederick Lawrence (Cambridge, Mass.: MIT Press, 1987 [1985]).

9. Lewis Mumford, *The Transformations of Man* (New York: Harper and Row, 1956), 110.

10. *TCA* 1:68.

11. *CP* 7.680, 687.

12. *CP* 7.679, 374.

13. Habermas 1987:114–15.

14. See my discussions of Morris in Rochberg-Halton, *Meaning and Modernity,* 1986.

15. Lewis Mumford, *Faith for Living,* 1940:70–71.

16. Rorty, *Contingency, Irony, and Solidarity,* 1989:182, 88.

17. Ibid., 177.

18. Ibid., 192.

19. Ibid., 16.

20. Ibid., 65.

21. Ibid., 52; italics in original.

22. Richard Rorty, "Science as Solidarity," in *The Rhetoric of the Human Sciences: Language and Argument in Scholarship and Public Affairs,* edited by John S. Nelson, Allan Megill, and Donald McCloskey (Madison: University of Wisconsin Press, 1987), 48–49, 50.

23. Mumford, *The Condition of Man,* 1944:368–69.

24. Rorty, *Contingency, Irony, and Solidarity,* 1989:119–20.

25. Jürgen Habermas, *The New Conservatism: Cultural Criticism and the Historian's Debate,* edited and translated by Shierry W. Nicholsen (Cambridge, Mass.: MIT Press, 1990).

26. *Charles S. Peirce: Selected Writings,* edited by Philip P. Weiner (New York: Dover Publications, 1958), 398.

27. John Dewey, *Human Nature and Conduct* (New York: Modern Library, 1957 [1922]), 155.

28. Rorty, *Contingency, Irony, and Solidarity,* 1989:53.

29. *CP* 7.559–62.

Chapter Eight

1. Euripides, *The Bacchae.* Translated by William Arrowsmith. In *Euripides V,* edited by David Greene and Richard Lattimore (Chicago: University of Chicago Press, 1959), verses 396–400.

2. Heinz Kohut, *The Restoration of the Self* (New York: International Universities Press, 1977), 206.

3. Marshall Berman, *All That Is Solid Melts into Air* (New York: Simon and Schuster, 1982).

4. Ibid., 125

5. Letter to Henry Osborn Taylor, January 17, 1905, in *The Letters of Henry Adams, Vol. 5: 1899–1905,* edited by J. C. Levenson, Ernest Samuels, Charles Vendersee, and Viola Hopkins Wimmer (Cambridge: Belknap Press, 1988), 627.

6. Mikhail S. Gorbachev, "No Time for Stereotypes," *New York Times* op-editorial, February 24, 1992.

7. See my op-editorial, "Cold War's Victims Deserve a Memorial," *New York Times,* March 10, 1990.

8. Doris Lessing, *The Sentimental Agents* (New York: Alfred A. Knopf, 1983), 192, 194, 195, 204.

9. Ibid., 66–67. To those familiar with intergalactic philology, I might add that the term "Krolgul," when pronounced with tongue in cheek, is a translation of the earth term, "Stanley Fish."

10. D. H. Lawrence, *Psychoanalysis and the Unconscious and Fantasia of the Unconscious* (New York: Viking Press, 1960 [1922]), 10–11.

11. Vaclav Havel, "Thriller," in *Vaclav Havel or Living in Truth* (London: Faber and Faber, 1986), 160–61.

12. Vaclav Havel, *Summer Meditations* (New York: Alfred A. Knopf, 1992), 5–6.

13. Quoted from Daniel Goleman, "Shamans and Their Longtime Lore May Vanish with the Forests," *New York Times,* June 11, 1991.

14. *Darwin: A Norton Critical Edition,* edited by Philip Appleman (New York: W. W. Norton, 1979), 140–41.

15. Heinz Kohut, *How Does Analysis Cure?* edited by Arnold Goldberg with Paul E. Stepansky (Chicago: University of Chicago Press, 1984), 18.

16. Robert Bellah, Richard Madsen, William M. Sullivan, Ann Swidler, and Steven M. Tipton, *The Good Society* (New York: Alfred A. Knopf, 1991). See also Jeffrey Goldfarb, *The Cynical Society* (Chicago: University of Chicago Press, 1991). I deal with the effects of automatizing consumerism in my chapter, "A Long Way from Home: Automatic Culture in Domestic and Civic Life," in my forthcoming book, *American Epiphanies.*

Acknowledgments

I would like to express my gratitude to A. C. Goodson, for inviting me to give the keynote address for the inaugural series on "Literature and Social Theory" for the Comparative Literature Program at Michigan State University, in October 1991; and to the coauthors of *The Good Society*—Robert Bellah, Richard Madsen, William M. Sullivan, Ann Swidler, and Steven M. Tipton—for inviting me to be one of the speakers at "The First Annual Good Society Conference: Sources of Public Philosophy in America" at Berkeley, in November 1991. Both occasions helped me to shape ideas which found their way into this book.

Earlier versions or portions of the following chapters of this book were published in the following: Chapter 2, from "On the Life Concept in Social Theory," in *Comparative Social Research* 11, no. 1 (1989): 319–342, (Greenwich, Conn., and London, England: Jai Press Inc.); Chapter 3, in Richard Münch and Neil Smelser, *Theory of Culture,* Copyright © 1992, The Regents of the University of California, Reprinted with permission of University of California Press; Chapter 4, in *Lewis Mumford: Public Intellectual,* edited by Thomas P. Hughes and Agatha C. Hughes, Copyright © 1990 by Oxford University Press, Inc., Reprinted with permission; Chapter 6, from "Jürgen Habermas's Theory of Communicative Etherealization" (1989), 12, no. 2: 333–353, and Chapter 7, from "Habermas and Rorty: Between Scylla and Charybdis" (Fall 1992), 15, no. 3: 333–358, in *Symbolic Interaction* (Greenwich, Conn., and London, England).

Index

Abduction, 21, 26, 58, 69, 175, 206, 213, 214, 229, 231, 240
Adams, Henry, 19, 68, 133, 163–165, 249–252
Adorno, Theodor, 145
Afrocentrism, 11–12
Alexander, Jeffrey, 17, 34
Alexander, Samuel, 40, 60
Angelou, Maya, 255–256
Apel, Karl-Otto, 222–223
Aquinas, Thomas, 186
Arendt, Hannah, 60–62
Aristotle, 73, 156, 172, 186–187, 200, 201, 236
automatism, 20, 26, 39, 63–64, 66, 87–89, 100–101, 121, 128–129, 135, 138–143, 157, 161–162, 165, 234, 243, 261, 269, 272, 279
automobile, 87, 125, 158
autonomy, 23, 26, 55, 66, 71–72, 75, 97–98, 113, 118, 128–130, 139–143, 157, 161–162, 177–181, 184, 197–199, 203–204, 211–214, 236–237, 239–243, 248, 263–264, 280
axial age, 56, 134, 276, 280, 284

Bacon, Francis, 104, 105
Baker, Houston, 12–13
Bakhtin, Mikhail, 96

Baldwin, James Mark, 47, 208, 227
Balick, Michael, 272
Barnes, Harry Elmer, 148
Baudelaire, Charles, 22, 51
Baudrillard, Jean, 83, 102, 282
Beard, Charles A., 148
Becket, Samuel, 201
Beethoven, Ludwig van, 265–267
Bellah, Robert N., 179, 241, 278–279, 295
Bentham, Jeremy, 101, 235–237
Bentley, Arthur F., 224, 231
Berger, Peter, 129
Bergson, Henri, 40, 51, 52, 131
Berman, Marshall, 22–23, 124, 248–252, 264–265
Bhagavad Gita, 152–153, 254
"big picture," the, 2–3, 8–9, 93, 124–126, 155, 158, 172, 268, 270, 276–280
Blake, William, 21, 139–140, 173–174, 260
Boehme, Jakob, 65
Bohr, Niels, 170
Bourdieu, Pierre, 34, 85, 92–93, 270
Branford, Victor, 122
Braque, Georges, 249
Braun, Wernher von, 160
Brooks, Van Wyck, 123, 148

Buddha, 56, 179
Burgee, John, 163
Burke, Edmund, 270–271
Burke, Kenneth, 200
Butler, Samuel, 25, 40

Calvin, Jean, 25, 66–67, 100
Camus, Albert, 86, 87
canon, 2–3, 8, 11–13, 15, 17, 29, 33–
    34, 43, 74–75, 126, 151–157, 172,
    194–195, 252–256, 277
capitalism, 17–26, 44, 54, 67, 70, 73,
    113, 128, 132, 135, 142–143, 158,
    176–177, 221, 231–232, 237, 251,
    254, 257, 262, 270
Carnap, Rudolph, 170–172, 221, 231
Ceausescu, Nicolae, 125, 142, 287
Chodorow, Nancy, 80
Chuang Tzu, 254–255
class, social, 5, 17–25, 29, 39, 145, 151,
    155, 256
"classics," and social theory, 10–11,
    13–35, 38, 123–124, 126, 151–
    157, 193–195
Clifford, James, 85, 93–99, 269
Coleridge, Samuel Taylor, 52, 58, 262
communism, 9, 14, 17–25, 86, 125,
    136, 142, 165, 221, 231, 237, 249–
    251, 254, 263, 269–270
community, 2, 4–6, 11, 25, 34, 56, 62,
    73, 75, 106, 125, 133, 156, 172,
    223–224, 232, 238, 262–264, 269,
    272, 280; communicative action, 62,
    88, 102, 117, 192, 217, 223, 225,
    228–230, 245; communicative ration-
    ality, 42, 61, 113, 188, 193–217,
    225, 232–233, 239, 243, 268, 276,
    279; communitas, 108
Comte, August, 19, 30, 281–282
contingency, 2–8, 50, 75–76, 82, 85,
    93–94, 97, 102, 109, 136, 139, 181,
    224–226, 229, 235–237, 241–243,
    245, 256, 262, 264–265, 269, 273–
    274, 277, 279
Cooley, Charles Horton, 40, 42, 89,
    122, 127
Coser, Lewis, 157

Cowley, Malcolm, 148
critical animism, 115
critical theory, 5, 18, 44, 89, 92, 126–
    129, 144, 192, 220–223, 231–232,
    262, 268, 272, 277
culture, 2–3, 8, 12, 19–20, 27–29, 33–
    36, 38, 42, 49–50, 52–54, 59, 62,
    67, 70, 73–75, 232–234, 238, 263–
    265, 273–280; and cultural studies,
    3–13; and cultus, 79–119

Darwin, Charles, 39–77, 127, 141,
    186–187, 232, 275
deconstructionism, 9–10, 35, 70, 128,
    182, 272
democracy, 22–23, 72–73, 118, 144–
    145, 146–150, 158, 162–165, 219,
    234–242
Derrida, Jacques, 1, 4, 9–10, 34, 83,
    88, 124, 225, 270, 277, 282
Descartes René, 20, 26, 34, 67–68, 83,
    174–175, 220, 231–232
Dewey, John, 2, 3, 4, 22, 40, 57–60,
    68–69, 76, 109–110, 122, 127, 128,
    146–150, 170–172, 176–177, 182,
    205–206, 215, 219–224, 229, 232–
    233, 238, 240–244, 253
Dilthey, Wilhelm, 40–43, 51, 61–62,
    69, 96, 109–110, 204
disenchantment, 26–29, 35, 112, 115,
    193–194, 225–226, 283
Dostoevsky, Feodor, 19, 22, 23, 37, 62,
    71–73, 134
dreaming, 27, 32–33, 84–85, 114–115,
    117, 130–131, 140–141, 186, 262–
    264, 267, 273–280
Driesch, Hans, 62–63
Dunbar, Paul Lawrence, 256
Durkheim, Emile, 11, 13–19, 29–36,
    53, 126, 130–131, 193–195, 200,
    207–211, 216, 220, 232, 249

Eckhardt, Meister Johannes, 66
Eco, Umberto, 34
Einstein, Albert, 249
Eisenhower, Dwight, 251
emergence, 21–25, 28, 33, 56, 60, 64,

67, 73, 76–77, 89, 93, 114–117,
127–141, 143, 146, 150, 154, 180,
198, 208–211, 212, 227, 232, 263,
265, 271, 273–280
Emerson, Ralph Waldo, 58, 146, 153,
176
empathy, 74, 116, 123, 133, 180, 246,
259, 264–265, 278–280
enchantment, 35–36, 113–119, 194,
230, 271–280
Enlightenment, 17–19, 21–24, 28–29,
33–36, 72–74, 104–105, 117–119,
135–136, 181, 184, 192, 211–214,
225–234, 242–246, 263–265, 277–
280
essentialism, 2, 54–55, 73, 85–86, 92–
94, 105, 116–117, 152, 255, 279
Eucken, Rudolph, 40
Euripides, 247
evolution, 17, 19, 29, 30–33, 39–48,
52–54, 58, 60, 62–67, 75–77, 82,
85–86, 89, 114–119, 126, 127, 129–
133, 136, 141, 154, 169, 180, 183–
189, 198, 203, 208, 210, 215–217,
223, 227, 230
experience, 1, 6–7, 20, 25, 27, 29–30,
33, 41–42, 49, 55, 62–64, 69, 81,
84–85, 88, 90–102, 106–111, 115,
130, 136, 143, 146–149, 155, 169,
173–176, 181, 184, 191, 196, 199,
204–211, 213, 216, 219, 224, 227,
231–234, 240–242, 246, 255, 262,
265–280

Farias, Victor, 9
feminism, 12, 80, 87, 97, 132–133, 277
Feuerbach, Ludwig, 3
fibrous structure of history, 135–137,
194
Fish, Stanley, 1, 5–8, 75, 256, 258 fn.7,
269, 277, 293
Flynn, John T., 148
Foucault, Michel, 282
foundationalism, 1, 6–9, 11, 16, 47–48,
51, 90, 143, 151, 169–171, 174–176,
183–184, 198–199, 208–211, 223–
226, 232, 233, 240

fragmatism, 3–8, 151, 183, 224–226,
243, 268
Frank, Waldo, 123
Franklin, Benjamin, 131
Frege, Gottlob, 174
Freud, Sigmund, 33, 40, 42, 101, 232,
259, 261, 278
Friedman, Milton, 144–145
Frisby, David, 51
Froissy, Juliette, 168
Fuchs, Ernst, 69
Fuss, Diana, 97–98

Gadamer, Hans-Georg, 42, 96, 109
Gaudi, Antonio, 40
Geddes, Patrick, 40, 122, 127
Geertz, Clifford, 10, 89–90, 96, 105,
123, 230
Gehlen, Arnold, 44, 62–65, 69, 76, 89,
115, 128, 233, 245, 263, 277, 285
"Ghost in the machine," 8, 13, 26, 27,
31–32, 34–36, 83, 87, 89, 99, 114,
127, 128, 142, 150, 174, 177, 183–
184, 232–233, 236, 242–246, 252,
264–265, 278–280
Giddens, Anthony, 34, 99–100, 109
Gilligan, Carol, 80
Glennie, J. Stuart, 56
Godelier, Maurice, 196–199
Goethe, Johann Wolfgang von, 52, 65–
66
Goffman, Erving, 200–202
Goldfarb, Jeffrey, 294
Goodall, Jane, 274
Goodson, A. C., 295
Gorbachev, Mikhail, 250
Gould, Stephen Jay, 75–76
Graves, Michael, 163

Habermas, Jürgen, 17, 34, 42, 44, 85,
88, 99, 102, 109, 117, 183, 188,
191–217, 220–246, 249, 262, 268,
270, 277–280, 285
Halton, Eugene, 177, 283, 285, 286,
287, 292, 293, 294
Havel, Václav, 79, 134, 161–162, 251,
255, 259, 264, 269–270

Hawthorne, Nathaniel, 118–119, 146, 253, 262
Hegel, Georg Friedrich, 17, 20, 24, 136, 137, 163, 166, 188, 195, 227
Heidegger, Martin, 1, 4, 9–10, 223, 239, 241–242, 270
Herder, Johann Gottfried, 64, 104–105
Heß, Rudolph, 44
Hirsch, E. C., 282
Hitler, Adolph, 28, 46, 51, 112–113, 128, 142, 146–150, 234, 239, 287–288
Hobbes, Thomas, 67–68, 72–73, 84, 100–101, 232, 274
Hobhouse, L. T., 40
Holton, Gerald, 159–161
homo faber, 58, 129, 131, 140, 257, 266–267
homo ludens, 266–267
homo rationalis, 260–262
homo sapiens, 68, 114–117, 139–141, 257, 266–267, 273–277
homo sentimentalis, 257–260
homo symbolicus, 75, 129–132, 266–267, 273–280
Horkheimer, Max, 145, 220–221
Hume, David, 173
Hussein, Saddam, 142
Husserl, Edmund, 42, 55, 204
Huxley, T. H., 52
Huxtable, Ada Louise, 288

ideology, 8–9, 11–15, 21, 82–85, 94–98, 114, 123, 128, 137, 151, 155, 162, 165, 253–255, 257–258
imagination, 11, 21, 23, 29, 30, 65, 68, 71, 74, 84–85, 91, 102, 127, 139–140, 147, 163, 173–174, 184, 186, 188, 191, 198–199, 245–246, 248–249, 265–267, 280

Jacobs, Jane, 123–125, 158–159
James, William, 40, 42, 47, 57–60, 97, 146–147, 172, 176, 220–222, 226, 253
Jaspers, Karl, 56
Jesus, 56, 71–73

Joas, Hans, 292
Johnson, Alvin, 145
Johnson, Phillip, 163
Jung, Carl Gustave, 33, 109

Kafka, Franz, 23, 80–82, 86, 112, 119
Kahn, Herman, 160–161
Kandinsky, Wassily, 42
Kant, Immanuel, 17, 26–30, 48–62, 70, 130, 143, 169, 183, 193, 204–205, 207–214, 220–234, 249
Kepler, Johannes, 66
Kierkegaard, Soren, 22
Kimball, Roger, 151, 253–254
Koestler, Arthur, 150
Kohlberg, Lawrence, 181, 193, 227
Kohut, Heinz, 179, 247, 261, 278–279
Krober, Alfred, L., 81–82
Kropotkin, Peter, 39–40, 45, 76
Kundera, Milan, 28, 91, 117, 257–261, 266

Langer, Susanne K., 150
Lao-Tse, 153
Lasch, Christopher, 179, 242
Lawrence, D. H., 37, 70–74, 123, 191, 199, 261, 274, 285
Lebensphilosophie, 39–77, 204
Lehman, David, 9, 281
Leibniz, Gottfried Wilhelm von, 65
Lem, Stanislaw, 229
Lenin, Vladimir, 249
Lerner, Max, 148
Lessing, Doris, 257–261
Lévi-Strauss, Claude, 32, 108, 123–124, 145, 193, 196–199, 230
life, concept of, 17, 19, 26, 28–29, 37–77, 81, 86–91, 100–102, 114–117, 126–133, 161–162, 167, 178, 191, 194, 203–207, 217, 219, 220, 231, 241, 243, 258, 260–265, 269–280
literary theories, 3–13, 16, 22–23, 58–60, 75, 93, 102, 122–124, 127, 207, 222, 256–261, 272–273, 281, 282
Locke, John, 27, 179, 241
Lodge, David, 7
logocentrism, 4, 164, 181, 272–273

Lorenz, Konrad, 44–47
Lowenthal, Leo, 145
Lucretius, 153
Luhman, Niklas, 17, 34, 87–88, 109
Luther, Martin, 25, 66–67, 183
Lynch, Kevin, 123
Lyotard, Jean-François, 83–84, 245, 277

MacIntyre, Alasdair, 156–157, 172
MacLean, Paul, 111
Madsen, Richard, 179, 241, 278–279, 295
Mahler, Gustave, 50
Malinowski, Bronislaw, 96, 171, 289
Man, Paul de, 9–10
Mann, Thomas, 285
Marinetti, Filippo Tommaso, 88–89
Marx, Karl, 2, 4, 10–11, 13f., 126, 136, 137, 157, 163, 194, 248–251
Mead, George Herbert, 11, 16, 40, 57–60, 68–69, 76, 127, 128, 169, 171, 176–178, 194–195, 205, 207–211, 215, 221–223, 232–233, 244
Mead, Margaret, 96
mechanical, 20–21, 35, 82, 84, 88–89, 110–114, 119, 127–144, 158–166, 176–183, 186–189, 212, 216, 221–222, 229–236, 243–246, 251, 257–261, 277–280
Megamachine, 23, 25, 34, 88, 133, 137–146, 157, 162–163, 263, 270, 272
Melville, Herman, 19, 25, 58, 71, 122, 127, 133, 146, 159, 176, 252–253, 260–262
Meštrović, Ivan, 102
metaphysics, 4–9, 24, 28, 38–39, 48, 59, 114, 167, 175, 178, 186, 189, 203, 225, 227, 230, 269
Miller, Donald, 159, 163
Mills, C. Wright, 14, 193
Minsky, Marvin, 88–89, 119
modern culture, 8, 19, 35, 42–43, 48, 50, 67–74, 84, 100–101, 111–114, 117–119, 124–125, 132, 137–144, 156–158, 162–166, 171–177, 182–189, 192–201, 203–207, 211–214, 221–222, 225–234, 242–246, 248–280; and social theory, 17–36, 42–43, 52–53
modernism, 2–13, 22–23, 50–51, 88–89, 90, 163–164, 171–172, 175–176, 201, 221–222, 248–249
modernization theory, 13–15, 22, 59, 192–194
Morgan, C. Lloyd, 40, 60, 154
Morris, Charles, 15, 169–172, 221, 231
Morris, William, 40
Moses, Robert, 125, 158–159
multiculturalism, 2, 9, 11–13, 93, 98, 150–157, 252–256, 272, 277
Mumford, Lewis, 21, 23, 24, 25, 56, 60, 75–76, 89, 111, 117, 121–166, 188, 194, 215, 226, 231, 233, 234, 238–239, 244–245, 252–253, 270, 284, 288–289
Münch, Richard, 34

nature, 3, 21, 27–28, 31–36, 37–77, 80–91, 104–105, 110–119, 121, 127–129, 154, 170, 175, 176, 180, 183–189, 197, 199, 208–211, 214, 228–233, 244, 249, 257, 262, 265–267, 270–280
Neurath, Otto, 170
Neuweiler, G., 45–46
Nietzsche, Friedrich, 4, 38–40, 51, 59, 71, 128, 235, 248, 251, 282
Nolte, Ernst, 192, 239
Nominalism, cultural, 29, 51, 53, 61–62, 67–69, 76, 84, 99–101, 111–113, 118–119, 143, 167, 175, 177, 179–180, 182, 196–197, 205, 221, 235, 268–270, 280; philosophical, 67–68, 76, 99–100, 167, 170, 173, 175, 177, 179–180, 182, 197, 209, 217, 229, 232, 236, 242, 245, 268–269, 279

Ockham, William of, 186
Ogden, C. K., 169, 171

organic, 3, 19, 26, 28, 30–31, 34–36, 38–48, 54–77, 86–91, 95, 100–105, 110–119, 121–166, 186, 188–189, 232, 233, 236, 241, 243–246, 263–267, 270–280

Orwell, George, 1

Paine, Thomas, 176

Parsons, Talcott, 11, 13–17, 34, 81–82, 84, 126, 145, 172, 193–194, 200, 221, 249

Peirce, Benjamin, 168

Peirce, Charles S., 21, 24, 26, 40, 47, 57–60, 66, 85, 92, 113, 114, 127, 140, 146, 159, 166–189, 206, 207–210, 213–217, 220–233, 240, 243–245, 252–253, 270–271, 277, 290–291

Piaget, Jean, 181, 193, 196, 208, 227, 230, 276

Picasso, Pablo, 249

Pigeonhole, Professor, 11, 16, 125

Pinter, Harold, 201

Plato, 152–153, 237

Plotkin, Mark, 272

pluralism, 2, 9–13, 93, 98, 158, 221, 225, 240, 254–255, 265

Poggi, Gianfranco, 283

Popper, Karl, 34, 201–202

positivism, 4, 6–8, 20, 26, 41–42, 61, 81, 85, 169–172, 174–176, 181–183, 187, 221–222, 229, 231–232, 281–282

posthistorical, 135–137, 164–165

postmodernism, 2–13, 75–76, 81–89, 93–98, 102–104, 113–114, 163–165, 182–184, 224–226, 234–246, 252, 256, 262, 280

poststructuralism, 32, 34, 80, 83–84, 89, 91, 93–94, 124, 145, 170, 182, 224–225

power, 5–7, 11–13, 19, 22–25, 28, 33, 39, 46, 51, 53, 55, 57, 62–64, 68–69, 71–72, 74–75, 77, 88, 91, 97, 100, 102, 104, 108–109, 111, 114, 116–118, 129, 130, 132–135, 137–139, 141–142, 144, 147, 150–151, 153, 156–159, 161, 163, 165, 174, 176, 185, 201, 204, 216, 219, 222, 234, 237, 243, 249–252, 257–263, 267, 269, 278

pragmatism, 3–8, 38–39, 57–60, 68–69, 167–189, 193, 205–211, 214–217, 219–246; and fragmatism, 3–8, 183, 224–226, 243, 268; neopragmatism, 3–8, 219–246

Quine, Willard, 15

rational choice, 10, 43, 70, 277

rationalization, 18–28, 34–36, 38, 70, 86–89, 112–114, 118–119, 138–144, 170–173, 182–186, 193–217, 226–234, 245, 251, 257–271, 275–280, 283

realism, 2, 5–9, 24, 60, 127, 157–166, 167–189, 233, 242, 252, 264. *See* virtual reality

reasonableness, 5, 7, 8, 11, 19, 28–29, 34–36, 38–39, 51, 64, 67–76, 82, 98–99, 104–119, 125, 139–149, 156, 159–166, 167–189, 191–217, 224–246, 254–255, 257–280

relativism, 3–13, 27, 75, 81, 93–99, 117–119, 151–157, 183–184, 192, 224–226, 234–246, 252–259, 268–269, 272, 276–280, 283

religion, 8, 10, 14, 16, 18–21, 23, 25–26, 29–32, 37, 53, 56, 70–74, 105–109, 115–117, 130–132, 134, 137, 139, 142–143, 177–179, 183, 197–199, 203, 205, 207, 210–212, 216–217, 225, 227–228, 230–231, 267

Reuleaux, Franz, 138

rhetoric, 5–8, 258

Richards, I. A., 169, 171

Richards, Robert, 47

Richardson, Henry Hobson, 127

Ricouer, Paul, 34, 88, 193

Rochberg-Halton, Eugene. *See* Halton, Eugene

Romanes, George, 47

Rorty, Richard, 3–8, 69, 75, 100, 146, 182, 188, 193, 222–246, 262, 269–270, 277–280
Rosenfeld, Paul, 123
Russell, Bertrand, 148, 170, 174
Ryle, Gilbert, 8

Sachs, Oliver, 100
Santayana, George, 122
Saussure, Ferdinand de, 32, 91, 98–99, 115, 168, 169–170
Scheler, Max, 42, 51–57, 71, 76, 101, 204
Schelling, Friedrich Wilhelm Joseph von, 52, 58, 65
Schutz, Alfred, 203–207
Scotus, John Duns, 166, 186
Searle, John, 151
Seidenberg, Roderick, 135–136, 289
self, 6, 21, 26, 31–33, 54–57, 59–60, 71–74, 85–91, 99–100, 113–114, 134, 136, 139–141, 154–158, 161–162, 177–181, 189, 199–203, 205–211, 215–217, 230, 236–237, 245–246, 257–269, 273–280
semeiosis, 34–36, 82, 85, 90–91, 169, 215, 259
semeiotic, 57, 60, 85–86, 168–189, 207, 210, 216–217, 253
semiotics, 9, 15, 82–87, 91–119, 123–124, 131–132, 169–189, 196–197, 209–210, 222, 230–233, 259, 271; biosemiotics, 86–87, 110, 113–114, 131, 166, 180, 184, 217, 233, 245, 267, 271, 273–280
Shakespeare, William, 12–13, 79, 253–256, 282
Shalin, Dmitri, 282
Shaw, George Bernard, 40
Sica, Alan, 283
Simmel, Georg, 15, 16, 19, 27–28, 42–43, 48–53, 57–69, 76, 126, 204, 220, 249, 283
Sjoberg, Gideon, 123
social theory; codification of, 1–36
sociobiology, 40, 43–48, 82, 84, 111

sociologocentrism, 4, 269, 272–273
sociology, codification of, 10–11, 13–17
Speer, Albert, 112–113, 287–288
Spencer, Herbert, 17, 19, 30, 39–47, 57, 232
spontaneity, 5, 6, 31, 35, 51, 59, 61, 71, 73, 77, 82, 100, 102, 117, 136, 158, 178–181, 201, 210, 236, 241, 245–246, 260–261, 264, 268–269, 271, 279–280
Stalin, Joseph, 9, 22, 51, 63, 72, 73, 142, 161, 221, 234, 249–250
Stanford University, 151–157, 289
Strauss, Anselm, 123
Stravinsky, Igor, 249
Strindberg, August, 40
structural functionalism, 13–17, 34
structuralism, 15, 32, 34, 49, 80, 83–84, 91, 94, 99, 108, 123–124, 130, 182, 193, 195–197, 201, 225, 230, 233
Sullivan, Louis, 40, 127, 163–164, 219
Sullivan, William M., 178, 241, 278–279, 295
Swidler, Ann, 178, 241, 278–279, 295
Synechism, 177–178

Taylor, Henry Osborn, 249
textualism, 2, 7–10, 34, 83, 86–88, 93, 95, 109, 132, 154
Thompson, J. Arthur, 62
Thoreau, Henry David, 58, 86, 146, 153, 176
Tipton, Stephen M., 178, 241, 278–279, 295
Tocqueville, Alexis de, 253
Trivers, R. L., 40
Turner, Edith, 80, 96–98
Turner, Victor, 74–75, 89, 96–98, 106–111, 117, 123, 130, 200
Twain, Mark, 259
Tyler, E. B., 81

Varnedoe, Kirk, 75
Veblen, Thorstein, 122, 144–145
virtual reality, 89, 136, 165, 264, 278

Wallace, Alfred Russel, 39–40, 141
Weber, Max, 11, 13–19, 25f., 52, 53, 67, 70, 96, 112, 117, 126, 131, 137–140, 142–144, 156, 193–196, 200, 202, 211–214, 216, 227, 230, 242, 249, 275, 283, 285
Welby, Lady Victoria, 169
Wells, H. G., 19, 28, 186, 250
Western Civilization and multicultural-ism, 151–157, 252–273

Whitehead, Alfred North, 40, 127, 174
Whitman, Walt, 146, 153, 176, 215
Williams, Raymond, 104
Winnicott, D. W., 179, 181, 201, 261
Wittgenstein, Ludwig, 4, 42, 51, 170–173, 204, 223–224
Wolfe, Alan, 129
Wright, Frank Lloyd, 40, 127, 148

Zapp, Morris, 7, 13